DEDICATION

For Jack, whose untimely passing deprived him of the pleasure of seeing his dedicated scholarship materialize in this wonderful edition. With thanks to the many individuals and institutions, both Japanese and American, who graciously introduced us to Japanese culture and history, beginning in 1968. Those introductions resulted in our enduring love and appreciation of Japan. Special thanks to the Japan National Tourist Association for their help in obtaining additional photos for this book. The authors would further like to acknowledge the Tuttle staff who helped to prepare this book, notably Cal Barksdale, Rob Goss, June Chong, Bambang Ari Setyabudi, Hendro Susetyo, Muh. Fivian Cahyanto, Raharjo, Fajar Wisnu Hardono, Chan Sow Yun and Yukie Ishihara.

Published by Tuttle Publishing, an imprint of Periplus Editions (HK) Ltd

www.tuttlepublishing.com

Copyright © 2012 John H. Martin and Phyllis G. Martin

Library of Congress Cataloging-in-Publication Data

Martin, John H.
  Tokyo : 29 walks in the world's most exciting city / John H. Martin and Phyllis G. Martin.
  – 1st ed.
     p. cm.
  Includes index.
  ISBN 978-4-8053-0917-9 (pbk.)
1. Tokyo (Japan)–Tours. 2. Walking–Japan–Tokyo–Guidebooks. 3. Tokyo (Japan)–History.
4. Tokyo (Japan)–Social life and customs. 5. Tokyo (Japan)–Buildings, structures, etc. 6. Architecture–Japan–Tokyo. I. Martin, Phyllis G. II. Title.
  DS896.38.M26 2012
  952'.135–dc22
2011013616

ISBN 978-4-8053-0917-9

Distributed by

North America, Latin America & Europe
Tuttle Publishing
364 Innovation Drive
North Clarendon, VT 05759-9436 USA
Tel: 1 (802) 773-8930
Fax: 1 (802) 773-6993
info@tuttlepublishing.com
www.tuttlepublishing.com

Japan
Tuttle Publishing
Yaekari Building, 3rd Floor
5-4-12 Osaki
Shinagawa-ku
Tokyo 141 0032
Tel: (81) 3 5437-0171
Fax: (81) 3 5437-0755
sales@tuttle.co.jp
www.tuttle.co.jp

Asia Pacific
Berkeley Books Pte Ltd
61 Tai Seng Avenue #02-12
Singapore 534167
Tel: (65) 6280-1330
Fax: (65) 6280-6290
inquiries@periplus.com.sg
www.periplus.com

15 14 13 12
10 9 8 7 6 5 4 3 2 1

Printed in Singapore   1207CP

Tokyo

29 **Walks** in the World's Most Exciting City

JOHN H. MARTIN AND PHYLLIS G. MARTIN

TUTTLE Publishing

Tokyo | Rutland, Vermont | Singapore

CONTENTS

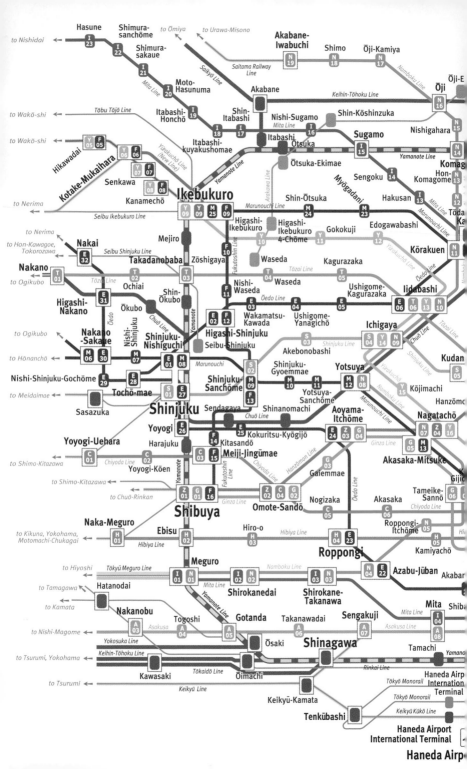

Central Tokyo Rail & Subway Network

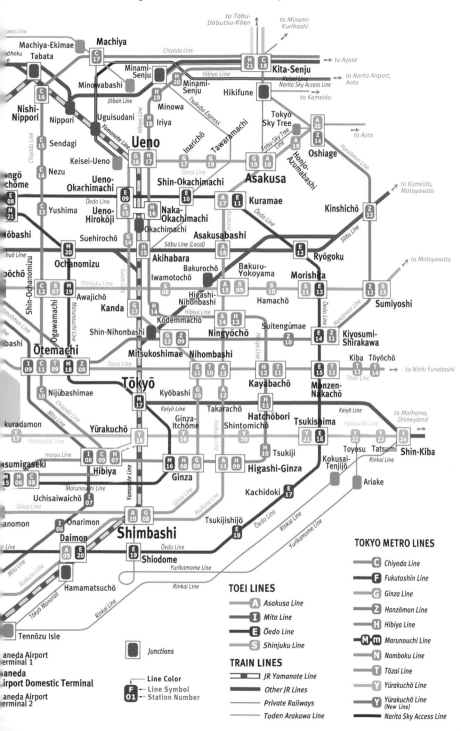

INTRODUCTION

Tokyo and Its Heritage

In 1590, Tokugawa Ieyasu, the powerful warlord of eastern Japan, was beholden to Toyotomi Hideyoshi, the military ruler over the nation. Hideyoshi, anxious to remove Ieyasu from Kyoto and the center of political power, offered to exchange certain of Ieyasu's territorial holdings near Kyoto for a grant of extensive lands in the underpopulated area in eastern Japan. Ieyasu's followers were aghast at their leader's acceptance of the isolated land at Edo Bay (Tokyo Bay) in exchange for his more valuable lands near the imperial capital. Ieyasu, however, had a vision he had not yet shared with them. Here, at the tiny village of Edo (*Edo* means "mouth of the river" or "estuary"), where the Sumida and other rivers poured into an almost completely encircled bay at the edge of the great Kanto Plain, he would create a mighty civil capital. And from here he and his heirs would rule all of Japan.

With the passage of time, with patience and guile—and with force—Ieyasu would bring

The shogun Tokugawa Ieyasu

this vision to reality. By 1598 Hideyoshi was dead, and, in the ensuing struggle among the daimyo (feudal lords) contesting for power, Ieyasu had by 1603 conquered all who stood in his way. As victor, Ieyasu moved the seat of civil and military control from an effete aristocratic court in Kyoto to the land at the head of the large and sheltered bay where he would build his capital. Thus Edo, the future Tokyo, began its modern existence. From here, as shogun ("barbarian-subduing generalissimo"), he ruled over Japan in the name of the powerless emperor and over the 176 "inside lords" (*fudai daimyo*)—those who had sided with him before his decisive and victorious battle at Sekigahara in 1603–as well as the 86 "outside lords" (*tozama daimyo*), who had not been farsighted enough to be his allies.

Ieyasu forced both the inside and the outside daimyo to supply labor, materials, and funds for the construction of an impregnable castle in Edo, and the work of creating moats, canals, walls, and a fortified residence went on until 1640. From 1603, and for the next 265 years, Ieyasu and his successors as shoguns were to rule the nation with unparalleled control. To both monitor and financially weaken any possible contenders for power, Ieyasu enforced the rule of *sankin kotai* (alternate attendance) on his vassals. Alternate periods of two years had to be spent by the leaders of the great clans at their Edo residence. Thus the great daimyo, the territorial lords, made their compulsory biennial passage from their domains to Edo, with the panoply and display required by Tokugawa shoguns. It was an ostentatious progress, which would keep them sufficiently impoverished. At the end of the period of attendance on the shogun, their return to their territorial homes took place with the same pomp. One half of the outside lords had to make their journey to Edo in March, while the other half returned to their homes that month. The inside lords made their biennial journey in alternate years in August.

In Edo, custom and honor forced these daimyo to live in splendid mansions befitting

The Yoshiwara pleasure district, with pedestrians among the teahouses and shops

their rank. On their return to their domains, they had to leave their women and children behind in their Edo palaces of Momoyama grandeur as hostage and warrant of their good behavior. (The Momoyama era in the late 1500s was a period of great artistic ostentation.) The expense of maintaining their territorial seat of power as well as an elaborate establishment in Edo, with the incumbent costly procession between the two locations, financially precluded any attempts on their part to mount a threat by force against the Tokugawa. As an additional precaution, the Tokugawa had barriers erected at points along the main highways into Edo, and here the rule of "No women out, no guns in" maintained the hostage system and kept the daimyo weaponless in the new capital.

For 265 years the Tokugawa ruled from their mighty Edo Castle, a fortress that only nature and time—and no military attack—would subdue. Its nemesis appeared in the form of earthquakes and fire, and these untoward events occurred on more than one occasion. When Tokugawa power finally came to an end in 1868, Edo was renamed Tokyo (*To*, meaning "eastern," and *kyo*, meaning "capital"). Then a 16-year-old emperor was moved from Kyoto to reign from the former castle grounds. Ostensibly, power had returned from the shogun to the emperor, but time would disclose the powerless nature of imperial rule, since the nation's new military leaders were the real power behind the throne and would both enhance and endanger the nation's place in the world. It is one of the ironies of history that in time a "blue-eyed shogun" in the guise of an American general would reign over Japan for a number of years, before a new and democratic form of government would issue from the political and economic centers beyond the Edo Castle, now become the Imperial Palace of Tokyo.

Thus Tokyo has been a major city for centuries, surpassing in size all of the great capitals of Europe since the 17th century. It is a city that, prior to 1868, witnessed the pageantry of the shoguns' days, as the great lords of Japan progressed in state behind their retainers along the Tokaido Road to their sumptuous mansions in the shadow of the shogun's castle. In more modern times, the city has seen the manipulations of the military attempting to make Japan a world power by employing the same and sometimes more brutal imperialistic means as those used by the nations of the West. It has faced as well the devastations of earthquakes and the "flowers of Edo," those all-consuming fires that swept periodically over Edo and old Tokyo and left it but ashes and a memory.

The *Eddoko*, the sons of Edo (and they were mostly sons, since until recent times men have always outnumbered women by two to one in the city), have always risen to the challenges that have rained down upon the city either by the forces of nature or the actions and laws of those who ruled over them. Despite the destructions of the 20th century, which leveled much of Tokyo—first in the Great Kanto Earthquake of 1923 and then in the fire-bombing raids of the spring of 1945, which in each case left more than 100,000 dead and saw a city of wood disappear in flames—there is a history and a continuity of tradition that has not died. Tokyo since the 1950s has been a phoenix revived. It is a city that offers visitors the most modern of façades and boasts towering skyscrapers that, it is claimed, can withstand future earthquakes. Yet the traditions of the past have been retained, despite all of the modernization visible in this early 21st century.

It is the intention of this guide to explore present-day Tokyo and selected areas near Tokyo in a series of walking tours with a view to the past that has made the present possible—a past whose memory still lingers in the urban life of an ever-changing city. In the following pages, the various intriguing areas of Tokyo will be explored on foot, with a narrative describing the buildings and neighborhoods, and the people and history behind them. This guide does not offer a compendium of restaurants (which can be found at every hand) or shops with their infinite variety of fine or expensive wares. On occasion mention will be made of particular department stores or specialty shops, for these cannot be ignored in such areas as Ginza, Shibuya, or Shinjuku, but the listings are not meant to be comprehensive. Museums are noted and some described in the course of a tour, but many of these require a separate visit in order to enjoy their extensive holdings. Each tour is so organized that one can leave it at a specific subway station and return at another time if the tour is found to be longer than desired.

Part of the pleasure of walking in Tokyo comes from viewing the architectural variety expressed in many of the unusual structures within the city. In the last quarter of the 20th century, Japanese architects (and some foreign architects with Tokyo commissions as well) became more imaginative and more daring in their architectural designs. Experimentation, innovation, creativity, and sometimes even extravagant conceptions have appeared on the face of the city. Witness the façade of one building on Meiji-dori near the Togo Shrine that has a jagged crack built into its construction, as though the building had been damaged by an earthquake. Or view the building near the Ebisu rail station that lacks the lower part of its façade, again as though a

cataclysmic event had exposed a portion of the inner building.

The walking tours that follow begin at that place where many visitors arrive in Tokyo, Tokyo Station. The walks then spiral out from the palace and the castle to encompass the variety that the city has to offer. The subway or other rail station from which each walk begins is indicated at the start of the walk, and specific instructions as to how to get there are provided in sidebars at the end. Thus, with the map of the city and the plan of the Tokyo subway lines provided herein, one can venture forth into a fascinating modern and ancient metropolis. Before striking out into unknown territory, one can always pur-

chase sandwiches from the many convenience stores in order to have a picnic lunch en route at a park or a shrine. These stores, which are open 24 hours a day, can also provide food for breakfast and dinners should one find restaurant or hotel dining prices too high.

No book on Tokyo, nor any individual who is interested in the capital of Japan as a living city with roots in a storied past, can afford to ignore the scholarly yet popular volume by Paul Waley in his *Tokyo Now and Then* or Edward Seidenstecker's *Low City, High City* and *Tokyo Rising*, or Sumiko Enbutsu's *Old Tokyo*. These volumes are essential guidance for anyone wishing further information on a most fascinating city.

Nihombashi, the commercial center of Edo in the early days, with Mt. Fuji in the background

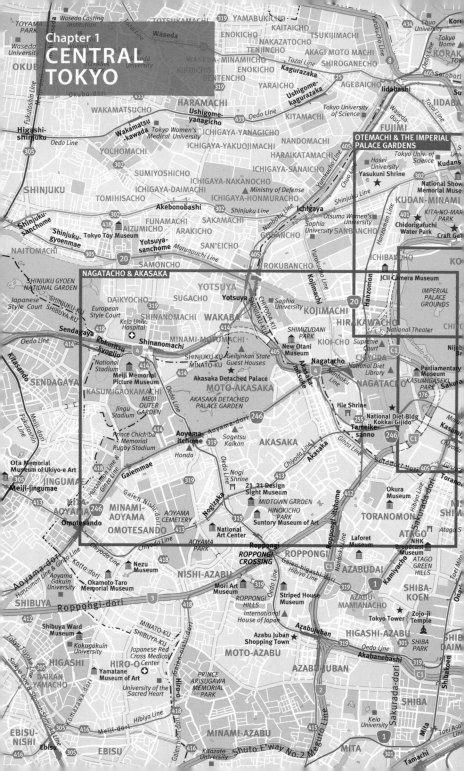

Chapter 1

CENTRAL
TOKYO

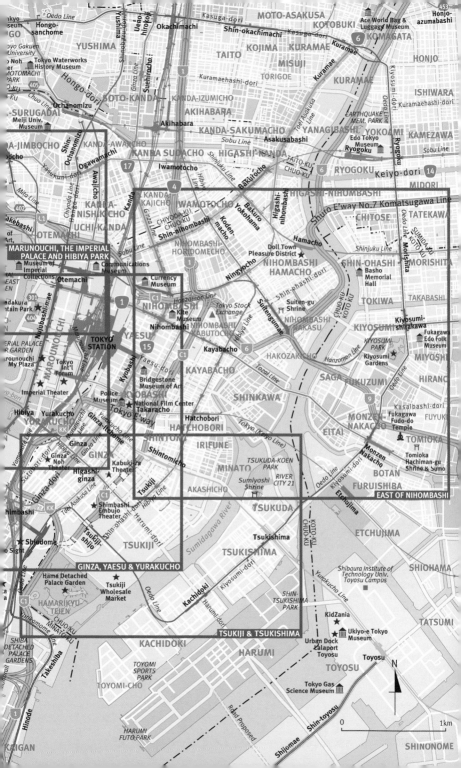

Walking Tour 1

MARUNOUCHI, THE IMPERIAL PALACE AND HIBIYA PARK

Within the Moat, the Blue-eyed Shogun, the Imperial Palace, the "Hall of the Cry of the Stag," and the Imperial Hotel

1. **Tokyo Station**
2. **Imperial Theater/Idemitsu Art Museum**
3. **The Imperial Palace Outer Garden**
4. **Hibiya Park**
5. **The Imperial Hotel**

When Tokugawa Ieyasu planned his castle in Edo in 1590, he chose to build it on the high ground above the inlet that spread inland from the great bay–then called Edo, and now Tokyo, Bay–in front of his new capital. Under his direction, Hibiya Inlet and various rivers in the vicinity of the castle were channeled so as to form canals and moats about the innermost portion of the city. Here, behind these watery barriers, the shogun's headquarters were to rise, protected by fortified walls and water-filled moats.

In front of the eastern side of the castle, the inlet was soon filled in, leaving an inner moat and, beyond the filled inlet, an outer moat. Earth for the project was taken from the higher terrain known as *Yamanote*, the "High City," to the west and north. On the newly reclaimed land between the inner and outer moats, an area called **Marunouchi** (Within the Moats) housed the mansions of the daimyo most favored by the Tokugawa shoguns. Additional fill was used to make the *Shitamachi*, or "Low City," to the east, where the common workers who supplied the daily needs of the daimyo and their entourages lived.

Ieyasu's most trusted, or "inside," lords resided in the castle enclave between the inner and outer moats. Today, Uchibori-dori, Inner Moat Street, borders the Imperial Palace grounds on the palace's eastern side, and a portion of this moat is still in existence. Sotobori-dori, Outer Moat Street, has in the

20th century become a ring road about the original central portion of Tokyo and the Imperial Palace grounds. It was only in the decades after World War II that the remaining portions of the outer moat were filled in, and thus Sotobori-dori now varies between being a ground-level roadway and, in part, an elevated and then underground roadway. In the northeast portion of the Marunouchi area, between today's Tokyo Station and the palace grounds, lay the mansions and dependencies of the Matsudaira lords in former times. To the south, in front of today's Imperial Palace Plaza, were the mansions of the Honda, the Sakai, and other favored daimyo.

For some 260 years, the most powerful military leaders of Japan occupied these lands. By the 1860s, however, the political and military power of the last two shoguns had gradually dissipated. The rule of *sankin kotai* (alternate attendance), which, after 1635, required both the inside and outside daimyo to spend two years in Edo alternating with two years on their own lands, was to come to an end. Then in 1868, with the victory of the adherents of Emperor Meiji over the Tokugawa shoguns, the mansions of all the daimyo were abandoned as the former provincial lords returned to their home provinces. By 1871, the deserted buildings were either used for government offices when these offices were moved to Tokyo from Kyoto, or were cleared for military drill grounds for a growing and ever more militaristic government.

By 1890, within 20 years of the imperial takeover of Edo, now Tokyo, the Meiji government and the military authorities required funds for the development of new establishments for their growing needs. Thus the land "within the moats" was put up for sale. The

Imperial Household did not have the funds to purchase the land, so the Mitsubishi, a leading mercantile and growing industrial family, were prevailed upon to acquire the vacant Marunouchi area in front of the palace grounds. Known derisively as Mitsubishi Meadow or the Gambler's Meadow by those who did not have the foresight to buy the land, the Marunouchi was intended by the Mitsubishi for a Western-style complex of buildings in anticipation of the industrial and commercial growth they foresaw for the nation. To this end, they hired Josiah Condor, an English architect who came to live in Japan in 1877 and who worked not only as an architect but as an instructor of architecture at the College of Technology (later to become Tokyo University). There he trained the first generation of Japanese architects in the technicalities of Western practice.

The three-story buildings that Condor designed for the Mitsubishi were redbrick structures with white stone quoins and windows and doors outlined in white stone. The new Western-style district he created was known as London Town. Its streets were lined with trees and the newest of modern appurtenances, poles to support above-ground electric wires. London Town, with its Queen Anne-style architecture extending to the not-too-distant Ginza area, with newly paved streets and brick-built structures, was the pride of the Meiji era. The sponsors of London Town hoped that it would quickly become the new commercial and financial center of Tokyo. The first building was completed in 1894, but unfortunately the Stock Exchange, the Bank of Japan, and other financial and commercial establishments remained in Nihombashi to the east. Success for London Town had to await the arrival of the railroad in central Tokyo.

The extension of the railroad from Shimbashi, south of the Ginza area, into Marunouchi finally became a reality in 1914. Dr. Tatsuno Kingo, a student of Josiah Condor, was named as the architect of the new **Tokyo Station** (where this walking tour begins), which opened in 1914. The thousand-foot-long redbrick Renaissance-style station was modeled after Amsterdam's Zentraal Station and faced east, toward London Town and the Imperial Palace. The plan to have an entrance on the eastern side of the station was stymied for years because the Sotobori moat still ran parallel to the railroad right-of-way on that

The old entrance to Tokyo Station in Marunouchi

side, and the Nihombashi and Kyobashi officials each wanted a bridge over the moat to go to their district. The dispute was not resolved and an eastern entrance to the station created until 1929. When the high-speed Shinkansen Line with its bullet trains came into being in the 1960s, this entrance was greatly enhanced, and a whole new, modern terminal structure was built behind the existing station, along with the Daimaru Department Store as a tenant facing the Yaesu Plaza, which covers the area of a portion of the former Sotobori moat.

Tokyo Station was meant as a memorial for Japan's victory over Russia in the Russo-Japanese War of 1904–1905, and its main entrance was reserved for use solely by royalty. The station remained central in name only, for it was the terminus for trains from the south while the station at Ueno (to the north) was the terminus for trains from the north and east. Not until after the Great Kanto Earthquake of 1923 could the two stations be linked, a possibility brought about by the earthquake's destruction of buildings between the two termini. The completion in 1925 of the elevated Yamanote Line, which circles a major portion of central Tokyo, finally achieved this linkage.

The early future of Marunouchi looked brighter when the Tokyo city and Tokyo prefectural governments agreed to share a new building in the former daimyo quarter. The redbrick, Western-style structure was to arise in Marunouchi with the prefectural offices to the right while the city offices were to the left. Each had the image of its patron before its portion of the structure: Ota Dokan, the founder of an earlier Edo Castle in the mid-1400s, was placed before the city sector of the building. Tokugawa Ieyasu, the second founder of Edo in the 1590s stood before the prefectural offices. (A new, modern city hall was erected on the site in 1957 under the direction of the noted Japanese architect Kenzo Tange. As with its predecessor, it was to be razed after 1991 when the city hall moved further west to Shinjuku.)

The new station became the front door to the city, and gradually office buildings in Marunouchi, as London Town came to be known again, filled the Mitsubishi Meadows between the railroad and the Imperial Palace over the next 25 years. The life of modern buildings is frequently all too short, and Condor's buildings were gradually replaced from 1930 on by newer and larger buildings. The last remnant of London Town, Mitsubishi Building #1, disappeared in 1967 in the post–World War II construction boom. The height limit of seven-to-eight floors (100 feet, or 45 meters) for the buildings in Marunouchi–out of respect to the adjacent Imperial Palace, which it would not be proper to overshadow–was to go the way of many such traditions after the 1950s, and today the financial and commercial headquarters of Japanese and international firms tower over the Imperial Palace grounds. Other traditions, such as the placing of an image of the Buddha under the roof of a building as protection against lightning, are no longer recognized.

1 TOKYO STATION

This tour of Marunouchi and Yurakucho begins at the western side of Tokyo Station, a bustling center whose daily train traffic could not have been envisioned by its original planners. Some 20 platforms above and below ground receive 3,000 train arrivals a day. A small park graces the area before the station, with the **Tokyo Central Post Office** on the left and a bus terminal to the right. A broad street leading from the plaza in front of the station to Hibiya-dori and the park before the

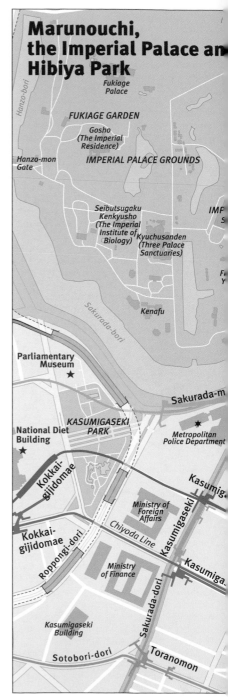

Marunouchi, the Imperial Palace and Hibiya Park

Hanzo-bori

Fukiage Palace

FUKIAGE GARDEN

Gosho (The Imperial Residence)

Hanzo-mon Gate

IMPERIAL PALACE GROUNDS

Seibutsugaku Kenkyusho (The Imperial Institute of Biology)

Kyuchusanden (Three Palace Sanctuaries)

Sakurada-bori

Kenafu

Parliamentary Museum ★

Sakurada-m

KASUMIGASEKI PARK

National Diet Building ★

Metropolitan Police Department ★

Kokkai-gijidomae

Kasumig.

Ministry of Foreign Affairs

Kasumigaseki

Kokkai-gijidomae

Chiyoda Line

Roppongi-dori

Ministry of Finance

Kasumiga.

Kasumigaseki Building

Sakurada-dori

Sotobori-dori

Toranomon

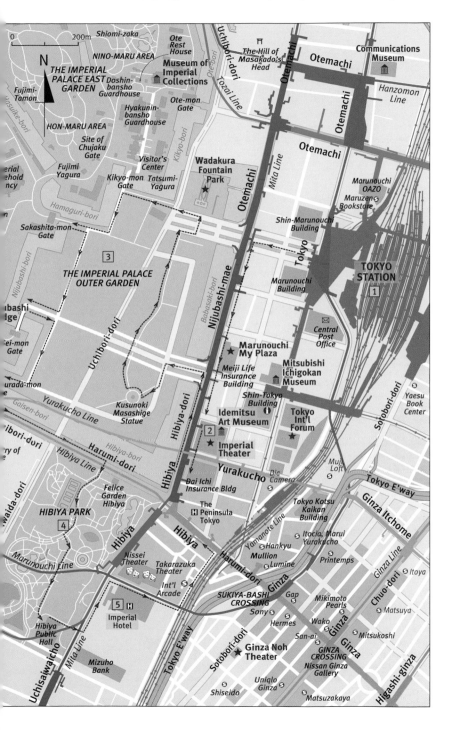

Imperial Palace was created in 1926. The skyscraper that dominates the beginning of this boulevard is the **Shin-marunouchi Building**, completed in 2007 to replace the previous 1953 building of that name that occupied the same site. At 650 feet (198 meters) in height, this 38-story building, designed by British architect Sir Michael Hopkins, is currently the tallest structure in Chiyoda ward. It stands across the street from another skyscraper, the 2002, 37-story **Marunouchi Building** (often called Maru Biru), which was built to replace the grand old 1923 building of the same name, an eight-story building that survived both the 1923 earthquake and the bombing of 1945 but was unable to survive Tokyo's 21st-century modernization. The two new Marunouchi buildings are packed with chic restaurants, fashionable shops, and high-end offices, and both represent the most modern face of Tokyo, as may seem fitting for one of the city's financial districts.

Two streets along the boulevard bring one to **Hibiya-dori** as well as to the Babasaki-bori (Moat in Front of the Horse Grounds) and the beginning of the Imperial Palace Outer Gardens. (The moat's strange name derives from a 1635 display of horsemanship presented before the shogun by a delegation from the then dependent kingdom of Korea.) When the capital was moved to Tokyo in 1868, three areas that were a portion of the castle grounds were gradually given to the public as parkland. These include the Imperial Palace Outer Garden along Hibiya-dori in front of the palace, the Imperial Palace East Garden, which contains the remains of the former Tokugawa castle, and Kita-no-maru Park, which was also part of the castle grounds. The Outer Garden has seen momentous events since it was separated from the Imperial Palace grounds. Here refugees from the destruction of the 1923 earthquake gathered, and here in August of 1945 a number of Japan's officer corps committed seppuku (ceremonial suicide), their deaths supposedly serving as atonement for Japan losing its war in the Pacific. In the 1950s and 1960s, it became a place for public demonstrations against unpopular government decisions, many of these gatherings being anti-American in nature.

Hibiya-dori extends along the moat before the Outer Gardens and the palace, with a range of modern office buildings on its eastern side. As you turn to the left from the boulevard leading from Tokyo Station and head south on Hibiya-dori, the buildings you see between the railway and the Outer Garden cover not only the site of the Matsudaira daimyo mansion and ancillary buildings but as well the building in which the shogun's chief Confucian advisor, Hayashi Razan, once held sway. Prior to the 19th century, the shogun's fire department was located where the **Meiji Life Insurance Building** now stands, across from the bridge over the Babasaki Moat. Edo never boasted an organization that could fight the "flowers of Edo," the outbreaks of fires that occurred all too frequently. Each daimyo and the shogun had men who could serve to protect their lord's property, but the common citizen was on his own in his warren of wooden houses in the Low City when fires broke out. Unfortunately, not even the daimyo's firefighters were always successful, and in the Long Sleeves Fire of 1657 even the shogun's castle was destroyed when flames engulfed it. The shogun's fire detachment can lay claim to fame even today on one score, however, for here at the location of the Meiji Life Insurance Building a son was born to one of the shogun's firefighters. He forsook his father's profession

Office buildings reflected in the Hibiya-bori Moat

when he came of age, and Ando Hiroshige made his name through his woodblock prints instead of the quenching of flames.

2 IMPERIAL THEATER/IDEMITSU ART MUSEUM

One full street along Hibiya-dori beyond the bridge over the Babasaki Moat is the Kokusai Building, the International Building. Within it is the **Imperial Theater** (Teikoku Gekijo), which opened in 1911. It was the first major Western-style theater in Tokyo, and it was generously ornamented with marble and enhanced with splendid tapestries reminiscent of the richness of the Paris Opera House. This 1,900-seat theater was initially intended for concerts and recitals as well as for Kabuki, but it proved unsuitable for this latter art form. In more recent years, after a 1966 renovation when the stage and its equipment were updated and a restrained decor pervaded the hall of the playhouse, it has been the home to many popular contemporary American musicals. The theater occupies the first three floors of the Kokusai Building. The main entrance to the building is found on its south side, and here are elevators that may be taken to the ninth floor and the **Idemitsu Art Museum**, which contains one of the finest collections of Asian art in Japan. (The museum is open from 10:00 a.m. to 4:30 p.m. [6:30 p.m. on Fridays]. It is closed Mondays and the New Year holidays. Entry ¥1,000.) Created by the president of the Idemitsu Oil Company, it has four large rooms that provide space for the display of the collection's riches. The main room presents objects from the museum's fine collection of Chinese ceramics, which range from prehistoric times through to the 18th century. Japanese ceramics are also well represented, with examples of Imari, Kutani, Seto, Nabeshima, and Kakiemon wares.

Another room in the museum shows selections from 16th- and 17th-century screens depicting episodes in *The Tale of Genji*, as well as prints with scenes of Kyoto and Edo before 1868. The ukiyo-e woodblock prints in the collection illustrate an art form that was popular from the 1600s through the 1800s, and these prints are complemented by Zen paintings and fine examples of calligraphy. An additional room holds the varied and very large collection of ceramic shards from Persia to southeast and eastern Asia. Chinese and Japanese lacquerware of the most excellent quality is also on view. Happily, the labels in the exhibition cases are in both English and

Guard tower on the Imperial Palace's outer moats

Japanese. Since 1972 the museum has branched into another area of art, with the acquisition of more than 400 works by the French painter Georges Rouault. Besides its artistic attractions, the location of the museum on the ninth floor of the Kokusai Building provides an excellent view of the Imperial Palace Outer Garden. In addition, a coffee shop offers a place for relaxation among the artistry of the Asian ages

Continuing south on Hibiya-dori, across the street from the Kokusai Building is the **Dai Ichi Insurance Building,** encompassing the full frontage of the street on which it sits facing the palace grounds. Built in 1938 to the design of Watanabe Matsumoto in what was the modern International Style, one particularly favored by authoritarian governments of the day, it had ten huge columns on its façade supporting two upper floors. One of the modern, fireproof buildings of pre–World War II Tokyo, it managed to survive the bombings and firestorms of the war years. Today the façade of the building has been covered over with a bland end-of-the-20th-century facing, while a new tower of 21 stories, designed by the American architect Kevin Roche, rises behind the original structure. Whatever character the front of the building once had, it has now been effaced. Here in the original building, from September 15, 1945, until April 11, 1951, General Douglas MacArthur, the "Blue-eyed Shogun" as the Japanese then called him (it was a Japanese folk belief that all Occidental gaijin had blue eyes) had his headquarters as the military and civilian representative of the victorious Allied forces at the end of World War II. His sixth-floor, walnut-paneled office was simply furnished with a conference table and a green leather armchair. In many ways, the general's office virtually became a museum after his departure, and now it is used by the head of the Dai Ichi Mutual Insurance Company.

3 THE IMPERIAL PALACE OUTER GARDEN

Crossing the street from the Dai Ichi Insurance Building and following the moat north on Hibiya-dori about a hundred yards, you reach a bridge leading into the **Imperial Palace Outer Garden** (Kokyo Gaien). In the Outer Gardens, which lie in front of the walls of the palace grounds, one can enjoy one of the few open spaces within this crowded city. This portion of Tokyo has seen many transformations in the 550 years since Ota Dokan in 1457 first built his fortified mansion and two other fortresses on the heights above today's garden. Then there was no garden, for Hibiya Inlet stretched this far inland, providing a natural moat before the fortified hill. The tiny town that Ota Dokan began below his hillside fortress received its name of Edo from its location, the word signifying "waterfront" or "mouth of the river." The town was to grow, but in the unpredictable politics of his day, Ota Dokan was assassinated at his lord's behest in 1486, and his fortified mansion and stronghold became derelict. One hundred years had to pass before a more massive castle would arise on the site and before Edo would see a renewal of its growth to become a major city.

This present parkland was created when Tokugawa Ieyasu moved his headquarters from Shizuoka to the site of Ota Dokan's castle in the 1590s. Ieyasu had Hibiya Inlet filled in with land from the hills of Kanda to the north, and the newly created land became the site of the mansions of the inside lords, the *fudai daimyo*, who were his closest allies. After 1868, with the fall of the Tokugawas, the Meiji government established its offices in the area in which the daimyo had lived. These offices were relocated from Kyoto into former daimyo buildings in Tokyo, a not too satisfactory arrangement. Relocation of the offices into more practical quarters was inevitable, and in the period after 1889 Marunouchi, as described above, was sold to the Mitsubishi family in order to raise funds for the proper housing of governmental functions. In 1889 the government offices were removed from that portion of what is now the Outer Gardens, pine trees were planted, and the land in front of the palace became a public park.

In 1897 a **bronze equestrian statue of Kusunoki Masashige**, given to the nation by the wealthy Sumitomo family of Osaka, was cast by Takamura Koun and placed within the Outer Garden. The creation of this statue by order of the Meiji government was part of its attempt to establish new heroes whose actions in the past showed devotion to the Imperial House and to the emperor. Such public images were meant to enhance the government's new creed of loyalty to the emperor and the need to be ready to sacrifice oneself for emperor and nation. These two virtues were evident in Kusunoki's life, first when he had defended Emperor Go-Daigo and his imperial prerogatives in the 1300s and then when he committed seppuku, or ceremonial suicide, after his defense of the emperor against Ashikaga Takauji's usurpation of power failed in 1336. Reverence to the god-emperor reached such ideological heights in the late 19th and early 20h centuries that at one time passengers in the trams that went by the palace were expected to rise from their seats and bow to the palace and the emperor within its walls. The fact that the Meiji defenders of imperial rule were themselves governing in the name of a powerless emperor, whose image they were using, was completely overlooked.

Kusunoki Masashige, samurai from the 14th century

A much lighter element was added to the northeast portion of the Outer Gardens in the 1960s, when a large fountain within a pool (**Wadakura Fountain**) was created to celebrate the wedding of the then crown prince (now Emperor Heisei). At the far end of the Outer Garden from Hibiya-dori, another moat separates the palace walls from the public park; these various moats encircle the 250 acres (100 hectares) of the palace grounds. The **Imperial Palace** today is located in the Nishi-no-maru, the Western Fortified Area, which was one portion of the shoguns' castle confines. The raised ground of the palace is faced with walls of huge stones brought by boat in the early 1600s from the Izu Peninsula some 60 miles (96 kilometers) to the southwest of Tokyo. These massive stones were dragged by teams of laborers supplied by the daimyo along paths covered with seaweed to ease the movement of the heavily loaded sledges from the bay to the castle grounds. Such fortified walls, before the development of modern gunpowder and explosives, could be breached only by treachery from within, by natural forces such as earthquakes, or through a siege that might starve a defending force into surrendering. In the more than 260 years of the enforced Tokugawa peace that followed 1603, these walls were neither breached nor attacked.

Most of the shogun's buildings in the Tokugawa castle were destroyed by fire in the years prior to the arrival of the Emperor Meiji to his new capital. His sojourn in the castle grounds was briefer than anticipated, since in 1873 the last of the Tokugawa buildings were destroyed by fire, and the emperor and empress were forced to move to the Akasaka Palace grounds, where they lived in a former mansion of a branch of the Tokugawa family until 1889, when a new palace was completed. This 1889 palace was destroyed in the air raids of early 1945.

When facing the palace grounds from the Outer Garden, to the right is the **Fujimi Yagura** (Mt. Fuji Viewing Tower) while to the left stands the **Fushimi Yagura**; these comprise two of the three remaining fortified towers of the Tokugawa castle. Toward the south end of the Outer Garden (to the left) the **Nijubashi** (Double Bridge) of 1888 comes into view along with the Fushimi Yagura, both of them rising out of the imperial moat. In the militaristic era of the 1930s and 1940s, the bridge, the Fushimi Tower, and the walls of

the palace grounds became a symbol of mystical patriotism for the Japanese. So mystical or mythical became the palace site where the god-emperor resided that when Emperor Hirohito at the end of World War II announced the capitulation of Japan, the more fanatical of imperial army officers performed the previously mentioned ceremonial suicide before the palace enclave as atonement for the loss of Japanese military honor.

The Imperial Palace (Kokyo) grounds are generally not open to the public except on two occasions: on the emperor's birthday on December 23 (from 9:30 a.m. to 11:20 a.m.) and at the start of the New Year on January 2nd (from 9:00 a.m. to 2:10 p.m.). On December 23 the emperor greets the public from the balcony of the Kyuden (Hall of State), while at the New Year holiday the imperial family receives the public from the same balcony. The Hall of State is a 1968 ferroconcrete, earthquake-proof and fireproof structure that serves as a reception and banqueting hall for official imperial events. The Kyuden consists of three buildings: the Seiden, where, in the Pine Tree Hall (Matsuno-ma), the Imperial family receives greetings from the prime minister and his cabinet in the annual New Year reception; the Homeiden, where formal dinners are held for foreign dignitaries; and the Chowaden, which has the balcony for imperial public greetings. The imperial private residence is in the **Fukiage Palace** in the western portion of the grounds, a structure that was constructed (1991–1993) to replace the unit built after World War II. (In Tokugawa times this 28-acre [11.2-hectare] sector provided land for the mansions of the three main branches of the Tokugawa family.) The private residence area has a gateway to the city through the Hanzomon Gate on the western side of the palace grounds. It is possible through advanced planning to have a tour of the palace grounds. This necessitates either telephoning the **Imperial Household Agency** (Kunaicho) at 03-3213-1111 (open 8:45 a.m. to 12:00 p.m. and 1:00 p.m. to 5:00 p.m. Monday through Friday) or applying online (via http://sankan. kunaicho.go.jp/english). Applications need to be made more than a day ahead of the proposed visit. Then a trip to the Kunaicho, at least a day before the visit, through the Sakashita-mon entry, with one's passport, enables one to obtain the permit for the tour. Tours start at the Kikyo-mon gateway at 10:00 a.m. and at

One of Tokyo's most photographed scenes: a glimpse of Fushimi Yagura tower behind Nijubashi Bridge

1:30 p.m., again with one's passport handy, and last one hour and fifteen minutes. The tours, of course, are given in Japanese.

The entry through which the public may go into the palace grounds on the two occasions when they may visit these private areas is by the 1888 **Nijubashi Bridge**. Although it is usually called the Double Bridge, the name originally referred to a Double Layer Bridge, a wooden bridge and then later a steel bridge with an upper and a lower level. A modern, single-layer steel bridge replaced the double bridge in 1964. Today, two bridges, one behind the other, give the Double Bridge a new meaning. In the foreground is a stone bridge of two arches, the Shakkyo-bashi, which is also called the Megane-bashi, since its two arches when reflected in the water form a whole circle and resemble a pair of spectacles (*megane*). During the public visitation to the palace, one moves through the massive gateway with its guard stations to the palace grounds, over the Nijubashi Bridge, through the **Sei-mon** (Main Gate), and into the Kyuden's East Garden in five or so minutes to the Hall of State, from whose balcony the imperial greetings are given.

Two other gates at the north end of the Outer Garden lead into the palace grounds: the **Sakashita-mon** (Gate at the Bottom of the Slope) provides an entrance to the brick structure that constitutes the Imperial Household Agency offices, the very conservative bureaucracy that safeguards and controls the heritage and activities of the imperial family. The buildings of the Household Agency stand before the **Momiji-yama**, the hill named for its maple (*momiji*) trees, an area more poetically known as the Hill of Autumn Leaves because of the lovely color of the trees' foliage at the end of the summer season. On this hill stood the Toshogu Shrine to the spirit of Tokugawa Ieyasu, one of the many shrines raised to his spirit throughout Japan that culminated in the highly ornate shrine in his honor at Nikko. The other gate, the **Kikyo-mon** (Bellflower Gate), is the entry for visitors and officials to the palace and for the delivery of supplies by tradesmen. Its name is said to derive from the family crest of Ota Dokan, which contained a bellflower.

Leaving the Outer Garden grounds from the southwestern corner, one exits through the **Sakurada-mon Gate** of the palace. It was one of the *masugata* gates that are described in the next tour, which is concerned with the original castle and its present site. Here on March 24, 1860, occurred an event that was to weaken the Tokugawa shogunate's rule and help to lead to its ultimate demise eight years later. At the Sakurada-mon (Gate of the Field of Cherry Trees) on a snowy morning, Ii Naosuke, lord of Hikone, and his guards with their swords sheathed against the snow, made their way to the castle grounds. Ii Naosuke was one of the more important advisors to the shogun, and he had signed the unequal treaties with the West, treaties opposed by the emperor in Kyoto, his courtiers, and even some branches of the Tokugawa clan. Assassins from the Mito branch of the Tokugawas, opposed to the agreements with the Western barbarians, fell upon Ii and his guards, leaving their bodies in the bloodied snow.

Ironically, walking through the Sakurada-mon Gate and crossing the **Gaien Hibiya** moat today and then Harumi-dori, one is faced by the white-tiled exterior of the 1980 18-story **Metropolitan Police Department** headquarters to the right, and the 1895 **Ministry of Justice** building to the left. The present police headquarters stands on the site of a pre-World War II jail, where the captured

fliers of General Doolittle's raid on Tokyo were held in 1942 before being taken to Sugamo Prison to be executed. The Ministry of Justice building was designed by two architects from Germany. They wished to combine the best of traditional Japanese and Western architecture in this new structure, but in the press for modernization in the 1890s, government officials insisted on a more Western style to the architecture. The original roof of the building was damaged in the 1945 air raids and was replaced with a flat roof that would have caused the architects even further unhappiness. It is one of the few Meiji period brick buildings still standing, and it and its grounds underwent extensive restoration in the 1990s.

④ HIBIYA PARK

Turning to the left along Harumi-dori, the northwest corner of **Hibiya Park** (Hibiya Koen) is at hand. Halfway down the street there is a path that leads through this 41-acre (16.4-hectare) park, which before 1868 held daimyo residences. Whereas Ieyasu's most dependable allies had their mansions in front of the castle gate in the Marunouchi area, the outside lords (*tozama daimyo*), who were not

Hibiya Park in bloom. The park makes for a lovely place to stop with a packed lunch during the walk.

among Ieyasu's allies prior to 1603, were permitted to lease lands at a further remove from the castle main gate. In what is today's Hibiya Park area, they were close enough for the shogun's spies to keep an eye on them, but they were not so close to the shogun and his retinue that they could act upon treacherous intentions. Here, beyond the outer ramparts of the castle, were the residences of the powerful Nabeshima clan of Saga on the island of Kyushu and of the Mori clan of Choshu in western Japan. (Sixty percent of the land in Edo belonged to the daimyo and their followers, who represented less than half the population of Edo, while 20 percent was occupied by commoners and another 20 percent was given over to temples and shrines.) The daimyo had to express their status by their show of splendor, and thus they built their residences in the extravagant, highly decorated Momoyama architectural style popular just before the turn of the 1600s. The original Momoyama mansions were destroyed in the Long Sleeves Fire of 1657, and the replacement structures were, of necessity, in a simpler style. New sumptuary laws together with the alternate attendance requirement –which entailed the expenses of a full entourage traveling to and from the home provinces and as well as the maintenance of mansions there as well as in Edo–were a crippling burden for the daimyo.

By 1871 the land once occupied by both the inside and the outside lords had been confiscated by the new Meiji government, and the land was cleared, leaving but a vestige of the past in the northeast corner of Hibiya Park, where a portion of the original wall of the **Hibiya Gate** of the former moat remains. What in 1903 was to become Hibiya Park was in the 1870s a dusty, military parade ground, and here in 1872 Emperor Meiji reviewed his troops. With the military wishing to create permanent Tokyo headquarters, their parade ground was moved to the then edge of the city in the 1890s. Plans were drawn for the building of Western-style government offices on the former military parade grounds. The subsoil was found to be too soft to support modern brick and stone structures, however, and, given the engineering of the day and the fact that this had once been an arm of Edo Bay before it was filled in, construction of modern buildings was out of the question.

Plans were therefore made to establish a park on the site, and it was opened to the public in June 1903. It was one of the first Western-style parks in Japan. Through the years, the park has accrued a number of amenities: the **Felice Garden Hibiya** on its Harumi-dori side; the **Hibiya Public Hall** of 1929 with its Art Nouveau touches on its southern side for concerts, lectures, meetings, and other cultural activities; a public library adjacent to the Hall; a café; two restaurants; a lake, ponds, lawns, flower gardens, and tennis courts; and a tier-seated, outdoor music area where today jazz, folk, and other popular music attracts young music lovers. In 1961 a large fountain was added to the park; it can be illuminated with seven colors at night. There is even a small museum devoted to the history of the park (open daily from 11:00 a.m. to 7:30 p.m. except on Mondays). The park is noted for its cherry tree blossoms in April, for its wisteria and azalea blooms in May, and for its magnificent display of chrysanthemums in November, this latter a festive event that draws many visitors. The park also contains a number of dogwood trees that were a gift from the United States in appreciation of the Japanese cherry trees that were given by Tokyo to Washington, D.C. In the unhappy days of the 1930s and 1940s, the park became an artillery battery, the lawns were replaced by vegetable plots, and, after the first American air raid by General Doolittle in 1942, anti-aircraft guns were put into place.

Mention has been made of the Imperial Palace Outer Gardens as a center for public dissent in the past. In 1905 some 30,000 protesters gathered at Hibiya Park to object to the terms of the peace treaty at the end of the Russo-Japanese War, and, as a result of the violence that ensued, martial law was declared by the government. In the 1950s and 1960s, protests were centered here against the Japanese government's relations with the United States. Hibiya Public Hall, which has served as the site of political party meetings, has had its unhappy incidents as well, the most notable occurring in 1960 when Asanuma Inejiro, the chairman of the Japan Socialist Party, was killed at the podium by a sword-wielding student.

5 THE IMPERIAL HOTEL

If Hibiya Park represented an early Western-style influence, there was an even earlier attempt at Westernization across Hibiya-dori on lands once held by the outside lords of Satsuma. After the nation opened its doors to the world in the 1860s, Japan was forced by the Western nations to grant certain extraterritorial rights to Western governments. These restrictions obviously bothered the members of the Japanese government, and numerous attempts were made to remove these limitations on Japanese sovereignty so as to permit Japan to assume its status as an equal with the European nations and the United States. One of the more futile of these attempts occurred in 1881 when Inoue Kaoru, the then foreign minister of Japan, had the Rokumeikan erected to the south of where the Imperial Hotel now stands. This Western-style, two-story, brick and stucco structure, designed by Josiah Condor, the British architect whose influence was so strong in Meiji Japan, was a potpourri of Western architectural styles. As Paul Waley describes it, it had Mediterranean arcades on both floors, being of a Tuscan nature on the ground floor and of a vaguely Moorish nature on the second floor. Verandas ran the length of the building, and the mix of styles was then topped with a roof that had overtones of France's Belle Epoque. A model of the Rokumeikan can be seen in the Edo-Tokyo Museum under one of the glassed floor panels.

The Rokumeikan was meant to be a social gathering place where foreigners and the cream of Japanese society (in Western attire) could meet and dance the popular Viennese waltzes that were the ultimate in modern social life of polite society, a place where each could enjoy the others' company. All the appurtenances of modern civilization were present: a ballroom, a reading room, a billiards lounge, and a music room. Other innovations of a Western nature occurred in these modern halls: invitations to gatherings were addressed to both husbands and wives in the European manner; there were garden parties and evening receptions. There was even a charity bazaar in 1884 that ran for three days. Surely this must have indicated to the Europeans and Americans (whom some Japanese still referred to as "red-haired barbarians") that Japan was now an equal to the West and should be treated as an equal.

The building was also intended to serve as a state guesthouse, since the former guesthouse in the Hama Detached Palace in Shimbashi, which had received American president Grant and his wife, had now fallen into disrepair. The suites for distinguished guests in the Rokumeikan could even boast an alabaster bathtub six feet (1.8 meters) long

by three feet (90 centimeters) wide. Unhappily, the significance of the name of the building was lost on the Westerners it was intended to impress. *Rokumeikan* means "The House of the Cry of the Stag," a literary reference to a Chinese classic that, as any learned Japanese would have known, referred to a place of convivial gatherings. Alas, the Rokumeikan did not bring about the abolition of extraterritoriality. The building soon lost popularity among the new Japanese elite of Meiji days, and a clamor from political rightists called for its demise as "an affront to Japanese honor." Abandoned as a cultural center, it became the Peer's Club in 1889, a mere five years after it opened, and it eventually came into use as a bank and an insurance office. In 1940 it was finally torn down. A remembrance of the Rokumeikan lingers in a most unusual location today. A Buddhist prayer hall in the Tomyo-ji Temple at Hirai in Edogawa-ku, Tokyo, houses one of the Italian bronze chandeliers from the ballroom of the Rokumeikan: so this 19th-century attempt at Western civilization has added a lamp of culture to the light of Buddhist faith.

The site of the Rokumeikan has been covered with modern edifices. One of the more striking examples is the **Mizuho Bank Building**, formerly known as the **Dai-ichi Kangyo Bank Building** across from the Hibiya Public Hall. This 32-floor building was erected in 1981, and its eastern and western walls are covered with gray granite, while the front has a stepped, glass-curtain wall. A sunken mall is entered from a plaza with a large clock, and the lobby holds the sculpture *Doppo la Danza* by Giacomo Manzo. Despite the failure of the Rokumeikan, a new Western-style hotel was being planned, and it came into being as the **Imperial Hotel** in 1890, sited adjacent to the Rokumeikan just to the north on Hibiya-dori. The new hotel soon became a center for both foreigners and the Japanese. A three-story wooden structure with verandas and arches and a mansard roof, it resembled its ill-fated next-door neighbor. It was not a large hotel, since it could only accommodate some two hundred to three hundred guests. Never-theless, it became the center for the smart set of its day. Within a year of its opening, it came into unexpected use when the nearby Diet chambers burned to the ground, and members of the Diet had to meet in the hotel until their new legislative meeting place was available.

The Imperial Hotel (center) looms over Hibiya Park.

The 100 rooms of the Imperial Hotel proved to be inadequate as Tokyo moved into the 20th century. In 1915 Frank Lloyd Wright was commissioned to create a new and more modern hotel on a portion of the site of the existing Imperial Hotel. Westernization achieved a new meaning in Wright's edifice, for in it he reworked an earlier design in a somewhat Mayan style that he had created for a client in Mexico and that the client had rejected as too unusual. The design produced a building that was Western and modern in ambience but pre-Western in its architectural conception. The building was seven years under construction, engendering the usual recriminations because it ran several times over budget as well as over its timetable for completion. Its opening occurred in 1922 just as the original Imperial Hotel in front of it burned down, and but one year before the Great Kanto Earthquake of 1923.

Wright made great claims for the fact that his building had proved to be earthquake-proof during that 1923 disaster. He credited its underlying "dish" foundation construction, whereby the building could float on the un-derground basin that he had designed specifically to circumvent the building's collapse. A similar design, in which a structure would "float" on piles sunk in the mud, had been used elsewhere in Tokyo. A number of these other buildings successfully survived the earthquake, some without the unfortunate settling that affected parts of Wright's building.

The vicissitudes of use, the uneven corridors and floors and other evidence of the 1923 damage, wartime neglect in the 1940s, the hotel's use by the U.S. military authorities after 1945 before its return to civilian service, and the rise in land prices that called for better use of the land on which the Imperial Hotel sat—all this brought this self-proclaimed monument to Wright's genius to an untimely end in 1967. Then it was razed for the new skyscraper Imperial Hotel and its later tower addition, both in the international style of the late 20th century. A Society to Protect the Imperial Hotel had been organized in 1967, but the Wright hotel closed its doors forever on November 15 of that year. A portion of the original Wright Building, including the forecourt, pond, and main lounge rooms, have been saved and scrupulously restored in Meiji Mura, the outdoor museum of Meiji period architecture near Inuyama outside of Nagoya. Again, here is one of those small ironies of history—for Wright's Mayan-inspired building was actually built not in the Meiji period (1868–1912) but in the succeeding Taisho era.

The post-1968 Imperial Hotel, though now beginning to show its age and look somewhat lackluster against the flood of modern luxury hotels that have swept through Tokyo since 2000, is still regarded by many as one of the city's best hotels. It is a far cry from the original Imperial Hotel of a mere one hundred rooms. In 1983 an additional unit, the Imperial Tower, was added to the 1970s building, and its first four floors are given over to luxury shops. It also boasts a collection of fine Japanese and international restaurants. The later Imperial Hotel is overpowering in its attempt at grandeur and has the ambience of an international airport terminal striving for recognition.

Just to the north of the Imperial Hotel on Hibiya-dori is the 1963 Nissei-Hibiya Building, which contains the **Nissei Theater** (Nissei Gekijo) seating 1,334 theater-goers. The theater offers ballet and opera in season and concerts and movies at other times. It provides a showy theater interior with its ceiling flecked with mother-of-pearl, its walls of glass mosaics and lights flashing within the walls and ceiling. Its lobby boasts an Art Deco ceiling and a marble floor, and it is thus as theatrical as some of the entertainment that appears on its stage or screen. Behind the Nissei-Hibiya Building is the **Takarazuka Theater** on the side street to the left of the Imperial Hotel. The street is now known as Theater Street; its sidewalks have been widened and its roadway narrowed in order to handle the festive crowds attending the theaters along its length. In the period of the United States military occupation of Japan after 1945, this theater served as the Ernie Pyle Theater for American troops, named for the famed World War II correspondent who was killed on Iwo Jima. Restored to civilian control as the Occupation ended, for almost a decade the Ernie Pyle had served as a movie and stage theater, its operation giving an exceedingly large Japanese staff employment that might not otherwise have been available to them in these postwar days.

The theater was eventually returned to Japanese control, and its spectacular music and dance extravaganzas, in which all the parts, male and female, are taken by young women, were resumed after a wartime and postwar hiatus. Aside from its multipurpose stage, there is a *hanamichi* (flower path) as in Kabuki theaters, which joins the stage at the Gin-bashi, the Silver Bridge. This obviously can bring the performers in closer contact with the audience. The Takarazuka revues are offered in the most lavish of settings and ornate of costumes, and these revues by the theater's Osaka/Kobe-based company have an immense appeal for adolescent Japanese girls and middle-aged matrons. Their attraction can be attested to by an incident from the war years: when the theater was closed for wartime reasons on March 4, 1944, the crowd was so large and in danger of becoming unruly that the police unsheathed the swords they carried so as to maintain order.

Continuing to the east on the street that runs alongside the Imperial Hotel, one arrives at the **International Arcade**, which is situated under the overhead railroad right-of-way. The International Arcade extends for one street in either direction as an enclosed market with a variety of goods meant to appeal to tourists: from electronic gear to new and used kimonos to souvenir items of great diversity. (Since the shops are open from 10:00 a.m. to 7:00 p.m., until 6:00 p.m. on Sundays, and some of the purchases are tax free, there is an added incentive offered to visitors.) To the north and still under the elevated structure are the *yakitori* stalls that are favored for snacks by both visitors and Tokyo residents.

Following the elevated tracks northwest for a hundred yards leads to Harumi-dori, where on each side of the street are stairs down to the several subway lines that intersect here, the Chiyoda Line, the Toei Mita Line, and the Hibiya Line, while an underground passageway connects the Yurakucho Line.

GETTING THERE

This tour starts at Tokyo Station, which is served by numerous JR train lines, *Shinkansen* lines, and subway lines. These include the Marunouchi subway line, the JR Yamanote Line, and the JR Chuo and Sobu Lines.

Walking Tour 2

OTEMACHI, IMPERIAL PALACE GARDENS, AND YASUKUNI SHRINE

A Flying Head, the Shogun's Castle, a Cultural Oasis, and the Japanese Valhalla

The Marunouchi financial district of Tokyo, which was explored in Walk1, has been described as the one-time site of the mansions of the inner lords of the Tokugawa shoguns from 1603 to 1868. Just to the north of Marunouchi is the **Otemachi district**, which also held the mansions of the Tokugawa's most trusted daimyo. This section is circumscribed by the main railway tracks on the east (to the north of Tokyo Station), by Uchibori-dori (Inner Moat Street) before the former castle walls on the west, by Eitai-dori on the south, and by the modern Shuto (Metropolitan) Expressway on the north. The mansions of the feudal daimyo have long since disappeared from Otemachi, and today Otemachi is the home of the barons of big business, for here may be found the offices of many banks, insurance agencies, and major commercial corporations.

1 THE HILL OF MASAKADO'S HEAD

The district is well served by subway and rail lines, since Tokyo Station is just to the south of the district, while Otemachi Station itself is served by the Toei Mita, Hibiya, Tozai, Marunouchi, and Hanzomon Lines. Exiting from the Marunouchi subway line brings one to the first point of interest on this tour: the 1964 eight-story Teshin Building, which houses the **Communications Museum** (aka Tei-Park) on its first four floors. Anyone interested in the various forms of modern communi-

nications will enjoy this museum, for the exhibits include matters pertaining to postal, telegraph, telephone, and other forms of tele-communication. Here one will find an extensive display of postage stamps (more than 200,000), and so it comes as no surprise to learn that there is a relationship with the Ministry of Postal Services. (The museum is open from 9:00 a.m. to 4:30 p.m. daily except Mondays; admission is ¥110.) The exhibits are labeled only in Japanese, but an English-language brochure is available upon request.

A rather unusual location can be found in the midst of this modern area of Tokyo. On leaving the Communications Museum, the east-west street should be taken to the west toward the grounds of the Imperial Palace. Just before Uchibori-dori and the Otebori Moat at the former castle grounds, surrounded by the Mitsui Bussan Building, the Long Term Credit Bank of Japan, and the Sanwa Bank, is a small open space upon which no modern financial organization has dared to build. Here is the **Hill of Masakado's Head** (Masakado-no-Kubizuka), a shrine at what was once the top of the bay when Marunouchi and adjoining areas were still under water. The object of veneration worshipped at this shrine by the early fishermen of Edo was Taira-no-Masakado, a headstrong warrior of the 900s. He not only took over eight counties in the Kanto (Greater Tokyo) region, but he set himself up in his domains as the new emperor—in defiance of Kyoto's emperor, whose claim to the throne, tradition held, was rooted in the divine origin of one of his ancestors. As the adage would have it, pride comes before a fall, and in 940 Masakado fell in battle. As was the custom of that and later times, the rebel's head was severed and sent to Kyoto as proof of the death of this usurper of royal power. True to his headstrong ways, it is said that Masakado's head flew back to Edo in one night to rejoin its body in its grave. The validity of the story was attested at the time by the brilliant lightning and pealing thunder that accompanied the head on its flight. As was only proper under the circumstances, a shrine to Masakado's spirit was raised over the site of his grave in order to keep his spirit from stirring up new troubles.

Centuries later, Tokugawa Ieyasu was not one to take chances. So troublesome a spirit might threaten his domains despite the passage of 700 years since Masakado was put in his place, but no thought could be given to moving the body from its grave since this might rouse the vengeful spirit of the former warrior. Thus Ieyasu let the grave remain undisturbed—as have all the corporate chairmen of the present day, since no structure has ever been raised over this very valuable piece of property. The shrine that honored Masakado's spirit, however, was another question. Ieyasu had the shrine removed to the Kanda Myojin Shrine not too far to the north, where Masakado can be honored today. There at Kanda Myojin, Masakado's spirit remains, albeit the story does not end there, for the Meiji government also foresaw a threat from this wayward spirit—but that tale has to wait until Walk 10 to be told. The small area of the Hill of Masakado's Head is enclosed by traditional Japanese walls as well as modern office buildings on three sides, but the slightly raised unit with memorial stones to the right at the rear of the plot remains a place of reverence. Offerings of flowers and the burning of incense occur a millennium after this intrepid warrior's death. Greenery throughout the small plot make the site a park, with ceramic frogs on either side of the memorial providing a lighter touch to so solemn a spot.

2 STATUE OF KIYOMARO

While warriors of the distant past still need to be placated, there is another side to the coin where noble statesmen are concerned. In the year 769, Wake-no-Kiyomaro, a member of Empress Shotoku's court, was sent on a mission. Her senior advisor (and lover), the Buddhist monk Dokyo, had designs on the throne for himself and hoped to succeed his royal mistress as the next emperor. The empress sent Kiyomaro, a trusted member of the imperial court, to the Hachiman Shrine in Kyushu to see if the gods favored Dokyo's accession to the throne. Despite dire threats

from the monk, Kiyomaro brought back the deity's pronouncement that only those descended from the imperial gods could sit on the throne. Kiyomaro suffered disfigurement at Dokyo's orders for bringing so untoward an answer from the gods. Sent into exile while monk Dokyo lived, he was returned to imperial favor by the legitimate successor to the empress upon her death.

This diversion into ancient history is relevant, for the large bronze **Statue of Kiyomaro**, which stands to the north in a small plot of greenery at the edge of the Otebori Moat, celebrates this eighth-century defender of the Imperial House. In 1854 Emperor Komei raised Kiyomaro quite posthumously to the first rank of the nobility and named him Go-o-myojin, a spirit to be honored. This was a powerless emperor's slap at the Tokugawa shogun of his day, his only way of showing his displeasure in those who ruled without consulting him. After Komei's death, his son became Emperor Meiji, who would see his advisors and supporters bring an end to the two and a half centuries of Tokugawa rule. The new emperor's advisors saw a similar value in the figure of Kiyomaro. Thus, on March 18, 1898, the noble and the divine status of Kiyomaro were once more confirmed

The statue of Kiyomaro near the Otebori Moat

Otemachi & the Imperial Palace Gardens

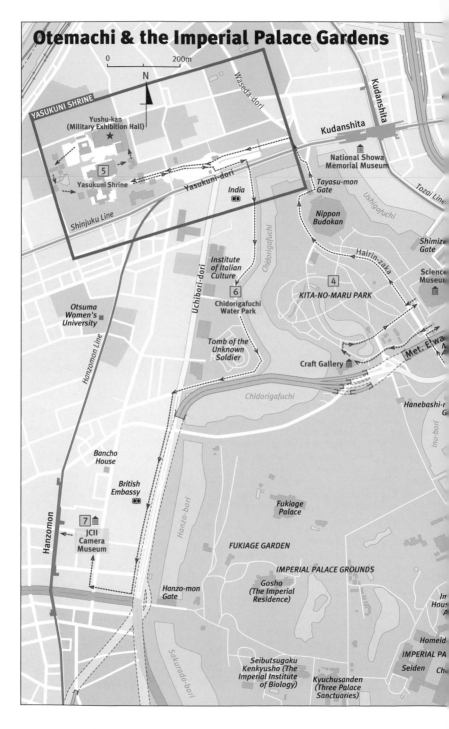

0 — 200m

N

YASUKUNI SHRINE

Yushu-kan
(Military Exhibition Hall) ★

Waseda-dori

Kudanshita

Kudanshita

National Showa
Memorial Museum

Tozai Line

5 Yasukuni Shrine

Yasukuni-dori

India

Tayasu-mon
Gate

Ushigafuchi

Shinjuku Line

Institute
of Italian
Culture

Chidorigafuchi

Nippon
Budokan

Hairin-zaka

Shimiz
Gate

Science
Museum

4 KITA-NO-MARU PARK

Uchibori-dori

Otsuma
Women's
University

6
Chidorigafuchi
Water Park

Tomb of the
Unknown
Soldier

Craft Gallery

Met. Ewa

Hanzomon Line

Chidorigafuchi

Hanebashi-r
G

Inu-bori

Bancho
House

British
Embassy

Fukiage
Palace

Hanzo-bori

Hanzomon

7 JCII
Camera
Museum

FUKIAGE GARDEN

IMPERIAL PALACE GROUNDS

Hanzo-mon
Gate

Gosho
(The Imperial
Residence)

In
Hous
A

Homeid

Sakurada-bori

Seibutsugaku
Kenkyusho (The
Imperial Institute
of Biology)

Kyuchusanden
(Three Palace
Sanctuaries)

IMPERIAL PA

Seiden   Ch

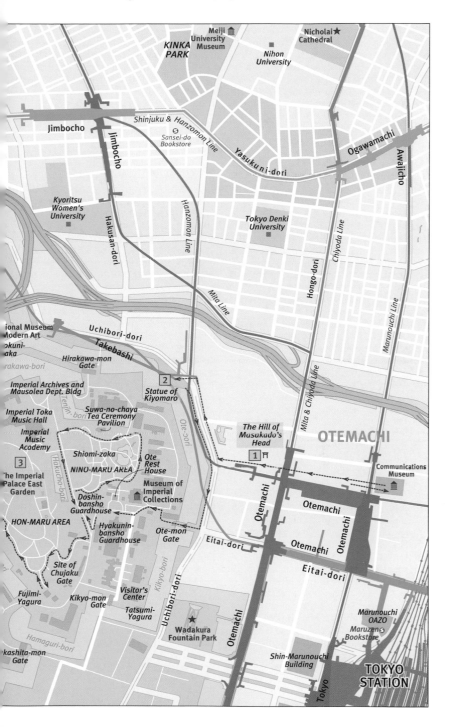

by imperial edict. In 1940, almost 90 years after Kiyomaro's elevation, his bronze image was raised at the edge of the Imperial Palace grounds by a later set of concerned advisors to Emperor Hirohito. In the 700s, this scholar had saved the throne. In 1940, the militaristic government sought to forestall any new threat to the throne. As a result, the statue of Kiyomaro still stands guard over imperial affairs at the edge of the Otebori Moat to the castle grounds.

③ THE IMPERIAL PALACE EAST GARDEN

The placement of buildings in Japan traditionally has to honor esoteric rules for the auspicious location of structures, lest they be built or oriented in a direction not favorable for their successful existence. In the case of Edo and the shogun's castle, this was a problem, since the castle site did not have the proper geographical orientation according to the rules of Chinese geomancy that were observed in Japan. Ieyasu, if nothing else, was decisive in matters like this. He decreed that Mt. Fuji to the west of his intended castle was truly to the north, and thus the castle site was properly oriented. Nonetheless, temples were built in Ueno to the true northeast (from which evil could flow, according to Chinese geomancy) as well as to the true southeast in the Shiba area as additional protection for the castle.

Walking back along the Otebori Moat to Eitai-dori, you come to a bridge that crosses the moat to the **Ote-mon** gateway and the shogun's former castle grounds, the site where Tokyo had its beginnings. The story of Edo Castle begins with Ota Dokan (1432–1486), who is credited with founding Edo. The top of the natural hill that overlooked the great bay of Edo and its inlets rose 65 feet (19.5 meters) above the water and thus provided a natural site for the largely earthen fortifications that Dokan created. Similar fortifications had been erected some two centuries before Ota Dokan made his stronghold here, but they had been of little consequence. Dokan's fortification did not have too long a life either, for his brutal murder in 1486, instigated by his feudal overlord of the Hojo clan of Odawara, led in time to the disintegration of his fort. By 1590, when Tokugawa Ieyasu chose the site for his headquarters, three small fishing villages and a few scattered farms at the foot of the future castle hill were all that comprised the village of Edo. The naturally defensive nature of the hillside was

obvious to Ieyasu when he entered Edo on August 1, 1590, and here he determined to build the strongest castle with the most intricate defensive system that Japan had ever seen.

The defensive stronghold that Ieyasu began in 1590 was not completed for another 50 years. By 1603 he had conquered all the contestants for civil power in Japan, and the work on the castle and its defenses could now be pursued with vigor, since the daimyo, the feudal lords of Japan who were subservient to him, were forced to supply labor, materials, and funds to create the castle that would keep them in fiscal serfdom. The dimensions of the stronghold beggar description, for they encompassed a 10-mile (16-kilometer) circle that stretched from the waterfront of the present Shimbashi area in the south to the hills of Kanda to the north. The outer fortifications that protected the area comprised some 110 entry gates, 30 bridges, an inner and an outer moat, and canals to serve as further barricades. The innermost moat was faced with stone walls 16 feet (4.8 meters) thick to protect the citadel where the shogun and his inner court resided. As was the case in European cities, the 19h century was to see the dismantling of the fortified walls of the city as it expanded and traffic increased. Thus, the outer walls and gates of the palace began to be dismantled in 1873.

The castle grounds themselves were always a protected and private area to which the public had no entry. However, in 1968, to celebrate the construction of the new Imperial Palace, which replaced the imperial buildings bombed in wartime, the inner grounds of the former castle complex were opened to the public as the **Imperial Palace East Garden** (Kokyo Higashi Gyoen). The inner walls of the complex divided the fortified hill into four areas called *maru* or citadels. The East Garden includes the Hon-maru (Central Keep), the Nino-maru (Second Keep), and the San–no-maru (Third Keep). The fourth fortified area consisted of the Nishi-no-maru (West Keep), which today forms the Imperial Palace grounds and is not open to the public.

The Imperial Palace East Garden, the former castle site, is primarily a garden complex today, since the various buildings and fortifications of the shogun's castle have long since been destroyed by fire. The Long Sleeves Fire

Right: *The Imperial Palace East Garden offers relief from the busy streets of central Tokyo.*

The Ote-mon gateway to the Imperial Palace East Garden

of 1657 was particularly disastrous for the castle, while the last major fire, of 1872, wiped out the remaining Tokugawa structures. The East Garden can be entered through several gates (*mon*), the Ote-mon, the Hirakawa-mon, and the Kita Hanebashi-mon, and these various gates can be reached from the Otemachi or Takebashi subway stations. (The garden is open from 9:00 a.m. to 4:30 p.m. in March through October and from 9:00 a.m. to 4:00 p.m. from November through February. The gardens are not open on Mondays and Fridays and are closed from December 28 to January 3 for the New Year holiday. Admission is free.) This tour of the garden begins at the **Ote-mon Gate**, since that was the main entrance to the castle in the days of its glory, and it provides an example of the type of defensive architecture employed in the 1600s. It is difficult today to envision the magnitude of the castle structures, for there were 99 gates—of which 36 were in the outer defensive wall that enclosed the 450-acre (180-hectare) heart of the shogun's castle. There were within this complex 21 large watch towers (*yagura*), and 28 munitions storehouses (*tamon*), aside from the residential buildings and ancillary castle structures.

To enter the castle grounds, one crosses the moat before the Ote-mon gateway, one of three such moats about the castle. These moats varied in size but were generally 230 feet (69 meters) wide and between 4 and 10 feet (1.2 to 3 meters) deep. On entering the

Ote-mon Gate, the visitor is given a small token, which must be returned when leaving the compound by any of its gates. The construction of the original Ote-mon Gate was the responsibility of Date Masumune, the daimyo of Sendai, and it was in two parts: the first or smaller gate was known as the Korai-mon (Korean Gate), while the larger of the two gates lay beyond a narrow courtyard. The inner Ote-mon gate was destroyed during the air raids of spring 1945, but it was rebuilt in 1967. The Ote-mon was a *masugata* gateway. That is, the outer and inner gateways formed a box. If an enemy were able to storm the outer Ote-mon, he then found himself in a walled, box-like courtyard with a second, larger gatehouse before him. Here he was under attack from more than one side, since slits in the gatehouse permitted the raining of arrows on the attackers. The chances of survival for attackers were slim. The roof tiles of these gates as well as other buildings often were topped with images of the mythical dolphin, intended to protect the structure against fire.

Beyond the Ote-mon were the four *maru* strongholds (or fortresses or keeps). At the foot of the hill beyond the Ote-mon was the Nino-maru, the Second Keep, while above it was the Hon-maru, the Central Keep. The Sanno-maru, the Third Keep, and the Kita-no-maru, the North Keep, lay below the Nino-maru. In Tokugawa days, the Kanjosho, the main office of the shogun's officers of administration and finance, was on the right just beyond the gate; the adjacent Otemachi and Marunouchi financial district of modern Tokyo echo this relationship from the castle past. Today the Sanno-maru Shozokan, the **Museum of Imperial Collections**, is on the right as one proceeds from the entry gateway. This modern, climate-controlled building of two large rooms is used as an exhibition hall for some of the 6,000 treasures of the Imperial Household, which were donated by the emperor in 1989. Thus a portion of the private artistic holdings of the imperial family, which are seldom otherwise available for public viewing, may be seen in this modern hall without charge. (Open the same days and times as the Imperial Palace East Garden. Admission is free.) The National Police Agency's Martial Arts Hall is on the left, while farther along on the right is the **Ote Rest House**, where beverages, maps, and souvenirs are available for sale to visitors.

The Hon-maru, the innermost sector of the castle, sat on the higher ground within the walls, and thus progress within the castle grounds calls for an uphill stroll. Walking up the slope, one arrives at the site of the **Ote Gejo**, the Dismount Gate, the point at which daimyo would dismount from their steeds or from their *kago*, those awkward "cages" in which a nobleman was carried on the shoulders of his retainers. Two walls remain, but the gate and the moat before it no longer exist. Here were two guardhouses to protect the

inner castle beyond the Ote Gejo Gate. To the right is the 1863 **Doshin-bansho guardhouse**, while on the left is the **Hyakunin-bansho**. The latter is the One Hundred Man Guardhouse, so named for the four platoons of one hundred men each who were drawn from the four major families or branches of the Tokugawa family to stand guard for the protection of the shogun.

To the left, a path leads to the Hon-maru (Central Keep), while to the right the path leads to the Nino-maru (Second Keep), which lies at the foot of the Hon-maru. The **Nino-maru** before 1868 served as the residence for the retired shogun, and its gardens were originally planned in 1630 by Kobori Enshu, the famed landscape artist of the 17th century. Today's garden, of course, is a reconstruction, but it contains all those elements essential to a traditional Japanese garden: a pond, a waterfall, stone lanterns, and a bridge. At the far side of the garden is the early 19th-century **Suwa-no-chaya tea ceremony pavilion**, a structure that once stood within the Fukiage Garden of the Imperial Palace.

The Nino-maru stands beneath the wall that supports the Hon-maru, a wall composed of the massive granite stones brought from the Izu Peninsula, 60 miles (96 kilometers) away, in the early 1600s. At its base is the **Hakucho-bori**, the Moat of Swans; the original 24 swans were a gift from Germany in 1953 after the East Gardens were opened to the public. A path from the Nino-maru Garden goes back to

The Suwa-no-chaya tea ceremony pavilion in the Nino-maru Gardens

The Fujimi Yagura (Mount Fuji Viewing Tower)

the Moat of Swans, and to the right of the moat is the **Shiomi-zaka**, the Tide Viewing Slope, which leads up to the Hon-maru. The slope today offers no view of Tokyo Bay or its inlets (now filled in), for the multistory buildings of the 20th century have obscured any possible view of tidal waters. In the 1600s, however, the slope was true to its name.

At the top of the slope once stood the Ote Naka, the Central Gate, leading into the Central Keep (Hon-maru) together with its guardhouse (*o-bansho*). The 1657 fire and the later 1872 fire destroyed the grandeur that once topped this hill, and the foundations of the main donjon and the Fujimi Yagura (Mt. Fuji Viewing Tower) are all that remain today. A **Rest House** on the left of the path at the top of the slope site offers a contrast in the photographs that are on display: one group shows the castle as it was in 1868; the other offers more recent photographs of the same sites.

The **Hon-maru** contained the Audience Hall, the residence, and other official buildings of the reigning shogun. At the southwest corner of the Hon-maru is the previously mentioned **Fujimi Yagura**, one of three such towers that still exist out of the original 21 that surmounted the castle walls. It was seriously damaged in the 1657 Long Sleeves Fire, but it was reconstructed two years later. At that time the decision was made not to re-build the rest of the fortifications of the Hon-maru, the Nino-maru, and the Sanno-maru. The nation was at peace, and such castles

were neither needed nor supportable when faced with the destructive force of modern artillery. Farther along the way is the **Fujimi Tamon**, the Mt. Fuji Viewing Armory, one of two remaining armories out of the 28 that once existed. Behind this arsenal was a well to supply water to the shogun's quarters. The well went down almost 100 feet (30 meters).

There were three main groups of buildings in this innermost complex of the Hon-maru site. Closest to the Fujimi Tower in an area now covered by a lawn was a group that contained the Halls for Affairs of State, the shogun's Audience Hall, and the Ohiroma, the Hall of One Thousand Mats (referring to tatami mats). It was in this grand hall that on the first and fifteenth of each month the shogun received his feudal lords. It was here also that the Dutch from the trading station of Dejima in Nagasaki were required to make the journey every four years to do obeisance to the shogun, to bring gifts, and to demonstrate the foolish ways of the Southern Barbarians—the uncouth Europeans who were best kept at a distance. A second group of buildings contained the shogun's private residence. A third group of structures consisted of the innermost quarters, which were adjacent to the Central Keep itself. Here were the shogun's sequestered halls for the women of his court, perhaps some five hundred to one thousand women consisting of his wives, his concubines, the ladies in waiting, attendants, servants, and cooks.

The pride of the castle was its five-story, 170-foot (51-meter) **Donjon** (Tenshukaku) or tower, which, given its location on the hill, soared 250 feet (75 meters) over Edo. It surveyed not only the bay but the five great highways that converged on Edo from throughout Japan. It had been erected under Tokugawa Hidetada, the second shogun, in 1607 and then rebuilt in 1640. All the buildings of the castle were white, save the Donjon, which was a stark black. Its lead roof tiles were covered with gold leaf, and golden dolphins surmounted the roof as protection against fires. Despite the protection these dolphins offered, the horrendous Long Sleeves Fire of 1657 destroyed this magnificent tower. The fire started with the burning of an accursed kimono in an exorcism ceremony at a Buddhist temple in the Low City. It then spread in the teeth of a gale and turned the city into a roaring inferno. Today nothing but the base of the Donjon remains, along with the tradition that all of the shogun's gold in the vaults beneath the tower melted. The whereabouts of this horde is still a puzzle and a challenge for those who imagine that it remains within the Hon-maru grounds. The base to the tower can be mounted by means of a slope for a view of the Hon-maru area.

A small granary building, the **Kokumotsu-gura**, is adjacent to the Donjon base, and this ceremonial structure was re-erected in the 1990s for a portion of the services concerned with the enthronement of Emperor Heisei. Other modern buildings are now located down a slope from the Hon-maru. These include the octagonal **Imperial Toka Music Hall,** created in 1966 for the then empress's sixtieth birthday. It is in the shape of an Imperial chrysanthemum petal, and the building by Kenji Imai shows the influence of Antonio Gaudi in its octagonal roof, which is shaped in the form of a peach flower. As a result, the hall has been nicknamed the Peach Auditorium. Imai used traditional Japanese motifs in the mosaic decorations of the external walls of the structure, a somewhat garish-looking building. Adjacent is the **Imperial Music Academy** and the unattractive, fireproof **Imperial Archives and Mausolea Department Building**.

One can leave the castle grounds at this point, if one so desires, through the **Hirakawa-mon Gate**, on the only wooden bridge over the moat, by taking the path from the Donjon base that runs behind the Archives and Mausolea Building and ultimately to Takebashi Station on the Tozai subway line. Alternatively, as this tour does, one can continue on through the Kita Hanebashi-mon Gate into the Kita-no-maru Park. The Hirakawa-mon was the main gate to the Sanno-maru (Third Keep), which disappeared at the time of the 1657 fire. This wooden gate was a *masugata* box gate, similar to the Ote-mon, where this tour began. It was the gate used by the women of the shogun's residence on the few occasions when they left the castle grounds. Adjacent to it is the smaller Fujo-mon, the Unclean Gate, through which those convicted of crimes within the castle or the bodies of the deceased were removed.

4 KITA-NO-MARU PARK

Continuing from the Hon-maru area, the **Kita Hanebashi-mon** (North Drawbridge Gate), leads into the **Kita-no-maru**, the North Keep, along the **Bairin-zaka** (Plum Tree Slope), a slope that, it is said, was planted with plum trees back in 1478 by Ota Dokan when he planned the fortress on this eminence. Ota Dokan used this area for the training of his troops, and later under the Tokugawa shoguns it became a walled area for the residences of collateral families of the shogun and for some of his highest officials. After the Long Sleeves Fire of 1657 the area was kept cleared as a fire break in front of the castle buildings. After the demise of the rule by the shoguns in 1868, the area was taken over by the military for barracks for the soldiers of the Imperial Guard who were charged with protecting the Imperial Palace. Kita-no-maru Park became a public park in 1969 in celebration of the birthday of the Showa emperor, Hirohito.

Down the Kinokuni-zaka slope, the **National Archives** and the **National Museum of Modern Art** (Kokuritsu Kindai Bijutsukan) by architect Yoshiro Taniguchi are on the right. (The museum is open from 10:00 a.m. to 5:00 p.m.; it is closed on Mondays, the New Year period of December 28 through January 1, and for up to a week when the exhibitions are being changed. Entry is normally 420 but is free the first Sunday of each month.) The museum, which was founded in 1952 and was relocated here in 1969, exhibits paintings of Western and Japanese artists in changing exhibitions on the first two floors (a fee is sometimes charged for these showings). The third and fourth floors exhibit paintings by Japanese artists since 1868, with the paintings chang-

Cherry blossoms line the approach to the Tayasu-mon Gate

ing four times a year since the collection exceeds 3,000 pieces.

The **Crafts Gallery** (Kogei-kan), with the same hours as the National Museum of Modern Art, is just a five-minute walk away. Continuing along the path that came from the Kinokuni-zaka and crossing the highway, after a few minutes' walk the Science Museum lies to the right while the Crafts Gallery is to the left. The Crafts Gallery is housed in a government-listed building that once served as the administrative headquarters of the Imperial Guard. It was at this site that the unusual revolt by 215 of the emperor's soldiers occurred, when they mutinied on August 23, 1878. They killed their officers, and, marching from their barracks to the Akasaka Palace where Emperor Meiji was then living, they protested the unfair division of rewards to those who had suppressed the Saigo Takamori revolt in Ueno Park and demanded a raise in pay. Severe punishment was meted out after the mutiny was put down, and, because of this insurrection, the military barracks were razed and the divisional headquarters was eventually located here. This 1910 formerly military, Gothic brick structure, in what has been kindly termed "19th-century Renaissance" architecture, is one of five remaining Meiji-period brick buildings in Tokyo. Exhibits are shown on the second floor of this Crafts Gallery building, and they encompass all of the various areas in which Japanese craftsmen have excelled: ceramics, bamboo, lacquer, metal, textiles, and others.

The **Science Museum** is the other museum in the Kita-no-maru Park. (It is open from 9:30 a.m. to 4:50 p.m. but closed on Wednesdays, entry ¥700. It is closed from December 28 through January 3.) The five-story, pentagonal-shaped museum is under the jurisdiction of the Japan Science Foundation, and it has fourteen sections of displays (primarily with Japanese labels) that appeal greatly to children, including workable models and space-age exhibits. It covers many aspects of science, from agriculture to nuclear science and from earthquakes to electricity—the latter topic being described by a robot that lectures to the children. The museum also has a laboratory, a workroom, and a library.

Beyond the museum complex lies the massive **Nippon Budo-kan**, the Japan Martial Arts Hall, constructed in 1964 for the Olympics of that year. The structure is reminiscent of the Horyu-ji Dream Hall south of Nara but on a more massive scale. Its octagonal roof is topped with a gold-leafed *giboshi*, an onion-shaped finial such as is often seen on the top of posts of rail fences at traditional Japanese temples. The building, which can seat 14,000 spectators, today is used for sports events, concerts, and other large gatherings—its first use as a concert hall occurred in 1968, when the Beatles came to Japan.

5 YASUKUNI SHRINE

The Kita-no-maru Koen is left through the **Tayasu-mon Gate**, a former *masugata* gate, on to **Yasukuni-dori** slightly to the west of

Kudanshita Station on the Toei Shinjuku and the Tozai subway lines. Yasukuni-dori here descends Kudan-zaka (Kudan Hill) to the Jimbocho area to the right, but this tour continues to the left on Yasukuni-dori. At one time this hill was higher and steeper than it now is, but it lost its top half for part of the fill needed to cover the marshy land at its foot as Ieyasu expanded the Shitamachi, the Low City, below his castle. The hill received its name of *Kudan*, nine steps, because it was so steep that it had to be cut in 1709 into nine stepped-sections for ease of mounting. The slope was further reduced in 1923 with the advent of the motor car. Strange as it may seem, there is a lighthouse (no longer used) at this point. Built in 1871, before as much of the land of Tokyo Bay was filled in and before tall buildings were erected, this beacon could be observed by boats in Tokyo Bay. Originally the lighthouse was in the Yasukuni grounds, but it was later moved to the south side of Yasukuni-dori.

Toward the end of the Tokugawa period there were barracks for the military at the top of Kudan Hill, but in 1869 it became the site for a "Shrine to Which the Spirits of the Dead Are Invited," originally called the Tokyo Shokonsha and now called **Yasukuni Shrine**. The shrine was intended to honor those who had died in the battles for the Meiji Imperial Restoration and the extinguishing of Tokugawa rule. In traditional Japanese custom, the spirits of the dead are enshrined here and can be feasted and entertained, not unlike the O Bon ceremonies of the Buddhist faith—a faith, ironically, that the Meiji leaders did not favor. The shrine was run by the army until 1945 and thus became the center of the most rabid nationalism. It still attracts right-wing militarists and extreme nationalists today.

In 1879 the Tokyo Shokonsha became the Yasukuni Jinja, the "Shrine of Peace for the Nation," on a more organized basis. Here horse racing took place until 1898, and there were sumo matches and the performance of Noh plays; in fact, a Noh stage was constructed on the grounds in 1902. In 1882, the Treasury (Yushu-kan), a military exhibition hall was built, and it today houses exhibits that honor the various wars Japan became involved in after 1868, down to and including World War II. (Open daily from 9:00 a.m. to 5:00 p.m., entry ¥800.) While commemorating the dead of the war, as is the purpose of the shrine, the displays, which range from the human torpedoes and even a Zero fighter and

a steam engine from the Bridge of the River Kwai episode, often seem to glorify the warlike in the Japanese past rather than the succoring of the spirits of the war dead. The labels of the exhibits, in Japanese, still offer the warped militaristic view of Japan's aggressive actions in Asia between 1895 and 1945.

With the war against China in the 1890s and then the Russo-Japanese War of 1905, the shrine became a memorial site to the dead of all Japanese wars since 1853, when the Imperial Restoration began. Soldiers heading into battle traditionally parted with the words "Let us meet at Yasukuni," where their spirits would be worshipped. As a result of the Japanese wars of the 1930s and 1940s, now 2,500,000 spirits are honored at the shrine. The more militant of Japanese nationalists who still see Japan's wars of the 1930s and 1940s as crusades to free Asia of Western imperialism have made the shrine a gathering place, as mentioned above. As a result, the visits to Yasukuni by members of the government have been the occasion for deep unrest among many of Japan's victims in past Japanese wars, particularly since even those who were convicted of war crimes, such as General Tojo, are also enshrined here, an action taken surreptitiously by the Japanese government, much to the outrage of other nations. In 2005 the Japanese courts indicated that such visits violate the Japanese

Shinto priests at Yasukuni Shrine

Constitution, but those of a nationalistic bent often act beyond the law. Though prior to 1945 the shrine was under military administration, the American occupation after 1945 had the shrine revert to non-governmental control. The shrine remains an unfortunate bone of contention for the Chinese, Korean, and other nations that suffered from Japanese imperialism.

The grounds are entered under the huge, steel **First Torii** (Daiichi Torii), a modern torii whose predecessor was melted in 1943 for use in armament production. Beyond it at an intersection of paths is the **statue to Masujiro Omura** (1824–1869), the first minister of War after the Meiji Restoration. He was in charge of the Meiji forces that defeated the shogun's supporters who held out in Ueno in 1868; just one year later he was assassinated. This statue in his honor was the first modern bronze statue in Japan when it was unveiled in 1888. Further along the path there is a **stone torii** and then the bronze **Second Torii** of 1887, and to its left is the **Hands-Washing Place** for ablutions before entering the inner shrine quarters. The path is lined with flowering cherry and with gingko trees and monuments to military men of the past.

The **Divine Gate** (Shinmon) of twelve pillars, with the imperial chrysanthemum of 16 petals embossed on its doors, follows, the **Shrine Offices** being to the left and the **Noh Theater** to the right. At the end of the path is the **Haiden**, the Hall for Worship of the spirits of the dead, and beyond that the sacred

Honden, the Main Hall, where the spirits are enshrined. Between the Noh theater and the Hall of Worship is the **Festivals Section**, while the **Hall of Arrival** is to the right of the Honden. Behind the Haiden is the **Treasury**, with the mementoes of Japan's wars mentioned above. Farther to the right-hand, rear of the shrine are the attractive Divine Pond, teahouses, and sumo ring.

The two major festivals of the Yasukuni shrine occur in the spring on April 21–23 while the autumn festival is held on October 17–20. At these times, in the tradition of the past, Noh dances, Bugaku, *Kyogen* farces, *biwa* music, folk music, kendo, and other activities to please the spirits of the dead are offered. These are festive occasions as are all Japanese commemorative functions for the dead. At these times, an Imperial Messenger presents imperial offerings at the shrine and reads the Imperial Message to the deities here enshrined. Commemorative services are also held each August 15, the day World War II ended for Japan. One other period of the year is particularly noted at this shrine, and that is the springtime blossoming of the many ornamental cherry trees on the shrine grounds.

6 CHIDORIGAFUCHI WATER PARK

Returning to the large statue of Masujiro Omura and crossing Yasukuni-dori, one can walk down Yasukuni-dori to the street that runs south along the Kita-no-maru Garden to Chidorigafuchi (Plover Depths), the pond that

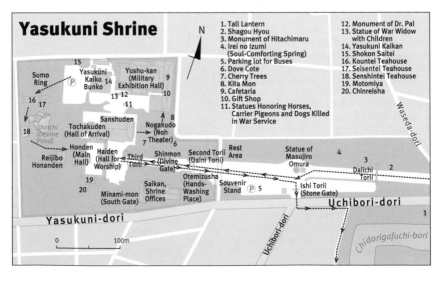

existed before the castle was built and that was included within the moat structure of the castle grounds. It takes its name from the perceived resemblance of this waterway to the wings of a plover in flight. **Chidori-gafuchi Water Park** is lined with some 90 cherry trees that in 1953 replaced the ones first planted here by Sir Ernest Satow (1843–1929), a British diplomat in the early Meiji period in the 19th century. The original trees were uprooted in the course of the construction of the Shuto Expressway.

The name "Water Park" refers not only to the moat but to the fact that one can rent rowboats for a pleasurable time on the waters of the park. Beyond this area, just before the Shuto Expressway and in a small park on the right is a hexagonal pavilion with a light green roof that has served since 1959 as the **Tomb of the Unknown Soldier**, a sacred spot commemorating the 90,000 unknown dead of Japan's wars. Under the roof is a symbolic, large stone sarcophagus. Each August 15, the anniversary of the end of World War II, the emperor makes his obeisance at this shrine, which remembers all those who died, regardless of their religion (unlike the Yasukuni Shrine, which is Shinto) or whether they were civilian or military. This visit occurs without the opprobrium connected with the Yasukuni Shrine for many non-nationalists and people of other nations.

Continuing along the western side of the Imperial Palace grounds, the handsome **British Embassy** is passed in the Bancho district of the city. In this sector the Hatamoto, the 7,000 guardsmen, drawn from the retainers of the shogun's domains, were stationed in an area that stretched to Ichigaya. Six regiments of these warrior guards lived here, each in his own district (*bancho*), and the district is still divided into six bancho blocks. After 1868, many of the Meiji nobility had their mansions here, and the area is still an upper-class residential district. Opposite the British Embassy, for example, is the modern **Bancho House** by the American architect Robert Stern, a combination office and apartment building.

Farther south along Uchibori-dori, the **Hanzo-mon Gate** to the Fukiage Imperial Palace is monitored by a police guard. At this place once lived Hattori Hanzo, the leader of the shogun's spies, those black-clad Ninja of tradition who were adept at infiltration, assassination, and acts of derring-do that still fill Japanese cinema and television with their

version of traditional medieval Japanese soap operas. The Hanzo-mon Gate has a more pacific reputation in modern times, since this is one of the entrances to the Fukiage area of the Imperial Palace private grounds. It was in this area that the Showa emperor, Hirohito, had his botanical laboratory and rice paddy fields. The emperor was unwittingly carrying on a tradition from the 18th century, for here the eighth shogun, Yoshimune (1716–1745) had an herb garden and a plantation for plant research. Just before the gate, on the left, is a small park that runs along the palace moat, and in it is a statue grouping of three nude, young male figures (such as the Tokugawa and Meiji governments would not have permitted). The park is a favorite place for lunchtime use by workers from adjacent office buildings.

The **Hanzomon subway station** lies two short streets along Shinjuku-dori to the west of the Hanzo-mon entrance to the palace, and it can be taken to other connecting lines as one leaves this area. However, the JCII Camera Museum offers a possible diversion before reaching the end point of this walk. It can be reached by taking the first right on Shinjuku-dori and continuing past two quick intersections and almost to the third.

7 JCII CAMERA MUSEUM (DIVERSION)

The **JCII Camera Museum** (open Tuesday–Sunday, 10 a.m. to 5 p.m.) was established by the Japan (Nippon) Camera and optical instruments Inspection and testing Institute (JCII) in the late 1980s. Although likely of limited interest to non-camera buffs, it is a must-see for photographers for its collection of several thousand cameras from Japan and overseas, which range from historic models and so-called "curio" cameras to modern gear. Of broader interest are the photographic exhibitions that the museum puts on regularly. To proceed to the Hanzomon subway station after your visit, return along the street by which you came and, at the first intersection, turn right. The station will lie before you when you reach the next cross street.

GETTING THERE

This tour starts at Otemachi Station, which is served by the Toei Mita Line, the Hibiya Line, the Tozai Line, the Marunouchi Line, and the Hanzomon Line. One can also walk to Otemachi Station in five minutes from Tokyo Station.

Walking Tour 3

NAGATACHO AND AKASAKA
High Culture, the Law, Politics, an Ancient Shrine, Commercial Palaces, and the Shadow of Geisha Times

Tokyo is, of course, the capital of Japan, and as such it has the nation's legislative chambers and its massive bureaucratic offices as major aspects of contemporary life. Few countries are as controlled by their bureaucracy as is Japan, and most of these offices of government are clustered about the National Diet Building so as to be certain, perhaps, that elected officials do not stray from what is considered best for the nation by the bureaucracy. The area geographically falls into two districts, **Nagatacho**, whose center is the Diet Building and the offices of the political parties, and then **Kasumigaseki**, where the governmental offices and ministries and the first skyscraper of modern Tokyo, the 36-story Kasumigaseki Building, are located. Kasumigaseki derives its name from the *seki* or 14th-century guarded barrier that once existed in this quarter. It was poetically named the Kasumi Barrier, the "Barrier of the Mists," a name that is perhaps appropriate even today for a government quarter.

Behind the political center of Tokyo and of Japan, situated on one of those fingers of hills of the original Edo's High City that stretch into the Low City where the commoners dwelled, is the Hie Jinja, a Shinto shrine of great antiquity that served to protect the shogun's capital and perhaps still protects governmental affairs today. It was the locus of one of the three great festivities that enlivened old Edo, days that are still enjoyed by modern Tokyo residents every other year, when the festival brings a colorful procession and excitement to the city. Below the Hie Shrine, in the flat land spreading from the Diet to Akasaka Mitsuke, is an area where the politicians and reporters, and today the minions of the television studios, continue to find places for relaxation, gossip, and the making of deals. Much of this activity has always been done in expensive restaurants on side streets off Sotobori-dori, the main street running through **Akasaka** and once the outer moat of the castle grounds. Here too are the luxurious New Otani and Akasaka Prince Hotels with their striking architecture and many amenities.

1 HANZO-MON TO NAGATACHO
Hanzomon Station on the subway line of that name is where this tour begins, and it starts where the previous tour ended. Walking from the subway station to the main street, Shinjuku-dori, the tour turns east toward the **Hanzo-mon Gate** and the Fukiage area of the Imperial Palace grounds. The most striking element in this part of Tokyo is the nine-story 1984 **Wacoal Kojimachi Building** by architect Kisho Kurokawa. As buildings go, it is not as tall and overpowering as some of the recent skyscrapers in the city, but its architectural design is rather striking. It has been described by some as an oversized sewing machine (not inappropriate considering that the sponsor of

the building is a garment manufacturer of lingerie whose main office this is). From a distance the design on its east side gives the appearance of having a baleful eye near the top of the building–or, so it is claimed, that is the manner in which Emperor Hirohito regarded it, for the building peers over the palace grounds. Synthetic marble and aluminum bands cover the façade of the structure, and the canopy over its entrance has been described as a giant flying saucer. The lobby of the building is interestingly decorated with mosaics from China, Korea, and Japan, and the reception area on the ninth floor is striking, with its high-domed ceiling. Exhibits are frequently on display, and the building has an Art Deco theater and a café-lounge.

Turning to the right on Uchibori-dori (Inner Moat Street), which runs along the palace moat, one comes to the **National Theater** (Kokuritsu Gekijo). This 1983 edifice provided the nation with its first state-owned theater, a center that offers productions of traditional Japanese performing arts. The theater sits on a rise, and its reinforced concrete structure is built in the *azekura* (log cabin) style of the Shoso-in Treasury of Nara, a 1,300-year-old wooden storehouse that the exterior of this building imitates. The theater has two auditoriums. The larger one to the left, seating 1,610, is primarily for Kabuki productions and ancient court music. The smaller auditorium, to the right, has 590 seats and is meant for Bunraku (puppet plays), *Kyogen* (farce), and other traditional forms of Japanese dance, music, and theater. The L-shaped lobby has displays pertaining to Japanese theater, ranging from costumes to scrolls about ancient performing arts. (These may be viewed between 10:00 a.m. and 5:00 p.m.) Adjacent is **Engei Hall,** a smaller, more intimate theater seating 300, which offers *Rakugo* and other forms of traditional storytelling or comedy. Ironically, the roof of the National Theater was used at one time by the writer Yukio Mishima as a parade ground for his private army. Mishima's concern that traditional Japanese values were being undermined by Westernization after World War II led to his ultimate attempt to persuade soldiers in the nearby Ichigaya military barracks to revolt. Laughed at by modern soldiers, who abjured the fiery militarism of the not-too-distant past, Mishima committed seppuku, his death actually coming about through his decapitation by one of his followers on November 25, 1970.

The Supreme Court of Japan

Just beyond the National Theater is the 1974 **Supreme Court of Japan** (Saiko Saibansho), a rather austere building in white granite that was designed by Shinichi Okada, who had studied architecture at Yale University. Many people find the interior of the building to be equally overwhelming. The building has the appearance of a bunker where justice has hunkered down, a not-too-inviting structure. (Tours are offered on weekdays in Japanese at 3:00 p.m.; closed from July 20 to August 31.) Perhaps in contrast to this less than graceful and almost windowless building, at the corner in front of the edifice is a piece of sculpture of three naked women in bronze–an art form that would hardly have been accepted in the decades and centuries before 1950. They complement the statue of three naked men in the park alongside the moat just to the left of the point where Shinjuku-dori meets Uchibori-dori, across from the Wacoal Building.

Continuing along Uchibori-dori, at the crossroads on the right side is the Miyake-zaka slope, which the overhead Shuto Expressway mounts. At this crossroads, the moat and Uchibori-dori, which diverges to the left, should be abandoned, as one heads under the Shuto Expressway into the street leading to the National Diet Building, passing the headquarters of the Socialist Party of Japan on the right. This area bore a more military outlook prior to 1945, for here after 1870 was located the War Ministry, while the headquarters of the General Staff Officers sat where the Parliamentary Museum is now located. Behind these structures was the official residence of the Minister of War. For a period after 1945 this area held the office of the U.S. Occupation Chief of Staff. In the years since World War II, these various military units have been replaced by more peaceful and democratic structures.

Nagatacho & Akasaka

0   200m

N

NAITOMACHI

SAMONCHO

SUGACHO

YOTSUYA

Marunouchi Line

Yotsuya

Y

SHINJUKU GYOEN
NATIONAL GARDEN

DAIKYOCHO

SHINANOMACHI

WAKABA

Kokuritsu-kyogijo

Shinanomachi

MINAMI-
MOTOMACHI

Geihinkan State
Guest Houses

Tokyo
Gymnasium

National
Stadium

Meiji Memorial
Picture Museum

Meiji Kinenkan
(Meiji Memorial
Hall)

9

AKASAKA DETACHED PALAC

to Indoor
Swimming Pool

KASUMIGAOKAMACHI

Oedo Line

MOTO-AKASAK

MEIJI
PARK

11

THE MEIJI
OUTER
GARDEN
(DIVERSION)

AKASAKA DETACHED
PALACE GARDEN

Jingu
Baseball
Stadium

Aoyama-dori

Gaien-nishi-dori

JINGUMAE

Prince Chichibu
Memorial
Rugby Stadium

Aoyama-
itchome

Aoyama-
itchome

Japan
Traditional
Craft Aoyama
Square

Canada

10

Soge
Kaika

German E
Asiatic Soc
(Göethe Inst

Honda

Choan-ji

Gaienmae

Gyokuso-ji

Watari-Um
Museum

Aoyama Bell
Commons

KITA-
AOYAMA

Baiso-in

MINAMI-AOYAMA

Oedo Line

Aoyama-dori

Gaien-nishi-dori

AOYAMA
CEMETERY

Nogizaka

21_21 Desi
Sight Muse

M
G

The Ritz-Carton
Suntory
Museum of Arts

Gaien-higashi-dori

TOKYO MID

Omotesando

Omotesando

Chiyoda Line

National
Art Center

AOYAMA
PARK

Fuji
Squ

R

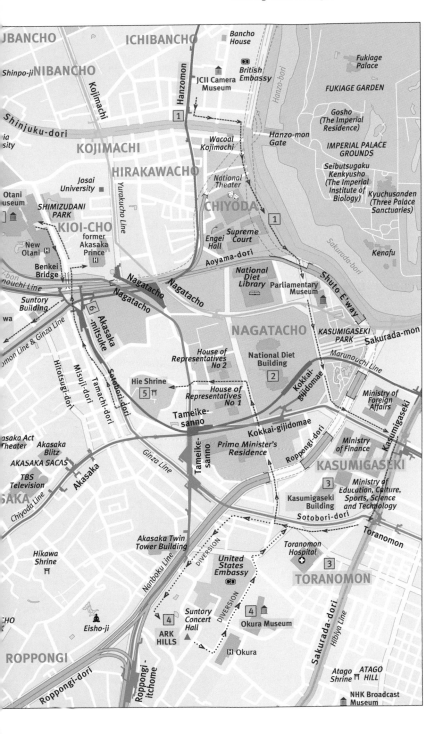

The National Diet Building

② NATIONAL DIET BUILDING

On the left along this street headed toward the Diet is the **Parliamentary Museum** (Kensei Kinenkan). (It is open without charge from 9:30 to 5:00 p.m. [last entry at 4:30] but is closed on Saturdays, Sundays, national holidays, the last day of each month, and from December 28 through January 4. Entry is free.) The museum was established in 1972 to commemorate the establishment of the Diet a century earlier. The first floor, as the building is approached from Uchibori-dori, contains the 1960 Ozaki Memorial Hall (Ozaki Yukio Kinenkan), which commemorates Yukio Ozaki (1859–1954), who was a member of Parliament starting with the session of the first Diet in 1890 and who served in the Diet for sixty-three years. A fearless opponent of the military in the 1920s and 1930s, he stood for parliamentary government at a time when it was being undermined by the Japanese military. He was also responsible for the gift in 1912 of the cherry blossom trees that grace the parks of Washington, D.C. The adjacent main portion of the Parliamentary Museum offers a model of the Diet on the second floor. The model is accompanied by an audiovisual slide presentation in Japanese and in English detailing the development of parliamentary democracy in Japan and the vicissitudes that the building and democracy have faced through the years. Special exhibitions are also presented from time to time.

Across the street from the Parliamentary Museum is the 1961 eight-story **National Diet Library**, with more than two million books in its six above-ground floors and its two below-ground levels. (It is open daily without charge from 9:30 to 7:00 p.m. [to 5:00 p.m. on Saturdays] except Sundays, national holidays, and the third Wednesday of each month.) The National Diet library has 30 branch libraries.

Ahead on the street we have been following lies the massive three-story National Diet Building on the right. But first attention should be drawn to a small "temple" on the left in the park. On the hill below the Diet is a small classical Roman temple, which covers the **Water Level Bench Repository**. It is from this marker that the height of the Japanese plains and mountains are measured. The marker is set at 80.3 feet (24.1 meters) above the level of the Sumida River. Between the mini-temple and the Parliamentary Museum is a plaza with a long pool with fountains, and beside it are three metal shafts 100 feet (30 meters) tall supporting a clock. This area is on a height above and overlooking the Sakurada-mon Gate of the palace and the government offices below.

The **National Diet Building** (Kokkaigijido) stands on the site of the mansion of Lord Ii, the leading minister of the Tokugawa shogun in the 1850s, who, with his guards, was cut down not far from here at the Sakurada-mon Gate entrance to the castle grounds in 1860. A park or plaza, as mentioned above, stands before the Diet, with a 164-foot (49.2-meter)-wide boulevard below it leading from the Sakurada-mon Gate and the Sakurada-bori moat of the Imperial Palace where Lord Ii was slain. There is a garden on either side of this boulevard, a Western-style and a Japanese-style garden, both created in 1964. Designed by the architects Yoshikuni Okuma and Kenkichi Yabashi, the granite and marble Diet Building, with a central clock tower rising 200 feet (60 meters) above the entry portals, was begun in 1920, but it was not completed until 1937. When facing the building, the House of Councilors, with 250 seats, is on the right, while the House of Representatives, with 467 seats, is on the left. Before World War II, the House of Councilors was the House of Peers, the Peers being the newly created nobility of the post-1868 Meiji years. The building is not open to the public, but it may be visited on the presentation of one's passport and a letter of introduction from a member of the Diet–which is to say that entry is seldom possible. Entry to the Visitor's Gallery when the Diet is in session may be obtained from one's embassy in advance of the date of the visit. It is possible to enter the grounds alone by requesting permission from the office at the rear of the Diet Building. (Such visiting hours are generally from 9:00 a.m. to 5:00 p.m. [last entry at

4:30] except for Saturdays, Sundays, and national holidays, depending on whether sessions of the Diet are in process.)

3 KASUMIGASEKI AND TORONOMON

To the south and east of the Diet Building are the many offices of the national government. Some 30 such offices lie to either side of Sakurada-dori, which runs southwest from the Sakurada-mon Gate of the Imperial Palace. Farther south Is the 1968 **Kasumigaseki Building**, the first of Tokyo's post-World War II skyscrapers and its first skyscraper of 36 floors. One reaches this structure by continuing along the street in front of the Diet Building and following that street as it bends slightly to the left. On the left one passes the **Ministry of Foreign Affairs Building** and on the right the **Ministry of Finance Building**. Turning to the right on Sakurada-dori and following this street as it bends to the right, one comes to Sotobori-dori at Toranomon. The Kasumigaseki Building lies to the right. With some 25 cafés and restaurants in its basement and lower floors, most open between 11:00 a.m. and 11:00 p.m., the building is a good place to stop for a break on the tour.

The **Toranomon** (Tiger Gate) area supposedly received its name when, in the distant past, a Korean diplomatic mission exhibited a large tiger in a cage at this former gateway at the Sotobori Moat. This area of Sotobori-dori is in the low land below two hills and was originally a marshland when Tokyo Bay extended close to the castle grounds. Here was a lake, Tame-ike, which today is the name of the intersection along Sotobori-dori to the west. Once a weir and a dam stood here, the dam serving to back up waters to keep the Sotobori moat about the castle filled. With time the lake shrank, and in 1910 it was finally drained to create the street Sotobori-dori, which from here leads to Akasaka Mitsuke.

4 ARK HILLS AND THE OKURA MUSEUM

If one continues along Sotobori-dori, the Shuto Expressway crosses overhead at Roppongi-dori. An optional and somewhat lengthy diversion to the left on this walk can take one along Roppongi-dori to the **Ark Hills** development with the ANA Hotel Tokyo, a luxury hotel that boasts a waterfall and a model Venetian gondola in its lobby. Here, too, is the **Suntory Concert Hall**, seating 2,000 people, a part of the Ark Hills development along with the hotel, restaurants, office space, and luxury apartments. The more ambitious who take this side jaunt may wish to follow the street behind the ANA Hotel up to the Hotel Okura where the **Okura Museum** (Okura Shukokan) is located at its front entrance. (Open from 10:00 a.m. to 4:30 p.m. but closed on Mondays, national holidays, and from December 29 through January 4; entry ¥800.) This museum, whose art objects were collected by Baron Okura, became the first private museum to open in Tokyo when it made its debut in 1917. Okura was a Meiji-era industrialist (armaments) who founded the Imperial Hotel and whose son founded the luxurious Okura Hotel. The museum was destroyed in the 1923 earthquake, but it was rebuilt in a Chinese style in 1928. The two floors of the museum display Baron Okura's collection of ancient art from India, China, Tibet, and Japan as well as exquisite ceramics, sculptures, bronzes, costumes, and lacquer ware from its many diverse holdings. Exhibits run for three to four months before being changed.

On leaving the hotel, the street before the Okura can be taken to the right, passing the large **United States Embassy** complex. In 1884 this property, assessed at $25,000, was given by the Japanese government as a perpetual gift of friendship with the United States. (Nonetheless, six years later the United States gave the Meiji government $16,000 for the land.) This 1976 structure was designed by Cesar Pelli, and the arrangement of windows on one side gives the appearance of the American flag in stone and glass. Continuing down hill to the Toranomon intersection with Sotobori-dori, a turn to the left brings one back to the point before the Shuto Expressway where this diversion began.

5 HIE SHRINE

From here, continuing west on Sotobori-dori and taking the first street on the right, one soon crosses Roppongi-dori and then comes to the **Prime Minister's Residence** on the left. Crossing the street and continuing straight, one passes the **House of Representatives' Office Building Number One.** The street between it and Building Number Two should be taken downhill to the left, and this brings one to the upper level of the Hie Shrine. (The two office buildings are of an uninspired modern architectural style.)

The **Hie Shrine** was created in the year 830 and was located in the outer reaches of the future city of Edo, but in 1478 Ota Dokan

The main building at Hie Shrine, starting point of the Sanno Matsuri, one of Tokyo's great festivals

removed it to the castle grounds as a spiritual protector for his stronghold. In 1607 Tokugawa Ieyasu moved it to the hill to the west of the castle, land on which the Supreme Court now stands, so as to protect the castle from the southeast in the same manner that the Kan'ei-ji Temple in Ueno protected the castle from the northeast. After the shrine burned to the ground in the Long Sleeves Fire of 1657, it was eventually rebuilt at its present site in the highly decorated *gongen* style favored by the Tokugawas. Its main façade faced the castle. Here it not only acted as a protector of the castle but served as the site for worship of the deity who protected the Tokugawa family. Each Tokugawa infant was brought to the shrine shortly after its birth to be blessed by the shrine deity. The Hie Shrine was the largest Shinto shrine in Edo in Tokugawa days, and it was given its name from the fact that it is a branch of the Hiyoshi (Hie) Shrine in Kyoto. (Open October to March from 6:00 a.m. to 5:00 p.m. and from April to September from 5:00 a.m. to 6:00 p.m. No entry charge.)

The shrine was destroyed in the fire bombings of 1945, and it was recreated in ferroconcrete in 1967. The deity of the shrine is Oyamakuni-no-kami, the god of the Kyoto shrine on Mt. Hiei who protected the city of Kyoto from the northeast, the point from which evil flows. As for the earlier castle, it serves now as the protector of the present palace and perhaps, since Meiji times, of the

Diet and government offices as well. This is but one of 3,000 Hie Shrines throughout Japan. The messenger of the shrine deity is the monkey, and thus monkey images can be found about the complex. One image of a female monkey holding its child (to the left of the main shrine building) is regarded as a symbol of maternal harmony, and thus the shrine has earned a reputation as being one which can grant fertility and then ensure safe childbirth to those who worship here. A shrine to the Shinto deity Inari is also on the grounds.

The main entrance to the shrine is on its eastern side, the side facing toward the hill on which the National Diet stands. A stone torii stands at the foot of the 51 steps that lead up to the roofed corridor that encloses the square before the Haiden (Prayer Hall) and Honden (Spirit Hall). The entry gate is guarded on either side of the passageway into the shrine by the seated Shinto guardians Yadaijin and Sadaijin, with their bow and arrows and sword. Before the Haiden a female monkey holding her infant is on the left while a male monkey is on the right. Both are clothed or draped with protective colorful cloth. To the right of the Haiden and the corridors are a series of smaller shrine buildings, including *kura* in which are stored shrine festive objects and the *mikoshi* in which the spirits of the deities are taken in procession every other year. Roosters strut freely about the grounds. The shrine museum is at the top of the steps from Sotobori-dori (open every day but Tuesday and Friday from 10:00 a.m. to 4:00 p.m.), and it holds many important swords once owned by the Tokugawa clan. Entry is free. The Sanno Festival (the Festival Without Equal) has always been one of the great festivals of Tokyo, and it takes place every other year from June 10 through 16 with a great procession on June 15. Some 50 *mikoshi* (sacred palanquins holding the god spirit), two imperial carriages, and 400 participants in Heian-period (800-1200) costumes participate in the procession, with the shrine officials on horseback behind the most sacred, oxen-drawn *mikoshi*.

On February 26, 1936, the shrine was the center of some political excitement. In that period, when the Japanese military was getting more out of civilian control, some 1,400 soldiers set out to "restore power" to the emperor and to bring wealth to the people. They executed two former premiers of government and the inspector general of military training, seized government buildings, and set up their headquarters below the Hie Shrine. Four days later, with little support from the military, the government, or the emperor, they surrendered. Nineteen of the ringleaders were executed—but they are remembered by those with a nationalistic and militarist bent on a memorial stone at their place of execution, which today faces the Shibuya Ward Office and the NHK Broadcasting Building in Shibuya.

6 AKASAKA MITSUKE AREA

On leaving the shrine, descend the hill that is lined with vermilion torii. The torii of this shrine are unique in that they have a triangular-shaped top rather than the normal slightly curved top bar these sacred gateways usually employ. (One can also descend the street that runs from the rear of the Diet Building to Sotobori-dori.) Descending the hill to Sotobori-dori, there are a series of streets running parallel to Sotobori-dori to the west that are noted for their restaurants. These streets in the **Akasaka district** took a new lease on life when the Kasumigaseki area became the seat of government after 1868, and they developed restaurants to serve the new government quarters. Some of the restaurants provided geisha entertainment. As the traditional and not-too-distant Shimbashi geisha area grew ever more expensive and exclusive, a new entertainment and geisha sector became established in this area between the hills not far from the Diet. It also at one time had its

The view from Benkei Bridge in Akasaka Mitsuke

seamier side, with "bath girls"—or prostitutes—who served visitors to Akasaka.

By the early 1900s the area was in its heyday, supported by politicians, businessmen, and the new breed of journalists. In more recent times these types have been augmented by staff from the nearby TBS television studios. Tourists frequent the restaurants as well, but the *ryotei* (geisha restaurants) have declined greatly with the passage of time. They can still be recognized by the huge limousines parked before the high walls behind which they sit. These are establishments that only the wealthiest can afford. The three streets to the west of Sotobori-dori—Hitotsugi-dori, Misuji-dori, and Tamachi-dori—are at the heart of this entertainment area. Misuji-dori, between Hitotsugi-dori and Tamachi-dori, has some of the major geisha restaurants.

Back on Sotobori-dori and continuing toward the overhead expressway is **Akasaka Mitsuke**, that crossroads of streets, subway stations, and the overhead Shuto Expressway (once again encountered in another of its branches). The Ginza, Marunouchi, and Hanzomon subway lines all have entrances here. As has been indicated, Sotobori-dori, which we have been following, was once the outer moat for the Tokugawa castle and was completed in 1636 by the third shogun, Tokugawa Iemitsu. The moats about the castle each had a *mitsuke*, a fortified gate, at the bridges that crossed the moat. As with the *masaguta* gates at the Ote-mon and the Sakurada-mon entrance to the castle, each *mitsuke* had behind the gate a fortified wall that formed a "box" within which any trespasser or enemy could be ambushed. It is claimed that there were 36 of these *mitsuke* about the moats. The gate at Akasaka Mitsuke is said to have been one of the finest of these defensive units, and it guarded the road (the present Aoyama-dori) that led from the castle to Shibuya. The last remnants of this gate and the one at Sotobori-dori at Toranomon were removed by the Meiji government in 1873.

Today, of course, the gate is missing but survives in the name of the area, Akasaka Mitsuke, which means "Red Hill Fortress Gate." Akasaka received its name of "Red Slope" from plants for red dye that once grew here. A portion of the moat does continue to exist, separating the lands of the Akasaka Detached Palace from the New Otani Hotel and running in part in front of the Akasaka Prince Hotel, where it is spanned by the **Benkei Bridge**. On the left of the Akasaka Mitsuke intersection is the **Suntory Building** (see Walk 13 for the Suntory Museum), which houses the Tokyo offices of beer, spirit, and soft-drink maker Suntory. Crossing under the expressway, ahead is the Benkei Bridge, while looming large to the right beyond the bridge is the 40-story **Grand Prince Hotel Akasaka**. This starkly white building shaped in the form of a folding fan in mirrored white glass and aluminum was designed by Kenzo Tange in 1983. It closed shortly after the Great East Japan Earthquake in March 2011 and was for a while then used to house evacuees from the Tohoku region who had been displaced by the earthquake and tsunami. Now empty, it is slated for demolition but was still standing as of publication.

7 NEW OTANI ART MUSEUM

Crossing the Benkei Bridge brings one to the impressive **New Otani Hotel** and its traditional garden. The 40-story main structure was built in 1974, and then in 1991 a 30-story **New Otani Tower** was added. Between the two units of the hotel, some 2,100 rooms are available for guests. The **New Otani Art Museum** can be found off the sixth-floor lobby of the original building. The gallery to the right offers paintings by noted Japanese artists, while the gallery on the left shows the work of Western artists and particularly the Ecole de Paris school. (The museum is open 10:00 a.m. to 6:00 p.m. except Mondays. It also closes during the New Year holidays. Admission is ¥500 but is free for those staying at the hotel.) The lower floors of the hotel offer a variety of gift shops and some 36 coffee shops and restaurants, which can provide a break in the tour if one wishes. The gorgeous traditional outdoor gardens of the hotel are well worth a visit; they were once a portion of the estate of Kato Kiyomasa (1562–1611), the lord of Kumamoto, and they are a fine example of a traditional Japanese garden. The garden can be entered from the corridor between the two buildings of the hotel, the door to the garden being next to the lounge.

Temple or shrine? Toyokawa Inari Shrine is unusually also known as Myogon-ji Temple.

8 TOYOKAWA INARI SHRINE

Returning to the Suntory Building, a turn to the right on its far side brings one onto Aoyama-dori. Walking along this avenue, at the second street on the right is the **Myogon-ji Temple** or **Toyokawa Inari Shrine**. This is one of those delightful anomalies of Japanese culture, for here is a Zen temple that has red lanterns such as are found only at Shinto shrines. There was a tradition for such a joint situation before 1868, when temples and shrines cohabited, but from that time on temples and shrines were forcibly separated by the new Meiji government. Shinto had always been an unorganized folk faith (unorganized, not disorganized). The advent of Buddhism in the 600s provided a faith that was highly organized and structured, and in time Ryobu Shinto (Dual Shinto) developed, whereby Shinto shrines were often run by Buddhist temples. There has always been a relationship between the two faiths (the Japanese are not as prone to sharp divisions between faiths as in the West), since in Japan each temple has a small shrine to the Shinto deity of the land it occupies.

What is the occasion for the seeming open confusion at this temple/shrine? According to tradition, in the early 1200s Emperor Juntoko's third son, Kanganzenji (who happened to be a Zen priest), was on a ship returning from China. In the midst of a terrible storm, when all seemed lost, the son saw the image of the Buddhist deity Dakini (who is also known as the Shinto deity Inari) riding on a white fox and carrying a rice bale on his back. The ship did not founder, and the son carved an image of Dakini on his return to Japan. This carved figure of a deity who has both a Buddhist and a Shinto aspect is said to be the *hibutsu,* the hidden image, at the altar of the temple. (It is pictured within the temple, even though the original may not be viewed.)

In the period from 1717 to 1736 there lived across the street from this temple a daimyo who served as a city magistrate. He had come from Toyokawa in the provinces, and he brought with him the image carved by the noble Zen monk, which he established in the branch shrine that he had built across from his residence. This daimyo, Oka Tadasuke, was noted for his beneficent rule as a magistrate, and he is credited, among other charitable acts, with having created the first fire brigades for the city—brigades other than those that served solely to protect daimyo

mansions in times of danger. Within the temple grounds, the main hall of the temple is guarded in a rather unusual manner by red-bibbed foxes, which normally grace Shinto shrines but seldom appear in Buddhist temples. There is a hexagonally roofed shrine to the noble magistrate on the left side of the hall, while to the right is a modern building, the **Akasaka Tokyo Toyokawa Inari Kaikan,** where one can have priests pray for whatever type of success one is imploring Dakini/Inari to grant. Even in these modern days there is a bit of the supernatural in such requests, for the priest uses "the wind of wisdom" in reading the Buddhist sutras that may help in the granting of one's wishes. This "wind" insures that while the priest may chant only from the first and last page of an extensive sutra, when the intervening pages are being quickly flipped the "wind of wisdom" sees to it that the entire reading is automatically efficacious. The hall also provides space where shrine events can be held.

Before the Kaikan is a statue of the Kodakara Kanzein Bosatsu, a Kannon image holding a child in its arms. This bodhisattva is prayed to for the birth of healthy children and for prosperity for the future family line. In addition to the shrine to the magistrate and the main Buddhist hall, Inari shrines can be found on the grounds, guarded by their fox images—to which some worshippers bring offerings from nearby restaurants. The approach to the main Inari shrine is lined with banners, given by worshippers as prayers for the granting of their wishes or for thanks for the successful fulfillment of their prayers. Along the path to the Inari shrine is the **Migawari Jizo** on the right, again an unusual situation where a Buddhist deity is worshipped in the approaches to this Shinto shrine. He is a favored deity, since he takes upon himself the problems or troubles afflicting those who pray to him. To the left of the Inari shrine are images of the Seven Gods of Good Fortune. At the far end of this busy and self-contained temple/shrine is the aforementioned Akasaka Tokyo Toyokawa Bunka Kaikan, a hall for wedding receptions, conventions, and other affairs both religious and secular.

9 AKASAKA DETACHED PALACE

Farther along Aoyama-dori on the right are the parklands of the **Akasaka Detached Palace**. Not too far within the grounds were the separate palace units of members of the

The Akasaka Detached Palace today serves as a state guesthouse for visiting dignitaries.

imperial family, the mansions of the former Emperor Hirohito's brothers, Prince Chichibu and Prince Mikasa and their families. While the palace, which was designated a National Treasure of Japan in 2009, cannot be seen on this walking tour, it shall be here described so that those interested in it can view it at another time. The Akasaka Detached Palace can best be seen by a seven-minute walk from Yotsuya Station on the JR Sobu Line. The palace itself cannot be entered, since it serves today as a State Guest House (Geihinkan), but the gardens and fountains may be visited.

Before the end of the Tokugawa regime in 1868, the land that the Akasaka Palace occupies had belonged to the Kii branch of the Tokugawa family. Taken over by the Imperial Household Agency in 1868, the Kii mansion had to serve as the Emperor Meiji's residence from 1873 to 1888, after the buildings of the Imperial Palace were destroyed by fire. The new Akasaka Palace was built for the emperor by public subscription, and it was completed in 1909 as the Togu Palace. The structure was created after the fashion of English, French, and German palaces in a vain attempt to be "as Western as the West" in imperial architecture. In part, the architect Katayama Tokuma, who was a student of Josiah Condor, modeled it after the Palace of Versailles in France, but, reflecting the era prior to the French Revolution, the original model for the Akasaka Palace hardly served as the best example for the turn-of-the-20th-century official dwellings.

To further complicate matters, an American architect's advice was also invited. The new palace had all the grandeur and many of the discomforts of European palaces of the past. There was, for example, but one bathroom, and it was in the basement. The emperor's bedroom was in one wing of the building, while that of the empress was in another wing. This may not have made for the closest of marital bliss, but on the other hand, it was the custom of the emperor to drop his handkerchief each evening in front of one of the ladies-in-waiting (a euphemism if ever there was one), who was thereby invited to his wing for that evening. The palace has seen changes through the years. Emperor Meiji, on his move to the Imperial Palace after 1888, gave the Togu Palace to the crown prince for a residence. After World War II, it temporarily housed the National Diet Library until 1962. Next it was the headquarters for the 1964 Olympics in Japan. Then in 1974 the palace was redone so it could serve as the State Guest House for heads of state when they visit Japan. President Ford of the United States in 1974, Queen Elizabeth of Britain in 1975, world leaders at the 1980 summit, and other heads of state have used the guest house. The various rooms are quite impressive: the Egyptian Room was the former Smoking Room of the original palace, while the Hall of the Feathered Robe (the former ballroom) has a painted ceiling inspired by the Noh play *The Feathered Robe*. The former dining room is now the Hall of Flowers and Birds. As indicated above, the grounds also contain the **Omiya Palace Park**, with mansions of the branches of the imperial family, which included a residence for the Crown Prince.

10 SOGETSU KAIKAN

Returning to Aoyama-dori, some three streets further along the avenue is the **Sogetsu Art Center**, a 1977 Kenzo Tange building of mirrored glass. The Sogetsu School of Flower Arranging was begun by Sofu Teshigahara, and he was succeeded as head of the school by his son Hiroshi Teshigahara, who is also well-known as the director of the film *Woman in the Dunes*. Today, Hiroshi's daughter, Akane Teshigahara, is carrying on the family tradition as the head (*iemoto*) of the Sogetsu School. The lobby, a cascade of stone, has sculptures by Isamu Noguchi, and flower arrangements here are often on a very large scale. A small theater is on the lower level and a café on an upper level overlooks the lobby and the street. There flower arrangements by members of the school as well as other Japanese artists may be seen, and traveling exhibits of contemporary art are frequently on view. Lessons in the Sogetsu style of flower arrangements are possible for a fee.

One can continue further along Aoyama-dori to the Meiji Shrine Outer Gardens, but this is recommended only for those who wish to see the 1964 Olympic sports complex or the Meiji Picture Gallery, a rather heavy-handed glorification of the life of Emperor Meiji in 80 pictures (described below). If one does not continue to the picture gallery, a return to Akasaka Mistsuke brings one back to the various subway lines that lie below that intersection. (One can also reach the picture gallery and sports complex by taking the subway from Akasaka Mitsuke to Gaienmae Station, which is close to the Gallery.)

11 THE MEIJI OUTER GARDEN (DIVERSION)

The 20 acres (8 hectares) of the **Meiji Outer Garden** are an extension in part of the former daimyo lands that became the Akasaka Detached Palace. This portion of the land was developed into the 120-acre (36-hectare) Aoyama Parade Ground for the military after 1868. Here in 1912 was held the funeral service for Emperor Meiji, and in recent years a major portion of the area has become sports grounds. On the left side of the Outer Garden can be found the units that were the center of athletic events during the 1964 Olympics: the **National Stadium**, which can seat 75,000; the two **Jingu Baseball Stadiums**, which can accommodate 66,000 and 12,000 respectively; the **Prince Chichibu Memorial Rugby Stadium**, seating 20,000; the **Tokyo Gymnasium**, for 5,300 spectators; and the **Metropolitan Indoor Swimming Pool** for 3,000.

A long walk into the grounds along the gingko tree-lined roadway leads to the **Meiji Memorial Picture Gallery** (Seitoku Kino Kaigakan—The Sacred Virtue Memorial Gallery), a building that in part resembles the National Diet, except that its center portion is domed rather than having a tower. (The gallery is open from 9:00 a.m. to 5:00 p.m. daily all year and admission is ¥500.) Construction of the gallery was begun within three years of the emperor's death in 1912, but it was not completed until 1920. It was one of the centers where Japanese nationalism was fostered by the government's militant Shinto agencies before the end of World War II. The hall contains 80 pictures, half in traditional Japanese style, half in a modern Western style, all glorifying the emperor and his life in a manner that raises him to the level of divinity—which nationalist forces found helpful in creating a post-Tokugawa Japan. The gallery is no longer supported by the government but is now operated by the Meiji Shrine Foundation. Thus it has to create income by selling charms, through the rental of the nearby **Meiji Memorial Hall** (Meiji Kinenkan) for weddings and meetings, and with the restaurant and a beer terrace in the same building. This hall was once part of the Aoyama Palace, and it was here that the Imperial Constitution of the 1890s was discussed in front of the emperor. (The **Kinkei Lounge** is the restored room where the Meiji Constitution was promulgated in 1890.) In general, today's public has shown little interest in this memorial gallery to the Meiji emperor, and it can be bypassed by the average tourist not interested in the glorification of an unimportant emperor who was a façade for his militaristic advisors.

When one has completed this diversion, the Sobu Line trains may be reached at the Shinanomachi Station to the right rear of the gallery or one may take the Ginza Line at Gaienmae Station on Aoyama-dori for return to other parts of the city.

GETTING THERE

This tour starts at Hanzomon Station on the Hanzomon subway line, which connects directly to major stations such as Shibuya, Omotesando, and Otemachi.

Walking Tour 4

TSUKIJI AND TSUKISHIMA

The Harvest of the Sea, the Shrine of the Fishermen Spies, the Foreigners' Enclave, and Dutch Learning

1. Tsukiji Market
2. Hama Detached Palace Garden
3. Tsukishima Island
4. Dutch Learning Area
5. Tsukiji Hongan-ji Temple

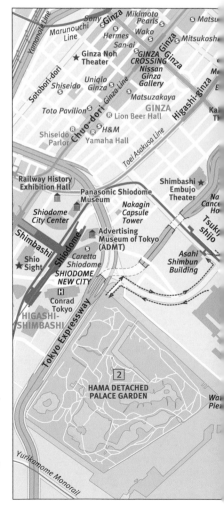

If Tokugawa Ieyasu were to return to Tokyo today, there is one area of his one-time capital that would utterly amaze him, and that is **Tsukiji**, to the east of Ginza. His astonishment would stem from the fact that this was still part of Tokyo Bay while he was alive. The very name of the district, Tsukiji, is a giveaway as to the change that has taken place over the centuries, since *tsukiji* means "reclaimed land," and that is exactly what it is.

When Ieyasu had the hills of Kanda to the north of the castle leveled to fill in Hibiya Inlet, the fill also helped to create solid land on the marshes of what became the Nihombashi and Ginza areas of old Edo. The creation of the Tsukiji sector began about 1650, but the area was greatly enlarged after 1657, the result of the Long Sleeves Fire of that year, which destroyed much of the city. The marshy sections to the west of Ginza were filled in order to create additional land where some of the daimyo could build their mansions and portions could be granted to certain temples. (The filling in of Tokyo Bay continues. In the four decades after 1945, one-seventh of the bay was filled in to create an additional 7 square miles [18.2 square kilometers] of dry land.)

A goodly portion of the land was granted to the heirs of Okudaira Nobumasa (1555–1615), with politics and marriage being involved with this grant. Nobumasa had been an ally of Ieyasu, and, in one of the many battles before Ieyasu became supreme, the enemies of Nobumasa killed Nobumasa's wife in revenge for his defection to Ieyasu's side. To atone for the loss Nobumasa had sustained, Ieyasu granted Nobumasa his eldest daughter in marriage. In time, Ieyasu even adopted his grandson from this marriage, giving him the new family name of Matsudaira. A descendent, Matsudaira Sadonobu (1759–1829), was one of the great Tokugawa administrators, and it was his family, living in the Tsukiji area, who were unwittingly to help in the founding of modern Japanese studies of the West. Even before the Matsudaira family set foot on their newly created land, others of a

less powerful group were living on one of the small islands, at the point where the Sumida River flows into the bay. Here on the island of **Tsukuda-jima**, now much enlarged, Ieyasu's son Hidetada had settled a group of fishermen from the Osaka area with a twofold purpose to suit his needs, one culinary and one political. Those purposes will be revealed when the fishermen's island is explored.

☐1 **TSUKIJI MARKET**
The fishing tradition remains strong in modern Tsukiji, in the shape of the **Tsukiji Central Wholesale Markets**, where this tour begins. Situated directly south of Tsukiji-

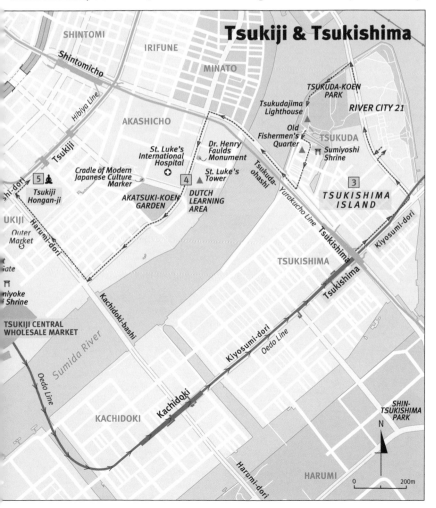

Shijo subway station, Tsukiji Market is one of Tokyo's earliest risers. The famed early-morning tuna auctions there are ideal for visitors to Tokyo keen enough or jet-lagged enough to get out of bed before sunrise, for they erupt into a frenzy of action at 5:30 a.m. and are one of the most worthwhile experiences Tokyo has to offer. With the tuna auctions dominating tourist brochure coverage of the market, Tsukiji has become known among foreigners primarily as a fish market, although it is actually a central market that handles all kinds of produce (fish, meat, vegetables, processed and dried fruit) with the exception of rice. This area was once the exquisite garden of the Matsudaira lords, difficult though that may be to imagine. From the beginnings of Edo in the early 1600s to the last century, the city's fish market lay to the north along the Nihombashi River at the far side of the Nihombashi Bridge. There the many white-plastered *kura* or storehouses and the fish market reigned supreme. The 1923 earthquake and fire, however, destroyed the area, and the market began to move to its present site, which became official in 1935 as new buildings were erected.

With the change in forms of shipping and packaging of bulk foodstuffs, the 1935 market has proved less than efficient. Plans have been

Tuna ready for auction at Tsukiji Market

Although primarily a wholesale market, Tsukiji also serves the needs of the general public.

suggested for moving the market to the south, but in 1991 a 12-year renovation program began. The revamped three-story market was to have multistory skyscrapers around it, with the market itself doubling in size and adequate parking provided for the vehicles flooding into the area each morning. Whereas much of the produce, particularly fish, came by boats in the past, today frozen bulk foods arrive by air and are then transported here by truck from Narita Airport, which can boast that it is Japan's leading fish port. It is estimated that 90 percent of the fish now arrives overland rather than by sea to the market's docks, with salmon from Canada and Chile, shrimp from Thailand, sea urchin roe from Maine, and tuna from Spain. So many fish have died to satisfy the Japanese palate that a monument has been raised outside the market to memorialize the fish that have given up their lives.

The largest fish market in Asia, the Tsukiji Market is owned and under the control of the metropolitan government of Tokyo. The figures for the number of market stalls, employees, and wholesalers who work here each day are staggering. It is estimated that there are some 1,677 wholesale shops that employ 15,000 workers. Work begins at 2:00 in the morning, while the auctions themselves start at 5:30 a.m. Some 3,000 barrows take the fish from the auction to the buyers' quarters. It is said that 60,000 individuals are within the market each day, 30,000 of them comprising wholesalers and retailers. Foreign workers have been on the increase as Japanese find this labor less to their liking. While the most exciting time to visit the market is when the auctions begin (registration for a visit starts at 5:00 a.m.), finding adequate transportation from one's hotel at that hour can be difficult. The auctions may also be off limits, as the market often places temporary bans or restrictions on tourists (both foreign and Japanese) in certain parts in response to complaints from the merchants that the visitors disrupt their work. Visitors are strongly advised to check the official market Web site (www.tsukiji-market.or.jp) before planning a trip and to make a note of how to behave properly while in the market. Later risers may wish to visit from around 8:30 a.m. to 9:30 a.m., before the market begins to wind down for the day. This is usually a safe time to avoid the visitor restrictions. As late as 1:00 p.m. there may still be plenty of activity, though the work day there is coming to an end.

Restaurants in the small streets that make up the Outer Market area (to the north of the main market) serve the freshest of fish at prices far more affordable than in the restaurants of nearby Ginza and so are a great place to stop for breakfast or an early lunch. Some of the restaurants have English menus for tourists, but as most are there to serve the market's workers, you may need to rely on the picture menus or the plastic food mock-ups in the shop windows to place your order.

2 HAMA DETACHED PALACE GARDEN

On leaving the front gate of the Inner Market (to the west), one is opposite the plant and offices of the *Asahi Shimbun* **newspaper**, where guided tours can be arranged. A ten-minute walk to the southwest along the street in front of the market—a street that gradually curves to the right—brings one to the entrance of the **Hama Detached Palace** (Hama Rikyu) grounds, now a public park. (Open daily from 9:00 a.m. to 4:30 p.m. but closed for the New Year holidays; entry ¥300.). The Hama Palace grounds originally belonged to a Matsudaira lord who filled in a portion of the bay to create wharves and warehouses to hold the rice he brought in from his Nagoya estates, the sale of which was to offset the expense of maintaining the clan's Edo mansion. The Matsudaira daimyo eventually gave the land to the sixth Tokugawa shogun, Ienobu, who in 1709 erected a villa and created gardens filled with pavilions, pine trees, cherry trees, and duck ponds. Unlike his predecessor shogun, who forbade the killing of any animals, Ienobu loved duck hunting, and thus there were three duck ponds in the grounds. The large pond in the garden was a tidal pond whose waters were continually cleansed by the flow of the tides. A floodgate still controls the filling and cleansing of the ponds by the tide.

At the end of the Tokugawa's rule over Japan, the grounds were taken over by the Meiji Foreign Ministry. The shogun's villa was burned, but it was restored in 1869 when a brick building with a veranda was built to house guests of state. It was here that former president Grant of the United States and his wife stayed on their visit to Japan in 1879. Emperor Meiji had his first carriage ride to the Detached Palace for his visit to Grant, and the emperor and the president held conversa-

New Tokyo and old: Hama Rikyu's Nakajima teahouse and Shiodome's skyscrapers

tions (through interpreters, of course) in a pavilion, a "floating" teahouse set in the midst of one of the ponds. This official guesthouse did not prove to be a success, however, and guests were soon put up in the new Rokumeikan opposite Hibiya Park. With ownership transferred to the Imperial Household Agency in time, the grounds continued to be used for outdoor parties for Meiji nobles and for receptions for foreign guests. The original brick guesthouse was later removed.

The Hama Detached Palace passed to the city of Tokyo after 1945, and it was turned into a public park the next year. Stands for snacks and a midday repast are available on the grounds of the garden. The 60-acre (24-hectare) park still holds a lovely tidal pond, which is spanned by staggered bridges shaded by wisteria-covered trellises. Of the three ponds in the garden, two are now fenced-in as nature and duck preserves. The pine-bordered shores of the ponds and cherry trees that flower in the spring add charm to the garden. The pavilion on an island in the middle of the larger pond, reminiscent of the one where the emperor and the president met in 1879, has been rebuilt with its veranda "floating" on the pond. A path along the northern side of the park leads to a pier where a water bus may be taken up the Sumida River to the Azumabashi bridge or to Asakusa. The boats leave from 9:50 a.m. to dusk for a 35-minute trip. The waterway at the Hama Detached Garden where the boats dock is enclosed with flood walls with floodgates, which can be closed in times of exceedingly high tides. Where once the park faced out of the bay, today it confronts one of the large man-made islands that have lengthened the Sumida River, which now flows in front of the park.

3 TSUKISHIMA ISLAND

Returning on foot to **Tsukiji-Shijo subway station** and taking the Oedo Line a quick two stops to the southeast leads to **Tsukishima Station**, the starting point of the next stage of this tour. As was mentioned earlier, in 1615 the recently established successor to Ieyasu as Tokugawa shogun had several motives for installing fishermen in this location. To begin with, the fishermen of Tsukuda in the Osaka area had assisted Ieyasu before 1603, and thus they were due a reward. They were therefore brought to these reclaimed mud flats at the entrance to the bay at Edo, an area that would grow as the bay was gradually filled in.

Tsukuda-jima (Island of Cultivated Rice Fields) originally consisted of two mud flats at the mouth of the Sumida River. In the early 1600s they were developed into two islands, the northern one being named Ishikawa-jima, since it was granted to Ishikawa Hachizaemon, the controller of the shogun's ships. The southern island became Tsukuda-jima, named for the fishermen's original home near Osaka. It was not until 1872 that the two islands were joined, and then in 1893 reclaimed mud flats to their south created the present large Tsukishima Island. The old fishermen's quarter has a branch of the Sumida River on its western side, while a narrow canal still exists on its northern and eastern sides. Its southern side has had its waterway filled in and replaced by the elevated highway leading to the bridge to Tsukiji.

The shogun's appreciation for past favors was not of the essence in this move, however. These fishermen were skilled in their trade, and they supplied the whitebait from the bay that garnished the shogun's tables. They fished in the dark of the night, burning firewood in metal baskets at the stern of their boats so as to attract the fish. As excellent watermen and navigators, they offered another purpose for the shogun: they could recognize any strange boats in the bay and thus serve as spies for the better protection of Edo and the shogun against any potential hostile forces. (A later shogun in 1715 enhanced his intelligence gathering by bringing skilled gardeners to Edo from Kii Province. Not only could they garden, but they were adept at entering the gardens of dissident daimyo by night and carrying out the shogun's less than charitable missions.)

One of the attractions of the island for Tokyo residents through the years has been the odor of soy sauce permeating the air here, for the fishermen developed a culinary delight by simmering fish in sea weed and soy sauce. Preserved in this boiled-down sauce along with salt, *tsukuda-ni* became a much desired delicacy. The island was known as well for a less happy association, for in the 1790s Matsudaira Sadanobu used it for a detention center for *ronin* (masterless samurai) who had lost their lord and thus their employment—as well as for vagrants. Both of these groups had become a political problem for the shogun, since they were often at the heart of brawls and riots. In a sense, what was being attempted was a halfway house where vagrants could be taught a trade. Later, for the 15 years after 1870, a prison was

The Sumida River with Tsukishima Island and the River City 21 skyscrapers on the right.

established here; it was subsequently removed to Sugamo in the Ikebukuro area. Three things remain of interest on the island, the Sumiyoshi Shrine, the old houses of the fishing village, which are all too quickly disappearing, and the River City 21 project that has been created in a former industrial area of the island.

We begin with the third of these attractions, **River City 21**. It has been indicated that once there were two islands, Ishikawa-jima and Tsukuda-jima, which are now joined. The former Ishikawa-jima is the northern half of the present island. Here the shogun's master of ships had his land in the 17th century, and here in 1854 the Mito branch of the Tokugawa built a modern shipyard. It became the first shipyard to launch a Western-style ship in 1876, and this small ship-building factory became the predecessor to the Ishikawajima Harima Heavy Industries, now relocated to the east of this area. Beginning in the 1980s, the factory and warehouse sites were cleared, and the new River City 21 appeared. This fascinating complex of high-rise apartments and office buildings is set in a park-like, landscaped area with a river promenade on three sides. Its architecture is strikingly modern, and thus this part of the tour should begin at **exit number four** of the **Tsukishima subway station**. This brings one to **Kiyosumi-dori**, and one should walk to the north away from the overhead highway. After a few short streets one reaches the new complex on the left, just before the bridge that crosses over the Sumida River into the

Fukagawa district of Tokyo. Steps or a ramp can be mounted to the park that encircles the River City 21 buildings on three sides, with a riverside promenade below at the water's edge. These 40-story buildings are also home to some of the most sought-after rental condominiums in Tokyo. A park, **Tsukuda Koen**, lies in front of these high-rise structures, and a **lighthouse** remains on its western side as a memorial to the beacon of the mid-19th century that once guided ships into the port of Edo. The new complex sits on a raised site above the dangers of tidal floods, whereas the older section of the island, closer to the subway line and main east-west street, are protected by high flood walls. A small canal separates River City 21 from the former Tsukuda fisherman's area, and thus a sluice in the riverfront with a red gate serves to control the waters of the Sumida River from flooding the canal at times of high water.

In their home near Osaka, the fisherman had worshipped the deity of the great **Sumiyoshi Shrine**. That shrine had been created by the Empress Jingu, who was deeply indebted to Sumiyoshi, the god of the sea. It seems that when the empress, then quite pregnant but determined to conquer Korea, made war against that country, Sumiyoshi had served as the pilot of her ship. When a huge storm threatened the survival of the ship and passengers, the god had a school of large fish support the boat in the high seas. Thus those involved with the sea are always beholden to Sumiyoshi, the deity of safety at sea. As a result, there are some 2,000 branch shrines of the Osaka main shrine throughout Japan. This small shrine is one representative. A large copper-plated torii provides an entrance to the shrine, with its unpainted and aged wooden buildings, and down the residential street beyond this first torii is a second stone torii. Behind it to the right is a traditional fountain for the cleansing of hands and mouth before approaching the Haiden, the Worship Hall, and the Honden, the Spirit Hall, of the shrine. Both these buildings have a copper-plated roof with the traditional *chigi* beams, a common feature in Shinto structures, to hold the roof in place, and they are joined by a roofed corridor or room. Thus the architecture of the shrine is typical of all Sumiyoshi shrines.

Smaller shrine units lie before the Haiden on the left and right side, while to the left of the Honden is an unusual brick *kura* (storage building) standing in front of and adjoining a traditional white plastered *kura*. The large inscribed *katsuozuka* (literally "bonito mound") *stone* on the grounds, behind the purification fountain, is a memorial to the fish that are caught each year for the *Tsukidani* delicacy, and services are held here in their memory annually. A *kagura* stage for religious dances is on the right side of the grounds. Aside from the usual stone lanterns, a pair of *koma-inu* (Korean lion-dogs) stand guard on either side of the path behind the stone torii. *Kura* to store the portable *mikoshi* used in shrine festivals are on the grounds. The Sumiyoshi Festival, which occurs on the first weekend in August every third year, is always a fascinating event. Then the octagonal *mikoshi* holding the god spirit is paraded through the streets behind a huge, golden lion's head. Traditionally, the *mikoshi* was brought to the river where it was partially immersed as a part of the procession, but since 1962 the flood walls built to protect the island have precluded this part of the festivities. Instead, the *mikoshi* is now paraded on a barge and doused with water as part of the festival, the offering of water to the deities being seen as religiously efficacious.

Since the shogun brought the fisherman from Osaka to Edo, they attempted to show their appreciation to him by having their shrine face toward the shogun's castle, and on festival days huge banners were raised so as to attract the attention of the denizens of the castle. Another festival related to Buddhist beliefs rather than to those of Shinto occurs each July 13, 14, and 15 from 7:00 p.m. to 9:00 p.m., when the residents of the area dance the traditional Bon Odori dance that is a part of the Buddhist festivity to honor the spirits of the deceased who return to this world for a few brief days each summer. Of interest also are the number of traditional wooden homes that still exist near the shrine, buildings that were fortunate enough to be spared in the 1923 earthquake and fire and then the 1945 fire bombings. The narrow streets and alleyways still retain some of the **original fishermen's houses**, though many have been modernized or replaced entirely so that the flavor of the old fishermen's quarter is gradually being lost. In addition, the old lighthouse that once guided ships to port now stands dwarfed by the very tall, high-rise apartments, a monument to times past.

④ DUTCH LEARNING AREA

Returning to the elevated highway under which the Yurakucho subway line runs, one must climb a set of stairs to the **Tsukudaohashi Bridge** to return to the Tsukiji mainland area. Until 1964 the only access to this island was by means of a ferry, which had existed from 1645 to 1964, for neither a bridge nor the later subway reached the island from Tsukiji, albeit the island had been connected by bridge to Fukagawa to the north since early in the 1900s. At the western end of the more recent bridge is a memorial stone recalling the ferry that traversed the river for so many centuries. In the early 1990s another novel bridge connected Tsukuda with the mainland, its single, inverted Y-shaped tower supporting the roadway over the river by means of cables. The Sumida River, a stream for pleasure boats with restaurants along the banks in centuries past, became less than desirable during the 20th century. Commercial and industrial sites took away the pleasurable aspects of the waterway, and then the high flood waters coursing in from the bay in the later 1940s led to the construction of the tall flood walls that effectively cut out any view of the waterway from riverside restaurants. In the last decades of the 20th century, this despoiling of the river was being reversed as new, modern buildings, many of them high-rise units, appeared along the banks of the Sumida. Attempts are being made as well to create promenades on the river side of the flood walls from the Tsukiji area up through Asakusa so as to return the waterfront to public enjoyment once more.

Once across the bridge, one is in an area that belonged to the Matsudaira lords. The whole sector was part of the retirement estate of Matsudaira Sadanobu in the 1700s, an area ennobled by the huge palace-residence of this important family. While nothing remains of the estate today, a remembrance of the Matsudaira palace with its outbuildings can be seen in a large model at the Edo-Tokyo Museum. Today the area has changed tremendously, but historic markers to **Dutch Learning** are encountered as the walk continues, and it may be well to provide some background to these markers. Here on Sadanobu's estate began a process that was to transform Japanese medicine, and which is in part remembered by the memorial stones in the neighborhood. Japanese medicine had always relied upon Chinese learning for its basic beliefs, but beginning in the 1770s this was to change drastically. A handful of Japanese physicians realized that much could be learned from Western sources: first, from the few Dutch medical books available to them, and then from the advice in the early 1800s of a Dutch physician, Philipp Franz van Siebold. The culmination came at the end of the 19th century, when St. Luke's Hospital was established—a hospital that exists still.

In 1770, Maeno Ryotaku, a physician and a retainer of the Matsudaira, journeyed to Nagasaki, where he was able to obtain a copy of a Dutch book on anatomy, *Ontleedkundige Tafelen.* Ryotaku had studied under Aoki Konyo, one of the early students of Dutch learning in Japan, and thus he already knew of this Dutch anatomy text. The only type of foreign books available in Japan were those in Dutch, often surreptitiously provided through the Dutch station at Dejima Island in Nagasaki due to the shogun's ban on anything foreign. Ryotaku, who had learned a smattering of Dutch, had developed a curiosity for greater European learning. (His mentor was nicknamed Doctor Potato by his contemporaries, since he had introduced the sweet potato as an edible staple to the diet.) With another physician friend, Sugita Gempaku, Ryutaku had the opportunity to perform an autopsy on a condemned criminal, and they were amazed to find that the anatomical plates in the Dutch book were a true representation of the human internal organs. By 1774 Ryotaku had translated the Dutch work

and thereby set Japanese medicine in new directions over the next century. With his appetite for more "esoteric" Western knowledge whetted, he mastered the Dutch language and went on to translate works on geography, military matters, and astronomy. This interest in Dutch learning (*rangaku*) was to expand among a group of Edo scholars, and thus the 19th century saw a gradual broadening of Japanese views. In 1826 Philipp Franz van Siebold was the first foreigner to teach modern European medical practices in Japan, and the revolution in the knowledge of modern medicine gathered steam.

Time moved on, and in 1858 another retainer of the Matsudaira clan, Fukuzawa Yukichi (1835–1901), was asked to open a school of Western learning on the clan property in Tsukiji. His students followed Dutch studies at first, but they then moved on to studies in English. Within a decade his school became the forerunner of Keio University, which today is south of Tsukiji in the Mita area of Tokyo. With the demise of the Tokugawa shogun's rule in 1868, the daimyo moved back to their estates and abandoned their Edo holdings, which in many cases were seized by the Meiji government. The Tsukiji area was not much in demand, since it was isolated from Ginza by various canals, and its space became known as the Navy Meadow, for the naval installation that existed here between 1858 and 1888. The Meiji government after 1868 was not happy with the unequal treaties forced upon Japan under the Tokugawa, and if Japan had to have foreigners in its midst, what better place to put them than in the comparatively isolated Tsukiji sector that had been abandoned by the daimyo?

To entice the foreigners to this somewhat out-of-the-way area, the government held out certain inducements. To begin with, they built a three-story hotel of 200 rooms. Since the foreigners ungraciously preferred to live in Yokohama, the hotel had to be sold to a Japanese entrepreneur four years after it was built. This grand if unsuccessful hostelry burned to the ground in 1872. Wooden houses of a vaguely Western nature were built for the foreigners who served in the legations and missionary enterprises that developed in Tsukiji. The American legation was here as well, and it remained until the extraterritorial status ended in 1899 and an embassy was set up in the Toranomon area of the city.

For the benefit of the foreigners, the Meiji

government even established a new Shimabara in the Shintomicho district, the area that in time would be occupied by the first Kabuki theater. Shimabara was the licensed, red-light district in Kyoto, and the new Shimabara brothel area in Edo had 84 teahouses, where one made an appointment to meet the more respectable geisha. It is said that there were 1,700 courtesans in 130 brothels aside from the 200 geisha (21 of them male) in 200 establishments—if these figures can be believed. Unfortunately the government did not realize that the few foreigners who were settling in the Tsukiji area were mostly Protestant missionaries, and thus the government's gracious accommodations found few foreign takers. The new Shimabara experiment folded in 1870, within one year of its creation. So much for one of the first major enterprises of the Meiji government.

Missionaries, teachers, and missionary physicians began to appear in Tsukiji. One such Presbyterian missionary from Scotland, from 1874 to 1887, was Henry Faulds, who opened a hospital close to the river. He noted that the illiterate among the Japanese used the print of their thumb for identification on documents. His scholarly paper concerning this discovery, which he submitted to the British journal *Nature* in 1880, led in time to the use of fingerprints as a source of identification for criminals in the West. Besides Fauld's hospital, schools and other medical facilities were established in this area by Western missionaries. One of them was to eventuate into Rikkyo University (now in Ikebukuro) and another into Aoyama Gakuin University (now in the Aoyama-Omotesando area).

The abolition of the unequal treaties led to a move by foreigners out of the Tsukiji area after 1900, and the earthquake of 1923 brought a temporary end to this sector as a residential area. One great reminder of the Western presence today is **St. Luke's International Hospital**, whose first buildings were replaced in 1933 and which has undergone modernization and expansion since the 1980s. St. Luke's was started in 1902 by Dr. Rudolf Teusler from Virginia, an Episcopal missionary. Unlike other Western-style hospitals in Tokyo, its records were kept in English rather than German. The Meiji government had previously turned to German medical schools and hospitals as a model for medical Westernization. The 1932 building was designed with colorful tile decorations by an

American architect in the Art Nouveau style, and its tower was topped with a cross. An inscription at one entrance notes that the hospital was an endeavor of Christianity in Japan. New buildings were constructed in the 1990s to meet the needs of modern medicine, and they occupy a major portion of Tsukiji just beyond the Tsukada-jima Bridge, creating a luxury area in which two skyscrapers, comprising the **St. Luke's Tower**, offer residential apartments for St. Luke's Hospital as well as a hotel, shops, and offices.

After crossing the bridge from Tsukada-jima, the first major cross street should be taken to the left. At the beginning of the second street is a small **granite memorial to Henry Faulds**, noting that "Dr. Henry Faulds, pioneer in fingerprint identification, lived here from 1874 to 1884." A small bubbling fountain behind the stone sends water coursing down a tiny channel along the sidewalk. The original American legation sat on the left in this second block from the bridge; the site is now covered by the twin high-rise buildings mentioned above. The area on the west of these twin towers was the location of the foreigner's settlement. Ahead on this street paralleling the river, in the **Akatsuki Koen**, is a bust to Philipp Franz von Siebold (1796–1866) who came to Edo as early as 1826 and gave lessons in medicine and surgery. A plaque dated June 18, 1988, next to the bust of Siebold explains that the memorial was presented to Chuo ward by Leiden University of the Netherlands and by the Isaac Alfred Ailion Foundation in cooperation with the *Asahi Shimbun* newspaper. The park has lovely fountains and a delightful children's playground.

Going back one street to the end of the block on which the twin towers mentioned above are located and turning to the left (away from the river), one comes upon a tiny triangular plot named the Nihon Kindai Bunka Koto Hajime-no-Chi (**Cradle of Modern Japanese Culture**). Two memorial stones erected in 1958 commemorate those Japanese who lived or worked here and brought Western knowledge to Japan. The larger stone to the rear, depicting an illustration from an anatomy book, is to Maeno Ryotaku and Sugita Genpaku and their associate Nakagawa Junen, who translated the first Dutch textbook on anatomy between 1771 and 1774. The second stone is to Fukuzawa Yukichi, whose 1858 private classes for the Matsudaira clan led in time to the formation of Keio University. Inscribed in the stone book are Fukuzawa's words, "Heaven created no man above another nor below." This egalitarian sentiment no doubt was a part of the reason that in 1901 the Meiji government would not permit Fukuzawa and his wife to be buried in the graveyard of Fukuzawa's family temple—for it was too near the Imperial Palace. This spiteful action was remedied in 1950 by the moving of their remains to the family temple graveyard. Another stone commemorates the fact that: "Here Dutch Studies Began."

The buildings of **St. Luke's Hospital**, begun by Dr. Rudolf Teusler in 1901, cover much of this area. Teusler not only introduced American medical approaches to health care, but he was concerned that his hospital offer medical care to all classes of society and not just the former samurai or Meiji official class. Curiously, opposite the entrance to St. Luke's in times past was the residence of Lord Asano, the unfortunate daimyo whose followers gained notoriety after his death as the 47 Ronin. On his disgrace, his lands were transferred to the Matsudaira clan.

5 TSUKIJI HONGAN-JI TEMPLE

Continuing southwest from St. Luke's Tower and the Faulds Monument, walking almost parallel to the Sumida River, the road comes to Harumi-dori, where a right turn leads in about 300 yards to the **Tsukiji Hongan-ji Temple**, an unusual-looking structure reminiscent of the architecture of India. The temple is a branch of the Jodo Shinshu sect of Amida Buddhism, at one time a militarily powerful religious group. In their Osaka headquarters in the mid-1500s, they were able to stand off Oda Nobunaga and his troops when he was the leading general as well as the civil ruler of Japan. In the 1590s Toyotomi Hideyoshi, Nobunaga's successor and Tokugawa Ieyasu's predecessor, disarmed the sect and offered it a location in Kyoto for their new headquarters. There they settled in what was, and is, a most luxurious site. When Ieyasu came to power in 1603, he still feared the arrogance of the sect, and thus he split the Kyoto Hongan-ji Temple and the Jodo Shinshu sect into two groups, the Nishi (West) Hongan-ji and the Higashi (East) Hongan-ji. As the head of the newly established Higashi group, he placed a disaffected relative of the leader of the main branch of the faith as the abbot in charge. Divide and

conquer, Ieyasu found, was better than a head-on approach when faced with potential opponents, religious or secular.

A subsidiary temple of the original sect (the Nishi Hongan-ji) moved to Edo in 1617 and was settled in Hamacho, the original Yoshiwara district. After its destruction in the Long Sleeves Fire of 1657, the temple was offered a site in the newly created Tsukiji area, and thus the Tsukiji Hongan-ji Temple came into being. The 1923 earthquake marked the ninth time the temple was destroyed by fire, and the decision was made to rebuild in stone. In the period of its greatest strength, the Tsukiji Hongan-ji had more than 50 sub-temples around it, a few of which survive here and there in the Tsukiji district today. In the 1935 rebuilding of the temple, Chuto Ito, the temple architect, wished to show the tie of Japanese Buddhism to its Indian heritage by creating a edifice reflecting that country's architectural traditions. The temple can seat 1,000 worshippers, and, as the central temple of the sect in the Tokyo area, it supervises more than 600 other temples in the Kanto region around Tokyo. Standing 114 feet (34.2 meters) tall and covering 70,600 square feet (6,354 square meters), it is one of the largest Buddhist temples in Japan. It offers daily services, supports a Sunday school, and on the third Saturday of each month offers an evening service in English and in Japanese for those interested in the Shinshu faith, which reverences the Amida Buddha. Within the Hondo, the front of the worship hall offers a golden façade, its *ramma* (transoms) above the golden altar intricately carved, while the altar area is embellished with golden furnishings, a Japanese Momoyama style within an Indian façade. A temple of the modern day, it offers soft seats for worshippers while a large organ is available for music during religious services.

Hongan-ji is where this tour comes to an end. Leaving the temple by the main entrance and turning right, a short walk east along Shin-ohashi-dori brings you to **Tsukiji Station** on the Hibiya subway line, which can be taken in one direction to Ginza or Hibiya and in the other to Akihabara or Ueno.

GETTING THERE
This tour starts at Tsukiji-Shijo Station on the Oedo subway line.

Walking Tour 5

NIHOMBASHI TO GINZA AND SHIMBASHI

The Quarter Where Pleasure Can Be Had, a Shopper's Paradise, Kabuki, and a New City "Where the Tide Ends"

The names of the original commercial center of old Edo and modern Tokyo–Ginza, Yurakucho, and Nihombashi–are somewhat flexible descriptions for the areas they encompass. Chuo-dori (Central Avenue) is the traditional heart of the Ginza district, and often foreigners have used the term *Ginza* as though that were the name of Chuo-dori. Although Chuo-dori extends to the north beyond the limits of this tour, we shall be concerned with that portion of the avenue that lies between the Nihombashi Bridge to the north and the Shimbashi rail station and the Shiodome area to the south. Each segment will be defined and described.

Ginza means "Silver Mint," for it was in this area in the early 1600s that the Tokugawa shoguns had their mint for the production of silver (*gin*) coins. (A stone monument in a flower planter of low evergreens at the edge of the sidewalk in Ginza 2-chome commemorates the birthplace of Ginza, the place of silver casting.) **Yurakucho** is just beyond the western quarter of Ginza; the elevated Yamanote and the Japan Rail tracks serve as a delineating boundary for the district on its western side. **Nihombashi** was the heart of the Low City in Edo times, and even into Meiji days it

was the commercial and financial center of the city. Nihombashi #1, for the purposes of this tour, is that portion of the district that lies to the south of the Nihombashi River. In Walk 6, the other part of Nihombashi, #2, will be combined with the adjacent Ningyocho district into which it merges geographically. This tour thus begins at Nihombashi Bridge, the "bridge of Japan," and proceeds down the eight portions of Ginza from 1-chome through 8-chome, deviating to the side occasionally for places of interest, then continuing into Shimbashi and terminating in Yurakucho. *Chome* is a city block. We start at **Nihombashi subway station**, and the walk itself can begin at the bridge. The Ginza subway line runs down the central axis of the walk, with stations at Kyobashi, Ginza Crossing (Ginza Station on Harumi-dori), and Shimbashi. Thus one can interrupt the tour at any of these points and pick up the route at a later time if desired.

1 NIHOMBASHI: THE BRIDGE OF JAPAN
In one sense, this is where any visit to Tokyo should begin. In the wonderful woodblock *Print #1* of his *Fifty-three Stages of the Tokaido*, Hiroshige shows the arched, wooden bridge that first spanned the Nihombashi River in 1603. Across the bridge in the print comes a daimyo's procession, the lance bearers holding their covered weapons aloft, the retinue following behind. In the foreground appear fishmongers, those workers who enlivened the riverfront for the next 300 years, here hastily making way for a procession they dare not block for fear of their lives. In the background are the roofs of the *kura*, the warehouses along the river, while fire towers fitted with alarm bells raise their ladder-like structures above distant buildings.

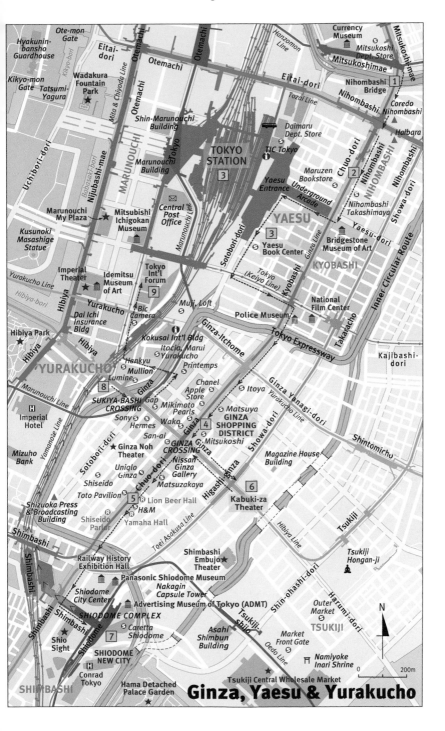

Ginza, Yaesu & Yurakucho

Nihombashi was the center of this exciting and boisterous community. The Tokaido, the great "Eastern Road" of Japan in the period from 1600 to the late 1800s, began at the Nihombashi Bridge in Edo (old Tokyo). This road was the most important connection between the imperial capital of Kyoto and the shogun's seat in Edo, the shogun being a military leader who ruled over civil life in the name of the emperor, giving the emperor the obeisance that tradition required while at the same time ignoring him politically as a powerless figurehead. From 1604, a milepost on the Nihombashi Bridge marked the beginning of the posts that counted off the 292 miles (467.2 kilometers) between the two seats of governance in the nation. The black pole on the bridge, which was the zero marker, began the count of the distance not only to Kyoto but to all the towns on the other highways from Edo. Four great roads departed from this point, two leading to Ueno and Nikko, and two to Kyoto: the Nakasendo Road through the mountains as well as the more heavily used Tokaido. Kyobashi ("Capital Bridge") to the south of Nihombashi Bridge was the first to be crossed on the way to Kyoto, but most of the rivers en route had to be forded, often with difficulty.

Nihombashi Bridge served a number of purposes apart from providing access between the northern and southern portions of Edo. At the south end of the bridge, felons were exposed in fetters. Adulterers and priests guilty of sexual offenses were among those so treated before they were led off to their deaths. Those guilty of murder were placed in a hole with only their neck and head protruding. Two saws were available for anyone who wished to cut off their heads—which in the long run the authorities would accomplish more quickly. Their severed heads were then mounted on a pike at the end of the bridge as a warning to any potential wrongdoers. An official notice board stood at the bridge, so the will of the shogun could be made plain. The announcement in 1702 of the fate of the 47 Ronin (see Walks 7 and 15) was so distasteful to citizens that the notice was ripped down almost as soon as it was posted. There was a "Lost Child Stone," where announcements regarding a missing child were placed on one side, while notices of children who had been found were put on the opposite side. In 1711 an improvement to the bridge brought the placement of the *Toki-*

A detail from the Nihombashi Bridge suggests its former grandeur.

no-kane, a bell that sounded the hours of the day, based on the lunar calendar with its twelve horary signs. Hours varied in length by summer or winter daylight in old Edo.

However, the **Nihombashi Bridge** where we begin is certainly not Ieyasu's 1603 arched, wooden structure whose raised middle section permitted boats to pass beneath it. In 1806, the bridge collapsed as hundreds fled to the south from a fire in the Echigaya warehouse, one of a number of times in which the bridge was destroyed. At the beginning of the 20th century, any replacement structure for this or any other bridge would have to support the traffic that trams and then automobiles engendered. Thus, in 1911 a modern stone and metal bridge of some charm, 161 feet (48.3 meters) long by 89 feet (26.7 meters) wide, was erected.

Four bronze Chinese lions stand on either side of the bridge at the northern and southern ends, while four seated dragons rest on either side of two bronze, obelisk-like light standards on the central balustrades. A copper plaque in the pavement at the center of the bridge, rather than the original black pole, today marks the point from which all distances are measured from Tokyo. Time heals all wounds, and in 1911 Tokugawa Yoshinobu, the 15th and last of the Tokugawa shoguns, was invited back to Tokyo from his exile in Shizuoka for the first time since 1868 to inscribe the word *Nihombashi* on the new structure. His calligraphic inscription of the bridge's traditional name appears in stone. A plaque on the western side of the southern portion of the bridge shows how the original wooden bridge appeared.

At the northeast side of the bridge is a commemorative **statue of Princess Otohime-sama**, the daughter of the Dragon King. (The Dragon King resided in the river and its waters, which flowed under the bridge.) The tale of Otohime-sama is the Japanese equivalent of the American story of Rip van Winkle. Urashima Taro, smitten by the princess's beauty, is said to have followed this daughter of the Dragon King to her home beneath the sea. They married, but when he later left her to return to his village, he found that years undersea were equal to centuries on land, and thus he was a stranger in the world to which he returned. The story is an entrancing one, but, alas, in 1964, in preparation for the Olympics of that year, an elevated highway was erected over the Nihombashi River, and the highway crosses above the bridge to the detriment of its attractiveness and, no doubt, to the dismay of the Dragon King. In 1991, on the 80th birthday of the present Nihombashi Bridge, a small terrace with benches was created at its south side, and steps were built down to a terrace from which one can obtain a better view of the 1911 structure. The terrace on the east side has a wall of ornamental water enhancing the small landing, although even from here the beauty of the bridge itself is still largely destroyed by the highway above.

② CHUO-DORI: TOKYO'S HIGH STREET

Stretching south from the Nihombashi Bridge along Chuo-dori, the first major crossroad is Eitai-dori. The **Tokyu Department Store**, founded in 1662 and once on the left in Nihombashi 1-chome, was an early shop in the area and developed into a major merchandising enterprise with numerous branches. Under the original name of Shiragiya, it was the scene of a tragic fire in which many of its female employees died. In the second-level basement of the modern building was the "magic well," which, it is claimed, emitted an image of the deity Kannon in the early 1700s. Nearby is the **Tokyo Daido Life Insurance**

Building, a thin building created by Kisho Kurokawa in 1978. The arcade running through the building has its shop windows arranged in staggered fashion along the walkway that traverses this long, narrow, interior thoroughfare, whose ceiling rises nine floors above the promenade. Adjacent is **Haibara,** which has been selling fine papers since the 18th century in a shop that resembles an old-time *kura* storage building.

Two blocks farther along Chuo-dori, in Nihombashi 2-chome, is **Maruzen** on the right, one of Tokyo's premier bookstores (open from 9:30 a.m. to 8:30 p.m daily). Maruzen has an unusual history, in that it first opened in 1869, right after the Meiji period began, and its intent was to bring Western writings to Japan so as to assist in the modernization of the nation. Besides several floors of Japanese books, it still stocks a wide variety of books in languages other than Japanese. It also sells Japanese crafts, and there is even a café on the premises. Across the way is **Takashimaya** *(*open from 10:00 a.m. to 8:00 p.m. daily*)*, one of the major department stores in Tokyo, with branches elsewhere in Japan. It has an exhibition gallery and restaurants on the upper floors, a fine kimono department, and food sales in the basement; and, as with all such stores, its roof garden offers bonsai and goldfish in season, along with a small Shinto shrine in honor of the deity of the land on which the store is located. It is worth being there at 10:00 a.m. sharp to watch the daily opening ceremony, when the big doors are slowly pulled open to reveal a line of uniformed staff bowing to the first customers of the day.

③ YAESU AND TOKYO STATION

Four minor streets beyond Takashimaya is the wide Yaesu-dori. Across the street on the left side of Chuo-dori is the **Bridgestone Museum of Art**, with the collection of Shojiro Ishibashi on the second floor of the Bridgestone Building. Shojiro Ishibashi's last name means "stone bridge," and thus the name of the company and gallery. While the art of the French Impressionists as well as modern Japanese paintings intrigued Ishibashi, he did not neglect to collect some ancient Greek and modern sculpture as well. (The museum is open from 10:00 a.m. to 8:00 p.m. Tuesdays to Saturdays and until 6:00 p.m. on Sundays and national holidays. It is closed on Mondays. Entry is ¥1,000.) The collection includes paintings by Rembrandt, Picasso, Rouault, Utrillo, and Modigliani among others, together with sculptures by Rodin, Moore, and Giacometti. Ishibashi also collected the work of post-Meiji Japanese painters in the Western style, such as Foujita.

Yaesu-dori, the broad street that intersects Chuo-dori, leads on the right to Tokyo Station, and beneath the street is an **underground arcade** of shops also leading to the station. Above ground, where Yaesu-dori meets Sotobori-dori, is the **Yaesu entrance to Tokyo Station**. This is the "missing" entrance mentioned in Walk 1 that took so long to create due to the dispute over where the Sotobori moat (now Sotobori-dori) should be bridged to the east. The name of *Yaesu* for the district is a reflection of Tokugawa Ieyasu's day. Will Adams, the shipwrecked English sailor who served Ieyasu so well as a naval advisor, had a fellow officer from his wrecked ship as a companion in Edo, Jan Joosten Loodensteijn. A Dutch seaman, Jan Joosten acted as Ieyasu's agent for trade with Southeast Asia. His residence was at the Babasaki Moat in front of the castle, then still an inlet of Edo Bay (in the area of today's Hibiya Park), where he lived with his Japanese wife. Jan Joosten's name became *Yayoosu* and then *Yaesu* in 17th-century Japanese mouths, and in 1929 the area called Yaesu after him was absorbed into the Marunouchi district. Thus for a while the name disappeared, but in 1954 it became current again, this time a bit farther to the north and on the opposite side of Tokyo Station, when the area was renamed Yaesu. (Joosten is reported to have died at sea near Indonesia in an attempt to return to Holland.)

Tokyo Station is the major hub for national and commuter transportation, albeit Ueno and Shinjuku Stations also are important centers for commuter lines and long distance travel throughout Japan. Mention has been made in Walk 1 of the original structure on the eastern side of the station, which copied the style of Amsterdam Central Station, and of the addition on the western side of the tracks of the new Shinkansen Bullet Train terminal. Ticket counters and information booths are available in the station, but with its various levels, including underground platforms and tracks, the station can be confusing to newcomers. Subway stations can be found in the lower reaches of the station, and the elevated Yamanote Line that circles a

An old street lamp in the Ginza district

major portion of the inner city also had its platforms in Tokyo Station.

In front of the Yaesu side of Tokyo Station is the **Daimaru Department Store** (open 10:00 a.m. to 8:00 p.m.). Daimaru offers the amazing variety of goods that one comes to expect in Japanese department stores. Its total of 14 floors above and below ground cover men's and women's fashions, interior design, sportswear, toys, deli goods, jewelry, and a variety of other goods and services and include restaurants.

Four short streets to the south on Sotobori-dori is the **Yaesu Book Center**, an eight-story building that includes a floor (the 8th floor) dedicated to foreign books and magazines. It also has a coffee shop and a library, where, for a small fee, one may rest and read. (The Center is open weekdays from 10:00 a.m. to 9:00 p.m. and weekends from 10:00 a.m. to 7:00 p.m.) Two streets farther down Sotobori-dori there is a cross street that is the first one to run to the east past the main line railroad tracks and Tokyo Station.

4 GINZA SHOPPING DISTRICT

Here one can regain Chuo-dori and Kyobashi Station via the Ginza Line, if one wishes, or walk back. The streets farther along Chuo-dori are at the heart of the **Ginza district**. Having arrived at Ginza, it is appropriate to look at the development of this portion of the city, which was one of the first areas to welcome the new world of Western architecture in the 1870s along with the amenities such buildings could offer. When the district was modernized after the 1872 fire, it only extended from Kyobashi to the Harumi-dori crossing. (Kyobashi was the first bridge over the beginning of the Tokaido Road to Kyoto, and thus its name—*Kyo* (capital) indicating its relationship to the ultimate destination of the road in Kyoto, and *bashi* meaning "bridge," of course. Now gone, it was a bridge over one of the outlets of the moats of Edo Castle.

Each block or *chome* in the Ginza district is numbered, the 1-chome block being the first square unit after Kyobashi (and the overhead expressway) between Sotobori-dori on the west and Showa-dori on the east. Ginza 4-chome ends at the Harumi-dori intersection. With the expansion of the Ginza district in time, there are now eight *chome*, which reach down to Shimbashi. Chuo-dori becomes a pedestrian's delight on Saturdays and Sundays from noon to 6:00 p.m., for then all traffic is banned from the street, and it becomes a place where the traditional *Gin-bura* or "Ginza stroll" has been popular for over one hundred years. The area's name, as indicated previously, is taken from the silver mint (*Ginza*) that Ieyasu established here in 1612 in the second *chome* after Kyobashi. The silver mint was later moved to the Nihombashi district after some financial indiscretions on the part of the mint operator, but the name *Ginza* remained. In 1872 Tokyo suffered another of its "flowers of Edo" fires, and this whole portion of the city disappeared in flames, with some 3,000 houses being lost in the Ginza and Tsukiji districts. By coincidence, on September 13, 1872, the first train from Yokohama arrived at Shimbashi Station farther down this part of the Tokaido, the highway that the railroad would soon put out of business. The new railroad terminus at Shimbashi was to bring new life to the Ginza area in the years after the fire, for, until the railroad was extended to Tokyo Station, Shimbashi was the front door to the new capital of Japan.

After the 1872 fire, the way was cleared for a fresh beginning, and the Meiji government made the most of it. Here in this still moated area—for the old defensive canals were not yet filled in—the first modern (that is, European-style) portion of Tokyo would arise, with two-story redbrick buildings and paved sidewalks. The transformation took ten years, but before 1874 had passed there were 85 gaslights illuminating the street at night, and within two years the lights were extended to Asakusa to the north and the palace to the

The Ginza Stroll on Chuo-dori between Ginza Crossing and Kyobashi

The Wako Building and its distinctive clock overlooking Ginza Crossing. Across the way is the Mitsukoshi Department Store.

west. Even the Kabuki-za Theater illuminated its performances by gaslight in 1877, though within ten years these lights would be replaced by electricity. In 1881 horse-drawn trams appeared, making their way along Chuo-dori to Asakusa, to be replaced in 1903 by electric trams.

The creation of this modern "European" city was placed in the hands of an English planner. In the next three years after the last embers of the 1872 fire had died, a thousand fireproof, redbrick buildings were erected in the Kyobashi area. At the time, there were but a handful of such buildings in the entire city, which was composed principally of wooden houses. Chuo-dori was lined with cherry, maple, and willow trees; in the long run, only the willows lasted. Unfortunately, this modern street was not a great success at first. Ventilation was poor in the new brick buildings. They tended to hold the dampness of the summer season, and it took pressure by the government to have them occupied. Success did come, but slowly, and by 1894 the Hattori Building at Harumi-dori and Chuo-dori had begun to change the area. Its clock tower became a rendezvous spot under which

friends could meet, and what had been a newspaper building was now to become a major store of quality products under the name of Wako. The building originally bore the name of Hattori Kintaro, a 22-year-old watchmaker who opened a shop in Ginza. By 1881 his watches were so well-made that they were given as gifts by the Imperial Household. He named his watches *Seiko*, or "Precision," a name and a reputation they have maintained.

Traffic, of course, increased with the advent of the automobile, and in 1921 it was decided that the roadway had to be widened, unfortunately at the expense of the trees that had graced the street. Modernization can have its pitfalls, however. The new 1923 roadway was paved with wooden blocks that were held in place by an asphalt binder. It was a setback when the asphalt caught fire and the roadway burned. The 1923 Great Kanto Earthquake saw the demise of the last of the two-story, redbrick buildings, and by 1930 Ginza was ready once more for a new beginning as larger buildings arose. The Ginza area now reached down to Shimbashi, and a new subway was built under Chuo-dori, reaching to Asakusa. (Ninety percent of Tokyo's subways, however, have been built since 1945.)

A wider street was created to the east of Chuo-dori after the earthquake, running from Shimbashi to Ueno, but this newly created Showa-dori never replaced Ginza as an exciting commercial street of shops. A new Hattori building, now renamed **Wako** for its new owners, replaced the original structure in 1932, and its clock remains a focal point at the Ginza Yon-chome (block 4) crossing at Harumi-dori, which is known as **Ginza Crossing**. The new building was designed by Watanabe Hiroshi, who is also responsible for the Dai-Ichi Insurance Building on Hibiya-dori and the National Museum Building in Ueno. Then came the war and U.S. military occupation, and Wako and the nearby Matsuya Department Store became Post Exchanges for the American military for a number of years. Department stores, beer halls (à la Czechoslovakia and Germany) were to open, while restaurants, coffee shops, and bars all created a lively center for the city. Department stores made the street the focus of women, who, while they do make purchases, also enjoy the simple art of *depaa-to deburi* ("browsing in the department stores") to view the latest in fashions, visit the exhibitions these store generously mount in special halls, and have lunch in one of their many restaurants.

The illuminated San-ai Building is for many the iconic image of the Ginza district.

5 A WALK THROUGH THE GINZA

This portion of the tour of Ginza begins at Ginza 1-chome and then proceeds down Chuo-dori to Ginza 8-chome at the Shimbashi subway station and Yamanote elevated rail line. Thus, starting at the overhead Tokyo Expressway where the Ginza district begins, the first locations of interest are in Ginza 2-chome, where **Itoya** is on the east side of the street. Itoya primarily offers office supplies and stationery but is noted for its crafts and hobby department as well as its selection of fine Japanese papers. It also has an exhibition gallery and a tearoom. A **memorial stone** in a planter at the curb, as mentioned earlier, marks the **site of the Ginza mint**, which closed in 1790 to be reopened in 1800 north of the Nihombashi River.

The **Matsuya** and **Printemps Department Stores** (albeit the latter is on Sotobori-dori) are in Ginza 3-chome, as are the flagship stores of international designer brands such as **Cartier**, **Chanel**, and **Gucci**. Also in Ginza 3-chome on the east-west street to the east of Showa-dori is the **Magazine House Building**, which can be recognized by its external pink-and-silver-tiled facade. This is the headquarters of a publishing house that specializes in magazines for young people, as may be surmised from the figures of Popeye and *Olive Oil at the main entrance (*Popeye* is also the name of one of its magazines). In Ginza 4-chome is the **Mikimoto** shop for the sale of Mikimoto's cultured pearls. In 1883, Kokichi Mikimoto discovered that it was possible to force oysters to create "cultured" pearls if a bit of irritant was placed within their shells. His success led to the opening of his shop in the Ginza in 1899, and it continues, having added an exhibition area to its premises. At the corner of Harumi-dori and Chuo-dori, is **Wako** (the Tiffany or Asprey of Ginza), owned by the makers of Seiko watches and selling the finest of luxury articles. It, too, has an exhibition hall.

This brings us to **Ginza Crossing**, which is the "Times Square" crossing of the district. Across the street, still in Ginza 4-chome, is

the **Mitsukoshi Ginza Department Store**
As with many department stores in Tokyo, the roof of the building offers a roof garden where plants (particularly bonsai) are sold, a children's playground exists, and, as always, there is a Shinto shrine so that the proper respect can be paid to the deity of the land on which the shops stands. In addition, it provides protection for business enterprise. Mitsukoshi Ginza also has a Jizo image on its roof, though Jizo is found in the Buddhist pantheon. This particular Jizo was found during excavations of a canal about 1870 as Ginza was being modernized, and it was placed in a small hall in Ginza 4-chome. The image disappeared in the 1945 air raids but was later found in the rubble. In 1965 it was given its home on the roof of Mitsukoshi, where this protector of children, pregnant women, and the dead can be reverenced.

South of the intersection is one of the eye-catching icons of Ginza: the 1963 **San-ai Building**, a 12-story glass cylinder whose floor divisions are illuminated with fluorescent lights. As a result, it is one of the many nighttime attractions in the area.

6 KABUKI-ZA THEATER

The **Kabuki-za Theater** sits at the corner of Harumi-dori and Showa-dori. For a visit, follow Harumi-dori east from Ginza Crossing to the next broad avenue at the corner of Harumi-dori and Showa-dori. Kabuki as a form of entertainment was a problem for the shoguns from Kabuki's earliest beginning and throughout the Tokugawa reign. Kabuki originated in 1596 in Kyoto when a woman involved in sacred dances at the great shrine of Izumo brought her dancers to the city. There they performed now secularized dances, and these gradually grew into plotless tales, many of which involved young men and prostitutes in the bathhouses. Some of her associates were quite experienced in these latter realms, and the rowdiness that resulted from these skits, for that is all they were, led in 1629 to the shogun banning female performers in Kabuki drama. The women's places were taken from 1630 to 1653 by rather attractive young men, some of whom were too sexually appealing to the Buddhist priests and the samurai who attended these performances—and who sometimes fell into brawls for the favors of particularly handsome young actors. Thus the shogunate banned this form of young men's

Kabuki—but not until after the shogun at the time had expired, since he, too, found the young men of Kabuki rather attractive. Thereafter the actors had to be mature males who took both the male and female parts in the dramas, as they still do today.

Kabuki began in Edo in the Yoshiwara licensed quarter at Ningyocho (see Walk 6). Periodically a streak of Puritanism would emanate from the shogun's castle, and in 1841 Kabuki was banished from the Hamacho's (Ningyocho) Yoshiwara district to a new Yoshiwara area beyond Asakusa and its temple, and there Kabuki remained while the Tokugawas were in power. In 1872, four years after the fall of the Tokugawas, the Morita-za Kabuki Theater moved from Yoshiwara to the area around the present Shintomicho subway station on the Yurakucho subway line and took the name Shintomi-za. Here Kabuki was quite successful under innovative management that brought new life to this stage form. The theater had come to this Tsukiji area since it was able to obtain land cheaply after the great fire that had destroyed the Ginza district in 1872. The land that the theater purchased had belonged to the defunct Shimabara licensed quarters that the Meiji government had permitted to become established on this recently filled ground.

Shintomi-za lasted but four years before it burned down in 1876, but it was rebuilt and reopened in 1878, and it was here that former president Ulysses Grant of the United States was entertained on his trip to Japan. The new theater made use of bright gaslights for its evening performances, and there was an attempt to raise the level of Kabuki drama over the coarseness that had developed in its Yoshiwara days. In short order Shintomi-za attracted other theaters to the district, one of them being Kabuki-za, and this new arrival became the great competitor to Shintomi-za after its establishment in 1889. The 1923 earthquake destroyed Shintomi-za, but this theatrical district soon obtained a legitimate theater that arose nearby in 1925 and that offered modern Western plays. It came to an end when it was destroyed in 1945 by air raids.

Kabuki-za remained, despite earthquakes and wartime bombing. It was a much larger theater than Shintomi-za, and it was to become the center for Kabuki in Tokyo. In its new home Kabuki was becoming a more elevated form of theater than it had been in the Yoshiwara. Moreover, various theatrical

The front of the Kabuki-za Theater before its renovation, slated for completion in 2013

techniques had been developing that were to make Kabuki both more dramatic and more spectacular as a form of entertainment. As early as 1758, the revolving stage had appeared in Kabuki to provide for a quick changing of sets. Trap doors in the stage could make for unexpected appearances or sudden disappearances. Black-hooded stagehands were brought into use to change scenery or props; their being all in black meant that they were not "seen," an artifice easily accepted by the public. The *hanamichi*, the "flower path," was found to be useful, for this runway extending into the audience permitted for entries and exits for the actors or for a place to strike one of those frozen and exaggerated poses that Tokyo audiences adore. The use of the *shamisen* softened, while drums and wooden clappers heightened, dramatic moments in the presentation. Costumes became ever more gorgeous and flamboyant, and a completely stylized form of acting developed, thereby creating an art form of its own.

Kabuki-za was damaged in the 1923 earthquake but was rebuilt in a modified flamboyant Momoyama style so as to give its exterior its distinctive look. Damaged in the 1945 air raids on Tokyo, it was reconstructed in 1950 and enlarged to seat up to 2,600 spectators. Despite campaigns to save the 1950 struc-

ture, it too was closed in April 2010, and the work started on a new Kabuki-za on the site, which is scheduled to open in 2013. It so happens that, after the destruction of the Shintomi-za and the damage to Kabuki-za in 1923, another Kabuki house arrived on the scene when the Shimbashi Embujo Theater opened its doors in 1925, two streets south of Kabuki-za. Aside from Kabuki, for years Shimbashi geisha offered their Azuma-dori, the spring and autumn dance plays, in the Shimbashi Embujo Theater. In 1982 the **Nissan New Building** was erected on the site of the Shimbashi Embujo Theater and incorporated in its multistory structure a replacement theater of the same name. Seating 1,428 theatergoers, the **Shimbashi Embujo** offers Kabuki, *buto* (traditional dance), and plays from the Meiji era as well as modern plays. (To reach the Embujo from Kabuki-za, walk southeast along Harumi-dori, then follow the second side street on your left for two blocks.)

Crossing Harumi-dori and returning to Chuo-dori, one comes to the **Matsuzakaya Department Store** in Ginza 6-chome. Ginza 7-chome offers the historic **Lion Beer Hall**, modeled on the beer halls of Munich and still retaining the original Bavaria-inspired interiors from when it opened in the 1930s, while the **Toto Pavilion** places all of its porcelain bathtubs and other related items on display. **Yamaha Hall,** with its pianos, and **Shiseido,** which has added boutique shops for its cosmetic products, are all in Ginza 7-chome as well. While shopping in Ginza was once known to be purely about high-end brands and luxury, Japan's lingering economic malaise has seen more affordable chain stores entering the area. The extremely popular budget fashion chain Uni-Qlo, one of Japanese business's greatest success stories in recent years, now has a large shop near the old Kabuki-za site. Swedish firm H&M, which also offers very popular fashion at affordable prices, opened its main Ginza branch in 7-chome to much fanfare in 2008.

Crossing into Ginza 8-chome brings us to the end of the Ginza district, but here is the **Shiseido Parlor,** which offers the weary a convenient coffee shop and is noted for its ice cream. This *chome* also boasts the architecturally unusual **Shizuoka Press and Broadcasting Building**. Virtually alongside the elevated railroad tracks, this building was designed by Kenzo Tange in 1967. This unusual structure consists of four asymmetrical boxes that are appended to a 187-foot-tall black shaft, the top of which is sliced off at an angle. It is one of the most striking elements

of the Tokyo skyline for visitors arriving on the Shinkansen Bullet Train.

Throughout the Ginza district, in the streets between Sotobori-dori and Chuo-dori, can be found many restaurants and small bars, all of which make the area an illuminated wonderland at night with their neon signs. Many of the bars and their "hostesses" delight in detaching the visitor from his or her money with their extravagantly priced beverages, so caution is the byword.

7 SHIODOME NEW CITY

Leaving Ginza 8-chome behind, Chuo-dori enters the **Shimbashi** and Shiodome areas. It was here that the first steam locomotive appeared in 1872 when it pulled into the new Shimbashi terminal of the Yokohama Line. The 18-mile distance was covered in 53 minutes. The pre-1923 station, destroyed by the earthquake of that year, was built on the site of the mansion of the daimyo of Tatsuno, where the 47 Ronin stopped to refresh themselves that snowy December night en route to their assassination of Lord Kira (see Tours 7 and 11). The original starting point of the 1872 railroad is remembered on a stone inscribed with the "0" milestone, and a bit of rail has been kept as a memorial to the beginning of modern transportation in Japan. Even

The old steam locomotive in front of Shimbashi Station

a 1945 steam locomotive has been preserved outside the current Shimbashi Station to commemorate the 1972 centennial of rail transport in Japan.

The original Shimbashi Station and freight yards are now but a memory. **Shiodome**, a new "city" within the city has arisen on its site. *Shiodome* means "where the tide ends," for this area, before it was filled in, was at the end of Tokyo *Wan*, or Tokyo Bay. The new **Shiodome complex** is on your left as you approach down Chuo-dori, and it begins with the **Shiodome City Center** skyscraper. (The area can also be reached by the Shiodome exit of the JR Yamanote Line's Shimbashi Station; from the Shiodome Station of the Oedo subway line; or from the Shiodome Station of the fully-automated New Transit Yurikamome monorail.) Built on the site of the original Shimbashi Station, the skyscraper has a replica of that rail terminus at its base, and, appropriately, the **Railway History Exhibition Hall** (open Tuesday through Sunday from 11:00 a.m. to 6:00 p.m.; closed Mondays and New Year holidays; entry free), which offer views of times past, ranging from woodblock prints of old Shimbashi to photographs of the heyday of rail traffic. Much of the development of the Shiodome complex of offices, apartments, shops, theaters, and museums is the result of the Dentsu Advertising Company's decision to create its skyscraper office complex, **Caretta Shiodome**, where rail cars once stood. The 48-story Dentsu Headquarters Building tower, designed by Jean Nouvel, overlooks Tokyo Bay and the surrounding city. Its views can be enjoyed from the restaurants on the 46th and 47th floors of the tower, which are reached by an elevator that ascends in a glass-enclosed channel.

On the B-1 and B-2 levels of the Caretta complex is the **Advertising Museum of Tokyo** (**ADMT**), sponsored by Dentsu, Japan's largest advertising agency (open Tuesday through Friday from 11:00 a.m. to 6:00 p.m. and Saturdays and Sundays from 11:00 a.m. to 4:00 p.m.; closed Monday; free entry). The story of advertising from broadsheets and woodblock prints to television and newspaper ads over the past three centuries is on display, and there is a research collection of over 100,000 digital images. Although the labels are in Japanese, the visual images can speak for themselves. This Caretta Shiodome portion of the Dentsu Building not only houses the advertising museum but has

stores, restaurants, and the 1,200-seat Dentsu Shiki Theater, where the latest in musicals from New York and London enhance the performances of Japanese theater art as well. The adjacent Matsushita Electric Showroom contains the small **Shiodome Museum**, formerly known as the **NAIS Museum** (open from Tuesday through Sunday from 10:00 a.m. to 5:30 p.m.; entry ¥600; entry fee varies with each exhibition), providing a changing exhibition of modern art as well as its permanent collection of works by the French painter Georges Rouault. Where once an abandoned rail yard stood, some 60,000 people today flock to one of Tokyo's new entertainment centers, set along its extended street plan. Once the original terminus of Japan's first railway between Yokohama and Tokyo, today it is where the **New Transit Yurikamone Monorail** begins its route, from its elevated terminus in front of the JR Yamanote Line station, along Tokyo Bay and over the Rainbow Bridge to Odaiba with its many museums, shopping malls, beach, and other entertainments. In the skyscrapers that surround the Shiodome monorail station are also many of Tokyo's most modern luxury hotels, such as the **Conrad** (in Tokyo Shiodome Building) and the **Park Hotel** (in Shiodome Media Tower).

The Shimbashi geisha quarters beyond the west exit from the Shimbashi stations became one of the most popular geisha sectors after 1868, for here the nouveau riche entrepreneurs and the new politicians of the Meiji era could relax and be entertained. The geisha of Yoshiwara looked down on this quarter and its customers, seeing these new governmental patrons of geisha divertissement as uncouth provincials and the Shimbashi geisha as of a distinctly inferior nature. Unfortunately for Yoshiwara, the 1923 earthquake pretty much finished off that traditional licensed quarter, since the Great Kanto Earthquake came not too many years after a major fire had hit the district. As a result, Shimbashi geisha and the *ryotei* restaurants in which they served both businessmen and politicians flourished. The postwar period after 1945 was a difficult time for the geisha as for everyone else, and the geisha district gradually faded from the scene. As of the end of the 20th century, some 150 geisha were still employed in the district, and they may occasionally be seen in the early evening heading to one of the 30 to 40 *ryotei* still in existence, when they have been called to serve their patrons. Sometimes these geisha arrive in a rickshaw—probably pulled by a university student in need of extra cash, for rickshaws have long since passed from general use. The district is filled with small restaurants, drinking establishments, and other shops. (It is one of those quirks of history that the first rickshaw was created by an upstate New York missionary to Japan for his invalid wife. The device quickly caught on and was useful until more modern conveyances made their appearance. Whether that missionary ever made use of the government's "New Shimabara" quarters is not known—but it is known that he was defrocked due to his amorous inclinations outside of marriage.)

8 YURAKUCHO

At Shimbashi, one can either take the elevated train line one stop to the north to **Yurakucho Station** or one can walk the same route by following the street that runs parallel to the elevated line. *Yurakucho* is a name with a history. When shogun Tokugawa Ieyasu first began his castle in Edo, he filled in the Hibiya Inlet of Edo Bay and at the same time created a series of moats around his castle. Sotobori, the "Outside Moat" on the east of the castle, ran roughly to the east of the elevated Yamanote rail line in the area behind the present Imperial Hotel and down past Tokyo Station. Oda Urakusai, the brother of Ieyasu's military commander, was one of the first to move into this area. He constructed his residence and a teahouse alongside the Sotobori moat. The teahouse was built in the *sukiya* style, a natural, light, asymmetrical style in keeping with the unostentatious and plain aesthetic of his day, for Oda was a devotee of the great tea master Sen-no-Rikyu of Kyoto.

Oda and his teahouse were to become place names in this area in time. A bridge over the moat near the teahouse became known as the Sukiya-bashi, "Sukiya Bridge"; the bridge lasted until the 1960s, when the Sotobori moat was finally filled in. The name still lives on in **Sukiya-bashi Crossing**, where Harumi-dori and Sotobori-dori meet, though neither the bridge nor the water it spanned any longer exists. The moat itself is remembered in the street that bears its name: Sotobori-dori. In this manner, Oda Urakusai's memory became attached to that portion of Edo where his mansion and teahouse had been, and it also still exists as Yurakucho, meaning the "Quarter Where Pleasure Can Be

Had." The pleasure for this 17th-century amateur of the tea ceremony was a spiritual pleasure, not the more sensual pleasures for which the area became noted in the last half of the 20th century. The meaning of *Yurakucho* was but a foretaste of what the centuries would bring.

After World War II, Yurakucho provided pleasures of a more dubious nature. Not too far away, at Chuo-dori and Harumi-dori, the U.S. military took over certain department stores to serve as Post Exchanges, where American troops could buy items not available on the local, impoverished, postwar markets. Many of these items found their way into the black market, which flourished under the elevated tracks in the Yurakucho Station area. At a time when jobs were not plentiful and food was equally scarce, small stalls sprang up under the elevated tracks where items of questionable ownership could be purchased or *yakitori* (grilled chicken) could be obtained. The area became a hangout for young Japanese girls willing to be picked up by all-too-willing American soldiers. The nearby Nichigeki Theater became notorious also, for it not only showed recent motion pictures but offered revues with a line of chorus girls and even striptease shows. As a result, after 1945 the area truly became a "Quarter Where Pleasure Can Be Had."

The postwar improvement of the Japanese economy, the departure of the occupying troops, the closing of the PXs, and then, in 1960, the filling in of the Sotobori moat in favor of an expressway changed the area once more. Today a few *yakitori* stalls survive, but the old Nichigeki Theater is no more. Between the elevated railway and Sotobori-dori at Harumi-dori is the modern **Mullion** or **Yurakucho Center Building**, which though now showing signs of age and no longer home to the recently closed Seibu Department Store, once helped to revive the Ginza area when it was losing some of its glamour to Shinjuku and Shibuya. The 14-story Mullion complex (with four floors underground, three of them parking areas) houses the modern **Hankyu**, separated by a pedestrian walkway from Lumine. The most noted element of the complex is the clock on the front of the building facing Harumi-dori. On the hour, between 10:00 a.m. and 9:00 p.m., the face of the clock moves up, a group of figures move forward from the clock's interior, and they then move to a musical accompaniment. Seven theaters lie within the building, one of which is a revived and more respectable **Nichigeki**, and the glistening elevators and hanging illuminations make the Yurakucho Center an intriguing and busy location.

In the side streets to the south of Sukiya-bashi Crossing between the overhead expressway and Chuo-dori, there are **numerous art galleries** offering many styles of paintings to prospective collectors. Heading east on Harumi-dori from the Mullion complex and Sukiya-bashi Crossing, one of Tokyo's 1,250 *koban* or small police stations can be observed. Most *koban* are rather utilitarian affairs, but the one here at Harumi-dori with its pointed roof is a more unusual unit of its kind. Before 1945, each *koban* kept a register of those who lived within the district, exercising the control needed by the police state that Japan once was. Today the units are there to assist local citizens, particularly to keep an eye on the elderly of their district, to provide information on the location of specific buildings in their district (given the somewhat confusing address system in Tokyo), and to offer whatever other help is needed by the public. Past the Sukiya-bashi intersection, on the right is the **Sony Building** of 1966, obviously a showcase for Sony products (open from 11:00 a.m. to 7:00 a.m.).

Up Sotobori-dori, to the north of the Mullion complex, is **Printemps**, a branch of the Parisian Au Printemps department store (closed Wednesdays). Heading west from Printemps, passing under the elevated rail tracks, to one's right is the massive **Bic Camera** home electronics store, where there are eight floors selling everything from the latest digital cameras, cell phones, and audio-visual equipment to more unusual items such as *washlet* toilet seats (electronic bidets) and high-tech massage chairs. The latter you can test for yourself near the sporting goods section on the third floor.

9 TOKYO INTERNATIONAL FORUM

Directly to the north of Bic Camera is the onetime site of the 1957 City Hall designed by Kenzo Tange, which replaced the earlier city administrative building described in Walk 1. As with its predecessor, Tange's City Hall is now but a memory, for it was torn down in 1991 when the new City Hall opened in Shinjuku. In its place the city has created the **Tokyo International Forum** by the

The cavernous interior of the International Forum is one of Tokyo's architectural highlights.

Argentine-born American architect Raphael Vinely, a convention and cultural center to enhance the life of residents of and visitors to Tokyo. Its active program is listed in English-language newspapers, and information concerning the program can be obtained at the Tourist Office on Harumi-dori. The Forum is really two buildings connected by a huge elliptical atrium, whose glass roof is 180 feet (54 meters) above the floor. The complex includes six halls for international conferences, four concert halls, shops, restaurants, and an exhibition hall on its lowest level. Its plaza is enriched with selections of sculpture.

This is where the tour ends, and if you aren't walking back in to Ginza to do some shopping, the nearest station to head for is **Yurakucho Station** on the JR Yamanote Line. You can reach it by retracing your steps south to the front of Bic Camera, which is adjacent to the station.

GETTING THERE

This walk begins at Nihombashi Station, which is served by the Tozai, Ginza, and Asakusa subway lines.

Walking Tour 6

EAST OF NIHOMBASHI TO FUKAGAWA AND NINGYOCHO
The Bridge of Japan, a Kite Museum, the Shrine of the Golden Helmet, the Low City Recalled, Sumo, and Doll Town

Nihombashi Bridge represents the heart of Shitamachi (literally, the "Low City"), the city of artisans and merchants in Tokyo's past centuries. In this tour we are concerned with that Shitamachi where commoners who served the daimyo and their retainers–who were arrayed around the Tokugawa castle and in the "High City" of raised land to the west–lived and strove to make a living. In time it was to become the entertainment, then the commercial, and finally the financial section of old Edo, aspects which are retained in this part of Tokyo today. Shitamachi began in the filled-in land in the Nihombashi and Ningyocho areas of Edo north of the Nihombashi River. After the Long Sleeves Fire of 1657, the area spread across the Sumida River and into Fukagawa as bridges began to be built and industries were moved eastward.

Nihombashi was the center of commercial life in Edo. It was also the heart of the male-dominated Shitamachi, where the inhabitants were primarily male workers. In the early years, Nihombashi grew as Edo grew–explosively. What began as a small village in 1590 was to swell to a population of half a million

some 40 years later and would number more than a million inhabitants before it was 90 years old. This swampy area at the head of Edo Bay benefited from the landfill operations begun by Tokugawa Ieyasu in the early 1600s that made Nihombashi and Ningyocho suitable for housing and commercial enterprises. Ieyasu encouraged immigration into his new military and civil capital, for producers of everyday wares and distributors of foodstuffs were needed by his court and by the 300 daimyo and their retinues. The craftsmen, tradesmen, fishermen, and merchants (many from the Ise region) who flocked to Edo created a lively population of commoners whose hard lives were all too frequently disrupted by the "flowers of Edo," those fires that burned down their warrens ("homes" is too luxurious a term) and their livelihoods. Between 1603, when Tokugawa

This "ground zero" milestone marker on Nihombashi Bridge marks the center of Tokyo.

Ieyasu became shogun in his new Edo headquarters, and 1868, when the Tokugawa rule ended, Edo suffered 97 major conflagrations.

This tour will start near **Nihombashi,** the "Bridge of Japan," which tied together this exciting and boisterous community. Along the south side of the river, the route will move to the **Kabutocho** district of the Nihombashi area, and then by subway (or on foot) to **Fukagawa,** that sector of Shitamachi across the Sumida River that blossomed after the Long Sleeves Fire of 1657. We will return from Fukagawa, with its intriguing museum of old Edo, and then go on to **Ningyocho,** the early licensed quarter where Yoshiwara first began, in order to explore this former district of pleasure before the tour returns once more to Nihombashi.

The banks of the river on either side of Nihombashi Bridge were busy, for here were the quays where vessels were unloaded and also the *kura* in which goods were stored. From 1628 to 1923, the north bank of the river between the bridge and today's Showa-dori was the location of the city's fish market, a flourishing enterprise that supplied one of the main sources of the city's food. Fishing vessels sailed into Edo Bay and, if too large, transferred their catches to smaller boats that would come up the Sumida River to the stalls where fish were sold. To the market stalls came the representatives of the shogun to requisition the best of the day's catch, making their selection before any other sales could begin. Delivery of the fresh fish was then made to the shogun's castle by way of the canals and moats that led to the stronghold above the Hibiya flats. The fish market was an unsightly place, for dead fish and the offal of gutted fish were all about—and it is not surprising that cholera often raged in the city. A marker on the north side of the river today provides a remembrance of the 300 years during which the fish market was here until it was forced to move to Tsukiji after the 1923 earthquake.

To the north of the river were many shops that supplied the daily needs of the city. Dried bonito and seaweed were available here in the 1600s because of the proximity to the fish stalls, and these items are still available in some shops on the north side of the river today. The district, too, would foster stores that in later years blossomed into large department stores, for trade was to pick up greatly after 1635, when the shogun required the 300 daimyo and their entourages to make the biennial procession from their home districts to Edo for a two-year stay in the shogun's capital. This requirement of "alternate residence" by the daimyo provided an additional populace to be served by Edo's fishermen, farmers, and tradespeople.

In the southeastern part of Nihombashi, in Hatchobori, were the lumberyards. The selling of lumber generated a great deal of wealth for entrepreneurs—since the constant fires in Edo necessitated constant rebuilding. One of the more noted lumber magnates was Kinokuniya Bunzaemon, whose rich villa lay to the north and east of Nihombashi River, in an area that adjoined Ningyocho and its Kabuki theaters, its Bunraku plays, and its licensed quarters of courtesans. Ningyocho was the red-light district of early Edo, particularly the area called Yoshiwara or "Field of Reeds," so named because it had only recently been swampland. Bunzaemon was a generous spender in this quarter, for, under the dual sources of Japanese religion, Buddhism teaches that life is brief while Shinto encourages the enjoyment of life. Money was to be enjoyed, and Bunzaemon dispensed his lavishly among the courtesans in Ningyocho. For those of a moralist nature, no doubt there must be a lesson here, for it is said that he died penniless due to his extravagant ways in Yoshiwara.

The lumberyards were moved from Nihombashi across the river to Fukagawa after the devastating 1657 fire, for the stock of wood in the lumberyards provided an ever-present danger to the welfare of the city. Fukagawa residents took a preventative measure by creating the Akiba Shrine, where protective amulets to the Deity of Fire were mass-produced and sold. Fukagawa thus became an extension of Shitamachi, reached by a ferry, for the Tokugawas would not permit the Sumida River to be spanned lest it provide too easy access to Edo proper from any potentially unfriendly forces. Trade necessitated shrines and temples, and some of these were relocated from Edo to Fukagawa after 1657. Not surprisingly, an unlicensed "licensed quarter" followed soon thereafter, and that section of Fukagawa in Meiji times eventually became the licensed Susaki quarter for sex.

1 THE KITE MUSEUM

We leave from the **Nihombashi Station** of either the Ginza or Tozai subway lines, which connect at Chuo-dori and Etai-dori. The Tokyu Department Store was established at this

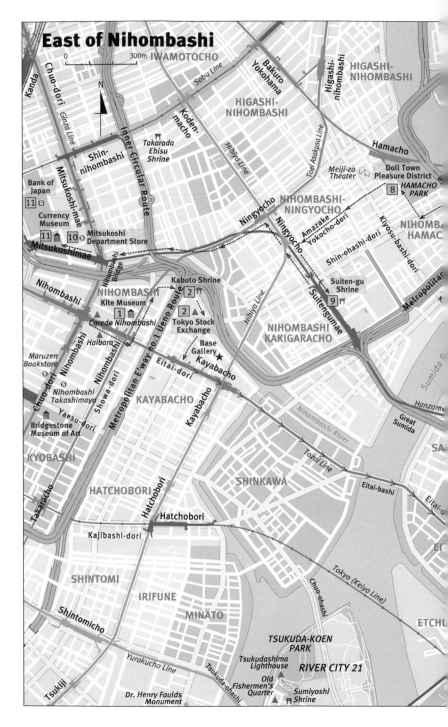

East of Nihombashi

0 — 300m

IWAMOTOCHO

Chuo-dori

Kanda

Ginza Line

Sobu Line

Inner Circular Route

Koden-macho

Bakuro-Yokohama

Higashi-nihombashi

HIGASHI-NIHOMBASHI

HIGASHI-NIHOMBASHI

Shin-nihombashi

Toei Asakusa Line

Hibiya Line

Mitsukoshi-mae

Takarada Ebisu Shrine

Hamacho

Meiji-za Theater

Doll Town Pleasure District

HAMACHO PARK

Bank of Japan

11 B

Currency Museum

11 🏛 **10** S Mitsukoshi Department Store

Mitsukoshimae

Ningyocho

Ningyocho

NIHOMBASHI-NINGYOCHO

Amazake-Yokocho-dori

Kiyosu-bashi-dori

NIHOMB HAMAC

NIHOMB HAMAC

Nihombashi

Nihombashi Bridge

Shin-ohashi-dori

Suitengumae

Suiten-gu Shrine

9 🛉

Metropolitan

NIHOMBASHI

Kabuto Shrine

2 🛉

Kite Museum

1 🏛

2

Coredo Nihombashi

Haibara

2 ▲ Tokyo Stock Exchange

Hibiya Line

NIHOMBASHI KAKIGARACHO

Metropolitan E'way no.1 Ueno Route

Base Gallery ★

Kayabacho

Maruzen Bookstore

S

Nihombashi

Eitai-dori

Sumida

Chuo-dori

Nihombashi

Nihombashi

Showa-dori

Nihombashi Takashimaya

KAYABACHO

Kayabacho

Kayabacho

Nihombashi River

Hanzom

Great Sumida

Yaesu-dori

Bridgestone Museum of Art

🏛

KYOBASHI

Tozai Line

SHINKAWA

SA

Takaracho

HATCHOBORI

Hatchobori

Hatchobori

Hatchobori

Eitai-bashi

Eitai-g

EI

Kajibashi-dori

SHINTOMI

Shintomicho

IRIFUNE

MINATO

Tokyo (Keiyo Line)

Chuo-ohashi

ETCHU

Yurakucho Line

Tsukuda-ohashi

Tsukiji

TSUKUDA-KOEN PARK

Tsukudashima Lighthouse

Old Fishermen's Quarter

RIVER CITY 21

Dr. Henry Faulds Monument

Sumiyoshi Shrine

intersection, and we start the tour by walking past the **Coredo Building** on its former site toward Showa-dori. Turning left at the end of the block, one sees the **Taimeiken restaurant**, whose proprietor created the **Kite Museum** that is on the fifth floor of this building. The museum's collection consists of some 2,000 traditional kites, representing the variety of regional styles across Japan and the rest of Asia, and these are not just for children. Adults not only collect kites but often enjoy kite battles, in which extremely large kites, constructed from the finest of strong paper, are flown by teams that work to move as well as restrain the heavy lines controlling the kites. The lines holding the kites are coated with powdered glass, and in aerial duels the operators of the kites maneuver their lines in order to cut the lines of their opponents' kites. A downed kite belongs to those who brought it to the ground. (The museum is open from 11:00 a.m. to 5:00 p.m. daily except for Sundays, national holidays, and the New Year holiday. Entry is ¥200.)

② **KABUTO SHRINE AND THE TOKYO STOCK EXCHANGE**

On leaving the Kite Museum, Showa-dori should be taken to the north toward Nihombashi River and the overhead expressway over it. A turn to the right at the street parallel to the river and past the expressway interchange brings one to the **Kabuto Shrine** (War Helmet Shrine), just on the other side of the overhead expressway. In the 11th century, the emperor dispatched one of his most trusted warriors to the eastern part of the country to subdue the "barbarians" from Hokkaido and eastern Japan who were preventing the spread of imperial power into this unsettled area. That warrior paused here at the Nihombashi River to pray to the Dragon God of the river for success in battle. On his successful defeat of the "barbarians," he buried his golden helmet (*kabuto*) here in homage to the god who had answered his prayer. A Shinto shrine still exists today at the site of the supposed buried helmet.

Just south of the shrine is the **Tokyo Stock Exchange**, which first opened in 1878. It became a lone holdout in what had been the financial sector of Tokyo after the Mitsubishi group enticed many of Japan's leading corporations to the Marunouchi area after World War I. After World War II, a new exchange building was constructed on this site, and in the plaza in front of the present 1985 building is the sculpture *Homage to the Sun*. An exhibition center offers information on the working of the exchange, while a "Hands Signal Robot" illustrates the signaling techniques used by the 1,800 workers on the floor of the exchange. The actual pandemonium of buying and selling in the exchange can be seen from a glass-walled viewing area set aside for visitors when the exchange is in session (9:00 a.m. to 11:30 a.m. and from 12:30 p.m. to 3:00 p.m.), after application at the reception desk.

③ FUKAGAWA FUDO-DO TEMPLE

Continuing south under the overhead expressway, then turning left onto Eitai-dori, a brief walk brings one to Kayabacho Station on the Tozai subway line, which can be taken to the next station to the east, **Monzen Nakacho Station** in the old Fukagawa area. Alternatively, one could continue eastward on foot along Eitai-dori, passing Kayabacho Station and in about 10 minutes reaching the **Eitai-bashi Bridge** and the wonderful view it affords. Looking south, the Sumida River opens into the bay and forks left and right around the striking site of Tsukishima Island and its towering residential skyscrapers. Continuing eastward from the bridge, the Monzen-Nakacho Station and the **Fukagawa**

Inari Okami at Fukagawa Fudo-do

area are reached in a half-mile. Fukagawa was a swamp in 1657 at the time of the Long Sleeves Fire that destroyed so much of Edo, particularly in the Nihombashi and Hatchobori districts across the Sumida River to the west. The fire gave an impetus to the reclamation of this low-lying area, so that the lumberyards could be relocated here, a river's width away from the city should fire break out again. The few fishing villages in this swampy sector thus became a center for the lumber trade, with its storage yard and docks. Fukagawa itself was to see fires and floods on more than one occasion. The 1923 earthquake destroyed much of the area, and the nights of March 8 and 10, 1945, saw almost half of Tokyo destroyed by American bombers. Out of the more than 70,000 deaths that resulted in those two nights of bombing, one-third occurred in Fukagawa. Floods also were always a problem for this low-lying district, and the floodwalls erected during the 20th century have protected the area from some of the backup of water from Tokyo Bay during typhoons and at other times of high water.

The lumberyards and warehouses brought men to work across the Sumida when there were no bridges to the rest of Edo. As a result, an unlicensed quarter beyond the jurisdiction of Edo magistrates developed to serve the workers. Fires in Yoshiwara that drove the courtesans out of their licensed quarter there and into Fukagawa contributed to this influx. A shrine and a temple that arose in Fukagawa led to the establishment of shops along the way, which were patronized by pilgrims and worshippers, and so teahouses, which stood among these shops, added girls to their staff. Soon arrangements could be made at these teahouses for "the geisha of the seven hills" or "hill place," as the red-light district of

Dragon-god trough at Fukagawa Fudo-do

Fukagawa was nicknamed. These geisha were not of the accomplished sort and were, in most instances, little more than prostitutes. After the 1958 anti-prostitution law came into effect, this unlicensed aspect of the quarter was to disappear entirely.

On leaving the subway station (from the front of the train, if one doesn't walk) a street to the right leads to the **Fukagawa Fudo-do Temple**, with a red torii heralding the temple and shrine to come. The street itself becomes the site of the temple market on the first, 15th, and 28th day of each month. At the top of the street is the Fudo-do (Fudo Hall); just before it on the right is the small **Eitai-ji Temple**, which once was within the grounds of the Tomioka Hachiman-gu shrine further along the way. In the iconoclastic Meiji period, when temples were separated from the shrines with which they were often associated, Eitai-ji was reduced to the small unit that still exists, its one building topped by a peculiar cupola. Beyond Eitai-ji a stone torii at the entrance to the Fudo-do has a large incense burner at the head of the steps to the temple, and a roofed ablution basin on the left is supplied with water which issues from the mouths of three rearing dragons. To one side, three fountains pour into a stone basin, and there is a gong that can be sounded by pulling on its rope to obtain the attention of the god.

This temple is a branch of the famed Fudo Temple at Narita, and thus it logically has Fudo as its main image, with his fierce-looking face and a large tooth protruding from

either side of his mouth. He is a benevolent deity, who carries a rope with which to bind evildoers, as well as a sword to smite evil. On either side of the Fudo image are multi-arm deities. A *ramma* (transom) before the altar is carved in the form of a dragon, and here also is an item worth noting in a Buddhist temple, a *haraigushi*, the sacred paper wand used by Shinto priests in purifying ceremonies. The *goma* rite is the important ceremony at the Fudo-do, and it occurs five times a day, at 9:00 a.m., 11:00 a.m., 1:00 p.m., 3:00 p.m., and 5:00 p.m. *Goma* sticks are cedar sticks on which one can write one's name, age, address, and a wish. At a set time, the priests place the sticks, one at a time, into the sacred fire, chanting sutras to a drumbeat. The burning of the *goma* stick makes the wish come true, according to temple tradition. Priests will also bless items over the fire, just as they will bless vehicles brought to the temple, although this latter ceremony is usually offered at Shinto shrines rather than at Buddhist temples. The temple itself was brought here from near Narita to replace the previous hall, which burned in 1945. One room at the rear is used for sutra copying by devotees of the temple, while another room serves as a small museum for the Fudo-do.

4 TOMIOKA HACHIMAN-GU SHRINE AND SUMO

On leaving the Fudo-do and returning to the main street, Eitai-dori, one is traversing the area that served as the licensed quarter in the past. Turning left at Eitai-dori and continuing

The main building of Tomioka Hachiman-gu Shrine in Monzen-Nakacho

for two streets, one finds a bronze-plated torii at the entrance path to the **Tomioka Hachiman-gu** on the left. This shrine, which attracted people to Fukagawa, was established in 1627, and it was famous in Edo times for the fact that sumo bouts were held here from 1684 on. As with all shrines, the grounds are entered through a torii. To the right are large stones commemorating noted sumo wrestlers: the middle stone lists the names of those who have achieved the rank of *ozeki*, the second highest rank in sumo. Stones to either side provide the statistics any devotee of sumo would want to know: the wrestler's height, the size of his hands, and the size of his feet.

A building on the left holds the shrine's two huge portable *mikoshi* (shrine palanquins) used during festivals to take the symbols of the deity in a public procession. Two buildings, the Haiden (Prayer Hall) and the Honden (Spirit Hall), with copper-tiled roofs that were rebuilt in 1968, lie at the end of the path. Behind these buildings is a hall with mementos of trades that once enriched Fukagawa—those of the rafters of lumber and the makers of sake. Beyond the shrine to the right is an exceedingly large stone known as the Yokozuna Stone, since it has inscribed upon it the names of those who reach the highest of sumo honors, the status of *yokozuna*. A tiny shrine to the right also honors the Shinto goddess Benten, while to the left behind the Treasury is a shrine to Ebisu. The shrine festival, when 50 very large *mikoshi* are paraded through the streets, takes place every third year (the next are 2013 and 2016). The three-day festival begins on a weekend in mid-August, and since this can be one of the hottest days of summer, much water is thrown on the shrine and its husky bearers as they jostle their way along the procession route.

5 FUKAGAWA EDO FOLK MUSEUM

A turn to the right on leaving the shrine takes one under the Shuto Expressway and to a major street where a left turn is made at the traffic light. Another turn to the right at a series of small temples puts one on the main north-south road, Kiyosumi-dori, which will lead in a 15-minute walk to the Fukagawa Edo Folk Museum. Just beyond this intersection, on the right, is a square, vermilion building in a courtyard. It is a **temple to *Emma*, the King of Hell**, and his fearful image overpowers this small hall. About three-quarters of

the way along the walled Kiyosumi Garden, on the right, which is the side of Kiyosumi-dori, are two temple posts at the entrance to a side street—an indication that the museum lies a block or two beyond the main road and these posts. Just before the museum is the **Reigan-ji Temple**, which retains one of the six Jizo images, nine feet tall, that once marked the borders of Edo at main roads leading into the city. The 1986 **Fukagawa Edo Folk Museum** (Fukagawa Edo Shiryokan) building can be recognized as a tall, windowless, white brick structure. (It is open from 9:30 a.m. to 5:00 p.m., closed the second and fourth Monday of each month and at the New Year period. Entry ¥300. It is a three-minute walk from Kiyosumi-shirakawa Station on the Toei Oedo subway line.) It is worthwhile to purchase the English-language guidebook that explains the purpose of the museum and elucidates the various sites within the complex.

A room off the lobby is filled with life-size figures (drawn on heavy plastic sheets) of the residents of Fukagawa during the Edo centuries, including a fortune-teller, a flower vendor, a hairdresser, and others. From this room one enters a balcony overlooking a huge exhibition hall in which a portion of Edo lies below. Here are the wooden houses of the 17th and 18th centuries, the fireproof *kura* in which merchants stored their valuables, riverside taverns, a greengrocer, and a watchtower where the alarm could be sounded should fire break out. The cycle of the day passes before one, for slowly the lights dim as the temple bell rings nightfall. Then, with the coming of dawn, a rooster crows, and the cries of the wandering vendors can be heard as the city awakens to another day. The variety of homes, from those of tenement dwellers to those of well-to-do merchants, can be entered when one descends to the lower level, and objects of everyday life are present as though life were still going on in these narrow quarters of the Sagacho district in 1840, the era portrayed in this museum. A side hall shows the changes that overcame this small area of Fukagawa, with dioramas of the outbreak of fire, the subsequent destruction, and then the process of rebuilding the community once more. Video units offer fine, brief films on the crafts and life of the earlier period in Fukagawa; many of these crafts are extant today.

The Sagacho district was rebuilt after the 1923 earthquake and the 1945 bombings, and two events today still recall earlier times. On the first Sunday in October, there is the Fukagawa Chikara Mochi (Fukagawa Strongman Contest), when the strength of local citizens is evidenced in a contest to see who can hold a 132-pound rice bag over his head the longest. Also in the October is the *kakunori* event (timberyard log rolling), where two men bearing a *kago* on their shoulders balance themselves on rolling logs in the water, trying to remain upright as they traverse a "road" of bobbling logs. A *kago* is the palanquin in which a daimyo could be carried on the shoulders of his servants when moving from one place to another.

6 KIYOSUMI GARDENS

Back at the main road, a turn to the right and then to the left at the next intersection will bring one to the entrance to the **Kiyosumi Gardens** (Kiyosumi Teien). This garden was once the part of a villa of Kinokuniya Bunzaemon, whom we encountered as a wealthy timber merchant in the Hatchobori sector of Nihombashi. In his more affluent days in 1688, this garden was designed as a stroll-garden with its lake, teahouse, and stone lanterns. The garden was to fall onto unhappier times as the years passed, but in 1878 Yataro Iwasaki, the founder of the House

of Mitsubishi, purchased the land and had the lake and garden restored and re-landscaped. Fifty-five rare rocks from all over Japan were gathered to enhance the garden and the villa that Iwasaki had built.

The garden eventually became a place of leisure for employees of Iwasaki's enterprises. The earthquake of 1923 extensively damaged the garden and its buildings, and thus the site was turned over to the city as a gift in 1924. It was restored to its former beauty, with a traditional house built at the edge of the lake, which is home to thousands of carp. (The garden is open from 9:00 to 5:00 p.m., closed at the New Year period; entry is ¥150. It is a three-minute walk from Kiyosumi–shirakawa Station on the Oedo subway line.) The lakeside building is a reproduction of the unit that was built by the government in 1909 to entertain General Kitchener of Britain on his visit to Japan. The park was the site of the funeral pavilion of Emperor Taisho in the mid-1920s. If one has purchased sandwiches or a *bento* en route, these can be enjoyed in the garden.

7 SUMO STABLES AND THE BASHO HOUSE SITE

The street beyond the entrance to the garden should be followed alongside **Kiyosumi Park**. Turn to the right onto the north-south street at the park's far end and then cross

The ornamental trees are a feature of Kiyosumi Gardens.

Kiyosu-bashi-dori (the bridge of that name over the Sumida River is one block to the left). At the second street on the right are sumo stables, one of which is the **Kitanoumi sumo stable**, while at the intersection beyond, on the southwest corner is the **Taiho sumo stable.** *Stable* may seem a peculiar term to use in conjunction with sumo, but it is the term for the places where sumo wrestlers train and live. Additional such units lie farther to the north near the sumo stadium—which will be covered in a later tour in this guidebook. Continuing on the main street and crossing over the **Onagigawa Canal** via the **Mannenbashi Bridge** (*mannen* means "one thousand years"—as in the wish "May you live one thousand years!"), the **Basho-an** is to the left across the bridge, between the north-south street being followed and the Sumida River to the east.

This is the site of the house in which the poet Basho was living when, on March 27, 1689, he set out on the wanderings that resulted in his *The Narrow Road to the Deep North*. The land on which Basho's small house stood belonged to the villa of Sugiyama Sampu, another of the lumber tycoons of the late 1600s. On these grounds, where Basho resided for ten years, banana trees (*basho*) grew. Basho humorously took his name from his neighbors' reference to him as "the old man of the banana trees." All that remains on the site today is a concrete torii, a stone monument, and a small Inari shrine. Symbolically these have meaning, but it is a meager reminder of the great poet who once resided here. A half-mile farther along the main street, after three streets on the right, is a three-story, white building on the left. This is the 1981 **Basho Memorial Hall**. The hall is of interest primarily to those who read Japanese, since the memorabilia connected with Basho are described only in Japanese. It contains examples of Basho's haiku, his letters, as well as an exhibition of travel clothes from Basho's day (open 9:30 a.m. to 4:30 p.m; closed Mondays; entry ¥100).

8 DOLL TOWN PLEASURE DISTRICT

The north-south street being followed reaches Shin-ohashi-dori, where a left turn should be taken toward Shin-ohashi Bridge. After crossing the bridge, continue on Shin-ohashi-dori until reaching the fourth side street on your right, which leads past Hamacho Park to Hamacho Station in the **Ningyocho** section of

Tokyo. (An alternative when you first reach Shin-Ohashi-dori is to turn right and walk one long block east to Morishita Station on the Toei Shinjuku and Oedo subway lines, where a train can be taken one stop to Hamacho Station.) The name *Ningyocho* ("Doll Town" or "Puppet Town") reflects the location here in the past of the Bunraku puppet theaters and the doll makers. Ningyocho once was primarily a pleasure district of Edo until a wave of Puritanism emanated from the shogun's office and forced the theaters to move to the north of the city in 1840.

As with much of Edo, the area was a swamp before Tokugawa Ieyasu began his project of filling in the low-lying lands to the east of his castle. In 1617, the area was chosen as the licensed quarter or pleasure district for the town, as it was sufficiently away from the castle and the residences of the daimyo yet in the midst of the growing Shitamachi area of the commoners who needed living and entertainment space in their work-wearying lives. The new pleasure district was named Yoshiwara (Field, or Plain, of Reeds), an indication of the nature of the terrain. Aside from the pleasures of what was basically a red-light district, two important Kabuki theaters were established here: the Nakamura-za and Ichimura-za Kabuki theaters, and Bunraku puppet theaters opened as well. Once the licensed quarter was created, Kabuki and Bunraku as entertainment forms came respectively from Kyoto and Osaka to enhance life in Edo.

Ningyocho had its problems. The 1657 Long Sleeves Fire destroyed the area, and Yoshiwara was eventually moved further north (beyond the great Senso-ji Temple at Asakusa), where a new cult of pleasure was to develop around cultured geisha. That is not to say that Yoshiwara did not have its common prostitutes, but it had restaurants and other forms of pleasure as well. The Kabuki and Bunraku theaters also moved to the north in 1841 as a result of the shogun's next bout of moralism, but the puppet craftsmen and the doll makers remained in the Ningyocho area. With the overthrow of the shogun's government in 1868, theaters and restaurants were to return to the area once more, and in the Meiji and Taisho eras (1868-1923) up to the 1923 earthquake, the area began again to flourish as an entertainment district.

The new post-1868 entertainment area centered about the Hamacho district, next to the Sumida River. Many of the Meiji military officials had their residence near the Sumida River, but Ningyocho itself remained a working district of traders and craftsmen. In the midst of this new, modern pleasure district, the Meiji-za Theater, with 1,770 seats, opened in 1893 for the new audience composed of the middle class and the military. The theater offered a newer, less formal form of Kabuki, and it was the first theater in Tokyo that was illuminated by electricity. In Hamacho also were the *machiai* (assignation houses), where geisha of the district could be summoned to entertain the well-to-do, new governing class. Thus an elegant geisha world developed in the *ryotei* (traditional restaurants) with views overlooking the river. At the end of the 20th century, 11 *ryotei* and 55 geisha still provided an ambiance of another era in Hamacho, although the view of the Sumida River is now gone because of the concrete flood wall and the elevated Shuto Expressway.

Hamacho Park was created after the devastation of the 1923 earthquake. The 1893 ferroconcrete Meiji-za Theater survived the 1923 earthquake, but a new disaster struck in 1945. Ningyocho was fortunate in the terrible firestorms that broke out in the 1945 March air raids on the city, since a shift in the wind took the fire away from that district. However, thousands seeking refuge in the theater were steamed alive by the intense heat created by the tornado of flames in the surrounding city.

Leaving Hamacho Park by the street that heads into town from the park's middle, one street on the right at the park finds the **Meiji-za** in a new high-rise structure, where it continues to offer a lively form of Kabuki noted for its fast pace and special effects. Amazake Yokocho-dori is the street being traversed, and it takes its name from a semi-alcoholic drink made from the lees of sake; it was considered non-volatile enough that it could be drunk by *ama* (Buddhist nuns). This street was the heart of the Ningyocho pleasure district from 1868 through 1923; previously it had been the southernmost limit of the original Yoshiwara. At the fifth intersection along Amazake-dori, a turn to the left on a major shopping street heads one toward the **Suiten-gu Shrine**. (A turn to the right would bring one to the entrance to the Hibiya subway line's Ningyocho Station; a plaque there indicates that this was once the site of the Kakigaracho Ginza, where the silver mint remained until 1868.)

9 SUITEN-GU SHRINE

Crossing Shin-ohashi-dori, the shrine is ahead on the left. The **Suiten-gu** (Celestial Palace in the Sea) is known for its relationship to pregnancy and childbirth. Its origin goes back to the battle of Dan-no-ura in Kyushu in 1185, when the child-emperor Antoku, his mother, and his grandmother-nurse leaped into the sea from their vessel to escape capture by the Minamoto forces pursuing them. The mother was saved, but the child and grandmother-nurse drowned, and this shrine is in honor of the boy and his mother, Empress Kenrei-mon-in. The mother is revered here as the deity who protects safe childbirth, while the boy-emperor is the patron of travelers. The shrine is a branch of the Suiten-gu Shrine in Kyushu, erected by Arima, the daimyo of Kurume in Kyushu. This branch shrine was originally created on the ground of Count Arima's former mansion on the Arima estate in the Shiba district south of Edo. The shrine was moved to Ningyocho in 1672, and a town grew up around it.

Stairs lead up to the raised level on which the shrine and its ancillary buildings are grouped. A bronze-plated torii stands well

Pregnant women rub this bronze statue at Suiten-gu to wish for an easy birth.

before the main building, and two bronze lanterns decorated with dragons and water symbols stand just before it. The main building is a modern structure of white plaster with a copper-tiled roof, and to the right of the main unit is a bronze statue of a dog with its newborn pup. Round projections on the base of the sculpture on which the image of the mother dog sits, as well as on the image of the baby dog, are frequently rubbed by visiting women, since these are talismans that are thought to bring about an easy birth. A four-pronged anchor also sits next to the stairs leading up to the shrine, a reminder of the fate of the young emperor who was drowned at sea.

The shrine is an exceedingly popular one, for here women come to pray for a safe and easy delivery in childbirth, and charms may be purchased to this end. The fifth day of each month is a festival and market day, and the shrine is most crowded on these days as well as on the Day of the Dog in the zodiac calendar—since dogs deliver their offspring so easily. Thus the charms for easy delivery are made of papier-mâché in the form of dogs (*inu-hariko*). Women come not only to pray but to purchase *haraobi*, a white cotton bellyband blessed at the shrine by the priests and sold at a stall between the torii and the shrine building. (It is said that the bands were originally made out of cloth from the red and white

bell-pull that is pulled to attract the attentions of the shrine deity.) These bands are intended to help in safe childbearing if worn from the fifth month of pregnancy on. The connection with childbirth and children, and the original location of puppet theater in Ningyocho, led to many doll makers and doll shops being centered in this district. Dolls have even affected local sweet foods, for one of the delicacies found in shops is the *ningyo-yaki*, a soft-baked confection in the shape of a doll, made from wheat with sweet bean paste in its center. Confections sold in the form of Suiten-gu charms can also be purchased in this area.

10 MITSUKOSHI DEPARTMENT STORE

On leaving the shrine, a little farther down the street is the entrance to Suitengumae Station on the Hanzomon subway line, from which this tour goes on to **Mitsukoshimae Station**, the next stop on the line. (To walk, follow the main street back to Amazake-dori and continue past it to Ningyocho Station at the next major intersection. Turning left here and walking west for 500 yards will take you first over Showa-dori and then to Chuo-dori, where you will see Nihombashi Bridge to your left and Mitsukoshi Department Store to your right.) As the station name indicates, the stop is in front of the **Mitsukoshi Department Store** (*mae* means "in front of"). The store, which has always been considered the finest

Staff greet customers outside Mitsukoshi Department Store, before the doors open at 10 a.m. sharp.

and most luxurious (and today the most old-fashioned) department store in Tokyo, had its humble origins as a dry goods store in 1673, a branch of the Kyoto Echigoya, a kimono shop. Mitsui Takatoshi, the owner of the shop, was an innovator in merchandising. He was the first to display his goods rather than bring out items one at a time for a customer to examine. He also sold at set prices, doing away with the time-consuming haggling over prices. Moreover, he sold for cash only rather than offering credit, since credit was sometimes difficult to collect. The shop was also the first one to employ women as salesclerks. From a modest beginning, the family enterprise grew beyond the Mitsukoshi Department Store, the successor to the Echigoya, and branched out into banks (the former Mitsui Bank), real estate (Mitsui and Company), and other commercial and industrial enterprises.

In 1908 Mitsukoshi built a Western-style, three-story building, modeled to a great extent after Harrods Department Store of London (indicating a fascination with English merchandise that is still evident today). In 1914 a five-story building with an escalator was created, and in 1935 the present structure came into being. English and other imported goods can be found throughout the store; the third floor even has a replica of Fortnum and Mason's tearoom in London, where tea is served. The **Mitsukoshi Theater** is on the sixth floor, and the **Mitsukoshi Culture Center** is adjacent. (The store is open every day from 10:00 a.m. to 7:00 p.m.)

[11] **BANK OF JAPAN AND CURRENCY MUSEUM**
Behind Mitsukoshi and one block to the north is the **Bank of Japan**. Here originally was the gold mint of the Tokugawa shoguns, set up in 1601. In 1790 when the silver mint was suspended because of irregularities in its handling, the silver and copper mints were moved here as well. From 1890 to 1896, the Bank of Japan building was under construction at this location, a project of Tatsuno Kingo, one of the four Japanese architecture students of Josiah Condor and later a student of William Burges. This was the first building in the new-to-Japan Western style of architecture, and it was inspired by the example of the neo-classical Berlin National Bank in Germany. A **Currency Museum** is located in the annex of the bank, offering a fascinating display of money from many nations and going back to ancient Roman and Chinese currencies. The heart of the collection is a retrospective of all the coinage of Japan. (The museum is open from 9:30 a.m. to 4:30 p.m. except Mondays, national holidays, and from December 29 through January 4. Entry is free. An English-language brochure is available, and exhibits are labeled in Japanese and in English.)

One last site of note is to be found near Mitsukoshi, and that is a reminder of William Adams, a one-time resident in Edo at 1-16 Nihombashi in Muromachi 1-chome. A plaque here, unveiled on July 28, 1930, reads:

In memory of William Adams, known as *Miura Anjin*, the first Englishman to settle in Japan, coming as a pilot on board the *Charity* in 1600, who resided in a mansion on this spot, who instructed Ieyasu, the first Tokugawa shogun, in gunnery, geography, mathematics, etc., rendering a valuable service in foreign affairs, and who married a Japanese lady, Miss Magone, and died May 16, 1620, at age 45 years.

Anjin is "pilot" in Japanese. Adams was a pilot on the Dutch ship *Liefde* (*Charity*) and a shipmate of Jan Joosten, who has been mentioned in conjunction with the Yaesu district nearby. Until 1932, this area where Adams lived was known as Anjin-cho after its noted resident. The monument to Adams is found on the second street to the right after crossing the Nihombashi Bridge and then two streets after turning to the right. In a small setback section before a low wooden fence is the memorial stone quoted above. Adams built an 80- and then a 120-ton ship for Ieyasu, among other accomplishments. He was given the daughter of a neighboring magistrate, Tenmacho, as his wife, for he was never permitted to leave Japan to rejoin his wife and family in Kent, England. He and his Japanese wife are buried in the cemetery in Yokosuka, where he was given an estate near the bay and harbor.

Nihombashi Bridge and the various Nihombashi subway stations are at hand for continuing on to the next destination.

GETTING THERE
This walk begins and ends at Nihombashi Station, which is served by the Tozai, Ginza, and Asakusa subway lines.

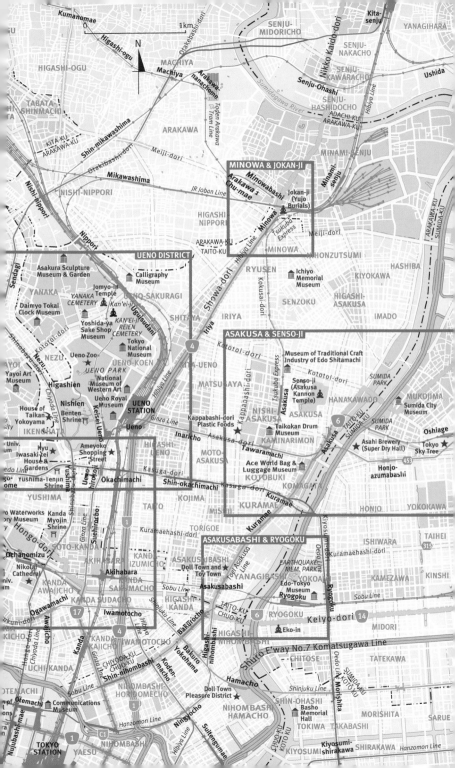

Walking Tour 7

ASAKUSABASHI, RYOGOKU AND YANAGIBASHI
A Geisha Quarter, the World of Toys, an Earthquake Memorial, Sumo Wrestlers, and Lord Kira's Demise

1. **Doll Town and Toy Town**
2. **Earthquake Memorial Park**
3. **Kyu-Yasuda Teien Gardens**
4. **Edo-Tokyo Museum**
5. **Sumo Stadium, Museum, and Stables**
6. **Eko-in Temple**
7. **Site of Lord Kira's Villa**
8. **Yanagibashi, Willow Tree Bridge**

A history of old Edo and then of Meiji Tokyo through the years could almost be recorded by the movement of the various pleasure quarters, licit and illicit. In Meiji days (1868–1912), the two most respectable geisha sectors of the city were in Shimbashi and Yanagibashi, the "New Bridge" and the "Willow Tree Bridge" districts. Shimbashi was the more recent of these two geisha areas, for it had its great days after 1868, with the establishment of imperial rule in Tokyo. It still continues today, albeit on a very much smaller scale. Yanagibashi, on the other hand, flourished during the last hundred years before the Tokugawa rule came to an end in 1868, and then it faded from the scene after managing to hold its own through World War I.

Yanagibashi, the Willow Tree Bridge, crossed the Kanda River just before its juncture with the Sumida River, and there boats arrived from Edo downstream. An unlicensed quarter soon sprang up around the bridge, and the geisha entertained not only in restaurants but on houseboats along the Kanda River, the waterway that was also the outermost moat about the castle. The delights of Yanagibashi were favored by native Tokyoites, who looked down on the brash Meiji newcomers who followed in the wake of the move of the capital from Kyoto and patronized the pleasures of Shimbashi. Inevitably, the attractions of the Yanagibashi geisha languished as times changed, and today its riverside restaurants would be hard put to continue, since flood walls have blocked the view of the river for the former buildings, which were only one and two stories tall. (Walls 15 to 28 feet above water level enclose the river for 15 miles inland as protection against high-water surges from Tokyo Bay during storms.) Thus, a bridge still remains at Yanagibashi, and the street from the Asakusabashi Bridge is, appropriately enough, lined with willow trees as it leads to the Willow Tree Bridge. The traditional Yanagibashi geisha area where the Kanda enters the Sumida is now little more than a memory, and the pleasure boats on which geisha entertained have undergone a change. This tour will eventually end at this site, with a reflection on the taking of one's modern pleasures on these two venerable rivers.

1 DOLL TOWN AND TOY TOWN
This walk begins at the **Asakusabashi Stations** of the aboveground JR or the Toei Asakusa subway line station. There are numerous wholesale districts in Tokyo, but the shops along Edo-dori between the Asakusabashi and the Kuramae subway stations of the Toei Asakusa subway line are the centers for wholesalers of fireworks, toys, dolls, and Christmas and New Year decorations. Maps of Tokyo often distinguish two sections of these wholesale shops, which lie not only along Edo-dori but also in the narrow streets behind this avenue. The first section, between the Asakusabashi and Kuramae Bridges, is referred to as Doll Town, while the section

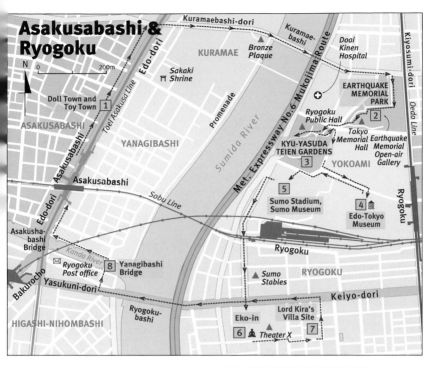

beyond Kuramaebashi Bridge is referred to as Toy Town. Both portions of the overall district can be enjoyable to explore on foot, with their specialized shops and the variety of goods offered by wholesale merchants.

Kuramaebashi, the Bridge in Front of the Kura, received its name in earlier years, since along the river stood a row of *kura*, granary storage buildings where rice received as a tax payment was stored in Edo days. Today, after lingering to explore the world of a child's delight at the wholesale toy and holiday decorations district, one can cross the **Kuramaebashi Bridge** to the far side of the Sumida River. The original bridge across the Sumida was a wooden one, and a bronze plaque on the right, just before the bridge is crossed, commemorates it with a drawing and a text (in Japanese). Below, between the flood wall and the river, a new promenade was built toward the end of the 20th century to return the riverfront to pedestrians once more. In this range of the promenade, the flood wall has been given a new facing so that it resembles the walls of the *kura* that once stood along the riverbank.

② EARTHQUAKE MEMORIAL PARK

Across the bridge, where a promenade exists on the far bank as well, the sector between the river and Kiyosumi-dori (which is the main north-south street) offers a number of sites of interest. South of the bridge, on the right, is the **Doai Kinen Hospital**, the memorial hospital built with American gift funds after the Great Kanto Earthquake of 1923. Just beyond the hospital, a path on the right leads into the **Earthquake Memorial Park aka Yokoamicho Park** and its museum and memorial hall, the Tokyo-to Irei-do (**Tokyo Metropolitan Memorial Hall**). In 1923 the site of the Memorial Hall was open ground, since the Army Clothing Depot had been moved to a newer site. When the earthquake struck at two minutes before noon on September 1, a time when cooking fires were lit in kitchens all over Tokyo, people fled from their damaged homes, which were now threatened by the spreading fires and raging winds that followed the massive tremor. Many in East Tokyo raced with their household goods to this vacant area on the east bank of the Sumida River. Flying sparks set these household goods on fire, and the whirlwind inferno generated by the heat of the burning houses in this eastern district caused the deaths of an estimated 40,000 people within this open area. More than 104,000 died in the entire city. The fires raged for 42 hours, during which 70 percent of Tokyo housing was destroyed. There were 1,700 aftershocks over the next three days, but, by the fourth day after the catastrophe, incense was being burned at the site of this holocaust in memory of the dead. Incense still burns here today.

Seven years after the earthquake, on September 1, 1930, a three-story, concrete memorial hall topped by a pagoda was erected on the site, and within are large urns containing the ashes of those who died. The hall has pews and an "altar" up front, while pictures of the disaster line the side walls. On September 1, 1951, the Memorial Hall was expanded to include a remembrance of the 100,000 or more who died during the bombing raids on Tokyo, when 851,000 houses were incinerated in March 1945. A two-story hall on the left hand side of the path into the Memorial Park has along its exterior the **Earthquake Memorial Open-air Gallery** of melted metal machinery, attesting to the ferocious heat generated by the fiery whirlwind that engulfed this area in 1923. Within the hall, the first floor displays artifacts and illustrative materials of

the earthquake and its fiery aftermath. The generous gift of blankets and clothing from the United States and France is also memorialized. On the second floor, paintings of the destroyed buildings in the city hang on the walls, while a relief model of the city in 1923 shows the devastated areas. Memorial services are held for the dead of the two disasters twice a year: on September 1 for the 1923 victims and on March 10 for those who perished 1945.

There is yet another memorial on the grounds, a stone that commemorates the death of 2,000 innocent Koreans, who were killed in the panic immediately after the earthquake, due to unfounded rumors that Koreans were responsible for looting and fires that followed the tremor. These rumors led to brutal attacks and the deaths of resident Koreans, who were set upon by Japanese mobs and killed without mercy.

③ KYU-YASUDA TEIEN GARDENS

Continuing along the south side of the Memorial Hall, a path toward the river leads to the **Kyu-Yasuda Teien Gardens**, with its large tidal pond to the left of the intersecting street. The garden had once been part of the estate of Zenjiro Yasuda, a financial magnate of the Meiji era. He was assassinated in 1921, and the land reverted as a gift to the city of Tokyo. Destroyed in the 1923 earthquake, the

The Kyu-Yasuda Teien Gardens in Ryogoku are at their very best in the fall.

garden has since been rebuilt, and the **Ryogoku Public Hall** now sits to one side of the park nearest the river. A large pond, encircled by greenery and with stone bridges over water courses as well as a small, traditional vermilion arched bridge (recreated in concrete) provides a restful area alongside the pond. (Open 9:30 a.m. to 4:30 p.m. Closed over the New Year holiday. Entry free.)

4 EDO-TOKYO MUSEUM

On leaving the Kyu-Yasuda Teien Gardens by way of the narrow street leading to the Sumo Stadium that lies ahead, a turn to the left at the end of the street leads to the **Edo-Tokyo Museum**, one of the most fascinating museums in Tokyo. (The museum is open from 9:30 a.m. to 5:30 p.m. [to 7:30 p.m. on Saturdays] but is closed on Mondays; it is open on Mondays if that day is a national holiday, but then it is closed the following day; it is also closed from December 28 to January 4; entry is free for permanent exhibition, a fee is required for special exhibition. Wireless headsets with English-language explanations of the displays are included with the price of admission.) Opened in 1993, this huge building, standing on four gigantic posts, offers a panorama of life during the 400 years of Edo/Tokyo since Tokugawa Ieyasu chose the high ground at the head of Tokyo Bay for his castle. Was it by chance or by intent that this 203-foot-tall museum approximates the same height as Ieyasu's castle?

The ticket offices are on the first floor and on the Edo-Tokyo Plaza. Escalators to the museum rise above the raised platform above which the museum stands on its four huge supports. These escalators (or adjacent elevators) take one to the sixth floor, where the tour of the exhibits begins, the sixth floor offering a mezzanine from which one can look down on the recreated buildings and the displays on the floor below. A reconstruction of the original Nihombashi wooden bridge is crossed to bring one to the beginning of the exhibition area. This mezzanine level offers the early history of the city, while the main floor below it takes the story of Edo into the years of early Tokyo and up to the 1964 Olympics. The exhibition area encompasses the fifth and sixth floor of the structure. Exhibitions are changed twice a month.

A full-scale reconstruction of the 19th-century Nakamura Kabuki Theater can be seen as well as the shogun's palace and one of the

The Edo-Tokyo Museum in Ryogoku

earliest "modern" buildings of the Meiji era. The exhibits of documents and artifacts of daily life range over a 300-year period, including even one of the earliest compact cars produced by Subaru. Various portions of the museum offer audiovisual displays for exploring areas of the city's history in depth. An auditorium for 450 and a gift shop on the first floor, coffee shops on the first and seventh floors, a Japanese and a Western restaurant, and a library concerned with the history of Edo-Tokyo on the seventh floor are among the amenities of this gigantic museum. There is even a stall on the outdoor plaza level where one can purchase *bento* lunch boxes, which can be enjoyed on Edo-Tokyo Plaza.

5 SUMO STADIUM, MUSEUM, AND STABLES

For many Japanese, however, there is another place on this side of the Sumida River that is of the greatest interest, and that is the **Sumo Stadium** (Kokugikan, "Hall of National Accomplishment"), the national center for sumo tournaments. Sumo has found a home for many years along the Sumida River. Sumo matches were held to the south in Fukagawa at the Tomioka Hachiman-gu Shrine in the late 1600s, later at Eko-in Temple from 1833 to 1909 (due south of the present sumo building at Keiyo-dori), and then in a sumo hall next to the temple until wartime damage ruined this hall. In 1984 a new sumo tournament stadium and a sumo museum in a five-story, ferroconcrete building was constructed on the east side of the Sumida River just to the north of Ryogoku Station on the Sobu railway line.

On leaving the Edo-Tokyo Museum, the Sumo Stadium is directly behind the museum, its entrance being on the side of the hall toward the river. The stadium can seat up to 10,000 spectators. The sumo ring with its round dirt mound (the *dohyo*) and the roof

A sumo tradition: the top-ranked wrestlers parade in the Kokugikan before the main bouts begin.

over the ring can be removed, the latter electronically, for occasions when the hall is used for activities other than sumo. Sumo tournaments are held here for 15 days in January, May, and September. The one-room **Sumo Museum** inside the main entrance is devoted to the history of sumo wrestling. (The museum is open from 10:00 a.m. to 4:30 p.m. without charge. It is closed on weekends and national holidays and the New Year period. During the three annual sumo tournaments, it is open only to sumo ticket holders.)

Leaving the Sumo Stadium and walking under the overhead rail line, to the south of Ryogoku Station, one comes to a collection of *heya*, the "**sumo stables**," in which wrestlers train and live. More than a dozen *heya* are run by retired sumo wrestlers, who have purchased the right to run such establishments from the Sumo Association. Between the rail line and the overhead Shuto Expressway further to the south are a number of shops serving the sumo world, particularly those selling clothes and footwear for men of the largest sizes.

6 EKO-IN TEMPLE

Walk under the overhead rail line, and where the main street splits, take the left-hand roadway. The street ends at Keiyo-dori, and across the street is the post-1945 **Eko-in Temple**

behind its very modern gateway. Keiyo-dori is the main east-west street in this area, since the Ryogokubashi Bridge over the Sumida River (to the right) connects this sector with the major portion of Tokyo. The Tokugawas, as has been indicated previously, were opposed to any bridges over the Sumida in their desire to keep hostile forces at bay. Unhappily, in the 1657 Long Sleeves Fire people were trapped by the inferno at the river's western edge, and over 100,000 perished, since there was no way across to safety. After that debacle, the Ryogokubashi was built in 1659, the first bridge to cross the river.

Although the Eko-in Temple was destroyed in 1923 and then again in 1945, it has been rebuilt in a modern but not outstanding architectural form. The temple was noted for two events in particular. It was here that the ashes of those who died in the 1657 fire were interred. A grand ceremony in honor of the dead was held at the interment by orders of the shogun. Located in close proximity to sumo stables, it's obvious that the temple must have had a relationship with sumo. When the sumo tournaments were moved from the Tomioka Hachiman-gu Shrine in the south in 1833, Eko-in became the site of the matches until 1909. After 1909, the Kokugikan, the Sumo Stadium next door to the temple, became the location at which the matches were held until the building was damaged in 1945 and razed thereafter. A large memorial stone, to the left of the path leading to the main hall of the temple, the Stone of Strength, commemorates this location as the home of sumo for so many years. Eko-in became a burial ground or a memorial place for many other than the dead of 1657. Even non-humans have been memorialized here, for example, the Bato Kannon, the Horse-headed Kannon, honors the spirits of dead animals. The spirits of stillborn children and aborted fetuses are also remembered here: in the area to the left of the temple hall, up against the rear fence are rows of tiny Jizo figures, some with bibs, some holding pinwheels in memory of the unborn.

7 SITE OF LORD KIRA'S VILLA

On leaving Eko-in through the rear exit, a turn to the left and then to the left again takes one along the street behind the temple. Just before the second cross street on the left is all that remains of the one-time splendid estate of Lord Kira. Kira was the daimyo who was to instruct Lord Asano in the subtleties of the shogun's court etiquette at the beginning of the 1700s. He did not train his pupil properly, since his honorarium, he felt, did not suit his status, and he was derisive of his pupil. As a result, Lord Asano performed inadequately at the shogun's audience. In a rage, Asano drew his sword to attack Kira, committing a capital offense by uncovering a sword in the castle. The penalty for such an action required ceremonial suicide on the part of the miscreant. So begins the tale of the 47 Ronin, which comes to its conclusion for visitors to modern Tokyo at Sengaku-ji Temple described in Walk 15. The subsequent event is worth recounting: On the snowy night of December 15, 1702, 47 of Asano's followers obtained revenge for their master's death by storming Lord Kira's mansion here to the east of the Sumida River. A very small park sits on **the site of Lord Kira's villa**; a white-tile-and-plaster wall protects the small enclosure. In the left-hand corner is the "head-washing well" where Kira's decapitated head was washed by his assailants before it was brought to their master's grave. There is also a small Inari shrine dedicated to Kira's retainers who died in the attack, and the story of the attack is portrayed here in reproductions of woodblock prints of scenes from the famous *Chushingura* Kabuki play that has immortalized the event.

The Kanda River and Yanagibashi Bridge where floating pleasure boats still offer food and drink as in olden times.

8 YANAGIBASHI, WILLOW TREE BRIDGE

Turning to the left at the corner of the memorial site and returning the one street to Keiyo-dori and then turning left towards the Sumida River, a 10-minute walk, brings you to Ryogokubashi Bridge (described above). Crossing over to the far side of the bridge, a righthand turn on the first striped crosswalk leads into a short, willow tree-lined street to the **Yanagibashi**, the Willow Tree Bridge. Here to the right, the Kanda River flows into the Sumida River, and here was once the noted **Yanagibashi geisha quarters** and the point at which one could take boats to the Yoshiwara and to where geisha entertained on pleasure boats. Today, pleasure craft still tie up here to provide a pleasant evening of food and drink for those seeking diversion from busy Tokyo life. The Kanda River can be followed for the short streets to Edo-dori, where, a few streets to the right, lie the Asakusabashi Stations of the elevated JR Line and the subway station of the Toei Asakusa subway line. These can take one back to the center of the city.

GETTING THERE

Asakusabashi Station, where this walk begins, is served by the JR Chuo-Sobu Line and the Toei Asakusa subway line. It can be reached within 20 minutes from both Tokyo and Shinjuku Stations.

Walking Tour 8

ASAKUSA, KAPPABASHI AND MINOWA

Tokyo's Oldest Temple, the Street of Inside Shops, a Golden Buddha, Plastic Delights, and a Famed Pleasure Quarter

1. **Tokyo Sky Tree (diversion)**
2. **Senso-ji (Asakusa Kannon Temple)**
3. **Asakusa District**
4. **Kappabashi-dori Plastic Foods**
5. **Jokan-ji Temple**
6. **Toden Arakawa Tram Line**

Asakusa was for two centuries the most exciting and dynamic area of old Edo and Tokyo. Its early importance as a religious center can even be pinpointed to an exact date, March 18, 628, for on that occasion two fishermen brothers, Hinokuma and Takenari Hamanari, caught a small gilt bronze image in their fishing net. According to tradition, they threw this unwanted object back into the river two times, but then it appeared in their net for a third time. So unusual an event seemed auspicious, and they took the image to their overlord, Haji-no-Nakatome, who enshrined it in his house and later built a hall for it, the traditional date for the hall being 645. Thus **Asakusa Kannon Temple** (**Senso-ji**) is the oldest temple in Tokyo. The two-inch gold image of Kannon has remained a *hibutsu*, a hidden image, within the temple since its earliest days, as it is too holy to gaze upon.

Scholars have speculated as to the origin of such an image, and a possible clue appeared after the 1945 firebombing, when the remains of the Hondo (Main Hall) of the temple were excavated prior to the rebuilding of the hall. Tiles and religious implements of the 600s and 700s were found. Could it be that the image was of Korean origin since images of this early time came primarily from the continent? Further speculation arises as to whether the image may have been tossed into

the river by the Mononobe adherents of Shinto belief, who resisted the incursion of the new Buddhist faith in the late 500s–for just such a reaction had taken place earlier in the Osaka region when the Mononobe had cast the earliest Buddhist images into the Naniwa River. That the image was found after the Mononobe had been defeated and Buddhism was being encouraged by the court lends credence to this supposition. At any rate, it is said that a great golden dragon danced its way from heaven to earth upon the discovery of this tiny Kannon, an auspicious sign if ever there was one.

Senso-ji (which is the temple's correct name, although it is often referred to as Asakusa Kannon Temple) has been rebuilt many times. The famous ninth-century priest Ennin is credited with building a new Kannon Hall for the temple in 864; another rebuilding occurred in the 900s; and then an additional remake of the hall occurred in the 1100s at the request of shogun Minamoto-no-Yoritomo. Naturally Tokugawa Ieyasu put his imprint on the temple with a new hall when Edo became his headquarters, and then in 1620, two years after his death, the initial memorial to this first Tokugawa shogun was erected on the temple grounds. When this memorial shrine burned, it was rebuilt in the Edo Castle grounds, and later this earliest of Tosho-gu Shrines was relocated to Ueno Park where it stands today.

1 TOKYO SKY TREE (DIVERSION)

The Ginza subway line ends at Asakusa Station beside the Sumida River, and one should take exit #1 onto Kaminarimon-dori. On leaving the subway station, the view across the Sumida River shows the 1989

Two Tokyo landmarks side by side. Tokyo Sky Tree (before completion) and Asahi Beer's Super Dry Hall

Super Dry Hall, aka the Asahi Brewery Building, by the French architect Philippe Starck. Some see the Asahi Brewery Building as beer glass–shaped with a bead of foam rolling down its side as Starck intended, but because of the shape of the giant bead most locals refer to the building as *unchi-biru*, "turd building."

Looming behind Asahi's offices is one of the newest additions to Tokyo's skyline, the **Tokyo Sky Tree** broadcast tower. Completed in 2011 to a height of 2,080 feet (634 meters) and visible from many parts of the city, the Sky Tree is the second-tallest man-made structure in the world. Besides its primary broadcasting function (it was constructed by a group of six TV broadcasters along with Tobu Railway), it has restaurants and an observation deck that provide sweeping views from almost 1,500 feet above the city. To get there as a diversion from Asakusa, cross the Sumida River on the Azuma Bridge at the eastern end of Kaminarimon-dori and continue east for approximately a half-mile until reaching the third major turning on your left. Taking this will lead you over a small river, after which the Sky Tree will be towering above you on your right.

Returning to the walk to Senso-ji, follow Kaminarimon-dori a block west to the Kaminari-mon gateway. The **Asakusa**

Tourist Information Center is on the south side of Kaminarimon-dori, and on Sundays it offers walking tours of the area in English.

2 SENSO-JI (ASAKUSA KANNON TEMPLE)

The Hondo (Main Hall) of Senso-ji lies a good distance beyond the initial gateway to the temple complex. The vermilion **Kaminari-mon** (Thunder Gate) to the temple gets its name from the two deities who stand guard on either side of the gateway. Raijin (Kaminari-no-kami), the deity of thunder, is on the left, while Fujin (Kage-no-kami), the deity of wind, is on the right. They stand here at the beginning of the long path to the temple as protectors of Kannon, and thus they act as a barrier to keep evil forces from impinging on the temple. A large red paper lantern, which is ii feet (3.3 meters) in size, weighs 1,482 pounds (667 kilograms), and is illuminated from within at night, hangs from the center of the gateway roof. It seems strange that the Kaminari-mon, so important an element at the entrance to the temple grounds, was not recreated until 1955 after its destruction by fire in 1865. No doubt the Meiji antagonism to Buddhism after 1868 had its effect here and discouraged the restoration of the gate. The heads of the two deities in the gateway are original, having been saved at the time of the fire, but the bodies are mod-

Nakamise-dori, the shopping street before the temple

ern. In 1978, on the 1,350th anniversary of the appearance of the Kannon image in the fishermen's net, a new pair of guardian images were donated to stand in the rear niches of the gate, a male on one side and a female on the other side, though these images do not quite have the attractive nature of the ones at the front of the gateway.

Beyond the Kaminari-mon stretches **Nakamise-dori**, the Inside Shops Street, within the temple grounds. Stalls have lined this pathway for centuries, but in 1885 the

SENSO-JI TEMPLE FESTIVALS

The temple enjoys a number of festivals throughout the year, and among these are:

March 18 **Kinryu-no-mai** (The Golden Dragon Dance) This festival celebrates the great golden dragon said to have descended from heaven when the golden Kannon was found. A golden dragon held by eight strong, young men is danced through the streets.

May 17–18 or the nearest weekend **Sanja Matsuri** A festival in honor of the three men enshrined in the Asakusa Shrine. There is a procession of over a hundred *mikoshi* (palanquins holding a god spirit), led by the three *mikoshi* belonging to the shrine. The bearers having fortified themselves with beverages sufficiently strong to enable them to carry the heavy *mikoshi*, there is a recklessness to the parade that is most exciting.

July 9–10 A visit to the temple on the 10th is equivalent to 40,000 visits. Chinese Lantern plants are sold at some 500 stalls. Holding of the "cherry" from within the lantern in one's mouth was said to ward off the plague, and thus the sale of the plants was quite popular. The festival now has branched out into the sale of bonsai, other plants, and ornaments for the garden.

October 18 A repeat of the March 18 festival.

December 17–19 **Hagoita-Ichi** A festival when New Year's decorations are sold. *Hagoita* (battledores and shuttlecocks), the former richly decorated with the faces of Kabuki actors, are available for the New Year festival battledore sport.

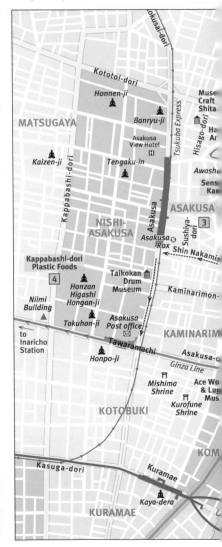

Meiji authorities had the stalls replaced by brick buildings from which the shopkeepers operate. Such modernization no doubt had another motive, given the Meiji rulers' antipathy toward Buddhism: a number of Buddhist sub-temples behind the stalls disappeared with the modernization. Today, moveable roof coverings can be closed over the street in inclement weather. A variety of small items ranging from *sembei* (rice crackers) to hair combs, paper crafts, toys, and articles of clothing can be found along Nakamise-dori. One hundred

and fifty shops are ranged along the 984-foot (295-meter)-long path between the Kaminari-mon gate and the Hozo-mon gate. As with much else in Tokyo, even Nakamise-dori was modernized and upgraded in other ways with time. Missing from the Nakamise-dori scene are the archery galleries of centuries past. These were presided over by attractive young women sufficiently made up that one knew the purpose of the back rooms of the galleries. Today Nakamise is far more proper than in past times.

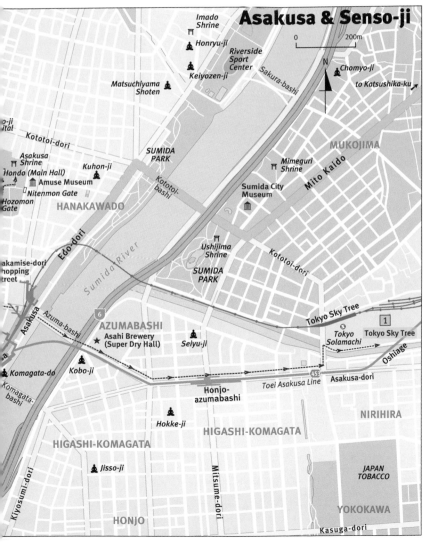

Senso-ji Temple's five-story pagoda and mighty Hozo-mon gateway at the entrance to the temple precincts

At the end of Nakamise-dori is the **Hozo-mon Gate**, the Treasury Gate, of the temple. When it was redone in 1964, the treasures of the temple were stored on its upper floor during the rebuilding of the Hondo, and the upper level still stores some 14th-century Chinese sutras (Buddhist scriptures). A large paper lantern hangs in the gate, while Deva Kings on either side of the passageway are there to protect the temple. At the rear of the gate hang two gigantic straw sandals, a gift from a provincial village to the temple, and these oversized sandals are almost as large as the Deva Kings they are supposed to fit. One of the most remarked-upon elements of the temple is the huge bronze incense burner that stands between the Hozo-mon and the Hondo. Smoke swirling from the incense sticks in the huge burner can be wafted to those areas of the body that are afflicted, for the smoke of this burner is said to have curative powers.

To the left of the Hozo-mon is the five-story, 183-foot (55-meter)-tall **Asakusa Pagoda**, which was rebuilt in 1973. Now made of ferro-concrete, the pagoda contains bits of the bones of the Buddha, a gift from Sri Lanka; the relics are in a golden container hanging from the ceiling on the uppermost floor. The pagoda is open to the public on three occasions each year: February 15, the anniversary of the Buddha's death; April 8, the anniversary of the Buddha's birth; and December 8, the date of his enlightenment. A temple office

is located within a portion of the pagoda through the door on the left.

To the right of the Hozo-mon and slightly back toward the rear of the Nakamise shops stand two large bronze images of Bodhisattvas (enlightened individuals who refrain from entering nirvana so as to be of help to those still living), the gift in 1687 of a rice merchant in honor of his deceased master. In front of the images is a memorial to a man who killed many people and who asked to be buried at this spot so that his corpse would suffer the penalty of being walked upon forever by temple visitors. Beyond, in the southeast corner of the temple grounds is a small hill, the Benten Yama, or Benten Mound, with a small red shrine (rebuilt in 1983) dedicated to the Shinto goddess Benten. The small hill is thought to be an ancient burial mound of the Kofun period (c. 250–538 A.D.), and a small bell on it once rang the hours of the day. The bell now is rung each day at 6:00 a.m. to signal the opening of the temple grounds, and it is rung 108 times at the end of each year at midnight to symbolize the 108 shortcomings to which mankind is heir.

Partway down the Nakamise, an opening leads to a side street with additional shops. Here behind the Nakamise stalls on this side street is a building that displays one of the one hundred *mikoshi* (portable shrines) that are paraded at festival times. The **Hondo** (Main Hall) that looms beyond the Hozo-mon Gate marks the end of the Nakamise. The

Hondo is 113 feet (12.6 meters) long by 107 feet (32.1 meters) deep and was rebuilt in ferroconcrete in 1958 as a protection against fire and earthquake after its destruction by fire on March 10, 1945, during the wartime bombings of Tokyo. Because the hall is of concrete, it is permissible to enter wearing shoes, since they cannot damage the floor. The hidden, sacred image of the Kannon is kept within the inner portions of the hall, and here monks chant sutras three times a day before the case that holds it. To the left of this case is an image of Aizen Myo-o, while to the right is one of Fudo Myo-o. Votive paintings, *ema*, are hung on the interior walls, works of the 1700s and 1800s. Having been removed before the air raids of 1945, the 50 painting have been preserved, and eight are on view. The temple is also known as the Kinryusan Senso-ji, the Golden Dragon Mountain Asakusa Temple, due to the legend of the descent of the dragon on the finding of the small golden Kannon. Therefore, a dragon has been painted on the ceiling of the Hondo, the work of Kawabata Ryushi, while the angels and lotus flowers surrounding it are by Domoto Insho.

To the right rear of the Hondo is the **Asakusa Shrine** to the two fishermen brothers, Hinokuma and Takenari Hamanari, and their master, Hajo-no-Nakatomo. Also known as the Sanja Sama Shrine, the Shrine of the Three Guardians, it was built at the orders of Tokugawa Iemitsu in 1649. A stone torii stands at its entrance with protective *kuma*

inu (Korean lion-dogs) beyond the torii. Such shrines have a Haiden (Prayer Hall), which stands before the Honden (Spirit Hall). In this case the Honden holds the spirits of the two brothers who found the Kannon image and their master who enshrined the image. A corridor in the form of a room, the Ishi-no-ma, connects the Haiden and Honden. The ceiling of the Haiden is unusual in that it is embellished with painted flowers. Commemorative stones on the grounds of the shrine honor notable figures of Tokyo theater, for the adjacent main street to the west was for many decades the center of entertainment in the Asakusa district.

To the right of the shrine, at the entrance to a commercial street is the 1618 **Nitenmon Gate**, which leads into the temple grounds from the east. It originally stood before the temple's Tosho-gu Shrine to Ieyasu, but the Meiji authorities removed it to the area of the Shinto shrine on the grounds. To the west (left) of the Hondo is the **Awashima-do**, the shrine of the guardian deity of women, a deity who attends to female ailments. Legend has it that the sixth daughter of the ninth-century statesman Sugiwarano-Michizane had served as a *miko*, a priestess, at the Sumiyoshi Shrine in Sakai (Osaka). Since shrines could not be defiled by blood, when she fell "ill in her lower parts," she was set adrift in a boat on the Inland Sea. The small boat landed at Awashima in today's Wakayama Prefecture, and there she prayed

The Asakusa Shrine holds the spirits of the "Three Guardians" of the golden Kannon

for women with similar problems. A cult developed around the former priestess, and shrines to her proliferated throughout Japan. Women often bring dolls to these shrines so the dolls can serve as substitutes, taking on the ailments of the donor; in time the dolls are burned in a religious service in order to render efficacious the prayers for relief from the ailment that has been transferred to the doll.

Custom in Japanese religions permits the spread and enrichment of the powers of deities. Consequently, the Awashima Shrine now also protects the art of sewing in addition to the health of women. On the eighth of February each year, women bring their worn-out needles to the shrine, and these are placed in a bean curd kept within the shrine, where they can be blessed and then properly disposed of. The Asakusa Awashima Shrine stands on the site of the 1620 Tosho-gu Shrine to Ieyasu. Next to it, on the left, is a very small hexagonal hall dating from the 15th to 16th centuries, which once covered a temple well but later was dedicated to the Buddhist deity Jizo. This particular Jizo is a most accommodating one, for not only can one ask his help, one can set the date on which this help is to be made manifest. West of the Hondo is also a small hall to Yakushi, the Buddhist deity of healing. Additional halls and memorial stones to the left of the Awashima shrine were created in the late 20h century.

Denpo-in is the residence of the abbot of the temple, and, although one cannot enter the priestly quarters, it is possible to visit the lovely garden surrounding the residence between 10:00 a.m. and 3:00 p.m. Permission is obtained by applying at the temple office in the pagoda, the second office on the left (after removing one's shoes). Denpo-in was once the site of the Honbo, the residence for the priests, and the present structure for the abbot's use was erected in 1777. The residence has an entrance hall, a Lion's Room where the shogun's courier was received, a reception room, and a kitchen. The entrance to the **Denpo-in garden** is on the south side of the complex, opposite the **Asakusa Public Hall** (where an exhibition of old Asakusa is mounted on the upper floors). The bell at the entryway of the garden is from 1387 and is one of the oldest bells in the city. The strolling garden was originally laid out in the early 1600s, and it is attributed to the great garden master, Kobori Enshu. A large pond in the

shape of the Chinese character *shin* (heart) is enhanced by colorful carp and turtles. A small teahouse from the 1780s was brought from Nagoya, and it is said to be a copy of a no longer extant teahouse designed by the great tea master of Kyoto, Sen-no-Rikyu.

Behind Denpo-in is the Chinzo-do, a small unit dedicated to the spirits of aborted children. Thus the bibs on the Jizo images, the colorful thousand-crane paper decorations, and pinwheels are offered to the spirits of the unborn. **Senso-ji Hospital**, behind the Hondo, is but one of a number of charitable endeavors of the temple. In addition, the temple runs a kindergarten, which has its entrance at the side of Nakamise in the Denpo-in grounds. In 1958 the temple opened the Senso-ji Social Welfare Center to give marriage and educational counseling and offer lectures to assist young women and housewives.

③ ASAKUSA DISTRICT

The **Asakusa District** around Senso-ji grew into one of the most active commercial and entertainment districts of Edo. Its development came in part from the location of the temple and from its stalls selling a variety of items along Nakamise-dori. Then, in one of the occasional bursts of puritanical zeal emanating from the castle, the shogun banned the licensed district in Ningyocho in 1657 and banished the Yoshiwara red-light district to the empty fields beyond the Senso-ji. Boats carrying pilgrims to the pleasure houses of Yoshiwara would stop at Asakusa, from which, after sufficient refreshment, they could continue to their destination. Around this convenient stopping place other divertissements grew up in time.

In 1841 another burst of purity befell the then shogun, and now Kabuki and Bunraku were also banished to Yoshiwara, though these arts stopped somewhat short of that location, settling to the west of Senso-ji. Here Kabuki developed its *arigato* style, which so captivated the citizens of Edo: a brash, over-stated style that would climax in exaggerated poses held at length to the delight of the audience. It was far different from the more courtly type of Kabuki enjoyed in Kyoto. Kabuki remained just to the west of the temple until 1872, when it began its move back to the Ginza/Tsukiji area.

Rokku, the sixth district, between Kokusai-dori on the west and the temple on the east, became a center for all forms of divertisse-ment, for here the shogun's government gave permission for a restricted area where the elements of entertainment of which they did not quite approve could flourish. The shoguns were Confucianist enough to wish decorum to reign, but they were also pragmatic enough to realize that the citizens of the Low City need-ed an outlet for emotions. Thus the govern-ment alternately permitted and banned certain amusements that the working class enjoyed. With the advent of the Meiji govern-ment and its attempt at Westernization, a park was created in 1876 on land taken from the temple pursuant to the government's anti-Buddhist policy. Two ornamental lakes, trees, and greenery were seen as an antidote to piety to the east and rowdiness to the west. The U.S. Occupation after 1945 returned the park land to the temple, and it has now been built over. On its site, among other structures, are Senso-ji Hospital and the old-fashioned **Hanayashiki Amusement Park,** which has some 20 rides for children. (Open daily 10 a.m. to at least 5 p.m. Admission is ¥900; attractions are charged separately.)

Once one has visited the Denpo-in gardens, any of the streets leading back toward Asakusa-dori will bring one to the covered gallery street of **Shin Nakamise** (New Nakamise). Shin Nakamise is crossed by the narrow Sushiya-dori and by the major north-south Kokusai-dori, and these two streets held many of the theaters of the area. The first theater in the modern sense opened in 1886 in Rokku, and by 1903 the first movie house, Electricity Hall, had made its debut. It lasted until 1976, when it disappeared forever. There were archery stalls, as previously described, vaudeville houses, variety theaters, acrobatic acts, opera, revues, cabarets, bars, strip-tease theaters, restaurants—all the varieties of mod-ern entertainment could be found in Asakusa. In 1890, the octagonal Twelve Stories Building was built, the tallest skyscraper in Tokyo, which even boasted an elevator. It lasted until 1923, when it lost its top four stories in the Great Kanto Earthquake and had to be demolished. (In the post–World War II period, the Jinten Tower, a one-half size copy of the Twelve Stories Building was erect-ed at the end of the street in which the Kaminari-mon Gate stands.) In 1927, the first subway line from the Ginza to Asakusa make the area ever more accessible. Until 1940, Asakusa was the place for entertainment, but

now the entertainment scene has moved elsewhere. Even the International Theater, the Kokusai Gekijo, with its line of dancing girls has gone. The 1945 bombing raids did inesti-mable damage to the district, and other, newer areas of entertainment, such as Shinjuku and Roppongi, now attract the younger crowd—and television has made a difference as well. The residue of these past times can still be ob-served in part on the street with theaters to the east of Kokusai-dori, but it is a pale reflec-tion of a more exciting time in the past.

4 KAPPABASHI-DORI PLASTIC FOODS

Take Kokusai-dori south, past the end of Kaminarimon-dori and on to Asakusa-dori, the next main street. Between Tawaramachi Station (which is at Kokusai-dori and Asakusa) and Inaricho Sation on the Ginza subway line is another wholesale district with some 50 specialty shops devoted to Buddhist and Shinto shrine furniture and ritual imple-ments. After the Long Sleeves Fire of 1657, many of the temples were moved from the heart of Edo to Asakusa, which became a new center for temples and shrines and so also for the shops that supplied them and their wor-shippers. **Honzan Higashi Hongan-ji,** for one, was founded here just to the north of Asakusa-dori and east of Kappabashi-dori. This temple was used by the shoguns to lodge envoys from Korea, and in the 1894 war with China the temple was used to house Chinese prisoners of war. (See the comments concern-ing Nishi Hongan-ji Temple in Tsukiji in Walk 4 for background to this temple.)

At the third street to the west of Tawaramachi Station on Asakusa-dori is the intersection with Kappabashi-dori. The inter-section cannot be easily missed, for atop the **Niimi Building** on the corner is the 39-foot (11.7-meter)-tall head of a chef with his tall white pleated hat. Along Kappabashi to the north of Asakusa-dori are 200 shops selling all manner of goods for the restaurant trade, including some that specialize in plastic *sampuru* (samples) of food. Foods in plastic that one sees in restaurant windows and display cases are available from these whole-salers, who offer souvenirs most visitors can-not resist. (Most of the shops are open from 9:00 a.m. to 5:00 p.m. but are closed on Sundays.) The tour of Asakusa can end here and the subway can be taken back to Ginza from Tawaramachi or Inaricho stations and other connecting subway lines. But perhaps a little more should be said about Yoshiwara, even though only one or two sites from this one-time pleasure quarter to the north of the district just visited still exist.

5 JOKAN-JI TEMPLE

Yoshiwara was the pleasure quarter for 300 years, with an emphasis on sex, a factor of everyday life that the shoguns had to accept when men in Edo outnumbered women by two to one, a situation that lasted until late in the 19th century. Female prostitution was licensed so the government could exert some control over the situation. There was male prostitution as well, since homosexuality was an accepted fact of life as well as a continuing attraction for both priests and samurai. Male prostitutes could usually be found around the temples, while female prostitution was centered in Yoshiwara to the north of Senso-ji from 1657, when it was moved here from Ningyocho by the shogun's order, until 1957, when the Diet outlawed prostitution.

Yoshiwara was a closed area of 20 acres (8 hectares), closed in the sense that it was entirely surrounded by walls and a ditch with but one entrance on its south side. This kept the women from escaping from the quarter, and it also kept patrons from leaving without honoring payment for services rendered. The gate was shut at night and not opened again until morning. The district was reached by boat from Yanagibashi to a landing just a short walk from the entrance to the five streets within the cloistered sector. The Ditch of Black Teeth (married women and courtesans blackened their teeth, an ancient custom meant to enhance female attractiveness) was crossed over a drawbridge, and then the O-mon (the Great Gate) brought one into Yoshiwara. If one were modest or wished to go into Yoshiwara incognito, there were shops outside the enclave that sold large straw hats to help mask one's identity.

Yoshiwara was not only an area for sexual gratification but a cultural center as well, a place where, in a society that was hierarchical and rigid in its social stratifications, all classes could meet. There were restaurants, some of which served as intermediaries to direct clients to assignations. There were the *ageya*, rendezvous teahouses, where the higher class of geisha, the *tayu*, met their clients. Both the geisha and the *tayu* could sing, dance, and carry on witty conversation and served as entertainers. But, though the geisha were

accomplished and provided social and cultural entertainment, the *tayu* were a cut above. Neither of these groups of women were prostitutes. In contrast was the separate group of *yujo*, whose primary purpose and attraction was sex.

The society of this demimonde was strictly regulated. *Tayu* wore their obi tied in front, a sign of their exalted status. *Tayu* and geisha, who were primarily entertainers, were distinctly superior to the common prostitutes on view behind lattice screens in the back streets of Yoshiwara. It is estimated that 2,000 to 3,000 women were in Yoshiwara, but in times of famine when women were desperate or when parents sold off unwanted daughters, this walled enclave could hold up to 10,000 women. Overcrowding and a lowering of standards gradually drove the better class of geisha elsewhere, and so Shimbashi began to flourish as the Meiji period wore on. The fire of 1911 seriously damaged Yoshiwara, and then the 1923 earthquake annihilated it. Some 200 brothels and teahouses were destroyed, and several hundred women were incinerated in the fires that followed. Today the area has lost whatever glamour it may once have had, and soaplands (brothels), massage parlors, and love hotels alone recall another era. At the end of the 20th century, it was claimed that there were 200 soaplands and 2,500 women employed in the trade in the Asakusa area.

One sad reminder of Yoshiwara's past can still be visited, **Jokan-ji Temple** in the Minowa area not far from the Hibiya Line subway station of that name. (To get there after visiting Kappabashi-dori, take the Ginza Line from Tawaramachi Station two short stops to Ueno Station, then transfer to the Hibiya Line, from where it is another two short stops to Minowa Station. The journey will take 10 to 15 minutes, depending on the connection) Known as the Dump Temple or Disposal Temple, here more than 11,000 girls who averaged not more than 22 years of age were buried in a common grave. These were the unfortunate women of the Yoshiwara, disposable wares who lie in unmarked graves. By 1900 the law permitted women who did not wish to remain within Yoshiwara to leave the enclave. That same year the Salvation Army arrived in Tokyo and published a tract, *Triumphant Voice*, encouraging the denizens of Yoshiwara to flee and offering them help. When the brothel owners tried to buy up all of the copies, the army benefitted from a strong boost in sales.

6 TODEN ARAKAWA TRAM LINE

If one does visit Jokan-ji, Minowa Station on the Hibiya Line is close at hand. Those who wish to partake of a diversion that has virtually disappeared from the Tokyo scene can take a ride on the last tram line still in existence in Tokyo. The Hibiya subway line's Minowa Station is under Showa-dori. Walking from the station to the north and continuing under the overhead elevated rail line, one comes to the the **Toden Arakawa Tram**

Line on the left at the end of a covered market. The 7.3-mile (11.7-kilometer) line wanders across Tokyo to its terminus at Waseda. En route one passes through an area of local housing that reflects ordinary Tokyo life away from the districts tourists normally visit. The line is nicknamed the *chin chin densha* line–the "clang-clang train line"–due to its noisy passage along its right-of-way. En route to the end of the line, one can stop at Oji Station to visit the **Paper Museum**, which is but a few minutes from the station in Asukayama Park, famed for the springtime blossoms of its cherry trees, planted by shogun Tokugawa Yoshimuni. Here a selection of paper from Egyptian papyrus, early Chinese paper, paper-making techniques, and exhibits of the various items made from paper during the years of Japanese seclusion under the Tokugawa may be seen. (The museum is open from 9:30 a.m. to 4:30 p.m. except for Mondays and national holidays. Admission is ¥300.)

This is where the tour ends. To return to central Tokyo, one can make the short walk back to Oji Station for either the JR Keihin-Tohoku Line or the Namboku subway line.

> ### GETTING THERE
> Asakusa Station is served by the Ginza subway line, Toei Asakusa subway line, and Tobu Isesaki Line. There is also a separate Asakusa Station for the Tsukuba Express.

The Toden Arakawa, the last tram line in Tokyo

Walking Tour 9

UENO AND NEZU

The Park Where Culture Abides, the Low City Remembered, a Shogun's Shrine, and Two Artists' Residences

Chinese geomancy always held an essential place in Japanese life, and it was particularly important for the siting of buildings and the plan of a city. When the Tokugawas made Edo their headquarters after 1603, it was necessary that the city be protected against the forces of evil, which, according to Chinese lore, flowed from the northeast. Thus in 1624, Hidetada, the second Tokugawa shogun, asked the long-lived priest Tenkai (1536–1643) to build a temple at the northeast corner of Edo as a protection for the new town. The new temple of Kan'ei-ji was to serve a purpose similar to the one offered to Kyoto by its Enryaku-ji Temple, a protection at its vulnerable northeast corner, the Ki-mon, the Devil's Gate.

The temple erected on Ueno Hill was befriended by the succeeding shoguns, and by 1700 it had 36 sub-temples on 294 acres

(117.6 hectares). As the shogun's temple, it was off-limits to commoners, and the fountain in Ueno Park in front of the National Museum now marks the site where Kan'ei-ji's huge main hall once stood. The temple's pagoda overlooked the city, and, after Tokugawa Ieyasu's death, the Tosho-gu Shrine to his spirit was raised on temple ground in the extravagant Momoyama style such as enriched his burial shrine at Nikko. Kan'ei-ji was truly the shoguns' temple, for it was here that a number of them were to be buried.

Originally, an arm of Tokyo Bay came up to the hillside of Ueno, but in time the low-lying marshland beneath the hill was filled in, and the new land became the Monzenmachi, the town in front of the temple. So huge a temple complex required services, and thus shops came into being in the town below the hill, a portion of the Shitamachi, or Low City, where the merchants and craftsmen lived. One modified arm of the inlet did remain, and it became the freshwater Shinobazu Pond.

1 HOUSE OF TAIKAN YOKOYAMA

To get to Ueno Park, Yushima Station on the Chiyoda subway line provides easy access as well as the starting point for this walk. One leaves the subway and gains Shinobazu-dori, the street under which the subway runs, then heads to the north. Shinobazu-dori bends to the left when it reaches Shinobazu Pond at the beginning of the park, and the street should be followed until one is alongside the second portion of the pond and opposite the Benten-do across the water. The walk on the left along Shinobazu-dori after leaving the subway brings one to the **House of Taikan Yokoyama** (Yokoyama Taikan Kinenkan), a traditional wooden house in the *sukiya* style favored in Kyoto. (The residence-museum is open from 10:00 a.m. to 4:00 p.m. Thursday through Sundays but closed for a month in midsummer and mid-December through mid-January. Entry is ¥500.) Taikan Yokoyama (1868-1958) was an artist who painted in the traditional Japanese *Nihonga* style but modified his techniques to include some from Western painting that differed from traditional Japanese approaches. Much of Yokoyama's life was spent in this wood house opposite Shinobazu Pond, which was rebuilt after the 1945 firebombing destroyed it. After his wife's death in 1976, 18 years after his own demise, the house was opened as a memorial. Some of the rooms are open to the public, and these include his tearoom, its 15 windows looking out upon his garden with a rivulet running through it. The tearoom it has a brazier mid-floor with a hanging teapot over it, a tokonoma–an alcove for displaying objects for aesthetic appreciation–and the artist's rare image of the deity Fudo from the 1100s. His adjacent studio workroom still retains his working tools. The upstairs bedroom was planned so that the garden could be enjoyed from above as well as on ground level. Selections of the work of the artist are on view, but aside from his art itself, the house and garden are fine examples of an artist's traditional home and studio. The small garden itself is a delight, with its rivulet, rocks, carp swimming in the pond, and stone lanterns. A pamphlet in English supplements the labels in Japanese.

2 AMEYOKO SHOPPING STREET

Returning to the foot of Ueno Park to the exit of the subway from which the tour began, one is at Kasuga-dori. A left turn here along that street will, after three more side streets, bring one to **Chuo-dori**, a continuation of the main shopping street in the Ginza area. This was a place of shops in Edo times, and so it still remains, with the **Matsuzakaya Department Store** being the largest example. Continuing along Kasuga-dori on the Matsuzakaya side, the first street on the left thereafter leads into the area known as Ameya Yokocho (more familiarly referred to as **Ameyoko**), which is situated under the elevated railway line that goes into the Ueno rail station up ahead. (Ueno Station is not only a stop on the Yamanote elevated line but a huge terminal for trains to the north and east of Japan. The station was first built in July of

The crowded entrance to the Ameyoko market

1883.) More than 500 shops crowd this quarter-mile (400-meter) bazaar under the rail line and spill out into adjacent streets. The name of the district, *Ameyoko*, combines two meanings: literally, the words *Ameya Yokocho* mean "Confectioners Alley"; and after the Korean War a pun evolved from the contraction of *American Market*, since this area sold black-market goods from American military Post Exchanges during those years. A new central market has been opened, but small shops operating under and around the elevated railway tracks continue the tradition of the Shitamachi, in which small-scale vendors have always operated in this district, and a tremendous variety of goods are available.

3 SHITAMACHI MUSEUM

Returning to Chuo-dori and Shinobazu Pond, Shitamachi, the Low City of the early years of Tokyo, is recalled in a delightful small museum at the foot of the pond and not far from the avenue. The **Shitamachi Museum** (open from 9:30 a.m. to 4:30 p.m., closed Mondays and national holidays, and from December 29 through January 3; entry ¥300) lies just beyond the shore of the pond. The devastation of the 1923 earthquake, the 1945 bombings of Tokyo, and the inexorable change to the face of the city in the post-1950s economic boom have gradually obliterated the traditional Tokyo of the period both before and after 1867. Thus the Shitamachi Museum was conceived in 1980 as an attempt to preserve aspects of the average person's life between 1867 and 1925. Change was to come much more rapidly after 1925, with the rebuilding after the Great Kanto Earthquake and fire. The museum helps to recall an era now gone, and the significance of the displays is made clear in a free English-language brochure; a more extensive booklet in English may be purchased. Here a 19th-century tenement has been recreated, a one-story space of some nine feet square (eight meters square) in which people lived and worked in close quarters with but scanty belongings. A merchant's shop, a copper boiler craftsman's workplace, and a shop selling inexpensive sweets each provide an aspect of the mercantile life of Edo-Tokyo days. An exhibition hall on the second floor of the museum displays clothing, children's games, and household items of the past, some illustrated by photographs as well as by video presentations.

4 BENTEN-DO

Behind the Shitamachi Museum, a roadway runs along Shinobazu Pond to a man-made causeway that leads to Benten Island. In creating the Kan'ei-ji Temple, based on the example of Enryaku-ji in Kyoto, the abbot Tenkai wished as well to copy other aspects of the city that had been Japan's capital for nearly a thousand years. An island was built in the middle of Shinobazu Pond for the shrine to the Shinto goddess Benten, one of the Seven Gods of Good Luck. Here Kyoto and its environs were in the abbot's mind, for the **Benten-do** on the island was in imitation of the shrine to Benten on Chichibu Island in Lake Biwa outside of Kyoto. A shrine on an island should be reachable, and thus in 1670 a causeway was built from the shore to the island. Destroyed in the 1945 bombing raids, this 17th-century shrine was rebuilt in 1958 in its original style, even to a painted dragon on the ceiling and painted autumn flowers on the panels alongside the image case. Benten, with her four-stringed lute, stands before her hall, and the shrine's annual summer festival helps to enliven the warmer months.

In Edo days, the pond was surrounded by places where one could eat and drink and admire the deep pink lotus flowers blooming in the water, and here the Bon Odori was

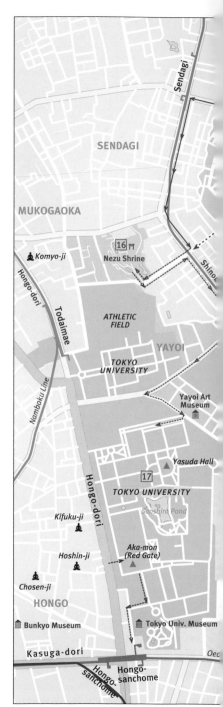

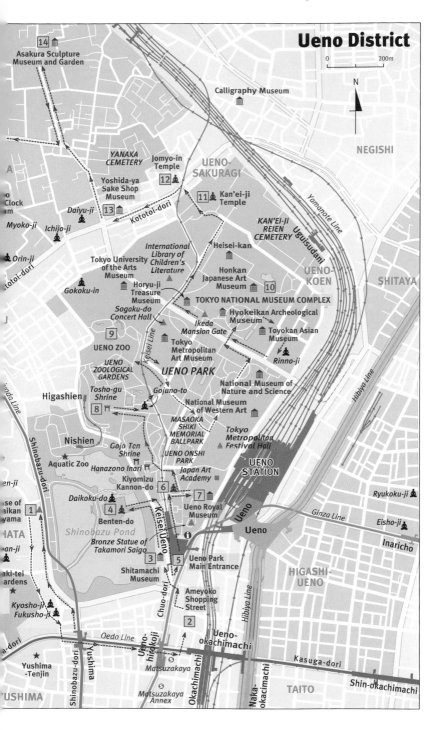

Ueno District

0   200m

N

14 🏛 Asakura Sculpture
Museum and Garden

Calligraphy Museum 🏛

NEGISHI

Yamanote Line

*YANAKA
CEMETERY*   Jomyo-in
Temple   **UENO-
SAKURAGI**

Yoshida-ya   **12** 🛕
Sake Shop
Museum

o
Clock
m   *Daiyu-ji* **13** 🏛

Kototoi-dori   **11** 🛕 Kan'ei-ji
Temple

Myoko-ji

*KAN'EI-JI
REIEN
CEMETERY*

Uguisudani

Ichijo-ji

totoi-dori   *Heisei-kan*

♨ *Orin-ji*   International
Library of
Children's
Literature   Honkan
Japanese Art
Museum   **10**   **UENO-
KOEN**   SHITAYA

Tokyo University
of the Arts
Museum

Gokoku-in   Horyu-ji
Treasure
Museum   **TOKYO NATIONAL MUSEUM COMPLEX**

Sogaku-do
Concert Hall   Hyokeikan Archeological
Museum

*Ikeda
Mansion Gate*   🏛 Toyokan Asian
Museum

9   Tokyo
Metropolitan
Art Museum   🛕 *Rinno-ji*

UENO ZOO   **UENO PARK**

*UENO
ZOOLOGICAL
GARDENS*   National Museum of
Nature and Science 🏛

onda Line   *Gojuno-to*

Higashien   Tosho-gu
Shrine   National Museum
of Western Art 🏛

8 ⛩   **MASAOKA
SHIKI
MEMORIAL
BALLPARK**   Tokyo
Metropolitan
Festival Hall

Nishien   Gojo Ten
Shrine   *UENO ONSHI
PARK*

Aquatic Zoo   *Hanazono Inari* ⛩

Japan Art
Academy ■

**UENO
STATION**

Kiyomizu
Kannon-do   **6** 🛕

Ryukoku-ji 🛕

Daikoku-do 🛕   **7** 🏛

1 ▲
*se of
aikan
yama*   **4** 🛕   Ueno Royal
Museum   **Ueno**   *Ginza Line*   *Eisho-ji* 🛕

an-ji   Benten-do   **Ueno**   **Inaricho**

*aki-tei
ardens*   *Shinobazu Pond*   🛈

Bronze Statue of
Takamori Saigo   **3** 🏛 **5** ↕   Ueno Park
Main Entrance

Kyosho-ji
Fukusho-ji 🛕   Shitamachi
Museum

Hibiya Line

Chuo-dori   Ameyoko
Shopping
Street   **HIGASHI-
UENO**

2

a-dori   *Oedo Line*

Yushima   Ueno-
okachimachi

★   *Matsuzaka*   **Okachimachi**   **Kasuga-dori**

*Yushima
-Tenjin*   ♨ *Matsuzakaya
Annex*   *Naka-
okachimachi*   *Shin-okachimachi*

USHIMA   *Keisei
Ueno*   *Keisei Line*   **TAITO**

The Benten-do in Ueno Park is set on an island in the middle of a pond.

danced to welcome the spirits of the dead back for their brief visit to this world each summer. The one-and-a-half mile (2.4- kilometer) circumference of the pond offered a new attraction after 1884, that of a racetrack circling the pond, including a royal grandstand alongside the track. The justification for a racetrack was that horsemanship was considered a necessary military skill for national defense. Happily, this "improvement" was removed in 1893. **Shinobazu Pond** (the "Pond Without Patience") is divided into three parts: the northernmost sector is a portion of the Aquatic Zoo and a haven for birds; while the western portion is available for boating; while the southern portion is noted for the pink-flowering lotus plants. On the hill above the pond is the Seiyoken restaurant, and nearby is the 1666 Toki-no-kane bell, which once sounded the hours for the temple monks. Also above the pond are two shrines. A tunnel of vermilion torii leads to one of them, the **Hanazono Inari Shrine**.

5 UENO PARK

Returning to Chuo-dori and passing the entrance to Keisei Ueno Station, one comes to the main entrance to Ueno Park. Here stands the **bronze statue of Takamori Saigo**, a reminder not only of the change from the government of the Tokugawa shoguns but of the battle fought at this site in 1868. On April 11, 1868, Takamori had worked out an agreement with the Tokugawa representative on Atago Hill in Edo, which led to the peaceful surrender of the city and the realm to the forces operating in the name of the Meiji emperor. On May 15, 1868, just one month later, 2,000 Tokugawa loyalists decided to fight the Meiji army despite the agreement that had ended the rule of

the Tokugawa shoguns. Gathering their forces on Ueno Hill on the grounds of the Kan'ei-ji Temple, here in front of the Kuro-mon, the Black Gate, they took up arms against the more modern army of the Meiji supporters. Besieged by Meiji guns and artillery, the loyalists (*shogitai*) were forced to surrender, but in their defeat they set fire to the many buildings of the Kan'ei-ji, the temple that served as the protector of the city. Along with the temple buildings, up to a thousand houses were destroyed in the conflagration that spread beyond the temple grounds, and the battle left 300 of the loyalists dead.

In 1898, a statue to Takamori Saigo (1827–1873), the general who won the day at Ueno for the Meiji, was unveiled at the entrance to what had become Ueno Park. He was honored in part for his efforts as chief of staff for the Satsuma and Choshu clans, those outside lords who led the revolt against Tokugawa rule, and for his victory at Ueno. The statue should have been erected in front of the Imperial Palace, but there was one overriding reason this could not be. In dismay at the new government's abolishing of samurai privileges and samurai status from 1870 on, Takamori led an abortive coup against the government he had brought to power. Ceremonial suicide

An Inari fox god in the Hanazono Inari Shrine

General Takamori Saigo, hero and outcast

ended the life of a man whom the government subsequently wished to honor but was perplexed as to how to recognize because of his treasonable act of rebellion.

After the emperor rehabilitated Takamori in 1890, the solution to the dilemma was to place the image in Ueno, the site of his victory, but to cloth him in a traditional kimono with his hunting dog at his side rather than in the uniform of a modern general of the Meiji military forces. This compromise satisfied all elements of the Meiji government, since Takamori's memory and reputation were to be respected even if these had not as yet been completely rehabilitated. Takamori's wife did not approve of the location or the garb of the statue, however. Behind the statue is a small stone-fenced area, which marks the spot where the *Shogitai*, the Tokugawa loyalists who had died, were cremated after the battle and their ashes interred. A small museum (open from 10:00 a.m. to 4:00 p.m., closed Thursday) commemorates the vanquished of 1868. A ukiyo-e print on the grounds describes the battle of that day in May.

6 KIYOMIZU KANNON-DO

Ahead on the left, beyond the *Shogitai* grave, is the **Kiyomizu Kannon-do** above Shinobazu Pond. Abbot Tenkai had this sub-temple built in imitation of Kyoto's Kiyomizu-dera Temple.

As an imitation it falls a good bit short of the intended goal, for it lacks the huge, intricate underpinning substructure that supports the Kyoto temple. The original copy of the Kyoto edifice was erected in 1631, but in 1698 it was relocated to its present, more auspicious position above the pond. As its main image, the temple holds a Thousand-Arm Kannon, which was sent as a gift from the abbot of the Kiyomizu-dera temple in Kyoto. The image that attracts the most attention in the temple, however, is the Kosodate Kannon, a Kannon to whom one prays in the hope of conceiving a child. Those who have been successful in conceiving often bring dolls as offerings to the temple, and these dolls may be seen in the left-hand corner of the temple. Here they remain until they are burned each September 25 in a service at 2:00 p.m. as priests chant sutras in a ceremony of thanksgiving to Kannon. This building was one of the few to survive the battle of 1868 (it was restored in 1994–1995), and above the entrance to the hall is a painting that details that 1868 battle. (The building is open from 9:00 a.m. to sunset without charge but is closed Mondays.)

The devastated Kan'ei-ji grounds posed the problem of their future use after 1868. The government favored the creation of a modern hospital on the site, but a consultant from Holland, Dr. Antonius Bauduin, argued per-

The annual cherry-blossom parties at springtime in Ueno Park

suasively that the grounds be used as a Western-style park and that the hospital be located on the former Maeda daimyo estate to the east (the future University of Tokyo site). As a result, Ueno became the first of five parks in the city, the most important ones being at former temple grounds in Ueno (Kan'ei-ji), in Shiba (Zojo-ji), and on a portion of the Asakusa grounds. (This latter was returned to the temple by the U.S. military after 1945, and it has now been built over.) In 1877, the first National Exhibition was held on the grounds of the park, as was the 1882 exhibition. At the conclusion of the latter, the Tokyo National Museum and a zoo were established in Ueno.

7 UENO ROYAL MUSEUM

Ueno Park became a cultural center through the years. Shinobazu Pond was annexed to the park in 1885, while the Tokugawa tombs in a portion of the old Kan'ei-ji Temple were separated from the park by a road. Behind the Kannon Hall is the **Ueno Royal Museum** (Ueno-no-Mori Bijutsukan), which offers a venue for changing exhibitions by artistic organizations, which may rent gallery space on the museum's two floors (open 10:00 a.m. to 7:00 p.m. daily; entry is free). Begun by Prince Takamatsu in 1971, it is an auxiliary of

the Japan Art Association. Behind the Royal Museum is the **Japan Art Academy**, an honorary organization with 150 members who are elected for life. The 1974 building was designed by architect Yoshio Taneguchi.

The **Tokyo Metropolitan Festival Hall** (Tokyo Bunka Kaikan) is the next building, designed by Kunio Maekawa in 1961. It has two auditoriums seating 2,327 and 611 respectively, and it also used for conventions. It serves primarily as a concert hall for all forms of classical music.

8 TOSHO-GU SHRINE

To the left (west) of the Festival Hall is a stone torii at the entryway to the Tosho-gu Shrine to Tokugawa Ieyasu. When Ieyasu died in 1616, his ashes were placed in an elaborate shrine that was built in Nikko. Additional shrines were ordered built to the deified Ieyasu throughout the nation, and the one on the Kan'ei-ji Temple grounds was established in 1627 and improved in 1651 by the third Tokugawa shogun. The pathway into the shrine is lined with 200 stone lanterns, one of which, the *Obake Toro* (Supernatural Lantern), stands 18 feet (5.4 meters) tall. Behind these are a double row of 50 bronze lanterns, all gifts from daimyo of the country, their name and the date of the gift recorded on each lantern. They were meant not for illumination but were involved in the purification of the sacred fire for important religious ceremonies. All of the lanterns survived the 1923 and 1945 disasters.

Before the bronze lanterns, as one approaches the main hall of the shrine, there is a kagura stage on the right for religious dances and then a roofed bell unit. On the other side of the path is a roofed ablution unit. *Koma-inu* (lion-dogs) on either side of the path protect the main building beyond. (A fee to enter the main hall is paid on the left, and then one walks to the left and around the vermilion fenced inner courtyard of the shrine, entering on the right hand side of the complex. The main building of the shrine is open from 9.00 a.m. to 5:30 p.m. daily, to 6:00 p.m. in July and August, but to 4:40 in the winter; entry ¥200.) The shrine is in the *kongen-zukuri* style, an ornate style much favored by the early Tokugawa shoguns. A Kara-mon (Chinese Gate) in front of the building is in the elaborate "Chinese" carved style with birds, fish, and other animals and shells. It is most noted for its carved dragons ascending on the right and descending on the left, said to be the work of the master carver of the early 1600s, Hidari Jingoro. Legend has it that the dragons were so real that they would descend and drink from Shinobazu Pond at night, and wire cages had to be put around the carvings to keep the dragons from wandering.

The main shrine building, the Konjiki-den, or Golden Hall, is in the ornate Momoyama style that was favored by the Tokugawas. The Haiden, the outer Hall of Worship, was decorated within by four paintings of lions on a gold background by Kano Tanyu. Two images of seated shoguns are in the middle of the room with a large dragon head at their side, while some 36 pictures of officials line the walls near the ceiling. Displayed at one side are a suit of the shogun's armor and his sword. The Haiden is connected by a corridor to the Honden. The Honden is where the spirit of Ieyasu is enshrined. The framed tablet on its front with the shrine name on it is in the writing of the Emperor Go-Mizuno of Ieyasu's day. The ebony steps leading up to the altar to Ieyasu's spirit is the one element in this small hall that is not gilded. A lion sits at the side of the steps to guard the approach to the shrine itself. The exterior gold finish of the shrine is in need of refurbishing from time to time, since modern pollution is deleterious to such a finish.

To the left of the shrine is the peony garden (9:00 a.m. to 5:00 p.m.; entry ¥600 when the plants are in bloom), where the winter peonies bloom from early January to mid-February, while the spring peonies are in flower from April to mid-May. Some 3,000 peonies of 200 different varieties are in bloom at a time, and an annual flower festival is held on April 17th. It should also be noted that the park has 1,000 cherry trees, and it is overcrowded in cherry blossom season with people enjoying the transient blooms of these trees. The 120-foot (36-meter)-tall vermilion pagoda (Kan'ei-ji Gojuno-to) to the Tosho-gu Shrine, a gift of the daimyo of Sakura Castle, is separated from the memorial buildings, since it is now within the confines of Ueno Zoo. Erected in 1631, it had to be rebuilt eight years later after a fire, and its top story is covered with roof tiles of bronze. It is not open to the public.

9 UENO ZOO

The adjacent **Ueno Zoo** (open from 9:30 a.m. to 5:00 p.m., but closed Mondays; entry ¥600.) is in two parts: The Aquatic Zoo on the shores of Shinobazu Pond is connected with the upper zoo area by a monorail train. The zoo is noted for its pandas and its monkey habitat, a "mountain" on which the monkeys roam freely, and its collection of 1,200 animals includes more than 950 species of wildlife. Opened in 1882, it was the first Western-style zoo in Japan.

10 TOKYO NATIONAL MUSEUM COMPLEX

Returning to the area of the park with its multi-museum complex, beyond the Festival Hall is the **National Museum of Western Art** (Kokuritsu Seiyo Bijutsukan). (It is open from 9:30 a.m. to 4:30 p.m. [5:00 in winter], and to 8:00 p.m. on Fridays, but is closed on Mondays and from December 28 through January 4. Entry is ¥420.) The initial building by Le Corbusier was erected in 1959, and a new building was added in 1979 by Kunio Maekawa. The core of the collection belonged to Kojiro Matsukata, president of the Kawasaki Shipbuilding Company, and it was originally housed in Paris. The collection, ranging from the Renaissance to the present, was seized by the French government during the World War II but was released by 1959 and came to the museum. Fifty-seven Rodin sculptures adorn the courtyard, and there are works by Cranach, El Greco, Rubens, Tintoretto, Manet, Cézanne, Monet, Dégas, Renoir, Picasso, and

Tokyo National Museum houses a magnificent collection of Japanese art and artifacts.

later 20th-century artists such as Joan Miró and Jackson Pollock. The Matsukata collection, primarily the art of the French Impressionists, is housed in the Le Corbusier building, while the remainder of Western art is in the newer building, where temporary exhibitions are also mounted from time to time.

Behind the National Museum of Western Art is the **National Museum of Nature and Science** (Kokuritsu Kagaku Hakubutsukan). (It is open from 9:00 a.m. to 5:00 p.m. daily, except to 8:00 on Fridays, and is closed Mondays and December 28 through January 1; entry ¥600.) Divided into various departments by typology, the museum endeavors to explore all the areas of modern science. It has five halls: the entry and Main Hall, a Natural History Hall, an Air and Space Hall, a Science and Technology Hall, and a Science and Engineering Hall. A good guidebook to the collections, in English, may be purchased at the museum shop. Across the way is the **Tokyo Metropolitan Art Museum** (Tokyo-to Bijutsukan). (It is open from 9:00 a.m. to 5:00 p.m., and closed the third Monday of the month and December 29 through January 3. Admission varies depending on the exhibition.) This redbrick building by Kunio Maekawa was opened in 1975, supplementing the earlier 1926 building. Housing an art school and studios, the museum displays the work of Japanese artists of recent decades (more than 2,600 items are in its collection) while offering rented space for temporary exhibitions,

some occasionally showing Western art. The museum library has more than 30,000 titles that may be used without charge. More than 50 percent of the building is underground so as not to intrude upon the park. In front of the building is the statue of Dr. Antonius Bauduin, who, after the 1868 destruction of the Kan'ei-ji Temple buildings, suggested that the temple grounds become a park.

To the left of the bust of Dr. Bauduin is the **Sogaku-do**, the oldest concert hall in Japan (1890), and the center for Western music when it was built for the Tokyo School of Music. It introduced Western classical music to Japan. Scheduled for demolition, it was saved by a public outcry, for it was seen as an historic and satisfactory concert hall. (The hall is open for visits on Tuesdays, Thursdays, and Sundays from 9:30 a.m. to 4:30 p.m.)

Continuing farther into the park, across the roadway is the huge **Ikeda Mansion Gate**, a gate that once stood before the residence of the Ikeda Lords of Inabe (Tottori) in the Marunouchi district of the city and was relocated here in 1954. An elaborate gateway, it has two guardhouses with Chinese-style roofs. Beyond the gate are four museum buildings around a large central courtyard, the four units of the **Tokyo National Museum** (Kokuritsu Hatsubutsukan). (Each unit is open from 9:00 a.m. to 5:00 p.m. and 8:00 p.m. on Fridays from April through December, and to 6:00 p.m. on weekends and national holidays, April through September. The museums are closed on Mondays and December 29 through January 1. Entry ¥600.) To the far left is the Horyu-ji Homotsuden, the **Horyu-ji Treasure House**, the original fireproof, concrete building created in traditional *azekura* (log cabin) architectural style. In 1878, under pressure from the Meiji government during the period when it was attacking Buddhism, the Horyu-ji Temple made a "gift" of 319 items to the Imperial Household from its trove of ancient artistic treasures of masks, paintings, sculpture, ritual implements, and furniture. This "gift" protected objects of inestimable historic worth when the art in many temples was being wantonly destroyed with official approval, and it also provided the temple with needed funds to guarantee its continued existence and necessary maintenance. In 1999 a new gallery designed by Yoshio Taniguchi (who also designed the new museum building for the Museum of Modern Art in New York City) was built and is a modern gem of steel and glass, surrounded by a garden and entered by way of a tree-lined path that ends at a rectangular pond in front of the gallery. (The Horyu-ji Gallery is open only on Thursdays, and then only if the weather is dry, so as to protect the ancient art within the building.) The quality of these early rare and exquisite pieces is similar to items on view at the annual Shoso-in exhibition in Nara.

On the left of the large courtyard and its fountain is the **Hyokeikan Archeological Museum**, which was built to celebrate the marriage of the Taisho emperor in 1909. It is in the Beaux Arts style then fashionable in Europe and America. It contains archeological finds from Japan in its nine rooms and is noted for its *haniwa* tomb figures and artifacts from prehistoric Japan through to the 600s. One curiosity in the collection is the wooden figurehead of Erasmus from the wrecked Dutch ship *Liefde*, which stranded William Adams and Jan Joosten in Japan in 1600. To the right of the large open courtyard, once the site of the residence of the abbot of the Kan'ei-ji, is the **Toyokan Asian Museum**, a 1968 ferro-concrete building by Yoshiro Taniguchi in traditional Japanese *azekura* (log cabin architectural style, housing the art of other Asian nations. The collection numbers more than 87,000 objects from China, Korea, Thailand, India, and Central Asia, and all are very fine examples of the art of these nations. The building has a cafeteria open to the public.

The main building of the National Museum complex, the **Honkan Japanese Art Museum** of 1937, with more than 100,000 objects in its collections, is at the far end of the courtyard. It houses the main Japanese art collection, the most extensive and the finest selection of Japanese art objects in the world. It includes paintings, ceramics, textiles, metal work, lacquer ware, and calligraphy among the various Japanese arts and crafts of the past. The objects are so numerous that they are rotated periodically in the 25 rooms in the building. In addition, two special exhibitions are offered each year, in April and May and then in October and November. The museum has an information and a research center.

Behind the Toyokan is the Jigen-do or **Rinno-ji**, the Memorial Hall to Abbot Tenkai, who began the Kan'ei-ji Temple in the early 1600s. His posthumous name is Jigen Daishi; thus Jigen-do (*do* means "hall") is what the hall was named when it was rebuilt in 1720 after a fire. It was one of the few buildings not destroyed in the 1868 battle. (The hall is also referred to as the Ryo Daishi [Two Great Masters], the first being Abbot Tenkai and the second the 10th-century priest Ryogen, whom Tenkai revered.) Toward the end of the 20th century the main hall was rebuilt again, and a temple office and hall for religious use have been added to the right. Four bronze lanterns with spiral and dragon-faced decorations stand before the hall. The Black Gate is one of two gateways into the complex, the one on the left, through which one enters, being the newer one. To the right of the bell tower is the original gateway, which once stood before the abbot's residence, but it was moved here in 1937 when the Honkan was built. It still shows the marks of the bullet holes it suffered in the 1868 battle of Ueno. The original Honbo (the abbot's residence) was located where the National Museum now stands, while the Kompuchu-do (the Main Hall with its large Buddha image) of the Kan'ei-ji stood where the large fountain in the park is now located.

Turning to the right when leaving the Jigen-do eventually brings one to a cross street beyond the museum complex and an entrance to the Keisei underground station. Ahead on the left is the **Tokyo University of the Arts Museum**, with an extensive collection of the arts of China and Japan. As a branch of a teaching university, its changing exhibitions often reflect the course of study in progress (open without charge from 10:00 a.m. to 5:00 p.m. but closed on Mondays). A right turn at the

Keisei rail entrance takes one past Kuroda Hall of the university and then the **International Library of Children's Literature** (Kokusai Kodomo Toshokan), where a **monument to Lafcadio Hearn** (Koizumi Yakumo) recalls an early Irish admirer of Japan.

11 KAN'EI-JI TEMPLE

A turn to the left at the road a little way beyond the library brings one to the entrance of the **Kan'ei-ji Temple** building. It is but a pale remembrance of the grandeur that once existed on Ueno Hill, when the full temple was in existence. Beyond the hall the temple cemeteries are on the right. As indicated earlier, the temple was built by the priest Tenkai at the request of shogun Hidetada in 1625 to "close" the Devil's Gate to the northeast of Edo. Tenkai had been active in the deification of Hidetada's father Ieyasu as a Shinto god after Ieyasu's death, and thus the abbot was able to rely on Hidetada to obtain funds for the temple from the daimyo of the nation.

The 36 temple halls and 36 ancillary buildings that resulted from Tenkai's efforts covered the hillside of Ueno. In 1647 Emperor Go-Mizuno's third son was made abbot of the temple, and such royal priestly leadership of great temples continued until the abolition of this practice by the Meiji government after 1868. The temple served the shoguns in an additional way, for the growing interest of the shoguns in the 1600s in Confucian doctrines led to the founding of the Confucian Academy on the temple grounds under the leadership of Hayashi Razan. This important academy was later moved to Yushima in Tokyo, where it remained until its dissolution. The Kan'ei-ji Temple buildings, with few exceptions, disappeared in the 1868 battle in the park. In 1879 the Hondo (Main Hall) of a temple built in 1638 in Kawagoe, 25 miles (40 kilometers) away, was moved to what was left to the temple of its former grounds, after much of its land had been confiscated for the new Ueno Park. This newly relocated hall came from a large temple that had once been administered by Abbot Tenkai. Four large bronze lanterns stand in front of the Hondo, and the hall retains the original main image of the Kan'ei-ji, a Yakushi image of the Buddha of Health. It is a *hibutsu*, a hidden image, which is never shown. The Shoro (bell tower) and other newer temple buildings lie behind the main hall. To the right of the Hondo, a new office and a meeting hall stand beyond the gate before them.

One historic room remains in the temple, the one in which the last Tokugawa shogun retreated after turning over power to Emperor Meiji in October of 1867 in Kyoto. Tokugawa Yoshinobu retired here on February 12, 1868, not knowing what his fate would be under the new government. On April 4 he was pardoned, and on April 11 Edo Castle passed to the Meiji government, and Yoshinobu left for his family lands. Since he had surrendered power peacefully and had opposed the Ueno uprising, he was granted the title of prince. Called back from exile in 1911, he presided at the opening of the new Nihombashi Bridge, and he outlived Emperor Meiji by one year, dying in 1913. He is buried in an adjacent cemetery close to the Nippori rail station, less than a mile from the Kan'ei-ji grounds.

The land in front of the temple has been used as a graveyard, and here is an historical marker at the grave of Ogata Kenzan, brother of Ogata Korin. Kenzan (1683–1743) was known for his ceramic art. Nearby is a huge memorial stone, the Mushizuka. Erected in 1821, it is a memorial to those insects killed to serve as models for the artistic work of Masuyama Masakata, also known as Sessai, head of the Ise Nagashima clan, who is best known for his four-volume work of insect pictures. The artist died in 1754. Behind the present main building of the Kan'ei-ji and extending behind the National Museum complex is the **Kan'ei-ji Reien**, the three cemeteries in which six of the Tokugawa shoguns' remains were buried. The elaborate mausoleums to these rulers were destroyed in the 1945 bombing raids, and thus only a portion of the gateway to the tomb of Tsunayoshi, the fifth shogun (1680–1709), with its carved lions remains (most easily seen from the road behind the National Museum main building). In the second cemetery, behind the National Museum, is the gate to the mausoleum of shogun Ietsuna (1651–1680), the predecessor to Tsunayoshi. Just the stone wall with bronze plaques and the remains of the gates remind one of the grandeur of the tombs that once stood here. (The grounds are open from 9:00 a.m. to sunset.)

12 JOMYO-IN TEMPLE

On leaving the Kan'ei-ji, a turn to the right brings one to Kototoi-dori, and opposite is the **Jomyo-in Temple**. Built in 1666, this was once one of 36 such residences for priests of the Kan'ei-ji. The Hondo (Main Hall) of the temple is a rather unattractive, square, reinforced-concrete unit, but it is the Jizos to the left of the entry gate that are of interest. The temple has a large seated Jizo image in bronze, and in the mid-19th century the then abbot of the temple vowed to erect in his temple grounds 1,000 images of Jizo, the Buddhist deity protecting children, the dead, pregnant women, and travelers. Having succeeded, he then vowed to increase the number to 84,000 Jizo images. Time ran out on the devout abbot, and the attempt by his successors to reach that elusive goal continues. Each image is numbered, and it is said that the count now reaches beyond 20,000. Each August 15 by the lunar calendar, the temple holds a very popular service, the Sponge Gourd Service. It is for those suffering with coughs and asthma, and the grounds of the temple are exceedingly crowded at this time with people seeking relief from their ailment.

13 YOSHIDA-YA SAKE SHOP MUSEUM

A turn to the right when leaving the Jomyo-in leads along Kototoi-dori and brings one, after the third traffic light, to an **addition to the Shitamachi Museum**. At the corner of the street is the **Yoshida-ya**, a former sake shop from 1910, a traditional-style building of the late Meiji era that appears to be much older. Within are the bottles, straw-wrapped wooden kegs, and porcelain jugs that contained the alcoholic beverages that delighted Tokugawa and Meiji patrons. (The museum shop is open from 9.30 a.m. to 4:30 p.m., but closed on Mondays; no entry charge.)

14 ASAKURA SCULPTURE MUSEUM AND GARDEN

One other artist's residence in the area lies to the north of Ueno Park. Turning as if to return along Kototoi-dori, but instead taking the left-hand road that leads away from Ueno Park, one follows the road for several small blocks until it briefly skirts the Yanaka Cemetery on the right and bends left (toward the northwest). The third side street on the right from here is a long, straight street that leads to the former residence of artist Fumio Asakura (1883-1964), now the **Asakura Sculpture Museum** (Asakura Choso-kan), a rather unprepossessing black structure on the outside (The house and sculpture gallery are open from 9:30 a.m. to 4:30 p.m. except Mondays and Fridays; entry ¥400.) Obviously a disciple of Rodin, Asakura created some 400 statues during his career. The building is entered through a modern wing, which holds

some of the artist's sculptures.

It is the interior of the house and its garden that continually attract visitors to this building. A traditional Japanese home, its has a tatami-matted tearoom overlooking the garden, with its pond and islands. The ferns, small bushes, and stepping-stones invite a stroll in this lovely enclosure. Within the house, an iron kettle steams over a small charcoal fire in a traditional burner. The artist lived here from 1908 until his death in 1964 at age 81. The less than attractive black exterior of the house reflects the fact that the studio wing of the complex has been created in reinforced concrete as a protection against fire and earthquakes, while the living quarters are in the traditional *sukiya*-style, a residence of wood and bamboo. The first room visited is the high-ceilinged studio room. Here are examples of Asakura's work, some life-size, some greater than life-size, some of nudes. One huge statue of a man in academic cap and gown is of Shigenobu Okuma, a statesman who was the founder of Waseda University. Another statue of a tall man is that of Shimpei Goto, another statesman and former mayor of Tokyo. Room two is the library, whose many books reach to the ceiling. A number of them are in English, including bound copies of the British *Studio* magazine. The third room is the guest room, with chairs, a couch, and more books as well as a display of the tools the artist used. A human skeleton and the skeleton of a cat that he employed for the study of anatomy are also in this room.

The enclosed garden in the center of the residence is the Goten-no-suitei, a Japanese landscape garden that incorporates water to symbolize the five Confucianist precepts of benevolence, justice, propriety, wisdom, and fidelity. The water comes from a natural spring. All the rooms surrounding the garden, on both floors, are tatami-matted, and thus shoes must be removed before entering these quarters. At the rear on the first floor are the original office and studio of the artist before the 1936 addition of the larger studio up front. There is a kitchen with its *kamidani* shrine up high to the kitchen gods. A living room and a tea ceremony room with a tokonoma follow, and then the bedroom with a display of Asakura's kimono.

Stairs to the upper floor have a rustic handrail and an internal "moon" window. Of the two rooms on this floor, the first has a large, low, bright-red Chinese lacquered table, while the second is the Poised Mind Room, with a tokonoma and a low table with an inlaid mother-of-pearl traditional scene. Old bronzes and ceramics are displayed on a shelf unit. The third floor also has two rooms, the larger of which is the Morning Sun Room, which contains a huge round table created from two exceedingly large pieces of wood. The ceiling is unusual in its attractive wood planking. A corridor runs along two sides of the Morning Sun Room, with *shoji* to cut the corridor off from the room if that is desired. The outer walls have windows of glass, which can be covered with draperies for privacy. An excellent English-language pamphlet concerning the house and its collections is available at the ticket counter on entering.

After your visit, retrace your steps along the long, straight street that brought you to the museum entrance, then turn right, heading west. From here, you may continue to the next site, the Nezu Shrine, or make a diversion to another small, curious museum in the area. To continue to the Nezu Shrine, proceed along this street until it crosses Shinobazu-dori at Sendagi Station and, turning left, descend Shinobazu-dori. About 50 yards after Shinobazu-dori turns to the southeast, it is intersected by a street that can be taken west (right) until the entrance to the Nezu Shrine.

15 DAIMYO TOKEI CLOCK MUSEUM

For the diversion, proceed along the street until the fourth turning on your left. This left-hand street can be followed for 200 yards, until the fourth turning on the right takes you down a short side street at the end of which, on your left, is the **Daimyo Tokei Hakubutsukan** (open 10:00 a.m. to 4:00 p.m. but closed Mondays, July 1–Sep. 30, Dec. 25–Jan. 14; entry ¥300). This is a museum of clocks from premodern times when the hours of a clock were indicated with the animal images of the Chinese zodiac. The clocks equated the amount of time in the day and the night—which caused constant upgrading of the timepieces as the day lengthened in summer and decreased in winter. This museum is of interest primarily to specialists. After a brief stop, walk straight ahead from the museum's exit and then turn immediately left onto a long, straight street that after less than a quarter-mile will cross **Shinobazu-dori** and lead to the Nezu Shrine.

16 NEZU SHRINE

The **Nezu Shrine** is noted for its attractiveness and for its long row of vermilion torii on the hillside leading to a shrine to the goddess Inari. The Nezu Shrine itself honors the sixth Tokugawa shogun, Ienobu (1709–1712) who succeeded his uncle Tsunayoshi, the Dog Shogun. Tsunayoshi was not only deeply reli-

A row of vermilion torii at the Nezu Shrine

gious but deeply superstitious. Born in the Year of the Dog, he forbad the killing of dogs under penalty of death. The first thing his successor did was to abrogate such senseless laws, and, under his more enlightened rule, for the first time the offspring of the imperial household were permitted to choose a profession other than that of the temple priests or nuns. At the tutelary shrine of Ienobu, the new shogun, the grounds are entered through a torii, with a pond on the right. The two-story vermilion Ro-mon main gate of the Nezu Shrine is similar to that at the Asakusa Kaminari-mon gateway, and this reveals a Buddhist influence on this shrine. The shrine was created at the time when Buddhism and Shinto were often allied, a situation to be destroyed by the Meiji rulers after 1868. The swastika symbol on many of the lamps within the shrine grounds also indicates a heavy Buddhist influence. The Shinto protectors of the shrine, Yudaijin and Sadaijin, with their swords and bows and arrows, are on guard in the gateway.

Beyond the Ro-mon, a *kagura* stage for religious dances is on the right while a roofed purification fountain is on the left. Then comes the inner gate, a Kara-mon gate, "in the Chinese style," a one-story vermilion gate in front of the shrine main hall, which contains paintings of the 36 classical poets. Purification by a priest is necessary before entering this restricted area. This hall is connected to the Haiden (Worship Hall), which stands before the Honden, the Spirit Hall, where the spirit of the sixth shogun is enshrined—vermilion on its outside but all ebony and gold within. The beam-ends of the structure are carved in the form of mythical animals, while carved pine and plum tree branches enhance the building. Damaged in the air raids of World War II, the shrine has been lovingly restored. Its ponds, its trees, its 3,000 azaleas that bloom in April and May all contribute to a shrine that understandably has been listed as one of the three Important Cultural Properties in Tokyo.

Returning to Shinobazu-dori and turning right, the road should be followed until it reaches Kototo-dori. A right turn onto Kototo-dori leads in a few minutes to Tokyo University, one's next destination.

⑰ TOKYO UNIVERSITY

Tokyo Daigaku (**Tokyo University**) is more familiarly known by the contracted form of its name, Todai. It is the most important university in Japan, and many of its graduates can be found among the bureaucracy that truly runs the Japanese government. Its 20,000 students are split into various colleges, a number of which have been moved away from the original 1880 campus as the school has expanded. Law and engineering remain at the main campus. The area to the north of the campus is the Yayoi district, a name given to one of the early periods of Japanese prehistory, since artifacts of that earlier time have been unearthed here.

Heading to the south, either by meandering through the campus or by continuing along Kototo-dori to Hongo-dori, then turning left and descending Hongo-dori, the university entrance at the **Aka-mon** (the Red Gate) was once the entry to the grounds of the mansion of the Maeda lords of Kaga. (Until 1923, a branch of the Maeda family still dwelled in a corner of the old estate.) In 1827, one of shogun Ienari's 55 offspring married into the Maeda family, and this gate was built in celebration of the event and remains intact. The university, as with many urban universities, is not that notable an architectural site. Perhaps its most famous building in the last half of the 20th century was **Yasuda Hall**, where in 1968 students barricaded themselves in the battle against the police and other forces, a virtual army besieging the campus, where all learning had temporarily ended. The Yasuda lecture hall was burned in the riot, and it has remained a shell as a reminder of more tumultuous times. On the campus is the **University Museum**, a six-story museum divided into numerous subsections and providing space for changing exhibitions.

Leaving the Todai campus by its southern exit onto Kasuga-dori, one will arrive at Hongo-sanchome subway station of the Oedo and Marunouchi subway lines, a convenient point for this walk to end.

GETTING THERE

The starting point of this walk is Yushima Station on the Chiyoda subway line. Ueno Park can also be easily accessed from a number of other lines: the Yamanaote Line and other JR lines at Ueno Station; the Ginza and Hibiya subway lines at Ueno Station; and the Keisei Line at Keisei-Ueno Station, which connects to Narita Airport. Ueno Station is also served by Shinkansen services.

Walking Tour 10

YUSHIMA, KANDA, JIMBOCHO AND AKIHABARA
Shrines to a Chinese Sage and a Rebel, the Bibliophiles' Paradise, Wholesaling Run Rampant, and Pleasure Deferred

1. **Yushima Tenjin Shrine**
2. **Kanda Myojin Shrine**
3. **Hijiribashi Bridge and Century Tower**
4. **Nikolai Cathedral**
5. **Meiji University Museum and Criminal Materials Exhibition**
6. **Jimbocho Bookstore Area**
7. **Koishikawa Korakuen Garden**
8. **Akihabara District**

When one looks at a topographic map of Tokyo, the hills of the High City stick out like fingers into the riverine land of the Low City. The **Yushima** and **Kanda** areas encompass both the high and the low sectors, and thus this tour will alternate between the slightly raised plateau as well as the former meadowland of the city. Here are ancient shrines to men of valor in centuries past as well as to failed usurpers of the throne. The wisdom of Confucius is enshrined not far from the major universities, which continue to search for wisdom of a type unknown to Confucius. Modern shrines to the inventive spirit of the industrial age of the 19th and 20th centuries can be found in a museum of transportation as well as in the commercial marts in **Akihabara**, where discounts are proclaimed on every corner. Then there is the realm of scholarly bookstores beloved by students and scholars, which is followed by another beloved retreat known as the Garden of Deferred Pleasure of a former Tokugawa lord.

1 YUSHIMA TENJIN SHRINE
Yushima Station on the Chiyoda subway line is where this tour begins. Leaving the subway by exit #3 onto Shinobazu-dori, one should briefly walk south, then take the second street on one's right to the **Yushima Tenjin Shrine** (Shrine to the God of Heaven) on the left-hand side of the street. The entrance is down a side street, so continue beyond the shrine and turn to the left to gain entry. Although the shrine goes back to the 14th century, it has burned down many times, and thus the present buildings date from 1885. It was one of the victims of the 1657 Long Sleeves Fire, when monks at the nearby Honmyo-ji Temple, just to the northwest of the Yushima Tenjin Shrine, burned a kimono with long sleeves that had been worn by three young women who had died suddenly. The "cursed" kimono was therefore set on fire. Unfortunately, a strong wind carried the embers of the burning kimono far and wide, leading to the destruction of much of the city. More than 1,200 houses and 350 temples were destroyed and 108,000 lives lost, and the houses of most of the working populace were consumed. Ironically, the next day it snowed.

On a ridge or bluff above the Kiridoshi slope, the Yushima Tenjin Shrine can be reached either by way of the steeper "male" slope to the right of the main hall or the easier "female" slopes. Kasuga-dori provides one of the female and gentler slopes; another such slope will be used when the shrine visit ends. The shrine is said to have been created in 1355 and then restored in the 1400s by Ota Dokan, the founder of the city of Edo. It is dedicated to the 9th-century statesman Sugawara-no-Michizane, who was posthumously enshrined as the deity of scholarship. Near as it is to Tokyo University and not too far from the other universities south of the Kanda River, it is a favorite among those of student age, who come to petition for divine help in their academic studies.

There was a time when this area was a favorite of the priests of the Kan'ei-ji Temple and the sub-temples of that great Buddhist complex not far away on Ueno Hill. These men enjoyed the local "teahouses" that were served by adolescent boys whose sexual favors they sought. The Tokugawa shoguns tried unsuccessfully on various occasions to rid the area of male prostitution, and the Meiji authorities too were intent on cleansing the neighborhood at the foot of the Yushima Tenjin Shrine of these "teahouses in the shadows" as well as the geisha quarter that existed here as well. The Meiji zeal was occasioned by a concern for nearby Tokyo University, for they wanted students to concentrate on their studies if Japan was to be the equal of the nations of the West. They did not want the young students to dally with the traditional divertissements of these quarters. One can imagine what success the Meiji leaders encountered, for even today the latest version of an old story can be recognized in the love hotels that abound.

Within the confines of the shrine property, there are two entrances leading to the Yushima Seido (the shrine's Sacred Hall) from the street leading off Kasuga-dori. The first, with a stone torii, is the minor entry, the main entrance being farther along the street at its

southeast corner with a bronze-plated torii at the entrance. Going in through the minor gate, a modern hall with offices and reception halls is to the left. On the right is a garden with a pond. Past the garden is a large rack to hold *ema* plaques, a rack so loaded with the prayers of students and others that it seems it should topple to the ground. Behind it is the main hall of the Yushima Tenjin Shrine, complemented on the right before it by a *kagura* stage for religious dances and ceremonies.

The Yushima Seido was created in 1632 on the grounds of the Kan'ei-ji Temple in Ueno (approximately where the statue of Takamori Saigo now stands) as a hall in which Confucian classics could be studied. The influence of neo-Confucianism, as Tokugawa Confucianism was known, was to become important, since by the 1600s establishment Buddhism had lost much of its spiritual influence. On the other hand, Shinto was so simple a faith—virtually nature worship–that it did not offer an intellectual challenge to the Tokugawa samurai. It was Hayashi Razan (1587-1657), a scholar of the Confucian classics, who was able to reinterpret Confucianism to satisfy the intellectual needs of the period. His version of Confucianism offered a foundation for ethics, and it provided a theory of government that seemed to undergird the political presuppositions of the Tokugawas. Omitting the metaphysics of Chinese tradi-

Ema votive tablets at the Yushima Tenjin Shrine

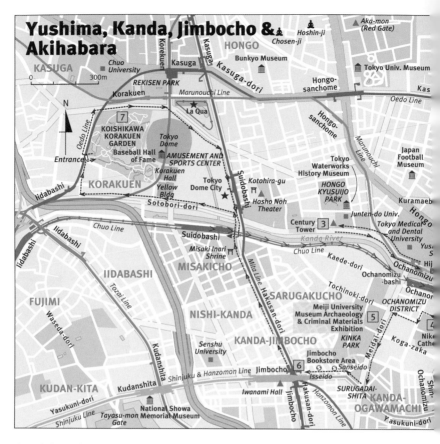

Yushima, Kanda, Jimbocho & Akihabara

tion while reinforcing the elements that gave a basis to the feudal system of obedience to one's superiors, the neo-Confucianism of Razan became the new ideology of the state.

In 1691, the devout shogun Tsunayoshi moved the Kan'ei-ji's hall for the study of Confucianism from Ueno to its present location, where in the second half of the 18th century it served as an academy for the ruling elite of the Tokugawa regime, much as the University of Tokyo was to serve in the 20th century. In fact, in 1872 the first teacher-training institute set up by the Meiji government had its origins here, and that new institute was to develop in time into the University of Tokyo, not too far to the north in the Hongo district, just beyond the Yushima Tenjin Shrine.

At the entrance to the shrine is the large, stone Nyutoku Gate with bronze doors, and the pistachio tree at the entrance had a significance for those coming to the shrine, for it

grew from a cutting from a tree at Confucius's grave. A ferroconcrete shrine office building and halls is to the right, winged dogs decorating the roof. Behind the building is a much greater than life-sized **statue of Confucius**, and it was in this area that the Shoheiko, the College of Confucian Studies, existed in Tokugawa times. Steps to the left of the image of Confucius lead uphill to the main shrine building on a higher level where there is a good-size wooden gate, and behind it to the right is the water purification basin, the only two items which survived the 1923 earthquake. Many broad steps lead up to a very large three-part gateway to the front corridor, which surrounds three sides of an inner courtyard, the shrine building itself forming the fourth portion of the court. This dark, bronze building, with its five massive doors, is most impressive. Large roosters surmount the roof of the shrine and two

is only a shrine, since the Confucian Academy is defunct.

After exploring the shrine, the grounds can be left by walking straight away from the main hall, noticing on the left, however, the "lost child" stone similar to one that stood on Nihombashi Bridge. The stone still stands in place, even though it is a much later replacement. On the left is a steep staircase, the "male slope" leading from the plateau down to the lower city. Continuing straight ahead from the main hall, one exits the grounds through the bronze torii. A marker just beyond it details the history of the shrine.

② KANDA MYOJIN SHRINE

On departing the Yushima Tenjin Shrine, the street leading south eventually crosses Kuramaehashi-dori, a broad, heavily trafficked street with a traffic light. Continuing beyond the crossing, a street on the right uphill brings one to the front of the **Kanda Myojin Shrine**. Located on the same hill as the Yushima Shrine, it looks out over the Low City to the east. It too has a "male" slope of steep steps as well as a less harshly inclined "female" slope. While the shrine is said to have been founded as early as 730, it has been on its present location since only 1616. In 730 it would have been solely dedicated to the deity Okuninushi-no-kami, the great deity descended from Susano-O-no-mikoto, who is the resident deity of Izumo, one of the two most important shrines in Japan. The Kanda Myojin Shrine originally was located in the Otemachi area near Edo Castle, where it was popular for having a local hero of the 900s, Taira-no-Masakado, who was later enshrined here as well. The original shrine was at the spot in the Low City where in 940 Masakado's decapitated head is said to have flown from Kyoto (as described in Walk 2) to rejoin his body after his abortive attempt to declare himself the emperor of Japan led to his death.

In 1616 Tokugawa Ieyasu had the shrine moved from the lowlands to this eminence, ostensibly to use the shrine site for the better securing of his castle, with its moats and walls. No doubt he was also moving the rebellious spirit of a man who had challenged authority, an attitude Ieyasu certainly would not permit. Despite this move, Masakado remained the popular deity with the towns-people, who respected his attitude, though they dared not emulate it. However, they could show their affection for this one-time rebel in

"devil dogs" appear on either side of the roof instead of the traditional dolphins found atop other buildings of this time.

The main hall, the Taisei-den, the Hall of Accomplishment, was rebuilt in the Chinese Ming style in 1935 (the earthquake of 1923 destroyed the former hall), and it enshrines the spirit of Confucius. Within the hall, an image of Confucius, flanked by his main disciples, was an imperial gift. (The grounds, with its statue of Confucius, may be entered from 9:30 a.m. to 5:00 p.m. free of charge.) Ties between the Chinese Nationalist government and the shrine were close, and a building beside the main gateway has reproductions of Confucian items in the Taipei National Palace Museum, a gift of the Lion's Club of Taipei. The shrine is no longer connected with the Japanese government, however, and it is operated by a private organization on behalf of the government. Today it the great festival that grew up with the shrine. Its *matsuri* (festival) is the oldest of the three great festivals of Tokyo, and in Edo times it was even permitted to pass through the grounds of Edo Castle both as an honor to the townspeople and to permit the denizens of the castle to enjoy the spectacle.

The festival had a political aspect as well, for it was held on the 15th day of the 9th month, the anniversary of the Battle of Sekigahara in which Tokugawa Ieyasu was victorious over all of his enemies and could thereafter assume complete civil control of Japan. Thirty-six large floats carrying musicians were drawn through the town by oxen. Portable *o-mikoshi*, sacred palanquins, followed, but most of these major floats were destroyed in the 1923 earthquake and fire. Since that time the festival has been moved to May 14 and 15 and is held in alternate years from those in which the Hie festival takes place, the Kanda festivities occurring in odd numbered years. The connection with the Tokugawa victory was thus belatedly severed. Today, three replicas of the emperor's palanquin and 76 *mikoshi* on wheeled carts from the district parade through the streets of Otemachi, Marunouchi, and Kanda. The participants are clothed in the garb of Heian times (796–1200). Once there were very large festival carts, but these are no longer practical components of the parade in as congested and traffic-ridden a city as Tokyo. Out of season, the shrine *mikoshi* are kept in the *mikoshi* hall to the left of the shrine's main hall.

If Ieyasu had his misgivings about a shrine to a rebel being so close to his castle, the Meiji authorities were equally as queasy about the Kanda Myojin. The emperor had been seen in 1868 as the actual ruler over Japan, and the authorities were disturbed when the emperor went to the shrine to do his obeisance to a somewhat questionable deity beloved by the common citizen. Thus they decreed that the spirit of the rebel Masakado had to be removed from the main hall of the shrine and be placed in a separate building. The main hall was destroyed in the 1923 earthquake, and in 1934, when the older generation of Meiji advisers was gone from the scene, the shrine was rebuilt (in ferroconcrete) and Masakado's spirit was returned to his rightful place in the main hall. The shrine was recreated in the ostentatious *gongen* style, which certainly would not have pleased the Meiji elders, since this was the style favored by their Tokugawa predecessors.

The shrine (open from 9:00 a.m. to 4:30 p.m.; entry free) is entered through a copper-plated torii and then through the two-story, vermilion Zuishi-mon main gateway (refurbished in 1976) with the Shinto guardians on either side of the passageway. The rear niche of the gateway holds the figure of a horse. At the foot of the hill below this main gateway is a large stone torii, and between the two gates were once traditional shops selling bean paste, pickles, and sweet sake; it is still possible to buy sweet sake with ground ginger in some adjacent shops. Beyond the two-story gateway a *kagura* dance stage is to the left, a gift of the founder of the Matsushita Electric Company, Konosuke Matsushita.

On the left stands a very large statue of Daikoku (also known as Okuninushi-no-kami) astride rice bales and with the traditional hammer in his right hand. Daikoku is a popular *kami* or deity, since he is concerned with the exploitation of land, the development of industry, and commercial success, as well as medicine. He is enshrined here together with Ebisu (also known as Sukunahikone-no-mikoto), who offers protection to commercial enterprises as well as medicine. These two figures helped to popularize the shrine in Tokugawa and later times. Beyond the statue of Daikoku is the purification fountain with a crouching dragon from whose mouth a stream of water flows into a basin, and on the far right is a long building containing offices and reception halls. A Lion Mountain was created in 1990 between this hall and the main shrine hall to celebrate the enthronement of the emperor. This rock "mountain" has water cascading down it and is graced by two stone lions from 1716.

Two stone lions stand before the Haiden, the prayer hall of the shrine, and the figure of a white horse stands on the right, since white horses are favored by Shinto deities. To the left and behind the main hall are small shrines to various Shinto deities and two *kura* (storage buildings) holding the *mikoshi*, the portable shrines of the Kanda Myojin. One of these *kura* on the left of the Haiden has glass doors so that the *mikoshi* may be seen, with large golden dragon heads resting on either side. Once one could look from the plateau on which the Kanda Myojin sits to the Shitamachi, the Low City, below the shrine, but today the high-rise buildings of modern Tokyo tend to disguise the difference between the two levels of this portion of the Kanda district. As with the Yushima Tenjin Shrine, the Kanda Myojin is noted for its plum blossoms in March and for its wisteria in May.

3 HIJIRIBASHI BRIDGE AND CENTURY TOWER
On leaving the shrine, one continues downhill to Hongo-dori and the Hijiribashi, the "Bridge of the Sages," over the Kanda River, once an outer moat of Edo Castle. A plaque on the far side of the bridge shows what the earlier bridge looked like. On the southern shore of the bridge is the district of **Ochanomizu** (Honorable Tea Water), so named from a spring of fine water that once existed here. The water was brought to Edo Castle daily, for its sweet taste enhanced the shogun's tea. In the distance to the right, the 21-story, twin-towered **Century Tower** in Ochanomizu was built in 1991 by Sir Norman Foster, whose skyscraper work in Hong Kong brought him fame. The Century Tower is supported by a huge steel frame on the exterior of the building, thereby freeing the interior of any columns.

4 NIKOLAI CATHEDRAL
The hill on the southern side of the Kanda River is known as Surugadai, for after Ieyasu's death land in this area was given to a number of his followers who came originally from the Suruga area near Shizuoka. Since the 1880s, it has been home to more than two dozen educational institutions, some of which, such as Chuo University, have now moved out of the center of the city in order to afford land for expansion. At the foot of the hill is the **Jimbocho district** of bookstores and publishers, a natural outgrowth of the educational establishments on this hillside. Just one street beyond the bridge is **Nikolai Cathedral**, the Russian Orthodox Cathedral, built by Ioan Nikolai Kasatkin (1836–1912). Kasatkin came to Hokkaido in northern Japan in 1861 as a chaplain and missionary of the Russian Orthodox Church, and he lived in Japan for the next 51 years. The 1884 cathedral, which was began construction in 1876, is the largest of the churches Kasatkin built. Josiah Condor was the architect for the building, using plans that came from St. Petersburg. The building originally had a much larger dome, but that collapsed in the 1923 earthquake and a smaller, flatter dome, 128 feet (38 meters) high, replaced the more traditional and larger Russian onion dome. (The cathedral is open

Stone lion on guard at the Kanda Myojin Shrine

without charge from 1:00 p.m. to 3:00 p.m. Tuesdays through Fridays.) The cathedral bells are rung at 10:00 a.m. and 12:30 p.m. on Sundays only, from the 95-foot (28.5-meter)-high bell tower, providing what was an unusual sound in the later 19th and early 20th centuries in this part of Tokyo.

5 MEIJI UNIVERSITY MUSEUM AND CRIMINAL MATERIALS EXHIBITION
Leaving the cathedral and turning to the left, at the end of the street another left and then a right turn takes one down a narrow street to Ochanomizu-dori. This area has the many buildings of **Meiji University**, and across the street to the right is the building that holds two of the university's public exhibits. On the fourth floor of the **Daigaku Kaikan Building** (University Hall or Ogawamachi School Building) is the **Meiji University Museum** (Meiji Daigaku Hakubutsukan). (It is open from 10:00 a.m. to 5:00 p.m. and closed on Sundays, and university holidays; no entry fee.) The museum exhibits artifacts from the Japanese Jomon era (before 200 B.C.) and *haniwa* figures from the Kofun tomb period (250–538). Archaeological items from Korea and China are also in the collection of more than 10,000 items. The exhibits are labeled in English and Japanese, and the maps and photographs offer further clear information. The museum itself is probably too specialized to be of interest to the average visitor. On the sixth floor is the **Criminal Materials Exhibition**, which includes instruments used in capturing criminals in the Edo period, as well as instruments of torture and execution.

6 JIMBOCHO BOOKSTORE AREA
On leaving the museum building, turning to the right and walking down Ochanomizu-dori takes one past the major buildings of Meiji

University and eventually down to Yasakuni-dori. At that intersection, the area to the left is filled with sporting goods discount shops, while the area to the right from Surugadai-shita all along Yasakuni-dori, primarily on the south side of the avenue, is the bookstore area of **Jimbocho**, with approximately a hundred bookshops. Along the far side of the street to the right is the **Sanseido Bookstore**, which has a huge stock of books in various European languages. The **Isseido shop** with an Egyptian-style façade follows, with books on East Asia, ukiyo-e prints, and art. (Many of these shops have special sales in October and November and are generally open throughout the year from 10:00 a.m. to 6:30 p.m.)

⑦ KOISHIKAWA KORAKUEN GARDEN

For a change of pace at the **Koishikawa Korakuen Garden**, leave Jimbocho by heading north on Hakusan-dori until it meets Sotobori-dori immediately after crossing the Kanda River, then walk west along Sotobori-dori before taking the third street on the right north for another 100 yards. (The garden is open from 9:00 a.m. to 5:00 p.m. and closed during the New Year period; entry ¥300.) Korakuen Garden today is but a pale reflection of what once was here during Tokugawa days, when this was the estate of the Mito branch of the Tokugawa clan. Then, at 63 acres (25.2 hectares), it was three times the size of the present 16-acre (6.4-hectare) landscaped park. The garden was constructed in 1629 by Yorifusa, the 11th son of Tokugawa Ieyasu and founder of the Mito branch of the clan. It took 30 years to complete in the *tsukiyama* style, resulting in a stroll garden in which the elements of design were meant to reflect classical scenes in Chinese and Japanese culture.

Its name, *Korakuen* ("Garden or Park of Deferred Pleasure"), refers to the Confucian virtue for a gentlemen scholar of concerning himself with the commonweal first and his own pleasure only thereafter. In earlier times, the garden area was a large, shallow lake and an arm of Tokyo Bay, but, once the arm of the bay was filled in, the garden preserved a portion of water for an ornamental lake and ponds. Yorifusa's son Mitsukuni continued the work on the garden, and the lake was created by the third shogun, Iemitsu. The miniature lakes and hills were intended to recall a number of classical scenic sites: Mount Lu Shan in China; the famed scenic West Lake in China; the Togetsu Bridge of

Arashiyama in western Kyoto. An isle in the lake with a shrine to Benten, the Shinto goddess, recalled a shrine on Chichibu Island in Lake Biwa. With winding paths, stone lanterns, arched bridges, a small teahouse, and a small Confucian temple, it was the most noted garden in all of Edo. All those elements that compose the garden and give it greater significance are made more understandable if one purchases the color guide in English. The estate of the Mito was taken over by the government after 1868 and used as an army arsenal. It was damaged in the 1923 earthquake but was partially restored before it was given to the city as a public park in 1936. The oldest of its type in Tokyo, this lovely stroll-garden park all too often receives too few visitors–making it possible to enjoy it in comparative solitude.

One cannot escape the amusement and sports center that has been developed on what was once the full extent of the Korakuen Garden. On leaving the garden grounds, the street that parallels the Kanda River should be followed toward the **Yellow Building**, which is difficult to miss, what with its yellow-and-orange-striped façade. Ten stories tall with a glass elevator, the building is dedicated to the sporting life and has bowling, boxing, and wrestling facilities. Behind it is **Korakuen Hall**, with additional sports facilities including a pool that doubles in winter as a golf-driving range. The only major facility on the site in 1936 was a baseball stadium, and these other sporting opportunities are post-1950 additions. The original baseball field is now covered by the 1988 **Tokyo Dome**, affectionately referred to by Tokyoites as the Big Egg. Home of the Yomiuri Giants, it can seat 50,000 spectators under its inflatable dome, and besides baseball it hosts soccer, football, and events other than sports. There is a **Baseball Hall of Fame** that is primarily of interest to the Japanese visitor (open March to September from 10:00 a.m. to 6:00 p.m. and from 10:00 a.m. to 5:00 p.m. from October to April. Entry is ¥500).

Baseball has become a Japanese addiction. Baseball games in large stadiums are available to a mass population. The game began in Japan in the early Meiji era, not too much later than in the United States. It was played first at schools and universities, and by 1903 Waseda and Keio University teams were competing against each other. Baseball was taken so seriously, and the attitude of the fans in the stands became so dangerous, that in 1906 games between the two universities had to be suspended. While resembling its American counterpart, the game has become thoroughly Japanese, and it is a team sport in which individual star are submerged.

The adjacent **Korakuen Amusement Park**, dating from 1955 and now named **Tokyo Dome City**, offers more than two dozen rides, parachute drops, and a 328-foot (93.4-meter) revolving observation tower. Besides the amusement park for children, the sports ground also has bowling, swimming, ice skating, a bicycle track, a swimming pool, a spa, a hall for judo (practice of judo can be observed between 3:00 and 5:00 p.m. by applying to the reception desk at the Kodokan Judo Hall). For the non-sportsman, movie theaters are available.

8 AKIHABARA DISTRICT

After exploring the Korakuen area, one can head back to Hakusan-dori and walk south back over the Kanda River for Suidobashi Station, and take the JR Sobu Line two stops east to Akihabara Station and the **Akiha-bara district** with its hundreds of discount shops. The name *Akihabara*, meaning "Field of Autumn Leaves," belies its modern commercial nature. What began as a black-market district after the World War II has grown into a gigantic discount center for modern communications equipment and supplies. Chuo-dori for the next number of streets is lined with a variety of these discount shops, large and small, as are the side alleys and the area under the railroad line. The larger ones offer tourist discounts in their tax-free shops on the showing of a passport. Adjacent to Akihabara Station is the **Atre 1 Akihabara**, which opened its doors in November 2010. It offers the normal selection of goods found in most department stores as well as items with which it competes with its neighboring discount rivals. Bargaining is a possibility in most of the shops in the district, particularly the smaller units. Given the pricing in Japan, many of the goods sold in the district can usually be found for less in Hong Kong and in New York City discount stores. When you are done exploring Akihabara, returning to JR Akihabara Station gives access to the JR Yamanote, Sobu and Chuo Lines for access to other parts of central Tokyo.

GETTING THERE

The starting point of this walk is Yushima Station on the Chiyoda subway line, which can be reached in less than 20 minutes from most major central stations.

Akihabara's Chuo-dori attracts crowds of electronics' shoppers and anime and manga fans.

Walking Tour 11

IKEBUKURO

A Shopper's Paradise, the City within a City, the Writers' Final Resting Place, and a Classic Stroll Garden

1. **Ikebukuro Shopping**
2. **Sunshine City**
3. **Zoshigaya Cemetery**
4. **Rikugi-en Garden**

It's hard to imagine while navigating the throngs of shoppers and office workers who seem perpetually to crowd **Ikebukuro Station**–where this walk begins–but the area's unlikely name, *Ikebukuro* ("Lake Hollow"), was once an apt description for this now mercantile hub. Previously a small, swampy hamlet out in the countryside beyond Tokyo, Ikebukuro came into its own only after the arrival of the railroads in the late 19th century. The introduction of the Seibu rail

line, and then the purchase of a local department store that was to be expanded in 1950 into the Seibu Department Store chain, helped in the development of this district. This Seibu store claims to cover more ground area than any other such store in Japan. In 1956, a subway line finally connected Ikebukuro with Tokyo Station, and now there are eight lines converging on the center of the shopping district. A rebuilt **Tobu Department Store** leads to an innovative "glass gallery," roofing a plaza and connecting a group of three buildings around the station of the Yamanote Line. (An underground walkway connects the east and west entrances/exits to the complex and the station, and modern escalators rise to the stores and the street.) The Tokyo Metropolitan

Less crowded than Shibuya or Shinjuku, the main crossing by Ikebukuro Station is still very busy.

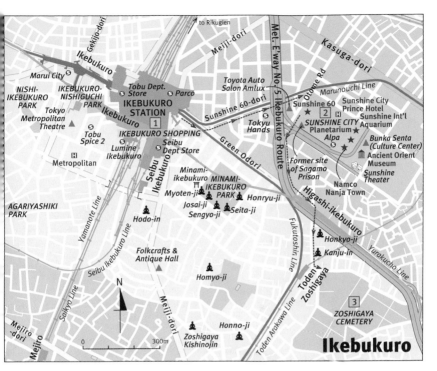

Theatre across the Metropolitan Plaza on the west side of the station offers concerts and theater performances and is home to the Tokyo Metropolitan Symphony Orchestra.

Just to the west of the commercial area is Rikkyo University (St. Paul's), which moved here from the Tsukiji district in 1918 in order to handle a growing student body that was attracted by its excellent programs. Begun by an American Episcopalian missionary, C. M. Williams, the new campus pursued two different architectural styles: Elizabethan England's architectural heritage can be seen in the classroom buildings, while the white, wooden faculty houses reflect a New England heritage.

Another institution transferred here from the Tsukiji area and welcomed by the local inhabitants for the jobs it promised was the Sugamo Prison. Here the American fliers shot down in General Doolittle's first air raid on Tokyo in 1942 were held and were executed; so was Richard Sorge, the dedicated Soviet spy who had wormed his way into the confidence of the German ambassador to Japan and of members of the Japanese premier's cabinet to gain valuable information for Moscow. Here too were detained the "Class A" war criminals, who were tried for starting World War II and held responsible for atrocities connected with the war. General Tojo Hideki was the last one hanged in the prison yard on December 23, 1948. (A memorial stone to the Japanese military officers who brought about the war in China and then the larger war in the Pacific has been placed here by unrepentant militarists.) The prison was returned to Japanese jurisdiction in 1958 and was then torn down in 1971, to be replaced by a rather optimistically named Sunshine City, a rather odd twist of history.

1 IKEBUKURO SHOPPING

The JR, Tobu, and Seibu rail stations and the Marunouchi, Fukutoshin, and Yurakucho subway stations are interconnected, and they form the heart of Ikebukuro. Here are the various department stores: Seibu, Tobu, and Ikebukuro Parco, fine stores that are a far cry from the black market that operated along the western side of the station as late as 1961. As with most department stores, Seibu, on the east side of the station, has food counters in its two basement levels, with some 300 vendors offering an amazing variety of foodstuffs. **Seibu Sports Ikebukuro**, the first sports specialty store of its kind in Japan, is now housed within the main store. Here are all the items needed for the sporting life, from fishing gear to skiing equipment to martial arts materials. **Parco** is noted for its high-end fashion but also houses a large branch of **Muji**, popular for its simple and low-cost, but fashionable, clothing and interior goods. To the east of the station are numerous cinemas, two large **Yamada Denki** home electronics stores next to rival **BIC Camera**, and even a **Tokyu Hands**.

West of the station is Rikkyo University, as previously mentioned, but also the **Marui Department Store**. Pride of place goes to the **Tobu Department Store**, since its Metropolitan Plaza contains not only a separate department store called Lumine but also the **Tokyo Metropolitan Theatre**. Tobu has five floors of restaurants, from the 11th to 15th floors of its giant main building, covering all tastes, while among its hundreds of stores are everything from high-end fashion brands to local budget fashion shop Uniqlo, which has a full two floors to itself, and even a Hello Kitty store.

2 SUNSHINE CITY

Leaving the station from the east exit, the wide Green Odori Street, with its central mall displaying a statue of two athletes balancing each other in the air, diverges to the left into Sunshine 60-dori. Taking this latter street, just beyond the expressway is the **Toyota Auto Salon Amlux** (open 11:00 a.m. to 7:00 p.m. daily but closed Mondays and the year-end holiday), a five-story temple of praise to the automotive age. Behind Toyota is the **Sunshine City** complex, the 1978 60-story **Sunshine Building**, until 1991 the tallest building in Tokyo. (A taxi from the east exit of the station is the quickest way to this area.) The complex of four buildings includes a hotel, a theater, a shopping arcade, a park, a planetarium, a culture center, an aquarium, an Ancient Orient Museum, a concert hall, and a trade promotion center. The management calls the complex a city within the city. An elevator can take one to the top of the Sunshine Building for its observation deck (open from 10:00 a.m. to 9:30 p.m.; entry ¥620) in 35 seconds, for a distant view of Tokyo and the Kanto Plain.

The 10th and 11th floors of the separate **Bunka Senta (Culture Center)** house the **Sunshine International Aquarium**, with 73 tanks and some 20,000 fish (open from 10:00 a.m. to 8:00 p.m daily (Apr. 1–Oct. 31), 10:00 a.m. to 6:00 p.m. (Nov. 1–Mar. 31; ¥1,800); closed December 31 to January 3). The **Konica Minolta Planetarium "Manten"** on the roof of the World Import Mart Building (open 11:00 a.m. to 8:00 p.m. daily, from 11:00 a.m. to 8:00 p.m. Sundays and holidays; ¥1,000) has 16 computer-controlled projectors presenting shows of the stars and planets. The **Sunshine Theater** is on the fourth through the sixth floors. The **Ancient Orient Museum** is on the sixth and seventh floors (open 10:00 a.m. to 5:00 p.m.; ¥500). The museum exhibits artifacts from pre-Islamic Egypt, Syria, and Pakistan excavated by a Tokyo University research group. Many of the artifacts were removed to save them before a proposed damming of the Euphrates River drowned the ancient sites. Glass and mosaics from ancient Iran, gold jewelry from the third century B.C. to the third century A.D., coins, painted pottery–the collections display the varied arts of ancient Near East civilizations. The **Alpa Shopping Center** portion of the complex has over 200 shops of all kinds as well as restaurants arranged around a plaza enhanced by a waterfall. The **World Trade Center** (or **World Import Mart**) on the sixth and seventh floor is meant to encourage world trade, while the adjacent **Sunshine City Prince Hotel** is one of the largest in the city with some 1,200 rooms.

3 ZOSHIGAYA CEMETERY

One place of some note to the southeast of Ikebukuro is **Zoshigaya Cemetery**. To reach it, walk one block west from Sunshine Building to the main, north-south street that runs under Metropolitan Expressway #5 and follow that street south until it joins Green-Odori. Another 50 yards along Green-Odori, a small north-south street should be taken south 200 yards to the northern end of Zoshigaya Cemetery. A cemetery with many ancient zelkovia trees, it is contains the graves of a number of literary figures of note in Japanese writings–Lafcadio Hearn, Soseki Natsume, and Kafu Nagai. (For those interested, the site is also five minutes from the Zoshigaya stop on the Toden Arakawa streetcar [see Walk 8].)

4 RIKUGI-EN GARDEN

For one of the most delightful gardens in

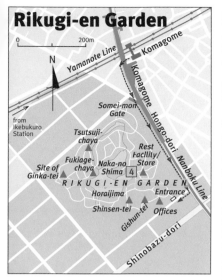

Rikugi-en Garden

0   200m

N

Yamanote Line

Komagome

Komagome Hongo-dori

Nanboku Line

from Ikebukuro Station

Somei-mon Gate

Tsutsuji-chaya

Fukiage-chaya

Site of Ginka-tei

Naka-no Shima

Rest Facility/ Store

4

R I K U G I - E N   G A R D E N

Horaijima

Entrance

Shinsen-tei

Gishun-tei

Offices

Shinobazu-dori

Tokyo, return along Green Odori to Ikebukuro Station, and take the Yamanote Line train three stops to Komagone Station. Leaving the station's north exit and walking south (left) down Hongo-dori, one is but five minutes away from the **Rikugi-en**, the "Garden of the Six Principles (of Poetry)" (open 9:00 a.m. to 5:00 p.m.; closed for the New Year holidays; entry ¥300). Begun in 1695 by Yanagisawa Yoshiyasu, a samurai and confidante of the fifth shogun, Tsunayoshi, the garden was seven years in the making and was designed to be a *tsukiyama* (stroll garden), with a path between hills and lakes. It became one of the favored resorts of the shogun. After the death of Yanagisawa in 1714, the garden declined. It was purchased by Iwasaki Yataro, the Meiji financier who became wealthy on Japan's wars between 1895 and 1905, and he had the garden restored. In 1934 the garden was donated to the city and has been open as a public park since then. As with other feudal "go-round" gardens, the attempt was made to have the scenery evince the 88 sites mentioned in the major Chinese and Japanese literary works. The particular desire was to exemplify the scenic spots cited in the ancient poetry collections of early Japan. There is a pond with an island and pine trees, a hill with a teahouse, all reflections of classical Japanese gardens. This lovely traditional garden can serve, perhaps, as an antidote to the many commercial enterprises described in this tour.

From the Rikugi-en Garden, the Yamanote Line brings one from Komagome Station back into central Tokyo.

GETTING THERE

Ikebukuro Station, the starting point of this tour, is served by numerous train and subway lines. These include the JR Yamanote Line and the Marunouchi and Yurakucho subway lines.

The Rikugi-en Garden, the "Garden of the Six Principles of Poetry"

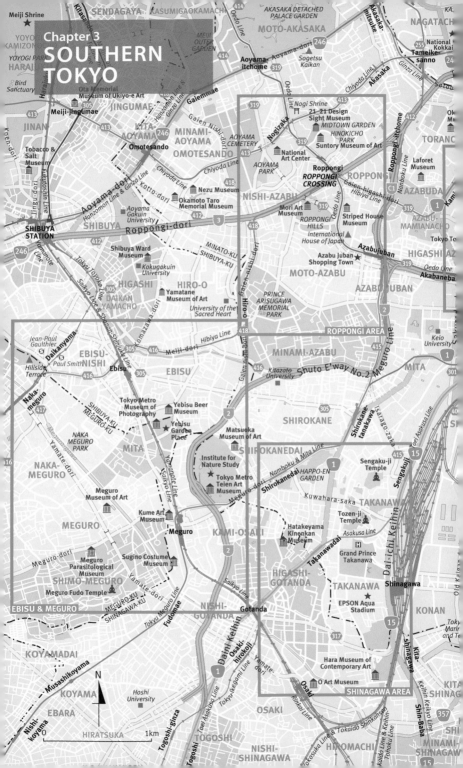

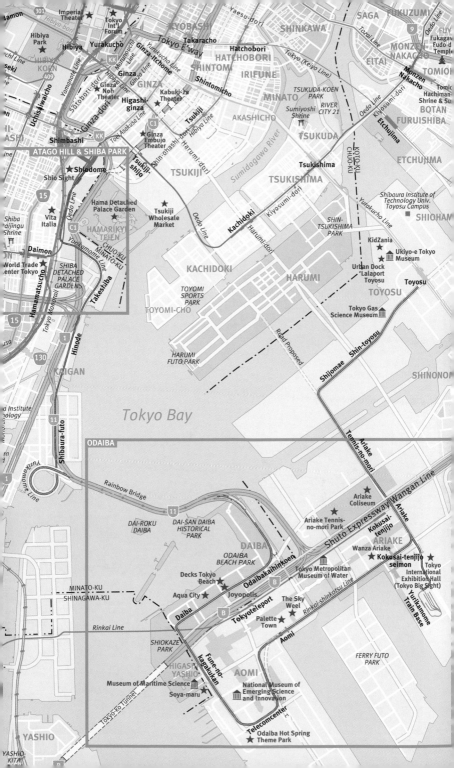

Walking Tour 12

ATAGO HILL, TOKYO TOWER AND SHIBA PARK
A Hill of Lost Causes, the Shoguns Defiled, Tokyo's Eiffel Tower, and a Former Nobleman's Garden

1. **Atago Shrine**
2. **NHK Broadcast Museum**
3. **Zojo-ji Temple**
4. **Tokyo Tower and World Trade Center**
5. **Shiba Detached Palace Gardens**

Tour 12 encompasses much of the history of old Edo as well as modern Tokyo, recalling the procession of daimyo along the old Tokaido Road from 1632 to the 1860s as well as events that led to the end of the shoguns' rule and the Meiji Restoration. There is, as

well, a tower taller than the Eiffel Tower in Paris, a vantage point that overlooks portions of Tokyo today, and a museum that documents the history of TV broadcasting in Japan.

1 ATAGO SHRINE
We start at Kamiyacho Station on the Hibiya subway line. Leaving the station from Exit 3, the first street on the right that goes under **Atago Hill** through a tunnel should be taken to the north-south street beyond. A left turn here brings one farther along that street to a torii in front of a very steep set of steps to the

The torii and steps that lead to the Atago Shrine

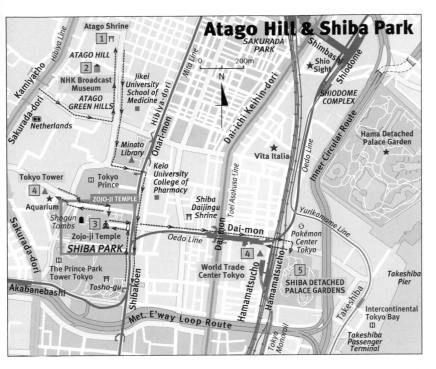

Atago Hill & Shiba Park

Atago Shrine on a hill 85 feet (26 meters) above sea level. Noted for its cherry trees, it is approached by the "male" slope of 85 steps, the adjacent "female" slope of 113 steps being but slightly easier to mount. Two bronze lions guard the approach to the "male slope." Once a view of the city and Tokyo Bay could be observed from the height of the hill, but modern buildings now preclude such a vista. The Atago Shrine, its teahouse, its gardens, stream, a small shrine to Benten (on a little island in a tiny pond), and another shrine to Inari, all make the hill a delightful park-like spot. The main deity of the shrine is the god who protects against fire, a needed deity, given the succession of the "flowers of Edo" that burned the city to the ground on too many occasions. Unhappily, the deity was unable to protect his own shrine, for it went up in flames during a 1945 air raid, and the present shrine building is a 1948 reconstruction.

Political and destructive events have marred the history of the site. It was here that the 18 samurai from Mito prayed before setting out to kill Lord Ii Naosuke, the shogun's chief advisor, one snowy day in March 1860.

Not too many years later it was here on March 13, 1868, that the leader of the Tokugawa forces met with Takamori Saigo of the imperial army in an attempt to avert an attack on the city by the imperial forces. Pointing out the city, temples, and shrines below, Saigo was cautioned that an attack could see the whole city destroyed by fire in the resulting battle. Common sense ruled on both sides, and thus the city was surrendered with no loss of life or destruction other than what occurred in Ueno by Tokugawa holdouts one month later. A less happy event occurred here on August 22, 1945, when ten imperial soldiers committed suicide jointly on the defeat of Japan and the loss of World War II.

Taking the "female slope" with its broader steps and more gentle landings, at the top of the hill is a modern one-story shrine office. On the left is the pond with a blue torii at its far end and multicolored carp swimming in the water. A small rivulet runs into the pond, and to the right of the rivulet is a shrine on either side of the small waterway. The near shrine is preceded by two red torii while the farther shrine is approached through a bronze-plated torii and then a blue-painted torii. Beyond, at the head of the "male slope" is a stone torii leading to a roofed, vermilion torii with solid doors. Large bronze lanterns stand before the main shrine building. The shrine has a small *mikoshi* (portable shrine) on the right in its Haiden (Prayer Hall) while on either side of the unit are large pictures of men on horseback negotiating the very steep shrine steps–a feat that few could accomplish successfully. The Honden (Spirit Hall) has a snowflake-like, golden hanging pendant above the innermost shrine area.

2 NHK BROADCAST MUSEUM

A path to the left of the shrine main hall brings one to the **NHK Broadcast Museum**. The initial NHK broadcasts emanated from this building, but today it serves primarily as a museum of early broadcasting. (It is open daily except Monday from 9:30 a.m. to 4:30 p.m., closed December 29 to January 4; no entry fee.) An early broadcasting studio can be observed in addition to other exhibits of the era before television became popular, as well as displays concerning television. Tapes of broadcasts are available in the library, and the history of broadcasting, the production of programs, and the use of the latest electronic means of broadcasting can be viewed.

3 ZOJO-JI TEMPLE

Returning down the "male slope" to the north-south street, this street should be followed to the parkland before the **Zojo-ji Temple complex**. (This park can also be reached by means of a ten-minute walk from JR Hamamatsucho Station or Onarimon Station of the Toei Mito subway line.) The Tokyo Prince Hotel will be on the right at the side of the park. Turning to the left and passing a vermilion gate to the temple, at the corner of Hibiya-dori, a turn to the right brings one to

Zojo-ji Temple, with the Tokyo Tower behind

the Onari-mon Gate, which was once the shogun's entrance to the temple grounds. A *Deva* king is on guard on each side of the gate's passageway, the one on the left with a pen and tablet, while the one on the right stands guard with a pike in his left hand. The Tokugawa paulownia leaves decorate the closed doors of the gate, once a brilliant vermilion. Continuing along Hibiya-dori, one comes to the great San-mon gateway, the only remaining structure from the Zojo-ji Temple's early days.

When Tokugawa Ieyasu established his headquarters in Edo in the late 1500s, he was concerned to assure the protection of his city by the deities. Accordingly, the great Kan'ei-ji Temple was built in Ueno to protect the city against the Devil's Corner, the northeast from which evil could flow. A protection to the city was needed from the southeast as well, and thus the Jodo sect, with Amida as its main Buddha, was established at the great Zojo-ji Temple, which came into being in the early 1600s. Second in size in Edo only to the Kan'ei-ji Temple in Ueno, the original Zojo-ji had been established elsewhere in 1393, but Ieyasu had it moved to its present site in 1598 to serve as the Tokugawa family temple. The materials to build the temple came by boat from Osaka and were brought from the nearby harbor to the site, for the temple was then close to the bay and the Tokaido Road.

At one time this magnificent temple, established on 164 acres (65.6 hectares), had 48 sub-temples and over 100 buildings. Meiji dislike of the Tokugawas, and then wartime bombing raids in 1945, reduced the temple and the mausoleums of the shoguns to little more than a memory. Not only did the Meiji government show its disdain for the Tokugawa family temple by confiscating much of its land

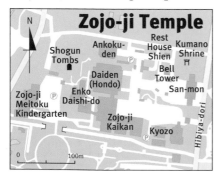

to create a park, **Shiba Park**, but the remains of the six shoguns buried here were in more recent times removed and placed within a small enclave to the rear of the main hall of the temple. Meiji religious fanatics set the temple buildings on fire in 1868 in order to cleanse "pure" Shinto from the influence of "foreign" Buddhist influences, and, when the temple buildings were rebuilt on a smaller scale, they were destroyed once more in 1909 in yet another blaze.

In the days of its greatness, the Zojo-ji was the central Jodo sect temple for the entire Kanto region, and it served as the main administrative and educational center for Tendai sect teachings. Its 48 sub-temples were served by 3,000 monks, and the compound was 15 times larger than the present 64-acre (25.6-hectare) site. The location of the temple was important, since the Tokaido Road between Kyoto and Edo ran beside it, and the Zojo-ji was not far from the last barrier or checkpoint on that road. On entering Edo, visiting daimyo could do their obeisance to the Tokugawa clan temple and the cemetery where shoguns were buried, for the shoguns were buried alternately here and at the cemetery at the Kan'ei-ji. To either side of the temple were the shoguns' tombs, an area entered through a black lacquered gate, and the ornamentation of the mausoleums reflected the extravagant architectural tastes of the late Momoyama period. Boardinghouses and refectories for the staff of the temples abounded, and the grounds included a pagoda and a pond with a Benten shrine on an island in its midst. An unnamed 17th-century gateway led to the Kodo-in Temple, which provided lodging for Tokugawa inside lords on their visit to the temple to offer their required respect to the shoguns' ancestors; it lay between the Dai-mon Gate and the San-mon Gate. Of all the temple buildings of the past, only the San-mon Gate, the plastered sutra storehouse, the gateway to shogun Hidetada's mausoleum, and one shogun's tomb, that of Ienobu (1662–1712), remains today.

The reconstructed black Dai-mon (Great Gate) lies to the west of the huge San-mon gateway, and it sits across the roadway leading to the San-mon. In 1605, a 50-foot-square, plastered Kyozo (Sutra Hall) was built near the San-mon (to the left of the San-mon along Hibiya-dori behind an entry gateway in the temple wall) to house the three versions of the *Tripitaka*, the complete canon of Buddhist

teachings, a gift from Ieyasu. (For the sake of safety, these ancient sutras, Sung and Yuan scriptures from China, are now kept in the modern, fireproof Zojo-ji office and reception hall within the temple grounds.) Some 18,000 scrolls containing Buddhist sutras remain in the red-lacquered, hexagonal sutra case within the Kyozo. This case can be revolved on its base by pushing upon its projecting handles, and one revolution of the case is equal to a complete reading of the sutras. Thus a simple rotation makes efficacious for the worshipper what otherwise would be a most onerous task. The Kyozo is open on four occasions annually, January 15, April 11–15, May 15, and September 15.

A second gateway lies to the left of the entryway to the Kyozo a little farther along Hibiya-dori, and it is the third and only other remaining structure from the original temple. This gateway, erected in 1632, once gave entry to the mausoleum of shogun Hidetada, the second Tokugawa shogun. It, along with the other shogun mausolea, was destroyed in the bombings toward the end of World War II, and the graves of the shoguns were later removed to a corner of the grounds behind the modern Main Hall of the Zojo-ji. The former burial area where daimyo came to pay their respects on their periodic visits to Edo is now covered by the Shiba Park golf driving range.

Returning to the great San-mon Gate, with its triple entryway on the west side of Hibiya-dori, the main grounds of the Zojo-ji can be entered here. Standing 69 feet (21 meters) tall and equally wide, this two-story gate was erected in the early 1600s in the Chinese style of architecture, and the gateway is the oldest wooden structure in Tokyo. It is known as the "Three Deliverances Gate," referring to the three evils of anger, greed, and stupidity from which the Buddhist faith should help to deliver one. On the second floor of this red-lacquered gateway are three images: the main image, Shaka, is seated on a lotus blossom, while at his side are two bodhisattva images (bodhisattvas are individuals who have achieved enlightenment but remain in this world so as to help others toward enlightenment), a small Monju seated on a lion on the left while on his right is a Fugen seated on an elephant. Sixteen *rakan*, early disciples of the Buddha, are also enshrined here.

Within the temple grounds a large stone image of Kannon stands between the gate and the roofed Suibonsha ablution unit on the left,

One of Tokyo's signature sights: Tokyo Tower

and behind these is the modern Zojo-ji office building, with a lecture hall and reception halls. Within this structure are preserved a number of the temple's treasures, including the sutras donated by Ieyasu. Beyond this modern unit to the left, up some steps, and through a gateway is a tea ceremony building, while farther to the rear are the temple's nursery school and its Meisho hall, with a large collection of books and maps of the Edo period (1603–1868). Returning to the path leading from the San-mon, on the right is the Shoro (Bell Tower), with its 11-foot (3.3-meter)-tall, six-foot (1.8-meter)-diameter bell weighing 33,000 pounds (14,850 kilograms). It is said the temple was granted the metal hairpins of the ladies of the shogun's court, which were melted as a contribution toward the creation of the bell in 1673. Also in this approach to the main hall is a pine tree planted by ex-president Grant of the United States in 1879.

The Daiden, the Great Main Hall, a 1972 reconstruction of the temple's Hondo (Main Hall), lies directly ahead of the San-mon Gate on a raised level (open from 9:00 a.m. to 8:00 p.m.). This reconstruction is in ferroconcrete, and the structure has a frontage of 158 feet

(48 meters) by 171 feet (52 meters) in depth. The frontage and the length of the steps (13.2 feet/48 meters) are derived from the Amida sutra, since the number 48 symbolizes the 48 vows made by Amida to save all sentient beings. The distance from the San-mon to the Hondo is 48 *ken* (about 48 feet) while the distance from the Dai-mon Gate to the Hondo is 108 *ken*, representing the 108 illusions or shortcomings to which mankind is subject. There are 25 stairs, symbolizing the 25 bodhisattvas who assist the Buddha. The Hondo has four large golden columns about the altar area, while four large golden hangings are pendent above the altar area in which is a golden Amida image from the 16th century.

To the right of and before the Hondo are hundreds of small images of Jizo, many of them wearing caps and holding pinwheels that turn in the breeze. Such small images so accoutered represent stillborn infants or young children who have died, and the images are decorated by grieving parents. To the right of the Hondo is the Ankoku-den, the Hall for the Safety of the Nation. Here is found the black Amida image that Ieyasu reverenced daily. Once covered with gold-leaf, the smoke of incense offered to it has long since turned the image black. It is kept within a case and is only shown publicly on January 15, May 15, and September 15. Behind the Amida is a row of many Jizo images. Jizo is a guardian of a number of aspects of life, but here the bibs and the pinwheels indicate that he is reverenced as the protector of children. To the rear of the Ankoku-den are the remains of six shoguns behind a handsome wrought-iron gate decorated with dragons. Of the six shogun tombs, with their magnificent architecture, only that of the sixth shogun, Ienobu, remains intact, and above the underground stone tomb holding Ienobu's ashes is a bronze Treasure Tower. To the south of the temple grounds, once a part of the temple, was the site of the Tosho-gu Shrine to the deified spirit of Ieyasu. From April 2 to April 7 there is a commemoration of the death of the founder of the Jodo sect, with a procession and religious ceremonies. The cherry trees of the temple are in blossom at this time.

4 TOKYO TOWER AND WORLD TRADE CENTER
On a rise behind the Zojo-ji Temple is **Tokyo Tower**, reached by a path at the side of the temple. (It is open from 9:00 a.m. to 10:00 p.m. year-round. Entry is free for the base of

the tower and ¥600 for the observation hall.) At 1,089 feet (327 meters) in height, it surpasses the Eiffel Tower, on which it is obviously modeled, by 100 feet (30 meters) but is dwarfed by the Sky Tree to the north. The viewing or observation hall is at the 820-foot (246-meter) level, and it is the main reason for visiting the tower. On clear days not only much of Tokyo but Mt. Fuji and a portion of the Japanese Alps can be seen. A wax museum, an aquarium, and a science museum located in the base of the structure are not exceptional sights. A restaurant and souvenir shops are on the lower levels as well.

Returning to the Zojo-ji and taking the street that leads from the San-mon and through the Dai-mon, one eventually reaches the **World Trade Center Tokyo**, which is just before Hamamatsucho Station on the Yamanote Line. The 40th floor of the Trade Center offers an excellent view of Tokyo Bay and the city of Tokyo. (Open 10:00 a.m. to 8:30 p.m.; entry ¥620. Inexpensive restaurants can be found in the basement of the building.) It is at this building that the monorail line to Haneda Airport, in operation since 1964, has its initial station.

5 SHIBA DETACHED PALACE GARDENS

Continuing under the Yamanote Line right-of-way brings one to the **Shiba Detached Palace Gardens** (Kyu-Shiba-rikyu Teien) (open from 9:00 a.m. to 5:00 p.m. but closed Mondays; entry ¥150). Three hundred years ago this was the residence of one of the more important Tokugawa officials, Okubo Tadatomo, councilor of state. The garden was created on land reclaimed from the bay in the Edo period and laid out in "go-round" style. Comprising miniature hills, ponds, islands with bridges, and walkways surrounded by pine trees and stone lanterns, it was a pleasant retreat on the waterfront. Today, the waterfront has receded due to additional landfill projects, but the garden remains a haven in the midst of rail lines, roads, and buildings of the modern age. As with all Tokugawa estates, it came into the possession of the Imperial Household after 1868, and in 1924 it was given to the city, which turned it into a public park.

Farther east, there are sites of interest along the waterfront. Today the **Takeshiba passenger terminal** for boats lies to the east of the Shiba Detached Gardens. The water-bus for the trip to Asakusa up the Sumida River

The Shiba Detached Palace Gardens, which sit on land reclaimed from the bay during the Edo era

leaves from the **Takeshiba Pier**, as do boats to the new Odaiba amusement and cultural island. Boats also leave from the Takeshiba pier for the Izu islands or just for cruises in the bay with variety shows for entertainment. The Shibaura area south of Hamamatsucho was filled in to create one of the first industrial zones for Tokyo, but the buildings were leveled in the 1945 air raids. The demand for supplies for the United States military in the Korean War led to a rebuilding of the area with warehouses and port facilities. The filled land of Takeshiba and to the south (the Hinode and Kaigan pier area) were, at the end of the 20th century, taken over by artists who here found appropriate loft space in the old *soko* (warehouses). The new monorail line from Shimbashi to the area has also made the waterfront more accessible. Mention has been made of the geisha section in Shimbashi, and as late as 1934 there were 133 geisha registered at the Kyodo Kaikan, south of Hamamatsucho and just to the north of Tamachi Station on the Yamanote Line, but times have changed and the hall has housed migrant workers in later years. The central hall from which the geisha were dispatched later became a 70-tatami-mat hall with a stage and was known as the Cooperative Labor Hall (Kyodo Kaikan) for community activities. Here the tour ends, and from the garden's main entrance one can return west, passing under the elevated Yamanote Line, for Daimon Station on the Oedo subway line.

> ### GETTING THERE
> This tour starts at Kamiyacho Station on the Hibiya subway line.

Walking Tour 13

ROPPONGI AND AZABU

The Last Samurai, Beverly Hills Transplanted, Roppongi Hills and Tokyo Midtown, and a Statesman's Garden

1. **Nogi Shrine**
2. **Tokyo Midtown**
3. **National Art Center**
4. **Roppongi Crossing**
5. **International House of Japan**
6. **Striped House Museum of Art**
7. **Roppongi Hills**
8. **Prince Arisugawa Memorial Park**

Roppongi is a popular part of the city due to its many restaurants and nightclubs, but it isn't the most physically attractive portion of Tokyo because its main intersection, Roppongi Crossing, is covered by the overhead expressway. Happily, at the end of the 20th century the area was greatly improved by the Roppongi Hills development, described below. The name *Roppongi* has historic antecedents: its meaning of "Six Trees" is a reference to the six Tokugawa daimyo—each of whom had the character for "tree" in his name—who once had estates in this area.

Roppongi history has been somewhat darkened by military events, for from 1868 to 1945 the sector to the north of Roppongi Crossing on Gaien Higashi-dori was primarily a military enclave, after the Imperial Army took over the land of the daimyo estates in the area in 1868. It was here that the drill grounds were relocated when the military gave up the land adjacent to the Imperial Palace that then became Hibiya Park. Later the War College for the Japanese army was headquartered on the site, and after 1945 the United States military used the former Japanese army grounds for its occupation forces.

The American presence brought an international note to the area, with new restau-

rants, cafés, and bars, but the departure of the U.S. military in 1959 led to the use of the compound by the new Japanese Defense Agency. The subway came to Roppongi in 1964, and by 1970 the sector took off as a restaurant and entertainment area appealing to the younger working set, who in decades past might have been attracted to Asakusa.

1 NOGI SHRINE

We begin at the **Nogi Shrine**, which was created for the spirit of one of Japan's most noted military figures, a general who was in command of Japan's forces in the fields of war at the end of the 19th and the beginning of the 20h century. General Nogi Maresuke (1849-1912) was the epitome of the role model held up to the youth of Japan by the Meiji government, whose leadership was drawn primarily from the military class of the pre-1868 outside lords of Japan. General Nogi not only lived for Japan and for the emperor, but he died for the emperor as well. His home, in which he and his wife committed seppuku, is part of the shrine to his spirit.

The Chiyoda subway line's Nogizaka Station exits on to Nogi-zaka (Nogi Slope) just before Gaien Higashi-dori. Here is **Nogi Park**, in which the general's house, shrine, and the Nogi Kaikan (Nogi Hall) are located. The latter is a 1968 building, and its design in red brick with stained glass windows is meant to reflect the type of architecture that was popular in the early years of Meiji rule. It was created to honor the general and his wife, and it serves as a wedding reception hall, for, since the disestablishment of Shinto shrines from government support after the World War II, shrines must raise money for their own support through commercial enterprises as

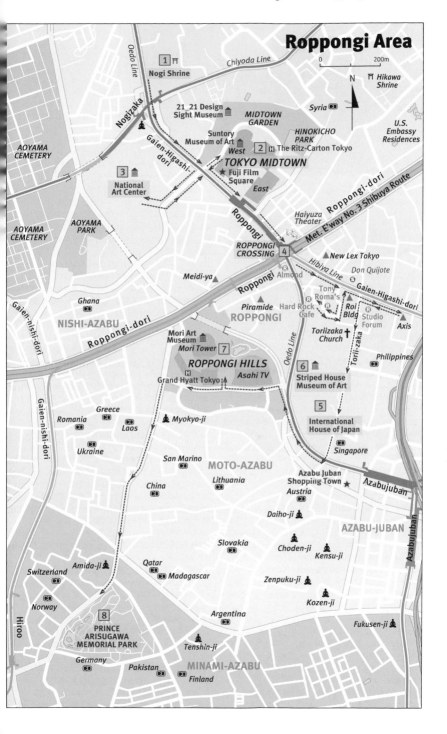

Roppongi Area

0   200m
N

⛩ Hikawa
Shrine

1 ⛩
Nogi Shrine

Chiyoda Line

Oedo Line

Nogizaka

21_21 Design
Sight Museum

MIDTOWN
GARDEN

Syria ☎

Suntory
Museum of Art

HINOKICHO
PARK

U.S.
Embassy
Residences

West

2 H The Ritz-Carton Tokyo

AOYAMA
CEMETERY

Gaien-Higashi-dori

3 ☐
National
Art Center

TOKYO MIDTOWN

★ Fuji Film
Square

East

Roppongi-dori

Met. E'way No. 3 Shibuya Route

AOYAMA
CEMETERY

AOYAMA
PARK

Roppongi

Haiyuza
Theater

ROPPONGI
CROSSING

4

▲ New Lex Tokyo

Don Quijote

Meidi-ya ▲

Roppongi

R
Almond

Hibiya Line

⊘ Don Quijote

Gaien-nishi-dori

Ghana ☎

NISHI-AZABU

Roppongi-dori

Piramide ▲

ROPPONGI

Hard Rock
Cafe

R Tony
Roma's ▲

R Roi
Bldg

R
Studio
Forum

Gaien-Higashi-dori

▲ Axis

Toriizaka
Church †

Toriizaka

Philippines ☎

Mori Art
Museum ☐

Mori Tower 7

ROPPONGI HILLS

Asahi TV

Grand Hyatt Tokyo ▲

H

Oedo Line

6 ☐
Striped House
Museum of Art

5

International
House of Japan

Greece
☎

Myokyo-ji

Romania
☎

Laos
☎

San Marino
☎

MOTO-AZABU

Singapore ☎

Azabu Juban
Shopping Town ★

Azabujuban

Ukraine
☎

China
☎

Lithuania
☎

Austria ☎

Daiho-ji 🧘

AZABU-JUBAN

Gaien-nishi-dori

Switzerland
☎

Amida-ji 🧘

Qatar
☎

Madagascar
☎

Slovakia
☎

Choden-ji ▲

Kensu-ji
🧘

Zenpuku-ji 🧘

Azabujuban

Norway
☎

Kozen-ji
🧘

Fukusen-ji 🧘

Hiroo

8

PRINCE
ARISUGAWA
MEMORIAL PARK

Argentina
☎

Tenshin-ji 🧘

Germany
☎

Pakistan
☎

Finland ☎

MINAMI-AZABU

Nogi Shrine, the resting place for the spirit of General Maresuke Nogi

well as from charitable gifts.

The general's house was situated across the street from the then army barracks, a street to be named Nogi-zaka in his honor after his death. A leading military figure in both the Sino-Japanese War of 1894–1895 and the Russo-Japanese War of 1904–1905, he was responsible on two occasions for the capture of Port Arthur in China. His generalship in the Russo-Japanese War was not particularly glorious, since 60,000 Japanese soldiers died in the capture of Port Arthur, including both the Nogis' sons, their only children. Feeling the disgrace of so pyrrhic a victory, he requested permission from the emperor to commit seppuku but was denied this act, since the emperor forbad the practice during his rule.

Appointed president of the Gakushu-in School (later a university), he was responsible for a few years for training the grandson of the emperor, a child who would eventually reign as Emperor Hirohito. The Gakushu-in had been founded in 1842 in Kyoto by the then reigning emperor for the training of the children of court nobility (as distinct from the less important children of the major daimyo). The school was transferred to Tokyo after 1868, and here it attempted to inculcate the ideals of the samurai in the children of the new peerage, drawn primarily from the families of the former outside lords, who had opposed the Tokugawa shogun.

With the death of Emperor Meiji in 1912, Nogi fulfilled the wish he had expressed to the emperor in 1905, and, as the emperor's body left the Imperial Palace for ultimate interment in Kyoto on September 13, 1912, the general's wife slit her throat while he performed seppuku, thereby fulfilling a very

ancient, though seldom followed custom, of following one's lord in death. The land about the Nogi residence was designated thereafter a shrine to this exemplar of Meiji virtues. The house has been retained and may be viewed, and a shrine to the general's spirit was created on the grounds. (The general and his wife were interred in nearby Aoyama Cemetery.) Destroyed in a 1945 air raid, the shrine has been rebuilt with a simplicity that reflects the temper of Shinto design. It is the work of architect Hiroshi Ohe, who also designed the Nogi Kaikan (Nogi Hall).

Steps from the street lead to a large torii, a public restroom on the left, and steps to the right mounting into the shrine grounds. At the top of the steps, on the left, a row of small vermilion torii leads to a small shrine, while the roofed ablution basin is on the left of the path. A modern shrine office unit is also to the left. Two *komu-inu* (lion-dogs) stand before a large stone torii, which marks the entry to the shrine proper. A very modern treasury building on the right has a sales counter at its nearest end. On the lower level of the building is a museum with a seated image of General Nogi and materials relating to his life. The Haiden (Prayer Hall) is ahead, and beyond it is the Honden (Spirit Hall), containing the general's spirit, the two buildings being connected by roofed corridors. Unusual globular units stand in front on either side of the Haiden: one's fortune slips can be attached to them when these are purchased. Steps lead up from the shrine grounds through what would have been the vegetable garden to the general's house farther up the slope. The simple **Nogi house** is said to have been designed by the general after a French barracks he had once inspected and admired in Europe when he was there as a student. It is a black, clapboard, wooden structure with as much charm as one would expect from an army barracks, and it was constructed in 1889 when the army moved its drill field from land adjacent to the Imperial Palace to the former daimyo estates across the way from the site of the Nogi home.

A boardwalk along the exterior of the house and large windows with sliding shutters permit one to look into the building, and on September 13, on the anniversary of the death of the Nogis, it is possible to enter it. A large reception room and the family living room are on the first floor, sparsely furnished with Western-style furniture of the day. The

The Tokyo Midtown complex includes a sprawling municipal garden dotted with modern artworks.

floors are generally tatami-matted, except for the wood-floored corridors. An eight-mat room on the second floor was the general's bedroom, while his wife had a six-mat room. Their sons slept in a ten-mat room in the attic. The death clothes, replete with bloodstains, are still shown, a rather gory glorification of the death of a belated samurai and his wife. Since the house is built on a slope, the lower, or basement portion, also contains rooms.

Adjacent, in four sections, are the brick stables, built in 1889 before the house was erected. Here Nogi kept the white horse that the Russian general Stoessel gave him after the Japanese victory at Port Arthur. (The grounds of the residence are open from 9:00 a.m. to 4:00 p.m. daily without charge. The grounds of the shrine are open at all times, and a flea market is held at the shrine on the second Sunday of each month.) The former military drill grounds across from the Nogi residence became the site of the Japanese War College in time. After 1945, it was occupied by the U.S. military forces, and it now houses the headquarters of the Japanese Self-Defense Forces.

2 TOKYO MIDTOWN

Returning to Gaien Higashi-dori and following it south for 250 yards brings you to one of Tokyo's more recent high-rise highlights. **Tokyo Midtown** has come to dominate the Roppongi and Akasaka skyline since it was completed in 2007–not surprisingly, as its main tower, at 814 feet (248 meters), is the tallest building in Tokyo Prefecture. The complex, designed by architectural firm Skidmore, Owings and Merrill and built by Japan's largest real estate developer, Mitsui Fudosan, is comprised of six buildings in all, containing a mixture of office space (Yahoo! Japan being one of the most famous tenants) and apartments alongside shops, restaurants, cafés, bars, galleries, and even a luxury hotel, the Ritz Carlton, which occupies the 47th through 53rd floors of the main tower.

Though you could easily while away half a day exploring the complex along with the crowds of tourists and Tokyoites who seem to find Midtown's allure too strong to resist, several attractions are worthy of special note. For shoppers, the five-story **Galleria** building has almost 800,000 square feet (73,000 square meters) of stores and restaurants that include a **Terence Conran** restaurant and

Coppola's Vinoteca, a wine bar featuring the wines of film director Francis Ford Coppola. For those with an interest in art and design, the most notable is **21_21 Design Sight**, a design gallery and workshop by renowned architect Tadao Ando and fashion designer Issey Miyake that showcases and nurtures the very best of modern Japanese design. It is located in Midtown's Design Wing on the western side of the complex. (Open 11:00 a.m. to 8:00 p.m., and closed Tuesdays and for the New Year holiday; entry ¥1,000.) In the more central Gardenside Building is the **Suntory Museum of Art**, with a collection of Japanese art that encompasses a changing lineup of paintings, ceramics, lacquerware, glassware, dyeing, and weaving (open 10:00 a.m. to 8:00 p.m. Wednesdays to Saturdays, and until 6:00 p.m. on Sundays; closed Tuesdays; entry fee varies with the exhibition). If you do choose to explore the complex, you will also find a collection of modern sculptures and other artwork scattered around Midtown's basement and first floor areas.

③ NATIONAL ART CENTER
Backtracking to and crossing Gaien Higashi-dori, the wide street leading west (there is a gas station on the corner) should be followed to reach the **National Art Center**. Designed by Kisho Kurokawa and reputedly built at a cost of some 40 billion yen, the sleek and cavernous National Art Center is a museum that focuses on 20th-century painting and various forms of modern art. With some 150,000 square feet (14,000 square meters) of uncluttered exhibition space, it is one of the largest art facilities in the country. (Open 10:00 a.m. to 6:00 p.m. daily, but until 8:00 p.m. on Fridays. Closed Tuesdays. Entry fee varies.)

④ ROPPONGI CROSSING
Returning again to Gaien Higashi-dori and continuing south brings one to **Roppongi Crossing**, situated above Roppongi Station. At Roppongi Crossing, one is just steps away from the numerous restaurants, nightclubs, and cafés found along Gaien Higashi-dori in both directions. Among these to the east are the **New Lex Tokyo**, and the **Roppongi Plaza Building**. Many nightspots are above the street level of their building, and listings for the venues most popular at any time can be found in the weekly free magazine *Metropolis*, available at numerous internation-

al hotels, restaurants, and bars in central Tokyo. **Little Beverly Hills**, as it was once nicknamed by expats, is down a street off Gaien Higashi-dori east of the crossing, It was so called for the American-named places such as **Tony Roma**, and the **Hard Rock Cafe** to be found there. A little farther east on Gaien Higashi-dori is **Studio Forum**, with wine bars and specialty shops.

Fashion has not been neglected, for farther along Gaien Higashi-dori is the four-story **Axis** (open from 11:00 a.m. to 7:00 p.m.), with upscale home interior offerings, galleries, and restaurants. In addition, on the left halfway back to the crossing is the **Roi Building**, of interest for shopping or dining.

⑤ INTERNATIONAL HOUSE OF JAPAN

From the corner on which sits the Roi Building, a street leads south to the **International House of Japan**, a private, non-profit organization established in 1952 with support from the Rockefeller Foundation, with the aim of promoting cultural exchange and intellectual cooperation between Japan and overseas. Here you will find a pleasant café, restaurant, and the lovely traditional Japanese garden of a former daimyo estate that belonged to the Kyogoku clan, the feudal lords of the fief of Tadotsu in what is now Kagawa Prefecture. The clan retained the mansion until the demise of the Tokugawa shogunate, upon which the then foreign minister of the new Meiji government, Kaoru Inoue, took possession of the house. It became known as the site of elaborate banquets, where Emperor and Empress Meiji, the Empress Dowager, and ambassadors of various countries could meet. In the years leading up to World War II, ownership in the property shifted between several well-heeled families; then after the war it found its way into the hands of the government, which in turn passed it over to the newly established International House. In the streets to the south and southwest is the Azabu district, with its many embassies, schools, and expensive residential quarters. The current modern structure was built in 1955 as a

The striking Kisho Kurokawa-designed National Art Center in Roppongi opened in 2007.

collaboration between three prominent Japanese architects, Kunio Maekawa, Junzo Sakakura, and Junzo Yoshimura, and was then expanded in 1976. Although modern and angular in design, it blends effortlessly with the former mansion's original garden, which was designed by the seventh-generation Kyoto landscape artist Jihei Ogawa and combines Momoyama and early Edo period influences. In October 2005 the garden was designated as a place of scenic beauty by Minato Ward.

6 STRIPED HOUSE MUSEUM OF ART

Heading briefly south from International House, then turning right and following the road as it bends northward, one comes in a few minutes to the **Striped House Museum of Art**, which is devoted to avant-garde sculpture. The museum derives its name from the striped effect of its facade, and it occupies the basement and three floors of the building. There is also an excellent bookstore in the museum. (It is open from 11:00 a.m. to 6:30 p.m., except on Sundays and national holidays; admission is without charge.) .

7 ROPPONGI HILLS

Backtracking about 50 yards south from the Striped House, one will see on the opposite side of the road the Tsutuya Bookstore, at the foot of a wide avenue that leads west to the Roppongi Hills complex. **Roppongi Hills** was the first of two huge urban redevelopment projects to revitalize this part of Tokyo, the other being Tokyo Midtown. While before Roppongi had been a watering hole that attracted young Japanese adults, foreign expatriates, and foreign businesspeople out for a night on the town, it now reaches a wider portion of the Japanese population as well as foreigners. Once a drab area by day that came to life in the evenings, it now throbs with even more visitors both by day and night. This change came about in 2003 when Minoru Mori, the head of the Mori Building Company, opened the spectacular new complex at one end of the Roppongi area. At a cost of $2.5 billion, Minoru Mori gambled that he could create a venue that would draw more people than even Tokyo's Disneyland could attract—and right in the middle of Tokyo rather than at its distant outskirts, where Disneyland is located.

Did Mr. Mori's gamble pay off? Well, in the first six months after the complex opened, some 26 million thronged the Roppongi Hills buildings and grounds. Today, it still attracts hordes of visitors. What is it that attracts so many? Spreading over 29 acres (11.6 hectares), it is slightly larger than Rockefeller

Louise Bourgeois's giant Maman Spider *sculpture lurks outside the entrance to Mori Tower.*

Center in New York City. It proffers so many attractions that the average visitor is said to spend the equivalent of $106 on a visit. There are offerings aplenty—some 220 shops, boutiques, restaurants, cafés, and bars; a nine-screen multiplex cinema, a Japanese garden and pond, the 380-room luxury **Grand Hyatt Hotel**, the **Mori Art Museum** atop the 52nd and 53rd floors of the **Mori Tower**, **Asahi TV**'s 800,000-square-foot broadcasting center, 840 units of apartments, an open plaza for performances, and a glass-enclosed **Tokyo City View observation deck** atop the Mori Tower—a true "city within a city." The observation deck, at more than 800 feet (250 meters) above the ground, offers panoramic views of the city that can stretch on a clear day as far as Mt. Fuji. It is open late into the evening for stunning nightscapes (open 10:00 a.m. to 11:00 p.m. daily, but until 1:00 a.m. on Fridays and Saturdays; fee ¥1,500).

There is a 100-foot (30-meter)-high entry pavilion at the base of the **Mori Office Tower** that leads into a 60-foot (18-meter)-tall glass center with a continuous spiral staircase rising to the upper floors, where a bridge 70 feet (21 meters) long leads into the office tower. Here high-speed elevators quietly lift one to 52nd floor and the **Mori Art Museum**, with nine galleries of 35,000 square feet (3,150 square meters) each, where changing exhibitions are mounted on this and the 53rd floor; the upper level is reached by an escalator. (Open from 10:00 a.m. to 10:00 p.m., Tuesdays to 5:00 p.m.. Entry fee varies with the exhibition.) Outside the entrance to the Mori Tower, near the **Roku-Roku Plaza** area, is Louise Bourgeois's striking giant sculpture of a spider, **Maman Spider**. It's an eerie sight that wouldn't be out of place scurrying around the shadows in Tolkien's Mordor.

8 **PRINCE ARISUGAWA MEMORIAL PARK**
Leaving Roppongi Hills for Roppongi Station (accessed most easily via the subway entrance in the basement of the Roku-Roku Plaza, in front of Mori Tower's main entrance), one can take the Hibiya Line one stop to Hiroo Station, where a turn to the left at the main intersection above ground brings one to the **Prince Arisugawa Memorial Park**. Alternatively, one can walk from Roppongi Hills, taking the road that runs south from the complex's western side and following it for about a half-mile to Arisugawa's northern end. The prince was a military leader at the

time of the overthrow of the Tokugawa shogun in 1868, and he later made his mark as a statesman. His lovely garden, on a rise overlooking a pond, with water-courses and bridges, is a period garden of the late Edo era and was donated to the city in 1934. Of historical note, but not quite worth a visit, is the rebuilt **Zenpuku-ji Temple** a few streets beyond the park. From 1859 to 1870 the temple buildings served as the diplomatic mission of the United States to Japan under Townsend Harris and his successors. A 1936 memorial stone placed by the America-Japan Society was removed during World War II, but it has now been reinstated, indicating that: "On this spot Townsend Harris opened the first American legation in Japan, July 7, 1859."

The temple is claimed to have been founded by the great Japanese priest Kobo Daishi (Kukai) in the early 800s, but it has been destroyed by fire on numerous occasions. One such occasion occurred in the 1860s when some fanatical imperial adherents, desiring to restore the emperor to power and expel the Western "barbarians," burned down buildings of the temple. Matters were further complicated when Townsend Harris's interpreter, the young Dutchman Henry Heusken, was killed one evening by anti-foreign samurai. Heusken was not permitted burial in the Zenpuku-ji Temple cemetery, since the temple was within the radius forbidden for burial of those not favored by the shoguns. He was thus buried in the Korin-ji Temple cemetery to the south of Prince Arisugawa Memorial Park. Curiously enough, even Fukuzawa Yukichi, the founder of Keio University, was also denied burial here at his family temple on his death in 1901, and he and his wife were also buried in Korin-ji, since Meiji officials considered him too advanced in his ideas. In 1977 Yukichi's and his wife's remains were reinterred at the Zenpuku-ji. The present temple structures are post-1945 buildings, though the replacement for the main hall is a very ancient temple building that was brought from Osaka to replace the main hall that was destroyed in wartime. Only the memorial stone remains to mark the first American presence in Tokyo.

> ### *GETTING THERE*
> This walk begins at Nogizaka Station on the Chiyoda subway line.

Walking Tour 14

DAIKANYAMA, EBISU AND MEGURO

Fashionable Living, a Beer Museum, a Nature Preserve with an Art Deco Villa, and Buddha's Early Disciples

1. **Daikanyama**
2. **Yebisu Garden Place**
3. **Institute for Nature Study**
4. **Four Temples, Buddha's Early Disciples, and the Great Priest Ennin**

Today, the **Daikanyama**, **Meguro**, and **Ebisu** areas of central Tokyo are considered among the most fashionably modern parts of the city, places where the rents are exorbitant and the cafés and restaurants are stylish and chic. But it doesn't take much peeking behind the modern façade of these areas to discover numerous remnants of both Edo- and Meiji-era Tokyo. This tour will pay visits to all three of these areas, beginning at Ebisu Station, which lies within easy walking distance of two of them.

1 DAIKANYAMA

To the west of the station along Komazawa-dori, one arrives in ten minutes by foot (or more quickly by taxi) at **Daikanyama**, an upscale residential and shopping center for the well-to-do of Tokyo, a place with a most delightful small square at its center. This suburban setting enjoys two of the architectural works by Maki Fumihiko, one being Hillside Terrace along tree-shaded Kyu-yamate-dori, with its offices, shops, and residences, a project that he realized over a period of two decades. Adjacent is his modern **Danish Embassy**, which has received architectural acclaim. The embassy is one of many in the area, which goes some way to explaining the profusion of well-heeled expats living here as well the cosmopolitan feel of Daikanyama's fashionable cafés and restaurants. A village atmosphere marks this expensive suburban enclave, where the **Hillside Gallery** offers contemporary art while expensive restaurants, luxury shops, and cafés enrich the ambiance of this small corner of the larger city. Just a few hundred yards south of Daikanayama is the equally expensive but more bohemian **Naka-Meguro** area, home to numerous hip fashion and design boutiques and small cafés and bars.

2 YEBISU GARDEN PLACE

Returning to Ebisu Station on the Yamanote Line, the moving Skywalk walkway takes but five minutes to bring one to **Yebisu Garden Place**. While the headquarters of the **Sapporo Beer Company** remains here at the Garden Place, its one-time brewery has been leveled in order to create an office, cultural, shopping, and hotel center with the 39-story **Yebisu Tower**, whose restaurants on the 38th and 39th floors offer not only a culinary respite but an overview of this portion of Tokyo. The **Mitsukoshi Department Store** has one of its branch shops here as does the **Westin Hotel** chain, but the brewing past of Ebisu is still in evidence in the **Yebisu Beer Museum** (Yebisu Biiru Kinenkan). While the museum

Yebisu Garden Place, in Ebisu

does not make beer, it thoroughly explores the art, craft, and science of beer making through interactive displays (in Japanese), and one can have a draft Sapporo beer at the end for a modest fee (open Tuesday through Sunday from 11:00 a.m. to 7:00 p.m.) The fee for the Yebisu tour is ¥500. This 40-minute guided tour includes tasting two kinds of beer. Behind the museum is another cultural attraction in the **Tokyo Metropolitan Museum of Photography** (Tokyo-to Shashin Bijutsukan), where changing exhibits by world-class photographers can be enjoyed. (Open from 10:00 a.m. to 6:00 p.m. Tuesday through Sunday but open until 8:00 p.m. on Thursday and Friday. Admission fees vary with each exhibition.)

3 INSTITUTE FOR NATURE STUDY

After crossing over the Yamanote rail tracks on the main street that runs east-west on the south side of Yebisu Garden Place, one turns left at the end of the street and walks south for almost a half-mile until reaching Meguro Station. From the southern end of the station area, turn left (east) along Meguro-dori, approaching and then passing under the overhead Shuto Expressway. This brings one in a few minutes to the **Tokyo Metropolitan Teien Art Museum** (Tokyo-to Teien Bijutsukan) and the **Institute for Nature Study**, with an entrance one street beyond the expressway. The museum was the one-time home of Prince Yasuhiko Asaka, the uncle of Emperor Hirohito and husband of the Emperor Meiji's eighth daughter, Princess Nobuko. (The prince served as the military general in charge of troops at the time of the Nanking Massacre in China.) The villa and its grounds were taken over by the government after World War II, and the villa opened to the public as a museum in 1983. The villa reflects the prince's residency for three years in Paris in the 1920s. It is not surprising, therefore, that this 1933 building was designed by Henri Rapin, an associate of René Lalique, in the Art Deco style that was popular in France in the mid-1920s. Art Deco touches can be found in various aspects of the villa, including the opaque glass doors by René Lalique in the entryway. As a museum, the villa displays temporary exhibitions on loan from other institutions. (It is open from 10:00 a.m. to 6:00 p.m. but closed on the second and fourth Wednesday of the month and December 28 to January 4. Entry fees to exhibitions vary, but to visit the garden area costs ¥200.) The landscaped grounds with a Japanese garden, pond, and large tea ceremony house are open to the public, as are a public tearoom and rest rooms.

The **Institute for Nature Study** adjacent to the villa is a 49.5-acre (19.8-hectare) wilderness that attempts to preserve the condition of the ancient Musashi Plain, which once lay to the west of Edo/Tokyo. The former estate of the Matsudaira daimyo of Takamatsu (from the mid-1600s to 1868) was taken over by the military for a munitions dump in 1868 and ceded to the Imperial Household in 1918. It became a public park in 1949 after the adjacent Art Deco villa had served as the prime minister's home for a few years after World War II. One can wander through overgrown meadowland and by swamps and ponds kept as they would have been before Edo was settled. The park contains 160 different varieties of trees, and the plants of the meadow and the aquatic flora recall those centuries when the Tokyo area was still virgin territory. (Open May through August from 9:00 a.m. to 5:00 p.m. and 9:00 to 4:30 p.m. the rest of the year. The park is closed on Mondays, from December 28 through January 4, and the day after national holidays. Admission is ¥300.) Since 1962, this reserve has belonged to the National Science Museum.

4 FOUR TEMPLES, BUDDHA'S EARLY DISCIPLES, AND THE GREAT PRIEST ENNIN

Beyond the Meguro Station area, there are a few temples of interest nearby. (In the distance to the west is the **Meguro Emperor** hotel.) Returning to the station area along Meguro-dori, the JR railway tracks should be crossed by means of the roadway bridge, and at the Sakura Bank building the narrow street to the left should be taken instead of following the main road to the right. After a quick right turn, the side street leads 100 yards to the small **Daien-ji Temple**, which was founded in 1630 but disappeared in the "Nuisance Fire" of 1772. Rebuilt in the 1840s, the temple is known for its 500 images of the *rakan*, the principal disciples of the Buddha. These were created as an offering to the spirits of those who died in the fire more than three decades earlier. Within the temple grounds, the sculptures are to the left against a wall, a series of *rakan* 11 to 12 rows high, carved in relief on stone. All are seated, but they differ in their stances and the implements they hold as well as in their individualized faces. Some look amused, some appear to be astonished, while others show disbelief or skepticism. In the foreground is a little pond with a fairly large Buddha on the left

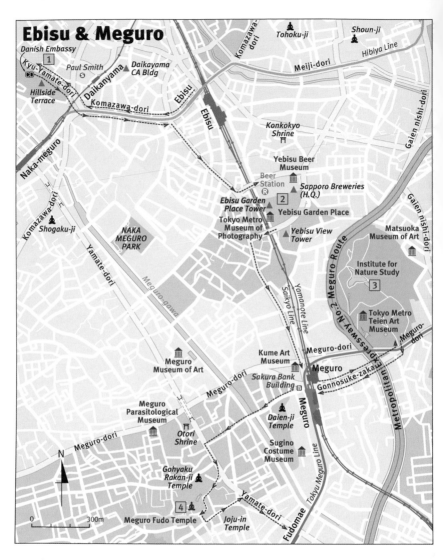

Ebisu & Meguro

seated on a lotus flower with a *rakan* on a lotus on either side. Numerous free-standing *rakan* have halos and extended ears, which denote their noble status. One is seated on an elephant on the right, while another is astride a monster on the left.

There are another 500 *rakan* not too far distant, and they can be seen by continuing along the street that brought you to Daien-ji until it comes to an end a quarter mile or so later at Yamate-dori. A turn to the left here brings one at the second street to the right to the **Gohyaku Rakan-ji.** This second temple of the 500 *rakan* is comparatively modern, for its main hall dates only from 1938. Its present site marks the relocation of a temple that was founded in the 17th century. These *rakan* were created by a monk named Shoun, who carved them, begging, as a monk traditionally did, for his sustenance. Fortunately the exceedingly religious mother of the fifth shogun, Tsunayoshi, learned in the late 1600s of his efforts to create the *rakan* images, and she prevailed upon her son to provide land for

Shoun to build a temple. Finishing 536 *rakan*, he then carved an image of Sakyamuni, the Indian prince who became the Buddha, and sat the *rakan* about him listening to him preach. The temple building to house the images came into being after Shoun's death, and the temple led a peripatetic life before settling in Meguro in 1908. The temple's ultimate salvation came from an unexpected quarter when it was befriended by a geisha who had married a premier of Japan at the turn of the 1900s. Becoming a nun after a life of various vicissitudes, she determined to see that the images were preserved. Many years after her death, and because of her efforts, a new hall was finally built in 1981 to house the *rakan* and the image of Sakyamuni. Additional images carved by Shoun, including one of himself seated in a chair, are here preserved. Some 300 of the original *rakan* have survived the various moves of the temple, and they still sit, enthralled by the sermon being preached to them by Sakyamuni. (The temple is open from 9:00 a.m. to 5:00 p.m. daily, entry ¥300.)

Adjacent to the Gohyaku Rakan-ji Temple, and on the hill above it, is the much larger **Ryusen-ji** or **Meguro Fudo Temple**. Legend relates that in 858 the great priest Ennin (794–864) carved an image of Fudo that he had envisioned in a dream and gave it to the village of Meguro. Ennin is said to have returned 50 years later to create a temple to Fudo, and the wooden figure he had carved became its main image. Today, as in the past, a pond stands before the temple, and a stream of water pours out of the mouth of two bronze dragons. The waterfall and the pond are a source of religious purification for those who brave its waters, particularly those hardy souls who stand beneath the stream in mid-winter. Above the pond is a small hall that originally housed the Fudo image before the post-World War II Hondo (Main Hall) was constructed. This latter hall not only holds the Fudo image, but it has a dragon painted on the ceiling by Ryushi Kawabata.

Above and behind the temple is the **grave of Aoki Konyo**, the instructor of Maeno Ryotaku, who first translated the Dutch volume on anatomy in the late 1700s. He was known by the nickname of Doctor Potato, since he introduced the sweet potato to the Japanese diet. The other grave of interest is located to the left of the temple gate, and it has a tombstone to a pair of blighted lovers whose story has become one of the staples of the theater. Gonpachi

One of the 500 rakan images at Daien-ji Temple

Shirai, the man in the tale, turned to robbery and murder to fund his visits to the courtesan he had fallen in love with in the licensed quarters. Caught, he was executed for his crimes and his body buried at this temple. When Komurasaki, his beloved, learned of his death, she fled the licensed quarters in order to kill herself over Gonpachi's grave. They are both buried here under a stone representing two birds who have become one in an embrace.

One street to the southeast there is another temple associated with Ennin. On his return to Ryusen-ji, he also carved an image of Yakushi for the **Joju-in Temple**. Yakushi is the Buddhist deity of healing, and Ennin always carried this image with him. On one occasion when he was returning from China, his ship was endangered by a storm, so he cast his Yakushi image into the sea. The waters calmed, and the ship was brought safely back to Japan. The image he then carved represented Yakushi on the back of an octopus in the sea, and it remains the main image of the **Tako (Octopus) Yakushi Temple**. Ennin endowed the image with the power of creating magic stones to cure disease, and believers still come to obtain the magical stones for cures for diseases and the removal of warts.

From here one can retrace one's steps to Meguro Station or walk east from Jojo-in to Yamate-dori, then turn right and follow Yamate-dori southeast to Fudomae Station on the Tokyu Meguro Line, where a train can be taken one stop to Meguro.

GETTING THERE

This tour starts at Ebisu Station, which is served by the Hibiya subway lines and the JR Yamanote Line.

Walking Tour 15

SHINAGAWA

An Ambassador Ambushed, the Finale to the 47 Ronin, a Bauhaus Museum, and a Garden Beautiful from Any Angle

1. **Sengaku-ji Temple**
2. **Tozen-ji Temple**
3. **Happo-en Garden**
4. **Hatakeyama Kinenkan Museum**
5. **Prince Takeda Mansion**
6. **Takanawa-mon Checkpoint on the Tokaido Road**
7. **Hara Museum of Contemporary Art (diversion)**

At first glance **Shinagawa** seems to offer nothing more than the hotels and con-glomeration of office buildings for which it is most known. For many expats in Tokyo, the chief reason for a visit is to catch the bus that heads to the outskirts of Shinagawa for Tokyo's main immigration office, where visas are granted and renewed. Yet among the hotels and offices, Shinagawa offers much worth exploring. The area retains many no-table historical sites, including one that brings us to the conclusion of the tale of the 47 Ronin that has been a recurring theme in these walks and has so delighted Bunraku and Kabuki aficionados. Here too, at the end of the Tokaido Road, was the gate through which the daimyo would have to pass to enter Edo, and which served as a checkpoint and safeguard of the shogun's power. Among the area's numerous temples, the Tozen-ji is asso-ciated with a major diplomatic incident toward the end of the shoguns' time, when anti-West-ern sentiment was rife among some of the shogun's supporters. Shinegawa also shelters the Happo-en Garden, a delightful example of Japanese landscape gardening.

1 SENGAKU-JI TEMPLE
This walk commences at Sengaku-ji Station.

Leaving the station from exit 2, one is at the foot of Isaraga-zaka, a road that goes up a slight rise (cross to the south side of the street at the traffic light). If one continues straight ahead and does not follow the road as it turns to the right, one arrives at the entrance to the **Sengaku-ji Temple**. The Sengaku-ji Temple of 1612 is famed for its association with the historic tale of the 47 Ronin, the popular story and Bunraku and Kabuki play (*Chushingura*) mentioned previously.

Oishi Yoshio, leader of the 47 Ronin

The final resting place of the 47 Ronin. Their former master, Lord Asano, is also buried nearby.

Here in the graveyard on his family temple grounds is buried Lord Asano, the unfortunate daimyo who was badly instructed by Lord Kira in shogun court etiquette and then scorned by Kira. This led to Asano drawing his sword to attack his spiteful teacher, a capital offense, since it occurred within the castle walls Condemned to perform seppuku, ceremonial suicide, the hapless Asano was interred at the Sengaku-ji. His loyal retainers, having dis guised their intentions and plotted revenge, killed Lord Kira on a snowy night on December 14, 1702, in Kira's mansion on the east bank of the Sumida River. Parading Kira's head through Edo, they placed it on the grave of Lord Asano to avenge his death. Remanded to the custody of the shogun's lords, the 47 were treated with respect for their loyalty to their former master. The shogun was in a quandary: the retainers had done what samurai ethics demanded, but they had assassinated a member of the shogun's court. Ordered to commit seppuku on February 4, 1703, the 47, ranging from 15 years of age (the son of Oishi Kuranosuke, their leader) to 77, they are buried in the same temple grounds as Lord Asano.

The temple (open without charge from 7:00 a.m. to 6:00 p.m., closing one hour early from October through March) is approached through a small gate with a guardhouse. Beyond the gate is a **statue of Oishi**, the leader of the ronin, holding in his hands a scroll on which is inscribed the oath that the 47 retainers took to avenge their master's death. Next comes the 1836 San-mon two-story gate. The temple Hondo (Main Hall) lies straight ahead, while a museum to the 47 Ronin is on the left. Taking the path to the left of the museum, on the right is the well in which the ronin washed Lord Kira's head before presenting it to the grave of Lord Asano. A set of steps leads up to the graves, and then a small building selling incense sticks to be burned at the graves is passed. On the right, past the small building, is the grave of Lord Asano's wife, while beyond is **Lord Asano's grave**. A short distance beyond and up a few steps brings one to the **graves of the faithful ronin**. Incense is always burning before the graves, placed there by those who continue to honor these men. Oishi is buried at the rear to the far right, and there is a roof over **Oishi's grave**, while his son's grave is in the far left corner, the burials having taken place in order of their precedence in serving Lord Asano. There are times when the area of the graves is almost obscured by the many burning incense sticks

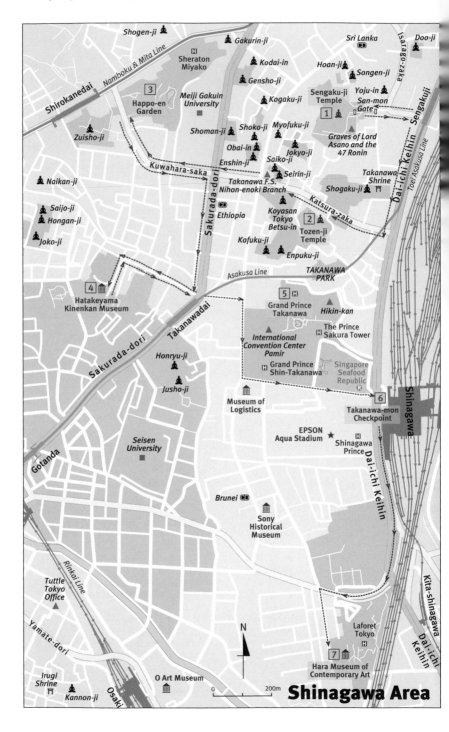

Shogen-ji

Gakurin-ji

Kodai-in

Sheraton
Miyako

Gensho-ji

Sri Lanka

Hoan-ji

Doo-ji

Songen-ji

Shirokanedai

Namboku & Mita Line

3

Happo-en
Garden

Meiji Gakuin
University

Kogaku-ji

Sengaku-ji
Temple

Yoju-in

San-mon
Gate

1

Sengakuji

Isarago-zaka

Zuisho-ji

Shoman-ji

Shoko-ji

Myofuku-ji

Obai-in

Jokyo-ji

Graves of Lord
Asano and the
47 Ronin

Takanawa
Shrine

Dai-ichi Keihin

Toei Asakusa Line

Enshin-ji

Saiko-ji

Seirin-ji

Naikan-ji

Kuwahara-saka

Takanawa F.S.
Nihon-enoki Branch

Shogaku-ji

Saijo-ji

Hongan-ji

Ethiopia

Koyasan
Tokyo
Betsu-in

Katsura-zaka

Joko-ji

Sakurada-dori

2

Kofuku-ji

Tozen-ji
Temple

Enpuku-ji

4

Hatakeyama
Kinenkan Museum

Asakusa Line

TAKANAWA
PARK

5

Grand Prince
Takanawa

Hikin-kan

Sakurada-dori

Takanawadai

Honryu-ji

International
Convention Center
Pamir

The Prince
Sakura Tower

Jusho-ji

Grand Prince
Shin-Takanawa

Singapore
Seafood
Republic

6

Shinagawa

Museum of
Logistics

Takanawa-mon
Checkpoint

Gotanda

Seisen
University

EPSON
Aqua Stadium

Shinagawa
Prince

Dai-ichi Keihin

Brunei

Rinkai Line

Sony
Historical
Museum

Tuttle
Tokyo
Office

Kita-shinagawa

Yamate-dori

N

Laforet
Tokyo

Dai-ichi Keihin

Irugi
Shrine

Kannon-ji

Osaki

O Art Museum

0   200m

7

Hara Museum of
Contemporary Art

Shinagawa Area

placed at each one by visitors.

Returning to the **Gishi-kan, the Hall of the Loyal Retainers**, one must purchase an entry ticket before visiting the building that holds the personal effects of the 47 Ronin (open from 9:00 a.m. to 4:30 p.m.). On the first floor are clothing, armor, helmets, swords, and other materials. Additional personal effects are displayed on the second floor, along with an image of Oishi and his son. Two cases on the side walls contain images of the 47 men as well as bows and arrows, pikes, drums, and musical instruments. In front of the memorial hall is a plum tree planted in memory of Oishi's 15-year-old son. Most of the buildings of the temple were destroyed in the 1945 air raids, and thus the reconstructed Hondo is not of the greatest interest. The two-story gate of 1836 is one of the few early structures remaining.

2 TOZEN-JI TEMPLE

The **Tozen-ji Temple** can be reached by returning to Sengaku-ji Station and following the heavily traveled Dai-Ichi Keihin Highway south until the juncture with Katsura-zaka, the first major roadway on the right. One should then follow Katsura-zaka west until the second street to the left, which leads to the temple. From 1859 to 1873, the Tozen-ji was assigned to the British legation, since it was sufficiently far from the center of Edo to keep the Western barbarians at a proper distance from the shogun, as was true of the American legation in the Zenpuku-ji. Sir Rutherford Alcock was the head of the legation in 1861 when 14 swordsmen attacked the legation staff. One legation attaché was wounded by a sword cut, while the visiting British consul from Nagasaki shot one attacker before being slashed on the forehead by another attacker. Edo paid a compensation for the injuries sustained, but the shogun's government was having trouble restraining some of its more rabid anti-Western allies. The building at the rear of the Zen temple held the legation, and the sword marks and the bullet holes are still visible on the pillars of the entrance to the hall. The three-century-old garden and the legation building can be visited by requesting permission at the temple. The temple itself now has modern buildings and a recent three-story pagoda, and the Tozen-ji remains an historic curiosity rather than an important site to be visited.

The Happo-en Garden is a wonderful example of Japanese landscaping.

③ HAPPO-EN GARDEN

A delightful garden respite can be found by continuing along Katsura-zaka as it crosses Sakurada-dori and becomes Kuwahara-zaka, bending north (to the right) and leading past a large elementary school to the main entrance the **Happo-en Garden**. "Beautiful from any Angle" is the meaning of its name. In the 17th century an advisor to the shogun maintained his estate here. With time his garden disintegrated, but it was restored to its lovely state once more by a 20th-century financier. It offers a Japanese-style garden with a pond, a Japanese-style restaurant, and a teahouse (which is open from 11:00 a.m. to 5:00 p.m. for a fee). Renowned for its beauty, especially when the cherry blossoms bathe the garden in pink from late March to early April and the azaleas bloom in summer, it is also a popular site for well-to-do weddings. Many people who wed elsewhere come to the park in traditional wedding clothing just to avail themselves of its backdrop for additional wedding photographs.

④ HATAKEYAMA KINENKAN MUSEUM

Returning from Happo-en along Kuwahara-zaka, one turns right at the intersection with Sakurada-dori and follows that avenue until it starts to bend to the southwest upon reaching **Takanawadai Station**. From here, one should leave Sakurada-dori on the street to one's right (leading west), and follow that street to the until the second left-hand turning, which leads to the **Hatakeyama Kinenkan Museum**. The estate on the wooded hill where the museum sits once belonged to the daimyo of Satsuma (Kyushu), and it still retains its noted garden, which can, unfortunately, only be observed from the outside. The museum is situated five minutes from the station. The Hatakeyama Museum is in a ferroconcrete building, and it possesses a very fine collection of Japanese paintings by the great artists of Japan's past as well as ceramics and lacquerware from the founding of Kyoto (794) to later centuries. Noh robes and Chinese and Korean artistic wares form another portion of the collection. The exhibitions of the museum's treasures are changed four times a year. (Between April and September the museum is open from 10:00 a.m. to 5:00 p.m., but it closes at 4:30 p.m. during the other months of the year. It is closed Mondays and for the year-end holidays, entry ¥500.)

⑤ PRINCE TAKEDA MANSION

Returning to Takanawadai Station, a walk east after crossing Sakurada-dori brings one to the grounds of the **Grand Prince Hotel Takanawa**, the former site of three imperial palaces that has now become a hotel center. In 1912 Katayama Tokuma, the architect for the Akasaka Palace, and Kozahiro Kigo were retained by members of the imperial court as architects. Here they created mansions in a French style for Prince Takeda and for Prince Kitashira, while the third mansion for Prince Asaka was in traditional Japanese style. Prince Takeda's property was noted for its lovely garden. After World War II, the properties were confiscated and placed on the market. The president of the Seibu rail system purchased the land and buildings in order to create the Grand Prince Hotel Takanawa in 1953 and the Grand Prince Hotel New Takanawa in 1983. The **mansion of Prince Takeda** (now renamed Kihin-kan) has been retained next to the 1953 hotel, and it is used for special events such as private banquets and weddings.

⑥ TAKANAWA-MON CHECKPOINT ON THE TOKAIDO ROAD

From the hotel grounds, continue east to Shinagawa Station, crossing the Dai-Ichi Keihin Highway again. A memorial stone before the station recalls the first train that came from Yokohama in 1872, but no stone or marker recalls the bustling licensed district that once operated here for 260 years, when the area lay just before the last barrier on the Tokaido Road before the entrance to Edo. The district is bustling now, with many hotels, offices, and shops, but it lacks the questionable character of the past.

Back at the highway it is difficult to realize that this broad, main north-south road to Yokohama was once the old Tokaido Road, which ran along the shore of Tokyo Bay, now filled in to form the railroad right-of-way and the port of Tokyo. On the raised land to the west were the mansions of the daimyo and later of the important figures of the Meiji government. Below, along the shore in Tokugawa days, were the houses of the commoners. It was in Meiji times and later that the filling in of the bay pushed the waterfront to the east. Across the bay were four small islands that in 1853–1854 saw some hurriedly constructed forts built to protect Edo against possible attack by the Western "barbarians." The appearance of Commodore Matthew C. Perry and the U.S. Navy ships that sailed into Japanese waters to demand the opening of the country to commercial intercourse had caused a panic in Edo. One such fort, no longer extant, was built at Shinagawa, roughly in the area east of the Sengaku-ji.

Just to the north of the subway station was once the Takanawa-mon, the most important gate to Edo and the checkpoint on the Tokaido where the rule of "no guns in, no women out" kept the daimyo from plotting against the shogun and his government. High walls on either side of the gate between the waterfront and the hills made for an effective barrier at this natural bottleneck. (Ota Dokan had taken advantage of the narrow passageway in the 1400s by building a castle here.) Obtaining clearance to pass through the gate could often take days, since the government took no chance of permitting interlopers into the capital. Today a mound on the north side of the Dai-Ichi Keihin Highway is all that remains to remind one of this last obstacle, the gate to Edo on the seashore and the last of the 53 stages of the Tokaido. Ieyasu's harbor (Minato) was located here when the bay came up to the highway.

Between the outer gate to Edo and the area to the south (Shinagawa) was a sector to serve the traveler on the Tokaido. There were inns of varying quality, and, as at all 53 stages, there were brothels to serve the passing travelers, a licensed quarter that did not have the reputation or esteem enjoyed by Yoshiwara to the north of Edo. Nonetheless it was a successful red-light district, patronized by samurai and priests. After all there were 3,000 novice priests not too far distant at the Zojo-ji, and Buddhism did not always demand celibacy of its monks or priests. The shoguns tried to restrict such activities by limiting inns to "two rice serving girls" in 1718, then permitting five such "rice servers" 50 years later. If one goes by the reported number of 1,358 "rice servers" at Shinagawa inns in 1843, either the road was overcrowded with inns or the number of "servers" at each establishment had increased drastically. Be that as it may, the advent of the railroad in 1872 was to see an economic decline for the inns, and the last stage of the Tokaido was to become no more than a memory.

From here, one may conclude this walk and catch a Yamanote Line train at Shinagawa Station for return to central Tokyo or make a diversion to an art museum not far away.

7 HARA MUSEUM OF CONTEMPORARY ART (DIVERSION)

Although the walk to the museum takes just 15 minutes, the route can be confusing, so it is best to hail a taxi. Then one can return on foot to Shinagawa Station if one so desires. The **Hara Museum of Contemporary Art** (Hara Bijutsukan) displays changing exhibitions of contemporary art, but perhaps of most interest is the Hara family's 1938 Bauhaus-designed home, in which the art is housed. An addition designed by Arata Isozaki houses the **Café d'Art**, where refreshments can be obtained. In warm weather, refreshments can be enjoyed in the garden in front of the café, amid modern sculpture. (The museum is open from 11:00 a.m. to 5:00 p.m. but remains open to 8:00 p.m. on Wednesdays; entry ¥1,000. It is closed on Mondays and for several weeks from late December to mid-January.) From the Hara Museum, one can walk back to Shinagawa Station, as noted, or ask the museum to call a taxi.

GETTING THERE

This walk begins at Sengaku-ji Station, which is served by the Keikyu Main Line and the Toei Asakusa subway line.

Walking Tour 16

ODAIBA
The City in the Sea, a Ferris Wheel, Classic Cars, Science Centers, Beaches, Hot Springs, and Maritime Displays

In the early 1600s, Tokugawa Ieyasu had a portion of the hills of the High City leveled in order to fill in the arms of Edo Bay, which lay below his castle. This helped to create the Low City (Shitamachi) where the plebeians would live who could serve the daimyo of Ieyasu's new capital. No one at that time could have conceived of the idea that such landfill operations would continue for another 400 years. Nonetheless, bit by bit, the arms of Tokyo Bay and areas of the bay itself were to become landfills as Tokyo expanded ever farther into the waters of the bay.

In 1852–1853 some of the islands at the top of the bay near the Sumida River were fortified under the fears that American warships might attack the capital, since the United States insisted that Japan open itself to full commercial intercourse with the world beyond its islands. The situation did calm down, and the incipient fortresses remained, albeit abandoned, as the Meiji government came into power in 1868. Tokyo's ever increasing population from early 1600 on had

Odaiba's Statue of Liberty replica with the Rainbow Bridge in the background

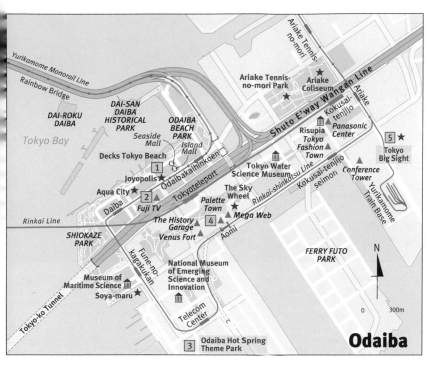

Odaiba

forced the government to reclaim low-lying lands, first in Ieyasu's day in the region below Kanda and in the swampy area that was to become Nihombashi. Later it was in Tsukiji and eventually in the Shimbashi and Shinagawa region that the waters were pushed ever farther away from the Tokaido road to the south of the city.

Finally, toward the end of the 20th century, the decision was made to create the **Rinkai Fukutoshin**, the "Ocean-Front, Sub-City Center" at the head of Tokyo Bay. Landfill began to create a 1,000-acre island that was to be connected with the heart of the city in 1993 by means of a new bridge to be called **Rainbow Bridge**, which could handle train, automobile, and pedestrian traffic. The financial crises of the 1990s slowed the project of creating the "New City," but by the turn of the 2000s new offices, apartment buildings, museums, shopping centers, restaurants, and places of amusement on the new island of **Odaiba** were under construction. A new monorail system was also created, starting at Shimbashi and serving ten stations along its new route by means of Rainbow Bridge. In addition, ferries from the Hinode Pier outside

of Shimbashi, as well as bus connections, would bring the thousands of amusement seekers who would patronize the new island with its various divertissements. (An addition to the Yurakacho subway line would also reach the island, where it connected with another line on Odaiba proper.) Suddenly, Odaiba became a fashionable place, where denizens of Tokyo could spend a pleasant evening or, even better, a happy weekend–for it is most crowded on weekends, when much of Tokyo can enjoy this "resort in the sea" offering sandy beaches in addition to an old-fashioned *sento* or bathhouse such as their forbearers enjoyed.

1 TOKYO BEACH AND JOYOPOLIS

When the Yurikamome monorail leaves its Shimbashi terminal, where this walk begins, its first stop on Odaiba after crossing the Rainbow Bridge is at the Odaiba Kaihin Koen Station. On exiting the station, the **Decks Tokyo Beach** building lies opposite, the first intimation one is entering a world that specializes in shops of all kinds: expensive boutiques as well as restaurants for seekers after fast foods or fine foods. Among other attractions,

The Fuji TV Building, an Odaiba landmark

this five-story seaside mall offers the young at heart the thrills of **Joyopolis**, a three-floor center with virtual reality technology and other more traditional amusements (open from 10:00 a.m. to 11 p.m.; ¥500 adult admission and separate fees for each attraction). "Decks Tokyo Beach" might see a misnomer—but the fact is that there is a boardwalk from which manmade beaches and grassy areas have been created, where one can relax and enjoy the view of Rainbow Bridge. If one five-story mall were not enough, there is also the **Seaside Mall** and the **Island Mall**. The latter, with its many Chinese restaurants offering a Hong Kong ambience, is meant to bring to mind Hong Kong itself.

2 FUJI TV, SCIENCE AND THE STATUE OF LIBERTY

The second stop on the island is Odaiba Station, where the four floors of **Aqua City** proffer its own combination of shops, restaurants, cinemas, and cafés. Between the first and second station, the **Fuji Television Building** is another quirk of modern Tokyo. In the 1960s, the city built Tokyo Tower, which is taller than the Eiffel Tower in Paris, which it resembles. Now another foreign attraction stands before the Fuji Building—a **copy of the Statue of Liberty** in New York City Harbor. Standing 150 feet (45 meters) tall, which is one-fourth the size of the New York City statue, it does come up taller than the copy on one of the bridges over the Seine in Paris.

(Poor Frédéric-Auguste Barthodli—not only is his Statue of Liberty now gracing what is basically an amusement park, but copies of this copy are often seen as decoration outside various love hotels throughout Japan, symbolizing another form of liberty.) The major attraction of the Fuji Building is its fifth-floor **"Studio Promenade,"** where one can watch television programs being recorded (open Tuesdays through Sundays from 10:00 a.m. to 6:00 p.m.). The building consists of two towers with a metal sphere high up that is connected to both buildings. Within, on the 24th floor are restaurants with a view over the bay and the city, while an observation deck is located on the 25th floor.

Between station number two (Odaiba) and station number three (Telecom Center) is the **Museum of Maritime Science (**Fune-no-Kagakukan) in the shape of a 60,000-ton cruise ship in concrete, a maritime form appropriate for a museum of shipping and shipping lore (open Tuesday through Sunday from 10:00 a.m. to 5:00 p.m.; entry is free). The museum offers everything from model ships to interactive displays concerned with shipping and the sea. Adjacent to and part of the museum are two ships that once saw active duty: the *Soya-maru*, which served as an icebreaker, keeping shipping routes open in the northernmost areas of the Japanese islands. Farther along and closer to the Telecom Center is the **National Museum of**

Emerging Science and Innovation (Nihon Kagaku Miraikan) (open Wednesday through Monday from 10:00 a.m. to 5:00 p.m.; entry ¥600). This is another interactive museum and is concerned with the ways in which modern science and technology will enhance life in the future. Often staff on duty will explain the exhibits and can answer questions, and its five floors include all aspects of the concerns of modern science, including environmental issues. Most exhibits labels are in Japanese.

3️⃣ **TELECOMMUNICATIONS AND HOT SPRINGS**
The next stop on the monorail is at the **Telecom Center** (open from 8:00 a.m. to 10:00 p.m.; entry free), which offers exhibits on radio, cell phones, and other forms of communication and is appealing to youngsters. (This imposing building offers another example of imitation—for the center can be seen as having been inspired by the architecture of the Grande Arche de La Défense in Paris.) An observation deck is on the 21st floor (open Tuesday to Friday from 3:00 p.m. to 9:00 p.m., and from 11:00 a.m. to 9:00 p.m. on weekends; closed Mondays; entry is ¥500). The major attraction in this area is the **Odaiba Hot Spring Theme Park** (Oedo Onsen Monogatari). There was a time when the *sento*, the public bath, was the social center of towns and cities before hot water and modern plumbing were available in homes. Here people would come to wash and then relax in the hot water pools, and here in the buff they could converse with their friends and neighbors. This "theme park" attempts to revive this aspect of Edo times—where one pays a fee and receives a *yukata* (a thin robe) and a towel, stores one's clothes in a locker, bathes at faucets, and is then free to luxuriate in a hot public bath (separated by gender). There are foodstalls that also bring back the sense of old Tokyo, and sushi and noodle dishes are reminders of the simpler fare of the past. All this (from 11:00 a.m. through to 9:00 a.m. the next morning; entry ¥1,980) permits one both to relax and to enjoy an aspect of earlier Japanese life. The source for the hot water for both the indoor and outdoor pools lies some 4,600 feet (1,440 meters) below the bay, and thus this is truly a natural spa.

4️⃣ **A FERRIS WHEEL AND AUTOMOBILES**
The next stop on the monorail is **Palette Town**, another mall and amusement park with indoor and outdoor attractions. Its most noted, and obvious component, is the 377-foot (113.1-meter) **Sky Wheel**, a Ferris wheel that rotates for 16 minutes as it takes one skyward and then back to the ground (open from 10:00 a.m. to 10:00 p.m.; fee). The **Mega Web** is Toyota's contribution to the entertainment world on the island. Not only can one see a variety of Toyota cars, but it offers two test-drive courses where one can try one's skill (if one has a driver's license). Electric cars can also be test-driven. (All this is free—and from 11:00 a.m. to 9:00 p.m.) In addition a **History Garage** is a showcase for classic cars of the past. The conspicuous spender is always in mind, for **Venus Fort** offers a mock Italian city and palazzo—with all the shops and restaurants that Odaiba deems requisite. In addition, there is a concert hall for popular music.

5️⃣ **TOKYO BIG SIGHT, FASHION TOWN, AND THE PANASONIC CENTER**
Continuing on to the next location by monorail, there is **Tokyo Big Sight** (Kokusai Tenjijo), consisting of four, huge, inverted pyramids on thick "legs." This is a convention center and huge exhibition hall for trade shows. Aside from its rather peculiar form, it cannot be missed, since there is a 50-foot (15-meter) inverted, red saw sticking up from the ground in front. Opposite this center is the **Tokyo Fashion Town**, where one can shop at the Wanza Ariake Bay Mall to see the world's tallest "Shower Tree," an indoor waterfall from which water gushes from a height of 115 feet (35 meters).

The last stop on this major extravaganza to popular tastes is Ariake Station, where the **Panasonic Center** is a main attraction, an obvious showcase for the company's advanced products. It includes areas devoted to universal design and eco-friendly housing, as well as the high-tech **RiSuPia museum of mathematics and science** and an area where visitors can test out the very latest Nintendo games.

> ## GETTING THERE
> This walk begins at Odaiba Kaihin Koen Station on the Yurikamome monorail, one stop from the Shimbashi terminal of the Yurikamome Line. You can transfer to the Shimbashi terminal from JR Shimbashi Station or the Shimbashi subway station on the Ginza Line.

Walking Tour 17

SHINJUKU
A District of Skyscrapers, City Hall, a Central Shopping Area, the Red-light District, and an Imperial Garden

1. **Shinjuku Skyscraper District**
2. **Tokyo City Hall**
3. **Park Hyatt Hotel**
4. **Tokyo Opera City**
5. **Japanese Sword Museum**
6. **East Shinjuku**
7. **Hanazono Shrine**
8. **Kabukicho and Golden Gai**
9. **Shinjuku Gyoen Garden**
10. **National Noh Theater (diversion)**

Take a walk through the bustling streets of Shinjuku, and there can be no doubt that one is in the heart of present-day Tokyo. It's a fact recognized by the metropolitan government, for in 1991 it moved its headquarters from the old downtown Yurakucho district to an area that has become more the center of the city and its suburbs, as people have moved from the old central city and into the outlying districts of Tokyo to the west. *Shinjuku* means "New Lodgings," a name it received in the 1600s when the Tokugawa requirement came into effect that the daimyo had to take up residence periodically in Edo. The Koshu Kaido highway came from the mountainous region beyond Tokyo toward the Japan Sea, and, having reached the Kanto Plain, the traveler still had a distance to go to reach the Tokaido Road and the last checkpoint or barrier at Shinagawa before reaching Edo. Thus it was that the shogun permitted "new lodgings" to be set up to the west of the city in the late 1600s, since Shinjuku was one of the five *guchi* or "mouths" granting entry to Edo. Only 20 years later, in 1718, this new post town was shut down due to a disorderly situation that had occurred in a local brothel.

A 50-year hiatus ensued before the post town was permitted to reopen, and in less than a decade this least traveled of all the highways coming into Edo had 52 inns with the appropriate number of "rice serving" girls to please the sexual appetites of travelers. The New Lodgings post town could boast of having one of the six licensed quarters in Edo for sex.

The modern period for Shinjuku began with the coming of the railroad, for a new Shinjuku center developed a mile to the west of the original post town. Today 11 rail lines converge on Shinjuku, with some three and a half million commuters passing through the station daily. Aside from the trains, there are some 30 bus routes that enter the district. Shinjuku has seen its fortunes change continuously since the first trains arrived here in 1885. The 1923 earthquake led to a movement of residents from the inner city to the outer suburbs, a movement that has continued since World War II as Tokyo has grown ever more populous. This has made Shinjuku the important transportation center that it is.

In 1924 Mitsukoshi opened a department store in Shinjuku, and the increase in such shopping facilities has continued ever since. This portion of Tokyo in the 1920 and1930s also became known as the "bohemian" section of the city, a reputation it was to enhance after World War II. The air raids of 1945 destroyed much of Shinjuku, and a new center for the traditional Kabuki theater from central Tokyo was planned for the area, though the plan was never realized. The sector designated for it, Kabuki-cho was instead to become a new pleasure quarter in both the old and the new sense of that term. As a result, in the 1960s pleasure became one of the great attractions for what became known as Higashi

(East) Shinjuku as theaters, bars, restaurants, and less reputable places grew in number.

Until 1965 an eight-acre reservoir existed to the west of Shinjuku Station, and its removal was to lead to development of this area for new high-rise buildings. In the 1970s Shinjuku began to attract corporations and financial organizations, and thus a business center was added to the district's attractions. In the 1980s and 1990s Nishi (West) Shinjuku became the locus for a new group of skyscrapers that have totally changed the complexion of the area. The Tokyo City government raised its tall towers for a new City Hall here in 1991. The towers' observation floors provide an excellent view of Tokyo Bay and Mt. Fuji on clear days. West Shinjuku has broad streets in a checker-board pattern around its skyscrapers, whereas East Shinjuku has retained its narrow streets, its alleys and lanes, and thus two contrasting parts of Shinjuku now abut, separated by the numerous rail lines that run into the station.

1 SHINJUKU SKYSCRAPER DISTRICT
This tour begins at the west exit of Shinjuku Station, a sector bordered by the **Odakyu** and the **Keio Department Stores** and rail terminals. The size of the station can be realized when one takes into account its 60 exits. The **West Exit Plaza (Nishi-guchi Chikahiroba)** to the station was created in 1966 with the development of the site of the former reservoir. Its exterior of precast concrete panels was an innovation in Japan in 1971. Opposite the station and the Keio Department Store are the bus terminal and the location for taking the limousine to the airport. Just to the south are **Yodobashi** and other noted home electronics and camera stores. Whereas there were no skyscrapers in West Shinjuku in 1960, today more than 20 of them tower skyward.

West Exit Plaza faces onto Chuo-dori (Central Avenue), which leads via an underground walkway to the heart of the post-1970s district in **Keio Plaza**, an area where numerous skyscrapers have arisen over a 21-year period, several of them hotels. At the corner of Chuo-dori and Higashi-dori (East Avenue) is the 54-story **Shinjuku Center Building**, which has a free observation deck on its 53rd floor. Just to the north is the **Sompo Japan Building**, its stone façade reminiscent of

A nighttime view of Shinjuku from the 45th floor of Tokyo City Hall

ancient Japanese castle walls. On its 42nd floor, it houses the **Togo Seiji Memorial Sompo Japan Museum of Art**, a museum named for the Japanese artist whose paintings of young women form the core of the collection. (He did commercial art for the insurance firm Yasuda Kasai Kaijo, which is today known as Sompo Japan, and is not among the great artists of Japan.) A very few selections of Western artists have been added to the collection, most notably the Van Gogh *Sunflowers* that set a record at auction when it was purchased by the museum for almost six billion yen ($40 million at that time). Other than a Renoir, a Cézanne, and a Gauguin, the collection is not outstanding. The gallery does look out upon East Shinjuku's love hotels and clubs, theaters, bars, and restaurants, and the view is an interesting one. (Open 10:00 a.m. to 6:00 p.m., closed Mondays; entry ¥1,000.) Next to the Sompo Japan Building is the Shinjuku Nomura Building of 50 floors with a free observation deck on the top floor.

Between Higashi-dori and Shinjuku's Central Park are nine square blocks that contain most of the high-rise buildings in West Shinjuku. Across Higashi-dori from the Nomura Building and occupying the northeast square is the blue, mirror-glassed **Shinjuku Mitsui Building** of 1974, which has an observation restaurant on the 54th and 55th floors. The basement level has a shopping plaza with restaurants, and its outdoor plaza is landscaped with trees and has fountains and a waterfall along with tables where one can dine. South of it in the east-central square are the two towers of the **Keio Plaza Hotel**, which has a collection of restaurants and bars on its 44th and 45th floors. The lobby of the hotel is enhanced by the artwork of Takamichi Ito. The southeast square contains the **Shinjuku Monolith Building** and the 32-story **KDDI Building** (International Telecommunications Center). The north-central square holds the six-sided **Shinjuku Sumitomo Building** of 52 floors, with a free observatory on the 51st floor. The building appears to be a triangle, despite its six sides, and its central hollow core is an open well from the fourth to the fifty-second floor. Its top three floors have fine restaurants. A glass roof floods the open space beneath it with light. The building is also the location of the **Asahi Culture Center** and **Sumitomo Hall**.

The northwest square contains the

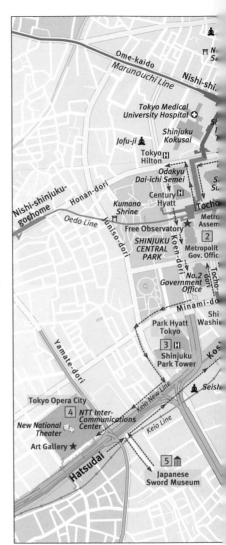

Shinjuku Dai-Ichi Semei Building and the **Hotel Century Hyatt**, while across Kita-dori (North Avenue) to the north are the **Shinjuku Kokusai Building** (International Building) and the **Tokyo Hilton Hotel**.

② TOKYO CITY HALL

The central square and the west-central square hold the 48-story, $1.2 billion, twin-towered **Metropolitan Government Office Building** (Tokyo Tocho, or City Hall) and the **Metropolitan Assembly Hall**, designed by

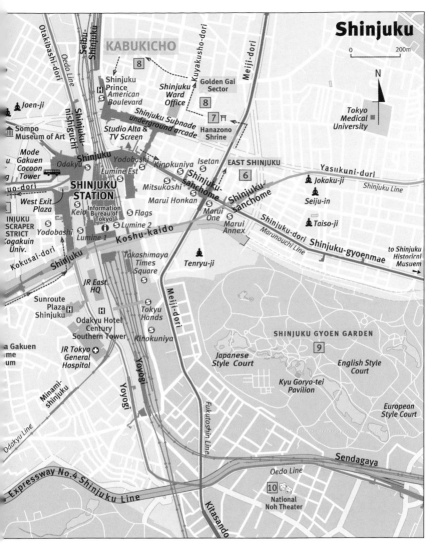

Kenzo Tange and built in 1991. Tange is reputed to have been inspired by the twin towers of Notre Dame Cathedral in Paris in his planning of the Tocho structure. Each tower has an observation floor. (The north tower observation floor is open from 9:30 a.m to 11:00 p.m,, while, the south tower observation floor closes at 5:30 p.m. The north tower is closed on Mondays while the south tower is closed on Tuesdays, and both are closed during the New Year holiday. Entry to the observation galleries is free.) From them, one has excellent views over all of Tokyo, and on clear days Mt. Fuji to the west and the Japanese Alps to the north can be observed. Above the large windows are photographic panels showing the view and identifying the buildings one can see in the distance. A coffee and desert bar in the center of the observation floor provides an added welcoming touch to the spacious hall. The Tocho's high-speed elevators reach the top of the building in 55 seconds. An inexpensive cafeteria is available in the Assembly Hall, and the large sunken plaza before the hall has a wall of falling water. A free shuttle bus runs between the plaza on the west side of the building and the west side underground plaza of Shinjuku Station, stopping at several of the major hotels and skyscrapers in the area.

3 PARK HYATT HOTEL

The south-central square holds the **Shinjuku NS Building** of 30 stories, with a multicolored, see-through glass elevator rising on one corner of the structure. Within the hollow core of the building is a 30-story tall atrium with a 24-foot water-powered clock by Seiko. A bridge on the 29th floor–the Sky Bridge–connects the restaurants floors for those who are not queasy about heights. The roof of 6,000 pieces of glass illuminates the core by day and by night as well, since in the evening it is illuminated artificially. (The NS in the building's name of is an abbreviation of "Nihon Seimei," as in Nihon Seimei Insurance Company.) Across Minami-dori (South Avenue) is the **Shinjuku Washington Hotel**, which has porthole windows and a curving white exterior. Opposite the Metropolitan Government Offices, across Koen-dori (Park Avenue) is **Shinjuku Chuo Koen** (Central Park), which occupies the equivalent of three squares. This park is patterned after parks in the West, with lawns, flowers, jogging paths, and a manmade waterfall.

On the south side of Chuo Koen on the avenue called Koshu Kaido is the **Shinjuku Park Tower**, a building with three linked towers topped with glass pyramids, another work by Tange Kenzo. The top floors, from the 39th to 52nd, house the **Park Hyatt Hotel**, with its famed New York Bar and Grill on the top floor offering stunning views across the city. It was at this bar where Bill Murray's character in the movie *Lost in Translation* would drown his woes. While one can walk from Chuo Koen, a free shuttle bus from the Odakyu Department Store arrives at the south side of the towers. An office building and hotel, the structure's third to seventh floors also hold the **Living Design Center Ozone** (open 10:30 to 7:00, closed on Wednesdays; entry free). The center is a museum of interior design that shows the influence of the English interior and household designer Conran. The first floor also holds Gallery One as well as Atrium, which offer photographic exhibitions (10:30 a.m. to 6:30 p.m.).

4 TOKYO OPERA CITY

Farther along Koshu Kaido to the west is **Tokyo Opera City**, which was created in 1997. It is a 20-minute walk from the Chuo Koen area, but the Keio Line subway from Shinjuku Station to the next stop at Hatsudai Station is an easier way to arrive at the Opera City. Here another 54-floor skyscraper is the centerpiece of offices, theaters, and even a sunken garden and a museum. The **New National Theater** here has a 1,810-seat opera house for opera and ballet, a 1,038-seat playhouse for drama and musical performances, and a 1,632-seat concert hall. It is called the New National Theater in contradistinction to the "old" National Theater in the governmental area near the Imperial Palace. The latter continues to offer traditional Japanese theater with Kabuki, Bunraku, and Noh. The museum in this complex is the **NTT Intercommunications Center** on the fourth floor of the tower building (open from 10:00 a.m. to 6:00 p.m., but closed Mondays; entry free). As may be inferred, this is a museum devoted to interactive displays concerned with modern communications. Restaurants can be found on the 53rd and 54th floors.

5 JAPANESE SWORD MUSEUM

One other site of interest on the outskirts of West Shinjuku is the **Japanese Sword Museum** (Token Hakubutsukan). (Open Tuesday through Sunday from 10:00 a.m. to 4:30 p.m., closed Mondays; entry ¥600.) It is but five minutes from the Odakyu rail line's Sangubashi Station (two stops from Shinjuku), and its collection of hand-forged, antique Japanese swords and scabbards reflects an art of metalwork at which Japanese craftsmen excelled. From the outside the museum is small and undistinguished (it looks like a regular house), but with 400 blades dating from the 1300s to 1800s–of which 25 are considered National Treasures or some other special designation–and exhibits detailing the forging process, it is worth visiting for anyone with an interest in Japan's feudal history or Japanese crafting.

6 EAST SHINJUKU

Returning to Shinjuku Station and leaving by way of the east exit, the eastern portion of Shinjuku is much more complicated an area, since it is the older portion of the district and does not have the checkerboard layout of the western part. Shinjuku-dori and Yasukuni-dori, running parallel to each other on an east-west orientation, divide the shopping and restaurant district from the pleasure sector of Kabukicho, the former enterprises being centered on Shinjuku-dori and the latter being to the north of Yasukuni-dori. Alongside the station to the east is the **Lumine Est**, and across Shinjuku-dori is **Studio Alta**, with its huge, external video screen marking the building as a television studio. A large underground promenade running beneath this area has many shops.

Turning down Shinjuku-dori away from the station, the **Kinokuniya Building** is on the left. The original Kinokuniya bookstore began here in a two-story frame building, and this 1964 structure offers a diversity of shops. The basement floor provide a variety of boutiques and restaurants, while the second through eighth floors house the stock of Kinokuniya's books. The seventh floor specializes in books in English. The complex has an art gallery and a theater seating 426.

Opposite Kinokuniya is the **Otsuka Furniture Building** lies to the south on Koshu Kaido. The following block (Shinjuku-dori) has the **Marui Honkan Building**, which houses the main Marui Department Store, and across the way is the large **Isetan Department Store**. On the other side of the road from Marui Honkan is the **Marui One** "gothic lolita" **Department Store**, which provides space for more than 50 clothing producers to display their latest fashions. To the east of Isetan between Shinjuku-dori and Yasakuni-dori, in Shinjuku ni-chome, is an area specializing in gay bars, which is most active in the evenings. The **Shinjuku Subnade** runs under Yasukuni-dori and beckons with a plethora of additional shops.

7 HANAZONO SHRINE

Turning to the left at the far side of Isetan onto Meiji-dori and crossing Yasukuni-dori brings one to the **Hanazono Shrine**, which dates back to before the founding of the Tokugawa city of Edo. It is claimed that Yamato-takeru-no-mikoto, the conqueror of the "barbarian" tribes in eastern Japan, is responsible for this shrine–the same warrior associated with the Kabuto (Golden Helmet) Shrine in central Tokyo. The Hanazono Shrine sits on the site of a garden that belonged to the Hanazono branch of the Tokugawa clan, which is why the name of this Inari Shinto

The Hanazono Shrine in eastern Shinjuku

shrine is also that of a daimyo family. Inari has many responsibilities, and one of them is the welfare of merchants. Hence this is a favorite shrine for local shopkeepers, who come here to pray for financial success. The shrine is entered off Yasukuni-dori through a large stone torii and then a vermilion torii. On either side of the entry to the shrine grounds are two large *kura,* which store the shrine's *mikoshi.* The shrine grounds run parallel to Yasukuni-dori, and thus there is a large torii on the right, then the water purification fountain. The large vermilion shrine building comprising a Haiden (Prayer Hall) and a Honden (Spirit Hall) is reached up a set of steps, and the gold and vermilion interior of the inner shrine is impressive.

8 KABUKICHO AND GOLDEN GAI

Between the shrine and the Shinjuku Ward Office are narrow alleys, now the haunt of prostitutes and touts, though prostitution was outlawed by the Diet as far back as 1958. Several of these lanes form an area known as the **Golden Gai**, with some 200 low-class bars between the shrine and Kabukicho. The area on the other side of the ward office, between it and Seibu Shinjuku Station, is the famed or notorious **Kabukicho district**.

In 1945 Shinjuku was virtually wiped out by the wartime air raids. The Kabuki theater in Ginza had also been badly damaged, and the idea of building a new home for the theater here in Shinjuku arose. The district was thus renamed in the atmosphere of blossoming hope for the opportunity to upgrade itself with a traditional art form. However, the hopes came to naught, because the Kabuki-za was rebuilt in Ginza. The name of *Kabukicho*, meaning "kabuki ward," endured nonetheless. The district has everything in the way of entertainment from legitimate restaurants, cinemas, nightclubs, pubs, pachinko parlors, and bars (it is said that there are 3,000 bars and eating and drinking establishments here) to sex shops, strip-tease shows, topless bars, no-panties bars, "soaplands" (a type of brothel), and transvestite and transsexual bars. In all, by some counts there are more than 130 sex-oriented establishments. Thus Kabukicho is the largest area in Tokyo dedicated to all forms of divertissements–which include, besides those mentioned above numerous theaters, discount shops, and other forms of amusement, legitimate or otherwise. Yet, at the same time, one can wander there without concern, so long as one avoids the hostess bars and other places where touts try to inveigle one in for an evening of fun and financial fleecing. The neon signs and the gaudy nature of the district have made it a popular place to seek an evening's entertainment, and it is always crowded with people of all ages and status in life. After World War II, the yakuza–underworld gangs–controlled much of the black market around the various exits to Shinjuku Station, and they are still present today, along with counterparts from other countries, overseeing the less-than-reputable establishments that they control. Allegedly, some 30 gangs are in existence.

NORTH AND SOUTH OF SHINJUKU STATION

Coming back to Yasukuni-dori and returning to the station area, in front of the Seibu Shinjuku Station is the **Shinjuku Prince Hotel**, embodying a somewhat different concept of a hotel, for its more than 500 rooms are on top of the first ten floors of the building, and the lower floors contain shopping arcades. The **American Boulevard** is the name of the ground-floor shops, which once specialized in American-made products but now carry all sorts of wares. In front of the Shinjuku Prince Hotel and running under Yasukuni-dori for six streets is the **Shinjuku Subnade**, the underground promenade lined with shops and connecting with Shinjuku-dori at Shinjuku Station.

Some distance to the north of Kabukicho are two buildings that stand out because of their unusual architecture. These are **Ichibankan** (Building One, 1969) and **Nibankan** (Building Two, 1970), by Takeyama Minoru. The buildings mock the government rules concerning warnings to low-flying aircraft by having a façade of black and white stripes that no plane could miss–if it were flying that low. The sides of Nibankan form a graphics display as an oversized billboard. The exterior of the buildings is opaque by day, but at night the interior lights provide a full view of the drinking and entertainment establishments within. To the northeast of Kabukicho is **Gunkan Higashi-Shinjuku Building (former Dai3 Sky Building)** by Watanabe Yoji. The building is composed of steel units that many think resemble mobile homes. This metal collage is topped by a water tank that looks like a battleship and is said to reflect the architect's fascination with this type of vessel, with which he was involved in World War II.

A modern shopping complex is situated just to the south of the south exit to Shinjuku Station, and a two-minute walk brings one to **Takashimaya Times Square**. This shopping complex not only has the major **Takashimaya Department Store** (open 10:00 a.m. to 8:00 p.m. daily), but **Tokyu Hands**, a multistory hands-on, do-it-yourself supply enterprise, the seven floors of an additional **Kinokuniya** bookstore, and two floors of restaurants.

9 SHINJUKU GYOEN GARDEN

The Marunouchi subway line can be taken at Shinjuku Station to the Shinjuku Gyoenmae Station, for the **Shinjuku Gyoen**. Lord Naito, the daimyo of Tsuruga, once had his mansion here after many of the daimyo mansions were relocated from the Marunouchi district following the Long Sleeves Fire of 1657. After 1868, the land was taken by the Imperial Household, and from 1917 to 1939 imperial receptions and cherry blossom–viewing parties were held here. After World War II, the land was given to the state, and the park was opened to the public. This public garden consists of 150 acres (60 hectares) in two parts: the northern portion is laid out as a Western garden in the French and English styles, while the southern portion is in the traditional Japanese manner with paths, artificial hills, islands in ponds, bridges, and stone lanterns (open from 9:00 a.m. to 4:30 p.m.; closed Mondays and from December 29 to January 3; entry ¥200). Within the garden is the **Kyu Goryo-tei Pavilion**, a pavilion in the Chinese-style given to commemorate the wedding of Emperor Hirohito in 1927. Cherry blossoms can be viewed in April (the prime minister holds a cherry blossom–viewing party here each year), and there is a lovely display of chrysanthe-

Shinjuku Gyoen is for many the finest park in Tokyo–and certainly well worth the ¥200 admission.

mums from November 1 to 15 annually.

This tour ends here, and one can return to Shinjuku Station for numerous trains and subway lines. Before that, however, three additional places in the area may be of interest and bear mention. To the north of the garden is the **Shinjuku Historical Museum** (22 San-ei-cho, Shinjuku-ku; open from 9:30 a.m. to 5:30 p.m., and closed the second and fourth Monday each month; entry ¥300). This excellent local museum is northeast of the Yotsuya Sanchome subway station and southeast of the Akebonobashi subway station. It is seven minutes on foot from the former station, but a taxi to the museum is the easiest way to find it. Models, including a huge one of medieval Shinjuku, as well as artifacts and documents illustrate life in old Japan when Shinjuku was still a post town. To the north of the museum on Yasukuni-dori is the **Jokaku-ji Temple**, an insignificant temple as temples go in Tokyo. However, a large communal grave identified by its tombstone as "a grave for children" is something quite other than that. This stone was erected by the innkeepers of the New Lodging's District in 1860, and it covers the graves of the many prostitutes who died young and were unceremoniously

dumped by the innkeepers who had employed these young "rice serving women," into a common grave at the Jokaku-ji, one of the two "dump" temples in Tokyo, the other being in the Yoshiwara district.

10 NATIONAL NOH THEATER (DIVERSION)

The last additional place of interest is another new theater in the area, which can be reached by taking the train from Shinjuku Station two stops to Sendagaya Station on the Chuo Line. This is the **National Noh Theater** (Kokuritsu Nohgaku-do), considered the most beautiful of the national theaters. It is an intimate space, rich in cypress wood, and has its own gardens. A ten-minute walk west from Sendagaya Station, it is just south of Shinjuku Gyoen, described above.

GETTING THERE

Shinjuku Station is the busiest station in Tokyo—and the busiest in the world by passenger volume—so there are plenty of ways to reach it. These include the JR, Yamanote, Chuo, and Sobu train Lines as well as the Marunouchi, Toei, and Oedo subway lines.

Walking Tour 18

HARAJUKU, OMOTESANDO AND AOYAMA

The Emperor's Spirit Enshrined, the Tokyo Olympics, a Japanese Champs-Elysées, and "Blue Mountain" Chic

1. **Meiji Shrine**
2. **Yoyogi Park**
3. **Togo Shrine**
4. **Ota Museum of Ukiyo-e Prints**
5. **Omotesando-dori**
6. **Aoyama**
7. **Nezu Museum**
8. **Tepia and Aoyama Fashion**

Walk 18 is one of contrasts, taking in historical sites such as the magnificent Meiji Shrine that was built to enshrine the spirit of the Emperor Meiji and his wife, the Empress Shoken—a highlight of any visit to Tokyo—and Omotesando-dori, which, though formerly known simply as the approach to Meiji Shrine, has become home to a concentration of brand-name fashion stores and the ultra-modern Omotesando Hills mall. The contrasts continue as the tour weaves through Harajuku's Takeshita-dori, a street crammed with boutiques flaunting the latest teen fashions, and then heads toward the cosmopolitan Aoyama area, known for its modern interior design stores, contemporary art galleries, chic cafés and bistros, and fashion boutiques. The two museums on this tour—the Ukiyo-e Museum of traditional woodblock prints and the Nezu Institute of Fine Arts, with its collection of ceramics, bronze work, paintings, and calligraphy from Japan and China—also provide a fine variety of tastes and styles.

One of the giant torii at Meiji Shrine

1 MEIJI SHRINE

Harajuku Station on the Yamanote Line is across Omotesando-dori from the edge of Meiji-Jingu Park and is the start of this walk. This 1924 station is a rather unusual one for Tokyo, since it is modeled after an English country rail station.

A bridge from Omotesando-dori leads over the railway right-of-way and into the **Meiji Shrine** through the Harajuku-mon (Harajuku Gate). (The grounds of the shrine are open from sunrise to sunset daily, without charge.) The memorial to the Meiji emperor is in two parts. The portion that holds the shrine to the emperor's spirit is the Inner Garden, while the portion with the Memorial Picture Art Gallery and the baseball, tennis, and rugby grounds is known as the Outer Garden (described in Walk 3). The Inner Garden consists of 178 acres (71.2 hectares) with 125,000 trees of 365 species from all over Japan. As the visitor walks down the path toward the shrine buildings, the former Imperial Gardens and the South Water Lily Pond are on the left. Here is the famed Jingu Nai-en iris garden, whose more than one hundred varieties of iris bloom in mid-June. The garden is said to have been designed by Emperor Meiji for the empress as part of the original Imperial Gardens in the suburban land that once formed an estate held by the Tokugawa family before 1868. (There is a fee for entry into the iris garden when it is in bloom.)

Emperor Meiji died in 1912. Empress Shoken died in 1914, and this shrine was begun in 1915 and completed in 1920. The Outer Garden was not finished until 1926. As with the shrine to the spirit of General Nogi (described in Walk 13) and that to the spirit of Admiral Togo (described below), this shrine deified the emperor whom the Meiji government used as a model to inculcate the myths of the military spirit and the superiority of the Japanese people, attitudes that imbued the educational system after 1890 and would eventually lead the military and Japan into the catastrophe of World War II. This and similar shrines were under military sponsorship until the end of that war. After the war, such shrines were made independent of government financial support and control.

The path from the entry gate turns to the left just before the shrine offices on the right. This new path is distinguished by the **O-torii**, the Great Torii. This 40-foot (12-meter)-tall torii, with a top beam 56 feet (16.8 meters) long, is the largest torii in Japan, and it was created from cypress trees said to be 1,500 years old. There is an ironic note to the construction of this torii: no cypress (*hinoki*) trees could be found in Japan that were large enough for the design of the torii, and thus the planners had to turn to Taiwan for the right tree. After the torii, the path turns to the right and leads to the Kita-mon, the North Gate, which opens on to the Honden, the building containing the enshrined spirits of the imperial couple. Created in 1915–1920, the shrine burned down during a 1945 air raid and was reconstructed in 1958. Paths leading off to the right or left can be followed to the far rear of the Inner Garden to the Homotsuden, the Imperial Treasure House, which holds personal belongings of the emperor and his consort. Built in 1921 of concrete, it is in the *azekura* (log cabin) style of construction of ancient Japanese treasure houses. The imperial memorabilia include not only personal objects and photographs of the couple but even the carriage drawn by a team of six horses that the emperor used at the time of the Proclamation of the Constitution in 1889. (The Treasure House is open daily from 9:00 a.m. to 4:00 p.m. from April to November and from 9:30 a.m. to 3:30 p.m. from December to March; entry ¥500.)

2 YOYOGI PARK

Backtracking to the entrance to Meiji Shrine, then turning right instead of heading eastward toward Omotesando-dori and Harajuku Station, the southwest roadway (Route 413) leads to the Yoyogi National Gymnasium and Yoyogi Park. Yoyogi Park has had a mixed history. In the late 19th century the Japanese army moved its drill ground from the Imperial Palace area and present-day Hibiya Park to the site opposite General Nogi's residence. When the War College was sited at that place, the drill grounds were moved to Yoyogi. After World War II, the grounds became "Washington Heights," with housing for the American military and their dependents. Then in 1964, after the departure of the American military, it became the village for the athletes participating in the 1964 Olympics. After the Olympics, the 22-acre (8.8-hectare) tract became a sports center. This park, with its many gingko trees, was one of three sites for the Olympics, the other two being the Outer Gardens (Jingugaien) of the Meiji Memorial Park and in Komazawa in the southern portion of Tokyo.

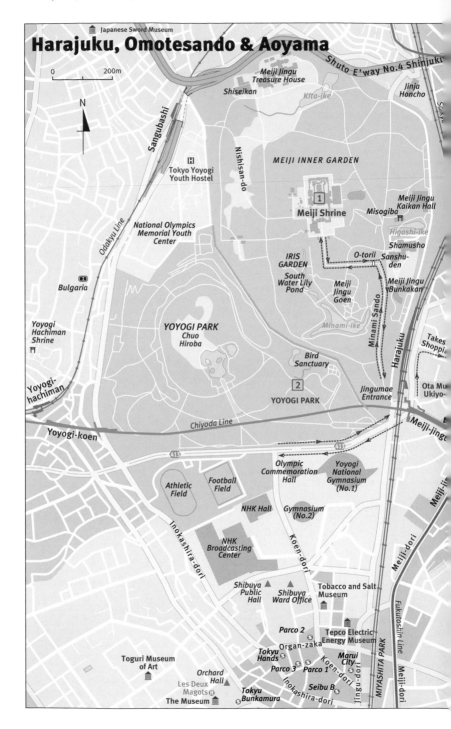

Harajuku, Omotesando & Aoyama

🏛 Japanese Sword Museum

0   200m

N

Shuto E'way No.4 Shinjuku

Meiji Jingu
Treasure House

Shiseikan

Kita-ike

Jinja
Honcho

Sangubashi

Nishisan-do

MEIJI INNER GARDEN

🅷 Tokyo Yoyogi
Youth Hostel

Meiji Jingu
Kaikan Hall

1
Meiji Shrine   Misogibo

Higashi-ike

Odakyu Line

National Olympics
Memorial Youth
Center

Shamusho

O-torii Sanshu-
den

IRIS
GARDEN

🆑 Bulgaria

South
Water Lily
Pond

Meiji
Jingu
Goen

Meiji Jingu
Bunkakan

Yoyogi
Hachiman
Shrine
🛉

YOYOGI PARK
Chuo
Hiroba

Minami-ike

Minami Sando

Harajuku

Takes
Shoppi

Yoyogi-
hachiman

Bird
Sanctuary

2

YOYOGI PARK

Jingumae
Entrance

Ota Mu
Ukiyo-

Chiyoda Line

Yoyogi-koen

Meiji-jing

413

413

Meiji-ji

Olympic
Commemoration
Hall

Yoyogi
National
Gymnasium
(No.1)

Athletic
Field

Football
Field

Inokashira-dori

NHK Hall

Gymnasium
(No.2)

Koen-dori

NHK
Broadcasting
Center

Meiji-dori

Fukutoshin Line

Shibuya
Public
Hall

Shibuya
Ward Office

Tobacco and Salt
Museum
🏛

Parco 2

Tepco Electric
Energy Museum

MIYASHITA PARK

Meiji-dori

Toguri Museum
of Art
🏛

Orchard
Hall

Les Deux
Magots ☕
The Museum 🏛

Tokyu
Hands

Organ-zaka

Koen-dori

Marui
City

Jingu-dori

Parco 3 Parco 1

Tokyu
Bunkamura

Inokashira-dori

Seibu B

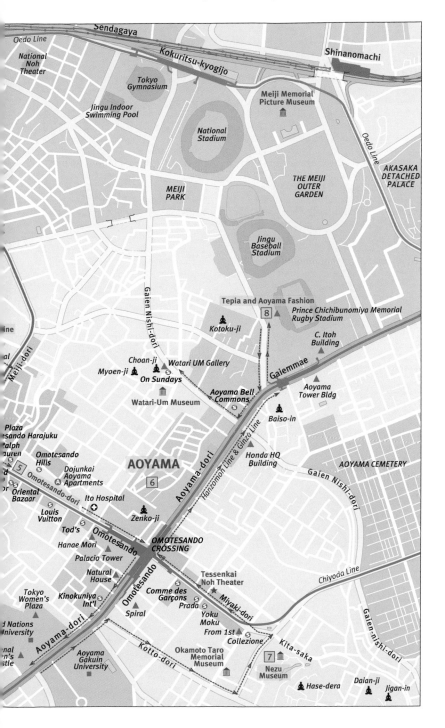

Two large structures designed by Kenzo Tange for the Olympics continue to serve athletics. **Yoyogi National Gymnasium** can seat 15,000 spectators, and it was originally devoted to swimming and diving events. Today, it serves as a venue for everything from ice hockey to major rock and pop concerts. An annex seating 4,000 is built in the shape of a snail with a tail, and it is the basketball court. (These buildings may be visited between 10:00 a.m. and 4:00 p.m. when they are not in use.) Various analogies have been employed for the unusual architecture of the main structure. It has been described as two huge comma shapes out of alignment, and as a seashell. The curved roof of tensile steel is hung between concrete masts so as to permit unobstructed sight lines within the structure, there being no posts or beams to hold up the roof. Adjacent is the **Olympic Commemoration Hall** of five floors, housing a research laboratory for sports as well as space for amateur sporting groups. Yoyogi Park beyond the Sports Center provides a green oasis in the midst of one of the largest cities in the world. (The park is open from 5:00 a.m. to 5:00 p.m [until 8:00 p.m. in spring and summer], without charge.)

3 TOGO SHRINE

Returning along Route 413 to Omotesando-dori, a left turn takes one alongside Harajuku Station to the first street on the right. This is

Shopping heaven for teens: Takeshita-dori

Takeshita-dori, a narrow street of fashions for teenagers and those who still dream of being teenagers. More than a hundred boutiques line this very crowded street, with shop names ranging from French to designations that are all-too-cute. It is best to avoid it on weekends, when all of young Japan seems to flock to this 900-foot (270-meter) mecca for teen fashion. At the far end of Takeshita-dori, which comes out on the larger Meiji-dori, turning left and walking some 50 yards along Meiji-dori leads to one of the entrances of **Togo Shrine**. The army had its enshrined spirit at the Nogi Shrine, and it was therefore necessary for the navy to have its leading admiral in the Russo-Japanese War deified as well. Admiral Togo Heihachiro had been the vanquisher of the Russian fleet in the Tsushima Straits in the 1904–1905 war, and thus he was one of the leading heroes of the early 20th century in Japan. The admiral headed the school in which the Emperor Showa (Hirohito) studied at the Togu Palace after 1914. Upon the admiral's death in 1934 at 87, his spirit was enshrined in this area near the Meiji Shrine in 1940, obviously a nationalistic enterprise by the military of the day.

A path leads from Meiji-dori into the grounds, a stream and a pond enhancing the wooded park before the Togo Memorial Hall, a modern building for multiple shrine uses including wedding receptions. Adjacent is the Togo Shrine, a ferroconcrete structure that in 1964 replaced the original unit, incinerated in a May 1945 air raid. In 1969 the Memorial Hall and the Treasury were added. A stone-roofed gateway leads into the inner shrine grounds, a corridor with paintings of the admiral's life on the walls. Between the Haiden and the Honden is a stage for religious ceremonies. A festival in honor of the admiral is celebrated each May 28, and a flea market is held on the shrine grounds on the first, fourth, and fifth Sunday of each month.

4 OTA MUSEUM OF UKIYO-E PRINTS

Returning along Meiji-dori, at the third lane on the right after Takeshita-dori is **La Foret**, with more than 100 boutiques for the younger generation on its five floors. Entering the lane just before La Foret and bearing to the left, one comes to the **Ota Memorial Museum of Art** (Ota Kinen Bijutsukan). (It is open from 10:30 a.m. to 5:30 p.m. and closed Mondays, approximately the last week of each month, and during the New Year period; entry fee varies depending on the exhibition.) The two floors of the museum exhibit changing selections from the 12,000 ukiyo-e wood-block prints which were collected by Ota Seizo, the president of the Toho Mutual Life Insurance Company. The prints included the work of the most noted Japanese artists in this genre. A pleasant coffee shop can be found in the basement of the building.

5 OMOTESANDO-DORI

Leaving the museum, one can continue along the lane to tree-lined **Omotesando-dori**, the Champs-Elysées of Tokyo, as it often used to be called. As the name *Omotesando-dori* (Avenue in Front of the Shrine) indicates, its original main purpose was as an entryway to the Meiji Shrine. In the period after 1945, with the American military forces billeted in so-called Washington Heights, the street began to blossom, with shops aimed at the occupying forces. Then came the 1964 Olympics when "Washington Heights" aka Yoyogi Park became the Olympic Village residence for athletes from around the world, and the street began to flower in earnest, as it continues to do. Expensive boutiques, internationally known clothiers, coffee shops, and restaurants make this gingko tree-lined avenue the equivalent, in Japanese eyes, of

The Tadao Ando-designed Omotesando Hills mall

Tod's on Omotesando-dori, designed by Toyo Ito

the Parisian avenue for which it was once nicknamed. Eventually Omotesando-dori is crossed by Aoyama-dori, and the continuation of both avenues from this intersection simply multiplies the number of exclusive shops that tempt susceptible shoppers.

Walking in the opposite direction from the Meiji Shrine, eventually on the right is the **Oriental Bazaar**, with its large stone Buddha at the entryway. The shop offers antiques and other items of a Japanese nature that appeal particularly to foreign visitors. While the green-and-orange faux temple façade of the Bazaar has long been something of an Omotesando institution, across the road is one of the newest highlights of the area—**Omotesando Hills**, an ultra-modern and very chic shopping mall designed by Tadao Ando, which opened in 2005. Inside are some 130 shops and 38 of the most sought-after apartments in the city.

Upon reaching the far end of Omotesando Hills, it is worth pausing for a look at the single, aging apartment block incorporated into the building's otherwise modern design. This is all that remains of the once foliage-covered **Dojunkai Aoyama Apartments** that were pulled down (amid much objection from some locals) to make way for Omotesando Hills. Part of the rebuilding efforts after the 1923 earthquake, this vestige offers a glimpse at what much of central Tokyo would have looked like between the 1923 disaster and the destruction of World War II.

Farther along on the right side is the 1978 reflective glass–skinned **Hanae Mori Building** by Kenzo Tange. It is the headquarters for the display of the designs by this couturière, and upscale antiques are offered for sale on the basement level. A more recent building from the beginning of the 21st century is Toyo Ito's **Tod's**, a fashionable footwear shop. Its façade, which is part of its structural integrity, is of a concrete webbing with polygonal glass filling its openings. Only 33 feet (10 meters) wide, the concrete web façade is thickest at the bottom and thinner as it rises—what the architect saw as a tree-form in concrete with 270 openings in its irregular façade. Six floors tall in an "L" shape (on two streets therefore), it has a roof garden.

Just a few feet beyond Tod's, sets of stairs on both sides of the street lead down to the Omotesando subway station, where the Chiyoda, Hanzomon, and Ginza subway lines can be taken by any who wish to interrupt the tour here. For those who wish to continue, Aoyama is just around the corner.

6 AOYAMA

Aoyama means "Blue Mountain," and the Omotesando-dori crossing with Aoyama-dori is the start of the **Aoyama district**. From Omotesando-dori, a turn to the right onto Aoyama-dori leads to several sites of interest. After the second street on the right is **Natural House**, for natural food items, while a little farther and across the street is the **Spiral** of the noted lingerie firm that built the Sewing Machine Building overlooking the Imperial Palace. The building was designed by Fumihiko Maki, and its nickname comes from the spiral walkway within that leads to the second floor (the first floor has a café open from 11:00 a.m. to 8:00 p.m.) and gallery and performance areas. Part art gallery, part theater, part boutique, it has a gift shop on the third floor, and the theater (Spiral Hall) is on the fourth. Women's lingerie made by Wacoal is on the upper floors. A nine-story structure as a cylindrical cone, with windows at various levels, it was planned to be asymmetrical. Across the street is **Kinokuniya** (not related to the bookstore chain), which sells foods, including foreign products. Since many of its signs are in English as well as Japanese, it is a favorite of foreigners.

Opposite Kinokuniya is Kotto-dori, to which we shall return shortly, but first **Aoyama Gakuin University** farther down Aoyama-dori should be noted. Begun as a Methodist missionary school in the Tsukiji area after 1870, it moved here to the countryside in 1883 and blossomed into a full-fledged private university. Across the way on Aoyama-dori is the **United Nations University** of 1993 designed by Kenzo Tange, a complex of glass and concrete units with exposed steel frames and glass walls. Beyond it is the 1985 **National Childrens' Castle** (Aoyama Kodomo-no-shiro), which includes everything from a swimming pool, gymnasium, concert hall for children, stage, and library with the latest in audiovisual and computer equipment in a complex to celebrate the U.N.'s Year of the Child. (Open from 12:30 p.m. to 5:30 p.m. from Tuesday through Friday and from 10:00 a.m. to 5:00 p.m. on Saturdays and Sundays; entry is ¥500 for adults, ¥400 for kids.)

7 NEZU MUSEUM

At the intersection of Aoyama-dori and Kotto-dori, a turn onto that street leads to a mishmash of record shops, nightclubs, galleries, interior design stores, restaurants, and antique shops. A left turn after the fourth street on the left brings one to the **Nezu Museum** (open 10:00 a.m. to 5:00 p.m., closed Mondays and the New Year holiday; entry ¥1,000, ¥1,200 for special exhibition). The museum holds the collection of Kaichiro Nezu (1860–1940), the founder of the Tobu railway group. He began to collect the finest of Japanese private art items from daimyo families who were in financial distress at the end of the Tokugawa era, and the collection is thus representative of all of the Japanese art forms. The collection contains very fine ceramics and early Chinese bronzes, textiles, calligraphy, and paintings from China and Japan. Holding 7,000 objects, only a portion of which can be shown at any one time, the museum mounts approximately eight exhibitions a year, generally based on a common theme. The collection includes seven National Treasures and 82 Imperial Cultural Assets. A delightful five-acre (2-hectare) garden with trees, a pond, waterfall, stupas, a tea ceremony house, and stone lanterns may be enjoyed after visiting the current exhibition.

Turning to the left, onto Miyuki-dori, the first building of note is **Collezione** by Ando Tadao, a sleek, rough concrete structure built in 1989. One street on is the **From First Building**, with a number of fashionable clothing boutiques and dining places. Farther up the street toward the Omotesando Crossing are the **Yoku Moku Confectionery Shop** (with café), the 2003 Herzog & de Meuron–designed **Prada Building**, with its convex glass façade creating the appearance of a crystal beehive, and the **Comme des Garçons** boutique. Across the street to the right is the **Tessenkai Noh Theater**. Within the building is a traditional Noh stage created from antique wood. The building is revolutionary in that its exterior walls are of concrete poured on the site, and instead of theater seats there are tatami mats for seating.

At **Omotesando Crossing**, a right turn on to Aoyama-dori leads to shops specializing in imported wares, as well as more clothing stores and restaurants, and after a quarter-mile from the crossing one comes to the intersection with Gaien Nishi-dori. Gaien-Nishi-dori runs north and south across Aoyama-dori, and its extension to the north of Aoyama-dori begins with the **Aoyama Bell Commons**, a popular spot for fashions and for dining at cafés or restaurants. The building even has gymnasiums for tennis and other indoor sports.

8 TEPIA AND AOYAMA FASHION

If one continues along Aoyama-dori and then takes the first left upon reaching Gaienmae subway station, for a brief diversion there is **Tepia**, designed by Maki Fumihiko, with exterior waterfalls flowing over marble cladding. The building holds various high-tech displays by companies that are creating new forms of communication. Restaurants, a health club, and art galleries add to the interest of advanced technology displays. Back on Aoyama-dori, at the Gaienmae subway station is the 1969 **Aoyama Tower Building** with its glass curtain walls, one of the early "modern" buildings. The red granite **C. Itoh Company Building** of 1980 a little farther along the avenue makes a colorful complement to the Tower Building. A 295-foot (78-meter)-high glass-lined interior open area contrasts with the external skin of the building and brings natural light into the structure.

Returning to the Aoyama-dori and Gaien Nishi-dori intersection and turning to the right, an amazing number of additional fashion and interior design shops line the street. After the fourth street on the left is the **Watari Um Museum**, a small museum of

FESTIVALS

A number of ceremonies take place at the shrine annually. Here are some of the most notable.

January 1 **Hatsumode** The "First Visit of the Year to a Shrine" brings some three million worshippers to the shrine.

Around May 1 to 3 **Spring Grand Festival** (Haru-no-Taisai) This festival to celebrate the coming of spring features performances of Noh and *Kyogen* traditional Japanese theater, as well as *bugaku* traditional music and dancing on the stage before the Honden of the shrine.

October and November Displays of chrysanthemums.

Around November 1 to 3 **Autumn Grand Festival** (Aki-no-Taisai) This festival to welcome in autumn features the same traditional performances as the spring festival as well as displays of traditional martial arts on the final day that include *yabusame* (horseback archery), archery, and aikido.

November 15 **Children's Day** Children of seven, five, and three (*shichi-go-san*) are brought to the shrine by their parents for a blessing. The children often wear traditional garb.

December 31 **Omisoka** The "Great Last Day of the Year," when people gather at the shrine to pray and the bells of temples throughout Japan are struck 108 times at midnight, signifying the casting out of the 108 failings to which humans are susceptible. The shrine is also a place where wedding pictures and family portraits are taken.

modern art in a building with a façade of alternating black and white stone designed by the Swiss architect Mario Botta. A pleasant café, a shop for gift and art books, and an art materials supply shop are on the premises (open from 11:00 a.m. to 7:00 p.m [until 9:00 on Wednesdays]. except Mondays). Adjacent is **On Sundays**, an excellent art bookshop run by the same company as Watari-Um.

Here the tour ends, and one can return to either Gaienmae Station for the Ginza subway line or retrace one's steps back to the subway line at Omotesando.

GETTING THERE

This walk begins at Harajuku Station on the JR Yamanote Line.

Walking Tour 19

SHIBUYA
The Faithful Dog, Teen Trends, and Museums Traditional and Offbeat in the Valley of Shibui

1. **Hachiko Statue**
2. **Shibuysa Shopping**
3. **Tobacco and Salt Museum**
4. **NHK Broadcasting Center and NHK Hall**
5. **Japan Folk Crafts Museum**

While the Omotesando district in the previous tour represents the sophisticated urban face of Tokyo, the brash, crowded streets of nearby Shibuya offer a very different side of modern Tokyo. The rail station in **Shibuya** is in a valley, and thus the tour of this remarkable area begins with the unusual sight of the Tokyo-Toyoko rail station on the fourth floor of the station building, the Ginza subway line passing through its station on the third floor, while the Yamanote Line is on the second floor. In all, eight rail lines con-

verge here to serve this commercial center. Shibuya, as with Ikebukuro and even Shinjuku, is a recent development in Tokyo's long history, and today is primarily known as a commercial center dedicated to satisfying the needs, but perhaps more the whims and desires, of young consumers. Where once there were love hotels along Shibuya's Koen-dori (Park Avenue, since it leads toward Yoyogi Park), today department stores and specialty shops abound. If one looks at the origin of the name *Shibuya*, meaning "Valley of Shibui," one has to recall that *shibui* for fanciers of the tea ceremony and its wares in centuries past referenced artistic tastes reflecting "austere elegance" or "restrained beauty." Such terms don't apply to this modern mecca for seekers after mercantile pleasures.

1 HACHIKO STATUE
No account of Shibuya can begin without mention of the statue of **Hachiko**, an Akita dog, which stands in the plaza of the station. Hachiko was the pet of a University of Tokyo professor, and the dog accompanied his master to the train station each day and then met him each evening. One day in 1925 his master died at work, but the dog continued his journey to the station for the next decade, seeking his missing master. The story so captivated the press and the public that a statue to the dog was created even before Hachiko's death in 1935. In fact, interest in the tale was so great that Hachiko still exists, since he has been preserved by taxidermy and can be visited in the Natural Science Museum in Tokyo. In recent years, the story even caught the attention of Hollywood, with Richard Gere starring in a Westernized version of Hachiko's story.

Hachiko, Japan's most loyal canine

Shibuya Crossing is Tokyo at its most congested and energetic

2 SHIBUYA SHOPPING

The plaza in front of the station has an always active large television screen by Sony on the outside of a building, similar to the one to be found at the Alta Building near Shinjuku Station. Jingu-dori rises up the slope from the station, and then Koen-dori (Park Avenue) diverges to the left toward Yoyogi Park, and this area is the center of the shopping district, complemented by side streets to the left with their many small shops. Directly ahead on Jingu-dori is the **Seibu Department Store** and its annex, a store that concentrates on the newest in high fashion. Returning to the station plaza, to the right of the station (when facing the station) is Dogen-zaka, a slope named for a brigand who robbed those coming up from the valley in times past. As with so many traditional tales, Dogen is said to have repented of his misdeeds later in life to become a Buddhist monk. At any rate, the slope is named for him, and today the hill is host to small shops and restaurants, with love hotels in the side streets renting rooms for the night or for several hours (for a so-called "rest" stay, though one doubts much resting occurs) at a time.

At the corner where Dogen-zaka begins is the **Shibuya 109 Building** (Shibuya Ichimaru-kyu), which is difficult to miss since its silver tower reaches toward the sky. This eight-story unit holds some 100 specialty shops that appeal to young women and teens, and its restaurants and cafés are open from morning through evening every day. The 109 Building sits in a triangular plot, with Dogen-zaka going off to the left while Bunkamura-dori (Culture Village Avenue) is on the right. Uphill on Bunkamura-dori, Sakae-dori takes off to the left, and at this new triangular corner is the main **Tokyu Department Store**, one of a number of Tokyu enterprises in central Tokyo. There are some 15 dozen restaurants on the eighth floor of the Tokyu store, in addition to some nine other floors above and below ground where you'll find everything from fashion and household goods to delicatessens and gardening supplies. Behind the store is the **Tokyu Bunkamura**, a unit that lives up to its name as a "culture village." Here are art museum, two cinemas varying in size from 150 to 1,260 seats, concert halls (the Tokyo Philharmonic has its home in the 2,150-seat Orchard Hall), boutiques, restaurants, and even a branch of Les Deux Magots of Paris. Farther uphill lies a small museum, the **Toguri Museum of Art** (open Tuesday to Sunday from 10:00 a.m. to 5:00 p.m.; entry ¥1,000), which specializes in Edo and Ming Chinese ceramics, a museum of interest primarily to collectors of ceramics.

Returning to the station and going up Jingu-dori to where Koen-dori diverges to the left, on the right is the **Marui Department Store**. Farther up Koen-dori on the left is **Shibuya Parco**, a three-part complex of boutiques, two of the centers being next to each other on Koen-dori. **Parco Part I** is the first you'll meet walking up Koen-dori; **Parco Part II** is next, while **Parco Part III** is behind Parco Part I. Parco I and II offer fashion shops (although as of this writing Part II is closed for an unspecified period), while Parco Part III provides interior design and cultural exhibits. Parco Part I has nine restaurants on the seventh and eighth floor as well as in the basement.

Turning left onto the street between Parco I, the **Tokyu Hands** store is ahead on the left. "Hands" began as a shop where hobbyists and those interested in working with their hands and in home improvement jobs could find tools and supplies. Now the store has branched into items ranging from gifts to interior decorative objects. The narrow streets within this general area are filled with bars, inexpensive restaurants, clubs, and small shops; one such alley is known as **Spain-dori**, due to its attempt to replicate Mediterranean façades.

③ TOBACCO AND SALT MUSEUM

Taking the street that runs between Parco I and Parco II in the opposite direction from Tokyu Hands (and crossing Koen-dori in the process), the road leads to Jingu-dori. Here a turn to the left brings one to the **Tepco Electric Energy Museum** (open from 10:30 a.m. to 6:00 p.m., closed Wednesday; free admission). A seven-story building of the Tokyo Electric Power Company, the museum offers interactive displays on all aspects of electrical power from the manner in which it is created to its various uses. If, however, one continues along Koen-dori from Parco I and II, at the second street on the right is the **Tobacco and Salt Museum** (open from 10:00 a.m. to 6:00 p.m. except on Mondays; entry ¥100). Until the 1980s, tobacco and salt were state monopolies, and the museum traces tobacco and its uses from the Edo period on. Rock salt sculptures and the story of the production of salt are also exhibited. The first floor has an information desk, shops, and a lecture hall. The second floor describes the "River of Tobacco" from South America to the world, and an intermediate floor offers the history of tobacco in Japan, illustrated by wood-block prints and video displays of the manufacture of cigarettes. The third floor deals with foreign and Japanese salt, while the fourth floor is devoted to

traveling exhibitions. The wood-block prints of tobacco in use are perhaps the most interesting part of the museum—as is the wooden Indian at the street level, holding tobacco leaves in his hand.

④ NHK BROADCASTING CENTER AND NHK HALL

Koen-dori leads past the **Shibuya Ward Office** and **Shibuya Public Hall** at the next major intersection. To the left is the NHK Broadcasting Center. As one of the curiosities of history, just south of the Shibuya Ward Office is a stone memorializing the nineteen soldiers executed here for their part in the February 26, 1936, revolt led by the most militaristic and anti-democratic elements of the army. The revolt attempted to bring down the government in order to institute military rule and prevent restrictions on the army's undeclared war in China.

The 23-story **NHK Broadcasting Center** was originally built as the information headquarters for the 1964 Olympics, and it became the center for NHK broadcasts after reconstruction in 1973. NHK, whose initials stand for Nippon Housou Kyoukai (Japan Broadcasting Corporation), is Japan's public television station, and the company is a fix-

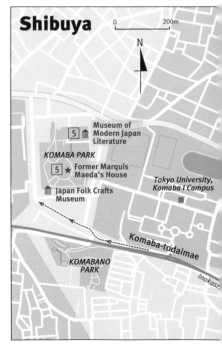

Shibuya 0   200m

N

⑤ 🏛 Museum of Modern Japan Literature

KOMABA PARK

⑤ ★ Former Marquis Maeda's House

🏛 Japan Folk Crafts Museum

Tokyo University, Komaba I Campus

Komaba-todaimae

KOMABANO PARK

Inokas

ture in modern Japanese life. An NHK fee collector figures prominently in the latest novel by Japan's most celebrated contemporary writer, Murakami Haruki. Tours of the broadcasting and television complex are offered without charge, but the guided tour is only offered in Japanese. There is viewing of current television programs as they are filmed in the studios of NHK (open 10:00 a.m. to 5:00 p.m., closed the fourth Monday of each month). Next to the NHK headquarters is the 4,000-seat **NHK Hall** for opera and concerts. Continuing along the street in front of the NHK Center past Koen-dori, the Olympic stadium lies ahead. At the end of Koen-dori, a right turn brings one to Omotesando-dori as well as Harajuku and Meiji-Jingu Mae Stations. Here one could begin Walk 18 if one wished, and explore Yoyogi Park, Meiji Shrine, and Omotesando, and Aoyama.

5 JAPAN FOLK CRAFTS MUSEUM

For those interested in Japanese folk crafts, however, a very worthwhile excursion can be made before concluding this tour by taking a train at Shibuya Station on the Keio Inobashira Line to Komaba-Todaimae Station, two stations from Shibuya. Leaving the sta-

tion by its main exit, the east exit, and following the main street west, a four-minute walk brings one to the **Japan Folk Crafts Museum** (Mingaikan, at 4-3-33 Komaba, Megura-ku, open 10:00 a.m. to 4:30 p.m., closed on Mondays; entry ¥1,000). This small museum was begun in 1936 by Yanagi Soetsu, and he and Hamada Shoji, Kawai Kanjiro, Bernard Leach, and Munakata Shiko (the first three craftsmen in ceramics and the last a woodblock print artist) sparked interest in preserving Japan's folk crafts, which were in danger of dying out in a modern, industrial world of mass-produced goods. The museum displays traditional crafts of ceramics, textiles, woodworking, lacquerware, glassware, and others. Across from the museum building is the Nagaya-mon, a long gatehouse that has been added to the collection.

GETTING THERE

This walk begins at Shibuya Station, which is on the JR Yamanote Line and the Tokyo Metro Ginza, Hanzomon, and Fukutoshin Lines. It is also served by the Tokyu Denentoshi and Tokyo Lines and the Keio Inokashira Line.

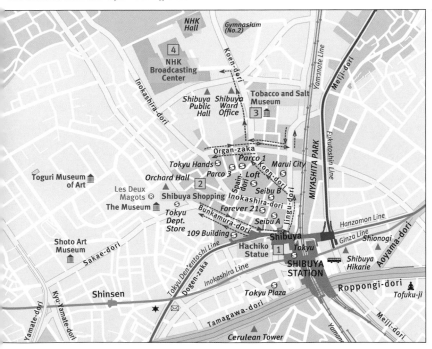

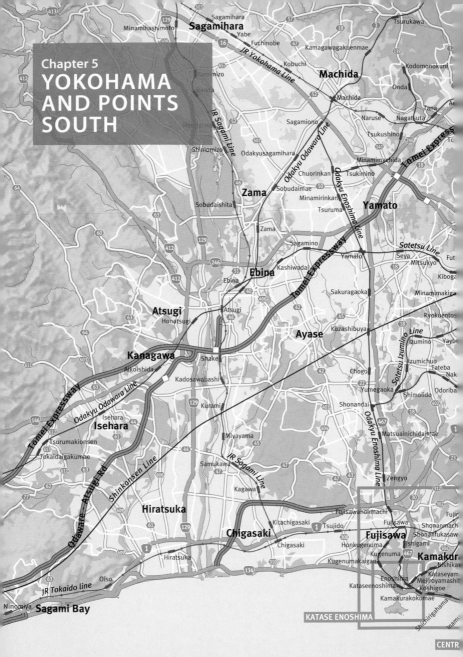

Sagami Bay

KATASE ENOSHIMA

YOKOHAMA OVERVIEW

Three Easy Excursions In and Around the Old Port City of Yokohama

Many guidebooks overlook Yokohama, which is a pity, since there is much to see here. Only 30 minutes from Tokyo Station, it is an easy trip, and one could return a number of times to explore the attractions of the city. The three different walking tours offered here can be done separately or combined. We begin with a brief history, and then in Walk 20 we describe **Kannai** (Inside the Checkpoint), the "downtown" section of the city and the area to which foreigners were restricted in the early years of settlement, as well as the **Minato Mirai 21** (Port of the Future 21) and the **Kangai district**, which lay beyond the checkpoint and today is part of greater Yokohama. Walk 21 explores **Yamate-cho**, that portion of the city on the heights above the bay to which foreigners moved after 1870 and which became primarily a European enclave. Here is the large **Foreigner's Cemetery** as well as various cultural attractions. Walking Tour 22 covers the **Sankei-en Garden** with its traditional buildings, an oasis of greenery not too far from the heart of Yokohama.

Yokohama is Japan's second largest city and one of the country's largest commercial ports, a prominence that no one could have foreseen when the little fishing village of 1859 was designated as the location for foreign consulates and chosen to serve as Japan's first overseas port. Several years earlier, on July 8, 1853, Commodore Perry's four U.S. warships, the "Black Ships" as the Japanese termed them, steamed into the waters down the bay at Uraga and presented the Japanese with gifts along with U.S. president Millard Fillmore's letter "inviting" the Japanese government to open its ports to international commerce. On his departure after a nine-day stay, Perry indicated that he would be back in one year for a positive answer, and thus on March 8, 1854, his fleet landed 300 hundred U.S. sailors and a brass band at the fishing village of Yokohama to continue the "conversation" he had begun the previous year. Perry's appearance created a

crisis in the Japanese government, which was split between those who wished to expel these "Western barbarians" and those who saw the need for Japan to open its ports or possibly face foreign military intimidation if not invasion, as was happening elsewhere in Asia. Thus the Treaty of Kanagawa was negotiated in 1858 at the village of that name, adjacent to the small fishing port that would become Yokohama, and four treaty ports were to be opened to the Western nations. The treaty guaranteed Western residents freedom of religion and granted foreign nations low tariff rates and the right of extraterritoriality. The latter two rights were to remain a bone of contention for the Japanese for the next 30 years before they were mutually revoked.

Kanagawa was to be one of the newly opened ports, but before long it was overshadowed and then absorbed by its neighbor, Yokohama. Thus when the agreed upon two-square-mile (5.2-square-kilometer) treaty port was opened on July 1, 1859, it was in the adjacent fishing village of Yokohama and not in Kanagawa, and the new town of Yokohama consisted of two parts, Kannai and Kangai.

For the next 35 years ships had to anchor in the bay and be unloaded by small boats because of the shallowness of the offshore waters, but nonetheless the city thrived, improved, and became the modern metropolis it is today. Yokohama has seen three great disasters in its fairly brief history: the Pig Pen Fire that began in its brothel quarter in 1866 and destroyed almost half the city; the Great Kanto Earthquake of September 1, 1923, which leveled 95 percent of the city and left 40,000 dead; and then the four-hour bombing of May 29, 1945, during which American bombers destroyed 50 percent of the city. Today Yokohama has been rebuilt, and in its Minato Mirai 21 project it is turning the former Mitsubishi Shipyards on the bay into a model of what can be done to bring excellent housing, cultural attractions and employment to a city that seems ever to be renewing itself.

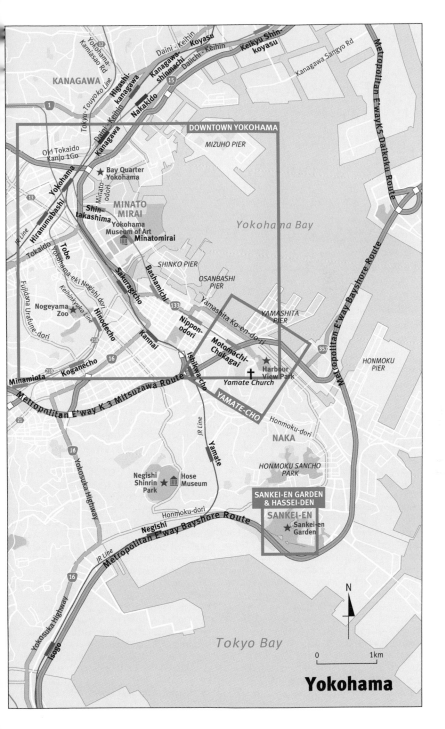

Yokohama

Walking Tour 20

OLD AND NEW YOKOHAMA

The Foreigners' Enclave "Inside the Checkpoint," a New Vision for an Old Port, and "Beyond the Checkpoint"

Kannai (Inside the Checkpoint) is the portion of Yokohama that was created for foreign settlement in 1859, when the port became the first town in Japan opened to foreign residents and to overseas trade. Yokohama, whose name means "side beach," was at first a mere tidal mudflat with but 80 fishermen's homes, and it was not where the foreign emissaries wished to set up their consulates. They much preferred the town of Kanagawa just a short distance to the north, since its single street lay astride the Tokaido (Great Eastern Road), the road between Kyoto, the emperor's capital, and Edo (Tokyo), the shogun's citadel. At the time, the Tokaido ran along the beach, which made Kanagawa favorable for a consular station as well as a port for foreign vessels. Ii Naosuke, the shogun's premier, thought otherwise, for a location for foreigners on the Tokaido was fraught with dangers. Along this road came the great daimyo, the feudal lords of Japan with their entourages, and many of these lords were opposed to opening Japan to the "barbarians" from the West. Since many of the "barbarians" were a brash lot, a confrontation would be inevitable and deaths of the foreigners—

and perhaps a pretext—would result.

Thus, Ii Naosuke had wharves, warehouses, and other commercial buildings created on the mudflats of the fishing village of Yokohama. The foreign emissaries were most unhappy with the location, but they had little choice, particularly since foreign shipping firms and merchants were quickly attracted to the new port. What irked the diplomats even more was that the new town was an enclave consisting of one district, the Kannai (Inside the Checkpoint or Barrier) for the foreigners, while the Kangai (Beyond the Checkpoint or Barrier) district was restricted for the Japanese who had to serve the foreigners. At first there were even four guarded bridges into Kannai, where all movement of foreigners and Japanese could be controlled. Times were to change, however, and it was not long before a new government and a different outlook on the part of the ruling classes led to the acceptance of foreigners and foreign ways. Yokohama boomed as a port, and it became the primary door for Japan to the rest of the world. Kannai still exists as a name, but its meaning as a "closed quarter" has long since passed into oblivion. Today **Kannai**, as it has been since the inception of the city, is the quarter of business and commerce, and at the end of the 20th century it had the added distinction of having a portion of its area become a planned center for the 21st century.

Yokohama is not often viewed as a tourist site, yet its attractions are worth exploring, particularly in light of its history as the first town created for foreign residence. In the 20th century the city has had its trials, being destroyed in the September 1, 1923, Great Kanto Earthquake, and then, just two decades later, being destroyed again in a four-hour bombing raid on May 29, 1945. Like the mythical phoenix, Yokohama has risen from its ashes, and its waterfront **Minato Mirai 21** (Port of the Future) announces the city of the future.

1 CHINATOWN

The first walking tour of Yokohama begins in the Kannai district, and it starts at Ishikawacho Station on the JR Negishi Line (change at Yokohama station to track #3 for the Negishi Line). From the northern exit of the station (at the rear of the train, if coming from Yokohama), Nishimon-dori (West Gate Street) should be taken to the east toward the bay, for a five-minute walk (a half-mile or 800 meters) away is Yokohama's **Chinatown** (Chukagai). At the end of Nishimon-dori, the street goes through the ornamental and colorful Hairu-mon (Entry or Main Gate) to become Chukagai-odori (Chinatown Avenue), a narrow main street of the Chinese sector of Yokohama. It is, of course, replete with Chinese restaurants and shops selling souvenirs, and it is a colorful area, with "Chinese-style" architecture enhanced by an occasional fearsome dragon decoration without which Chinatown would be incomplete.

This, the largest of three Chinatowns in Japan, was set aside for the Chinese residents of the city by the Japanese government in 1863. The Chinese originally came as the servants of Western merchants, many of them serving as treasurers (*comprador*) to Western firms while others came as craftsmen who could make the clothing and other essentials needed by foreigners. Revolutions in China brought additional Chinese in time, and it became a refuge for those plotting to overthrow the Manchu dynasty; these revolutionaries included Sun Yat-sen and Chang Kai-shek. Today Chinatown is home to 2,500 Chinese, and it boasts some 500 shops, restaurants, bars, and even that most Japanese of pastimes, pachinko parlors. Its restaurants run the gamut of Chinese food preparation from Szechuan to Shanghai, Guangdong, and Beijing cuisine. One of the main attractions, other than shops and restaurants, has been the **Kuan-Ti Miao Temple**, dedicated to Kuan Yu, a Chinese warrior who serves as the patron deity of Chinatown. Originally built in 1887, the temple burned down for a second time in 1987, and it has been reconstructed despite the internecine disagreements between the local Chinese partisans of Taiwan and Beijing. In 1990, it was rebuilt as the **Kantei-Byo** (open from 10:00 a.m. to 8:00 p.m. daily, no admission charge), a shrine to

One of the four entrance gates to Chinatown. The streets are just as colorful beyond the gateway.

Sangokushi, to whom the Chinese can pray for good fortune and good business. Two blue dragons in a leaping stance are situated at opposite ends of its roof, glaring ominously at any who oppose the future of trade and the enhancement of Chinatown.

Four Chinese-style gates mark each of the cardinal points of entry into the Chinatown. At the far end of Chukagai-odori is the Higashi-mon (East Gate), which is but 550 yards (500 meters) or a few minutes from the Marine Tower and the waterfront. The south gate leads toward the **Nakamura River** (Central Village River), across which is the Motomachi shopping street described in Walk 21 on the Yamate-cho (the Bluff) portion of Yokohama.

② HEPBURN MEMORIAL MARKER AND THE YOKOHAMA DOLL MUSEUM

Walking along the street that parallels the Nakamura River and its elevated expressway, and heading toward the bay, just before the overhead walkway that crosses the river for the Bluff and French Hill is a memorial marker on the left in a flower bed. It commemorates the **Reverend James Curtis Hepburn**, the man who created a Japanese-English dictionary in 1867 and whose Romanization of Japanese characters and the pronunciation system for Japanese bears his name. Hepburn was one of many missionaries who flocked to Japan once Yokohama was opened to the West. A number of these missionaries were medical men, and Hepburn was one of the more humanitarian of these medical Protestant ministers, for he would treat Japanese and Chinese patients in his house without charge if they could not afford to pay for treatment. He and his wife began a school that eventually became Meiji Gakuin University. Thus an historical marker has been erected to commemorate his and his wife's work in Japan between 1859 and 1892.

An elevated walkway ahead leads to the Bluff (Yamate-cho), and at its side to the left is a tall building housing the **Doll Museum** (Yokohama Ningyo-no-ie), which exhibits more than 3,500 dolls from 141 countries throughout the world. Only a portion of the collection is on view at any one time, and the displays change periodically. (Open 9:30 a.m. to 5:00 p.m., but closed the third Monday of each month; entry is ¥300. The building can be entered at the ground level or from the elevated bridge.)

A Hina doll set for Girls' Day

③ KAIGAN-DORI (SHORE DRIVE) AND YAMASHITA PARK

Beyond the Doll Museum one comes to Kaigan-dori (Shore Drive), sometimes called Yamashita Koen-dori (Yamashita Park Street). The street runs between **Yamashita Park** at the waterfront and the major buildings that face the park and the bay. The park extends for two-thirds of a mile (1 kilometer) along the waterfront, and from it Yamashita Pier, Osanbashi Pier (South Pier), and Shinko Pier (Central Pier) jut out into the bay. At an earlier date, the waterfront esplanade was known as the Bund, a term derived from the British relations with India, since it is a Hindu and Persian term meaning "quay" or "embankment," but Kaigan-dori is its present name. Yamashita Koen (Park at the Base of the Hills) was only developed as a park in 1925 after the debris from fallen buildings leveled in the great 1923 earthquake was used as fill to create the land for it.

The park runs from **Yamashita Pier** to Osanbashi Pier, its south end at Yamashita Pier being raised since a flood control pumping station lies beneath this upper end of the park. The raised portion has an ornamental water cascade descending from its upper reaches to the street level of the park. There is an excellent view from this vantage to the Kannai district of the city, the waterfront and bay, and the Minato Mirai 21 district that lies ahead to the north on the bay front. The **Guardian of the Waters statue** (Mizu-no-shugoshin-zo) that sits among fountains in the park was a gift to Yokohama and its people from its sister city of San Diego. The **Mogul Water Tower**, with a mosaic ceiling, stands as a memorial to Indian deaths suffered in the 1923 quake, and it is composed of debris from the disaster. **Osanbashi Pier** (South Pier) was built between 1889 and 1894, providing a proper place for ships to dock and be unloaded. The pier was formerly used by ocean liners that put into Yokohama, and, since many of the ships came from the United States, it was also known as the "Meriken Pier." (Open daily from 9:00 a.m. to 9:30 p.m.; the rooftop is open 24 hours a day.) Cruises of the bay can be taken from the waterfront for various lengths of time ranging from 40 to 60 to 90 minutes, and luncheon cruises are also available. Of interest at a small pier off the park is the permanently moored, former luxury liner *Hikawa-maru*, an ocean liner built in

One of the statues that dot the harbor area

Yokohama in 1930 that sailed between Japan and the West Coast of the United States from 1930 until 1960, making 238 crossings in its time. Now retired from service, it was closed at the end of 2006, and then reopened in 2009 on the 150th anniversary of the founding of Yokohama. From the same pier a ferry can be taken to the Minato Mirai 21.

Across from the park is the **Marine Tower**, a 10-sided, openwork, metal structure rising to 348 feet (106 meters), which was erected in 1961 to belatedly commemorate the centenary of Yokohama's existence since its founding in 1859 as a port city. The first floor houses a tourist information unit and restrooms, while the second floor offers souvenir shops and a restaurant and bar. The third floor is a wedding hall, and the fourth houses another restaurant. The observation floor is at the 328-foot (100-meter) level, and from here there is an excellent view over the bay and the port. On clear days, often in the winter, Mt. Fuji can be seen, but at all times of year the view of the city lights at night is enchanting. The building is topped by a lighthouse lamp at 417 feet (106 meters), which serves as the highest inland lighthouse in the world. Its light is visible over the bay for 24 miles (40 kilometers). To the

south of the Yamashita Park and pier is the 1989 **Yokohama Bay Bridge**, a suspension bridge that rises 180 feet (55 meters) above the water and extends 2,821 feet (860 meters) from shore to shore as it crosses the bay. Beneath its main span is the Sky Walk, which runs 1,050 feet (320 meters) from the far (east) Daikoku Pier end of the bridge to the Sky Lounge, a circular observatory. (The Sky Walk and Sky Lounge are open from 9:00 a.m. to 9:00 p.m. between April and October, and from 10:00 a.m. to 6:00 p.m. in other months. Closed Tuesdays and Wednesdays. Entry is ¥600.)

Heading to the north along Kaigan-dori is the **Hotel New Grand**, consisting of a charming older portion and a swank, high-rise addition. It was at this hotel that General MacArthur stayed on the evening of August 30, 1945, on his arrival at Atsugi airbase to begin his tenure as the head of the American occupying forces in Japan. It was from the New Grand Hotel on September 2, 1945, that he went to the *USS Missouri* battleship in Yokohama Bay to accept the Japanese government's surrender, thereby ending World War II. The Hotel New Grand replaces the original hotel built in the 19th century, and this 1927 edifice had an 18-story addition appended to

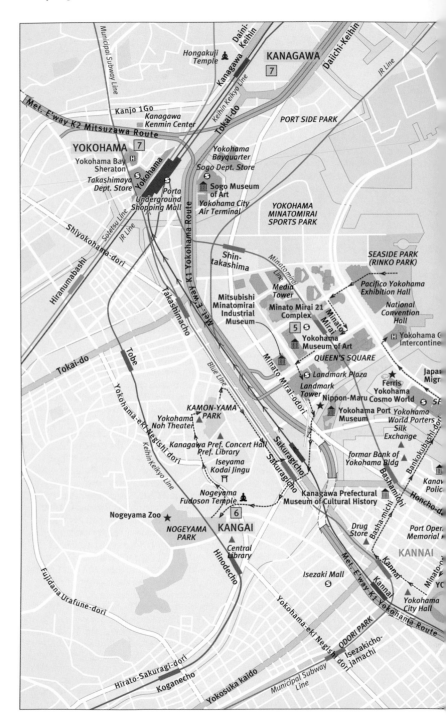

Hongakuji
Temple

KANAGAWA
7

Daini-Keihin

Kanagawa

Keihin Kekyo Line

Daiichi-Keihin

JR Line

Municipal Subway Line

Met. E'way K2 Mitsuzawa Route

Kanjo 1Go

Tokai-do

PORT SIDE PARK

Kanagawa
Kenmin Center

YOKOHAMA
7

Yokohama Bay
Sheraton

Yokohama
Bayquarter

Yokohama

Sogo Dept. Store

Takashimaya
Dept. Store

Porta
Underground
Shopping Mall

Sogo Museum
of Art

Yokohama City
Air Terminal

YOKOHAMA
MINATOMIRAI
SPORTS PARK

Sotetsu Line

JR Line

Met. E'way K1 Yokohama Route

Shin-
takashima

Minatomirai Line

SEASIDE PARK
(RINKO PARK)

Shiyokohama-dori

Hiranumabashi

Takashimacho

Media
Tower

Pacifico Yokohama
Exhibition Hall

Mitsubishi
Minatomirai
Industrial
Museum

Minato Mirai 21
Complex

Minato Mirai

National
Convention
Hall

Tobe

5

Yokohama G
Intercontine

Tokai-do

Yokohama-eki Negishi dori

Blue Line

Yokohama
Museum of Art

Yokohama
Noh Theater

KAMON-YAMA
PARK

Minato Mirai-odori

QUEEN'S SQUARE

Japar
Migr

Kanagawa Pref. Concert Hall
Pref. Library

Landmark
Plaza

Ferris
Yokohama
Cosmo World

Keihin Kekyo Line

Iseyama
Kodai Jingu

Sakuragicho

Landmark
Tower

Nippon-Maru

Yokohama Port
Museum

SF

Yokohama
World Porters

Sakuragicho

Silk
Exchange

Nogeyama
Fudoson Temple

Bankokubashi-dori

Nogeyama Zoo

6

Kanagawa Prefectural
Museum of Cultural History

formar Bank of
Yokohama Bldg

Basha-michi

Kanav
Polic

NOGEYAMA
PARK

KANGAI

Drug
Store

Honcho-d

Port Oper
Memorial

Central
Library

Basha-michi

KANNAI

Hinodecho

Fujidana Urafune-dori

Isezaki Mall

Kannai

Met. E'way K1 Yokohama Route

Kannai

YC

Minato

Yokohama
City Hall

Yokohama-eki Negishi dori

ODORI PARK

Isezakicho-
dori, Iamachi

Hirato-Sakuragi-dori

Koganecho

Yokosuka kaido

Municipal Subway
Line

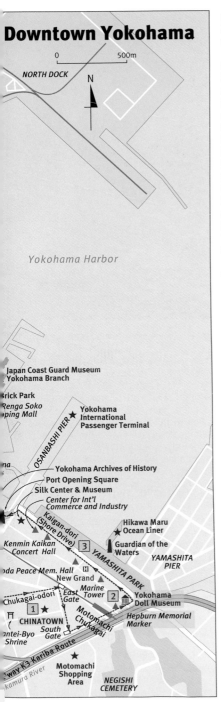

Downtown Yokohama

0　　　　　500m

NORTH DOCK

N

Yokohama Harbor

Japan Coast Guard Museum
Yokohama Branch

Brick Park
Renga Soko
Shopping Mall

Yokohama
International
Passenger Terminal

OSANBASHI PIER

Yokohama Archives of History

Port Opening Square

Silk Center & Museum

Center for Int'l
Commerce and Industry

Kaigan-dori
(Shore Drive)

Hikawa Maru
Ocean Liner

Kenmin Kaikan
Concert Hall

Guardian of the
Waters

YAMASHITA
PIER

YAMASHITA PARK

Toda Peace Mem. Hall

New Grand

Marine
Tower

East
Gate

Yokohama
Doll Museum

Chukagai-dori

Motomachi
Chukagai

Hepburn Memorial
Marker

CHINATOWN

South
Gate

Kantei-Byo
Shrine

Expressway K3 Kariba Route

Kamura River

Motomachi
Shopping
Area

NEGISHI
CEMETERY

it in 1991. A small formal garden in the French style in a courtyard behind the old wing adds to the 1927 building's charm.

On the following block toward the Osanbashi Pier is the **Toda Peace Memorial Hall** of the Soka Gakkai Buddhist religious organization. Next to its modern headquarters is an 1880s house, which now is its youth center. Originally, this Victorian building served as the headquarters of a British trading company. Farther along Kaigan-dori on the next street is the modern **Kenmin Kaikan**, a hall for concerts, plays, and other forms of entertainment. Next comes the **Center for International Commerce and Industry** (Sanbo Center), often referred to simply as the "Trade Center," and in the lower level of the building is a restaurant arcade. There is also a tourist information office in the building.

At the end of the block at the foot of the Osanbashi Pier is the **Silk Center** (Shiruku Senta) in a building erected in honor of the centenary of the founding of the city in 1859. In the early days of the city, the site of the Silk Center was the home to Jardine Matheson Co., the trading firm that had its headquarters and outlet in Hong Kong and was at one time heavily involved in the opium trade with China. The Japanese, having learned from China's unhappy experience with British and American traders and the opium business, had expressly forbidden the incursion of opium into Japan under the trade treaties signed with the West. The present nine-story Silk Center Building has two basement levels, one of which serves as a shopping arcade, while the first floor contains offices of airlines and shipping firms as well as a tourist information center and shops. The second and third floors are occupied by the **Silk Museum** (Shiruku Hakubutsukan). Raw silk was a major export to the West (virtually 80 percent of all exports) in the early years of Yokohama's existence as a port, and the city was the primary shipping outlet for this Japanese textile. The museum provides handsome exhibits that tell the story of silk from silk cocoons to the rich finished products of silk looms. (Open daily from 9:00 a.m. to 4:30 p.m., closed Mondays and New Year. Entry is ¥500.) The fourth floor of the building houses the Silk Trading Floor.

At this point, Kaigan-dori bends as it continues to the west, and the roadway opens to form the **Port Opening Square** (Kaiko

Hiroba) to commemorate the 1854 treaty between Japan and the United States, which was signed here on what was then the beach of the small fishing village of Yokohama. The square on its east side faces the beginning of Osanbashi Pier, and it is enhanced with fountains and trees and a **monument to U.S.-Japanese Friendship**. On the north side of the square is the **Yokohama Archives of History** (Yokohama Kaiko Shiryokan), which sits on the actual site of the signing of the Kanagawa Treaty by Commodore Perry. (An historical marker recalls the event.) At the northwest corner of the square is the **Yokohama Kaigan Kyokai**, a church begun in the 19th century by Protestant missionaries. The present building is a replacement for what was one of the earliest Protestant churches in Japan. Built in 1871, it was rebuilt ten years after its 1923 destruction in the earthquake.

The **Yokohama Archives of History** is in two buildings, and the older, more attractive unit in an 18th-century Georgian style was the former consulate of the United Kingdom. The archival collections consist of more than 140,000 items relating to the opening of the port to foreigners as well as other aspects of the city's history. The first floor holds the archives' permanent exhibition, while changing exhibitions are mounted on the second floor. Materials on Perry's visit to Japan as well as early English-language newspapers in Yokohama (on microfilm) form a rich resource. The archival display building has a tearoom. (The building is open from 9:30 a.m. to 5:00 p.m., and closed Mondays. Entry is ¥200.)

Continuing along Kaigan-dori, on the next block is the **Kanagawa Prefectural Office**. Its original building is connected by an overhead pedestrian bridge to its newer addition, and it has a selection of useful tourist materials on Yokohama and travel to elsewhere in Japan. At the next intersection, the street leading to the bay opens onto the **Shinko Pier** (Central Pier), a second pier created to handle Yokohama's growing overseas trade. It was built in 1916, destroyed in the 1923 earthquake, and then rebuilt. At its entrance is the **Yokohama Customs Office** with a Moorish tower and an exhibition on its second floor. Adjacent is the **Prefectural Police Headquarters**. Rather than proceed along Kaigan-dori, however, turn left onto Minato-odori. As one walks away from the waterfront, one comes to Honcho-dori, a street that in its

The clock tower of the Port Opening Memorial Hall

early days sported many drinking establishments favored by foreign sailors, whose praise of the street as an "all right" place became, in their mispronunciation of its Japanese name, "Hunky Dory." As a port city, Yokohama had more than its fair share of drinking establishments, with the resultant disorderly conduct. In the late 1950s, when container ships altered world shipping and docking practices, the port died, and it honky-tonk nature decreased markedly. At the corner of Minato Odori and Honcho-dori is the **Port Opening Memorial Hall** (Kaiko Kinen Kaikan), a structure erected in 1910 to commemorate the 50th anniversary of the port. It is easily recognized, since it has a tower with a clock face on each of is four sides, and it now serves as a public hall with a theater on its second floor for events of various kinds. The building is noted for its late Victorian redbrick-and-granite façade and its stained-glass windows on the second floor. It is open daily except on Mondays.

4 YOKOHAMA PARK

Continuing on Minato-odori for several blocks, past the Bank of Japan building on the right, brings one to the north side of **Yokohama**

Park (Yokohama Koen). The park has a peculiar heritage. Knowing the predilections of foreigners and the seamen who would be coming to Yokohama once the port became active, Ii Naosuke, the shogun's premier, had a delightfully landscaped park with fountains created on an artificial island–as the location for a high-class brothel for foreigners. The Miyozaki brothel district was surrounded by a moat and had one wooden bridge as its entry and exit, and it opened for business in November 1859, just four months after Yokohama came into existence for Westerners. It was modeled after the famed Yoshiwara red-light district of Tokyo, and experienced managers were brought from the Tokyo and Kyoto brothel quarters to operate it. In time the pleasure quarters, as it was euphemistically called, became less high-class, and it soon had a variety of pleasure units, ranging from 18 select houses of assignation to 85 lesser establishments. Then there were low-class establishments, where the girls were on display behind bars. (The term *girls* is used rather than women because most of the 1,400 "entertainers" did not live to any great age.) Many of the individuals had been sold to the brothel owners, and they existed virtually as slaves within the complex, with little chance of freedom. On their usually early deaths, they were deposited in a mass unmarked grave by the brothel owners. Outside these "pleasure gardens" lurked prostitutes, ever anxious for business and ever fearful of the police. That venereal disease was rampant in early Yokohama can hardly be questioned. The town had a reputation with seamen worldwide as a lusty village. In other respects the pleasure quarter served less carnal pleasures as well, for here were teahouses and geisha houses, where trained entertainers acted as hostesses and could sing and dance for the pleasure of diners who could afford such expensive entertainment.

A fire within the brothel area on November 26, 1866, found the girls trapped within their quarters, the one exit being too narrow to accommodate the throng fleeing the fire. The death toll reached 400 girls, many of whom flung themselves from the windows of their buildings to escape the flames only to perish from their fall. The pleasure quarters thereafter were moved farther from the center of the town. The 1866 conflagration was referred to as the Pig Pen Fire, and during the 14 hours in which the fires raged, it obliterated not only the pleasure quarter but a goodly portion of the city as well. One-quarter of the foreign sector and one-third of the Japanese sector of the city were reduced to ashes. In the rebuilding that followed, the city became one of brick and stone buildings instead of the flammable structures that had sprung up since 1859. In 1877, the former brothel sector was turned into a true public park to serve both the foreigners and Japanese, as many foreigners had homes in the area thereafter. Today, a stadium has been built within the park, occupying much of the grounds, and one of the Baltard buildings that once graced Les Halles in Paris has been re-erected here.

Turning away from Yokohama Park onto the main street that passes before Yokohama City Hall and Kannai Station, both on the left, one reaches Basha-michi (Horse Carriage Road) at the fourth intersection. Basha-michi runs from Kannai Station to Shinko Pier. The street was created in 1867 after the great fire of the previous year, and it then had to be widened in the 1870s to carry the heavy traffic of the foreigners in their horse-drawn vehicles. It was then that it received what is now a rather antiquated name. While it seemed a wide street at the time of its creation, today it is merely another city street that is not particularly remarkable. With redbrick sidewalks, gas lamps, and embedded pictorial tiles of scenes of early days of the city in the pavement, an attempt has been made to return to the look of the period before 1900. The attempt is a noble one, but the tall buildings of the late 20th century that line the street belie any effort to recreate a past that no longer exists.

Returning to the waterfront by turning right onto Basha-michi, one comes after several minutes to Benten-dori. On the left beyond the intersection is the **Kanagawa Prefectural Museum of Cultural History** (Kanagawa Kenritsu Rekishi Hakubutsukan), a neo-Renaissance European-style building from 1904 that was bought by the prefecture in 1967 to become a museum of local history and natural history. Its collections reflect the long history of Kanagawa Prefecture and not just of Yokohama alone. The exhibits range from period rooms of a small farmhouse of the past, to an office of Edo times (1603–1868), to tools and artifacts of daily life from prehistoric times (Jomon and Yayoi periods) to those of the beginning of the modern era in the prefecture. Three special exhibitions are mounted annually in a special hall. (Open from 9:30 a.m. to 5:00 p.m. except Mondays, the day following national holidays, the last Tuesday of the month, and the New Year period. Entry is ¥300.)

Two blocks farther, at the intersection with Honcho-dori, the colonnaded former **Bank of Yokohama** (now Yokohama Island Tower) occupied a corner position for many years. In 1996, the 30-foot (9-meter)- tall, 1,300-ton façade of the 65-year-old building was physically moved on rails to a new location at the intersection, since a subway was being constructed under its former site. That additional subway line reaches from JR Yokohama Station and Sakuragicho Station to serve the Minato Mirai development through Bashamichi Station. After the station, the street approaching the waterfront has become Bankokubashi-dori, and this wider avenue brings one to the end of Kaigan-dori. A short detour to the right along Kaigan-dori reveals the **Nippon Yusen (Japan Shipping) Building** with 16 Corinthian columns. This 1936 structure now houses the small **NYK Maritime Museum**, which includes ship models and shipping-related items as well as a library and small café. (Open from 10:00

a.m. to 5:00 p.m., closed Mondays and the day after National Holidays. Entry ¥400.)

Returning to Bankokubashi-dori, ahead lies **Shinko Pier**, with a Ferris wheel rising on the left and two redbrick warehouses on the right. Here ends the first part of this tour, covering the old center of Yokohama, the Kannai (Inside the Checkpoint) sector in which foreigners were at first restricted to this transplanted foreign community within Japan. From here, our attention turns to Yokohama's modern face (although even among the harborside skyscrapers one is never far from remnants of Yokohama's past), as the tour moves to the glistening and highrise Minato Mirai 21 complex and then on to the Yokohama Station area.

One of the fields in which Japanese industry excelled after World War II was the building of large ships, many of which were laid down in the Mitsubishi Shipyard in Yokohama. Indeed, the booming economy of the period after 1950 in Yokohama led to the revitalization of the city, and particularly of its Kannai area, after the city's destruction twice in a 20-year period. This renewal received its initial impetus from the need by

Yokohama from the bay. The Akarenga is in the center, with Landmark Tower dominating the skyline.

the United States for materials during the Korean War, in which the U.S. and the U.N. were involved. Then the economic boom years of the 1980s saw a further growth in the city as more land in the bay was filled in for industrial expansion,

In time, a worldwide glut of ships led to the closing of the Yokohama yard, and a plan to revitalize the area of shipyards, rail yards, and piers was undertaken. The goal was to create a new district in Yokohama named Minato Mirai 21 (Port of the Future, 21)–"21" referring to the 21st century. The undertaking was begun in 1983 with a completion date set for the year 2000, by which time a branch of the city subway would extend from Yokohama Station to the area and continue along Honcho-dori. It was anticipated that this renewal would bring in clean industry and reverse the situation in which thousands of Yokohama residents daily commuted to Tokyo to work. An estimated 200,000 jobs would be created, and housing for some 10,000 people would be generated in the new international sector. The plan called for the creation of a major art museum for the city, a convention center, and a maritime museum, as well as high-rise housing. The land was cleared, the new art museum was built, and an International Exhibition was held on a portion of the cleared land in 1989. However, hampered by the economic downturn of the 1990s, the project has not moved to completion as quickly as had been hoped, and the redevelopment of the area is continuing.

5 MINATO MIRAI 21 COMPLEX

The Minato Mirai 21 complex is connected to the Sakuragicho rail station by an overhead, glass-enclosed walkway that is 257 yards (230 meters) long and offers a choice of a moving sidewalk or a regular pedestrian sidewalk, but our entry will be via Shinko Pier, where we left off. The grounds of Minato Mirai are graced with fountains and trees, and this former working pier now houses a variety of elements that both complement and have become integral to it. To the right as you walk through Shinto Pier are the old brick warehouses at the bay side, which were built between 1910 and 1917 and have been restored to form the **Red Brick Park**, which comprises the **Aka Renga Soko Shopping Mall** and a large convention center. Off to the left at the

Red Brick Park, a renovated warehouse complex that contains the Akarenga Shopping Mall

western end of Shinto Pier is **Yokohama Cosmo World Amusement Park**, whose 345-foot (105-meter)-diameter steel Ferris wheel takes 15 minutes to complete a full circle. Cosmo World offers everything from carousels to a roller coaster. (Open Monday through Friday from 11:00 a.m. to 9:00 p.m. and from 11:00 a.m. to 10:00 p.m. on weekends. Closed some Thursdays.)

The street running past Cosmo World and across a small bridge brings one to the **Minato Mirai 21 complex** proper. Looming above is the 32-floor **Yokohama Grand Intercontinental Hotel**, which has added a whimsical touch to the skyline (if so large a building can be described as "whimsical") in that it is shaped like a sail. Adjacent to the hotel is **Queens Square,** another shopping mall, and just beyond the hotel and overlooking the bay is the **National Convention Hall** and a separate Exhibition Hall, which can supplement conferences and conventions with its displays. In front of the complex is **Seaside Park** (Rinkai Park), with lawns, fountains, and flowers along the bay side providing a place to relax and enjoy the skyline of a revived Yokohama port city."

Leaving Seaside Park and heading west, one passes the Convention Hall on one's left. Continuing to walk away from the water, one can then take the second turning to one's left. From here, the next right (at the end of the street) leads past the Minato Mirai subway station and on to the **Yokohama Museum of Art** (Yokohama Bijutsukan), the second largest art museum in Japan. Its permanent collection includes paintings by Cézanne, Magritte, Dali, and Japanese artists as well as paintings relating to Yokohama. Changing exhibitions of high quality, often borrowed from overseas collections, take place a continuing basis. The building was designed by Kenzo Tange, who, it is said, redesigned a portion of it in the planning stage after he had visited the then new Musée d'Orsay in Paris. The resemblance between the huge hall of the Yokohama Museum of Art and that of the Musée d'Orsay is more than a coincidence. The Yokohama Museum of Art is unusual in that it provides not only galleries of art but workshops and classrooms for those wishing to work in various fields of the creative fine arts. (Open from 10:00 a.m. to 6:00 p.m., closed Thursdays, the day after national holidays, and at the New Year period. Entry fee varies with the exhibition.)

Shortly after the Museum of Art, on one's left, comes what is arguably Yokohama's best-known sight, the American architect Hugh Stebbins's **Landmark Tower**, a 972-foot (296-meter)-tall structure that cost

$2,500,000 to build. This 70-story building surpasses the 1990s' Tokyo City Hall by 165 feet (50 meters). Its large central atrium is five stories high, and its first 48 floors are given over to offices, while floors 49 through 70 form the Royal Park Hotel. The Sky Restaurant is on the 68th floor, while the Sky Garden observatory is on the 69th, and on a clear day the Sky Garden offers a view of up to 50 miles (80 kilometers) in all directions. The tower's elevators can whisk one to the top in 45 seconds. (The Sky Garden is open daily from 10:00 a.m. to 9:00 p.m., but remains open until 10:00 p.m. on Saturdays and daily from July to September. Entry ¥1,000.) The building is owned by the Mitsubishi Estates, and it provides 200 shops (open from 11:00 a.m. to 8:00 p.m.), restaurants (open from 11:00 a.m. to 10:00 p.m.), and a large and a small hall for cultural events on its fifth floor. In front of the tower is the **Landmark Plaza**, yet another mall filled with shops, restaurants, and cafés.

The **Mitsubishi Minatomirai Industrial Museum** lies opposite Landmark Plaza, and it covers the development of current and future technology in the areas of communication, energy, the global environment, and the oceans. Various passenger ship models are on view as are active displays such as a ship's navigation program and a simulated helicopter flight that takes one over Mt. Fuji. (Open from 10:00 a.m. to 5:00 p.m., closed on Mondays except when a national holiday falls on a Monday, in which case the museum is closed the next day. Entry is ¥300.)

Immediately west after the Mitsubishi Museum one can turn left onto Minato Mirai-odori, the main north-south street. After 200 yards, Minato Mirai-odori leads, on one's left, to the 1989 **Yokohama Port Museum** (Yokohama Minato Hakubutsukan), whose historical exhibits of shipping and the port of Yokohama span the period from the arrival of Commodore Perry and his "Black Ships" in Yokohama Bay to the present time. As part of its exhibits, the adjacent *Nippon Maru* **training ship** is docked in an 1896 ships' basin of stone. The Nippon Maru, built in 1930 and once known as the "Swan of the Pacific," was a sailing vessel used to train naval students, and in the course of its active life it circled the globe some 46 times before being decommissioned in 1984. (The museum and the ship are open 10:00 a.m. to 5:00 p.m., though may close an hour earlier or

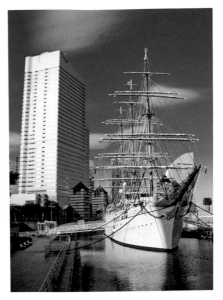

The Nippon Maru, *a former training ship*

later depending on the season. Closed on Mondays and the day after national holidays. Entry is ¥600.)

From the Yokohama Port Museum one can see **Sakuragicho Station** about 100 yards directly south. To the right is the overhead moving walkway that connects Sakuragicho Station with the Port Museum, the Landmark Tower, and the Yokohama Museum of Art.

6 KANGAI (BEYOND THE CHECKPOINT)
Sakuragicho Station was the original terminus of the Tokyo-Yokohama railroad of 1872, and a monument on its rear side commemorates its opening. Later, when the rail network expanded, the station was bypassed in favor the new Yokohama Station, which was situated away from the port area in order to provide a more direct connection between Tokyo and Osaka. Today Yokohama Station has become a hub of department stores and underground shopping passageways as well as a transportation center. Crossing through the underpass from Sakuragicho Station to the other side of the railway right-of-way, one enters the greater portion of Yokohama that is seldom visited by tourists. This was the original area for Japanese citizens when Yokohama was founded, part of **Kangai** (Beyond the Checkpoint or Barrier). Here in the **Noge**

district, with its *oden* and *yakitori* food stalls, small bars, and streets festooned with red lanterns, some flavor of old Yokohama still exists. The district includes two parks, a temple, a shrine, and shopping areas. The **Nogeyama Fudoson Temple** (Naritasan Yokohama Betsu-in) is directly behind the rail station by two streets to the west, and it is a branch of the great Naritasan Temple to Fudo near Narita International Airport. The Nogeyama Fudo Temple is noted for its fair, which occurs three times a month, on the 1st, 15th, and 28th.

To the southwest of the temple and about a half mile (800 meters) west of Sakuragicho Station is the Nogeyama Koen, the public Noge Hill Park, which contains two gardens in Japanese style given as gifts by well-to-do local citizens. The park is noted for its springtime cherry blossoms and its beautiful chrysanthemum display from mid-October to late November, as well as its seasonal flower displays throughout the year. The city has added to the park's ambiance by purchasing the former residences of wealthy resident merchants, which are open to the public without charge. Within the park, the **Nogeyama Zoo** presents some 1,200 animals of 200 different species. (The zoo is open from 9:30 a.m. to 4:30 p.m., closed on Mondays or the following day if a Monday is a national holiday. No admission charge.) Adjacent is the Nogeyama recreation ground, which contains a swimming pool, an open air theater, playing fields, and a view over the city and the port.

To the north of the Fudo Temple is the **Iseyama Kodai Jingu**, the Ise Hill Great Shrine (15 minutes on foot from the rail station), a branch of the important Grand Shrine at Ise. Created in 1870, the shrine holds the spirit of the Shinto tutelary deity of Yokohama, and its grounds are reached through a 33-foot (10-meter)-tall cedar torii. Its annual festival is held from May 14 through 16. With its double cherry blossoms in the spring and its various festivals, the shrine attracts 1,500,000 Japanese visitors a year. It is open daily without charge.

Beyond the Ise Hill Shrine and half a mile (800 meters) from the rail station to the north is **Kamon-yama Park**, which is noted for the loveliness of its cherry blossoms in mid-April. The park receives its name of *Kamon* from the statue of Kamon-no-kami, the post-humous name of Ii Naosuke (1815–1860), the Tokugawa premier who arranged for Yokohama to become a city back in 1859 and who was assassinated by anti-foreign radicals in 1860. When the bronze statue in his memory was first mounted in Hikone, the former premier's home district, it was found with its head removed the following day, an act that shows the intensity of the anti-foreign feeling at the time. Repaired, the statue was melted down 80 years later during World War II, after the anti-foreign attitude had resurfaced once more. Recreated in 1954, the statue now stands atop a hill overlooking the port that Ii Naosuke brought into being in 1859. The mid-April bloom of the park's double-petal cherry blossoms makes for a striking sight, with Landmark Tower looming behind. The Kanagawa Prefecture Concert Hall, a public library, and a youth center are adjacent.

To the west of the Negishi rail line between the Sakuragicho and Kannai Stations is the **Isezaki Mall**, with large department stores, movie houses, and a variety of shops. The mall extends for one mile (1.5 kilometers) behind Kannai Station and is linked to it by an underground mall. Directly to the west of Kannai Station is **Odori Koen**, a narrow park seven-tenths of a mile (1.2 kilometer) long on land reclaimed from the Yoshida River. It has a Stone Square with an outdoor theater and a statue by Rodin, while the park's Water Square has a fountain and a statue by Henry Moore. Its "forested" area is called, appropriately, the Green Wood, small though it is.

From Sakuragicho or Kannai Stations a train can be taken one stop to Ishikawacho Station, where Walk 21 begins. Alternatively bus #8 from Sakuragicho Station can be taken for Walk 22 to the **Sankei-en Garden**. The train can, of course, be taken back to Tokyo if one has toured enough for one day. Trains run every five to ten minutes for the 30 minute run to Tokyo Station.

7 THE KANAGAWA DISTRICT AND YOKOHAMA STATION

There are two other sites that should be mentioned, even though the first one is no longer worth visiting for historical purposes, and that one is the **Kanagawa district** of Yokohama. (*Kanagawa* is also the name given to the prefecture of which Yokohama is the capital city.) Historically, Kanagawa, the portion of the city to the north of Yokohama Station, is important because it was here that the initial foreign consulates were set up, and

Picnicking under the cherry blossom at Nogeyama Koen

it was here also that, at the Hongaku-ji Temple, Townsend Harris worked out the commercial treaty that opened Japan to intercourse with the rest of the world. Today Kanagawa has been swallowed by greater Yokohama. Its beach, along which ran the Tokaido Road (between the emperor's palace in Kyoto and the shogun's castle in Edo), is but a memory. The bay has been filled in, and modern industry and housing have obliterated the historic past.

However, just a quarter mile (500 meters) north of the Yokohama Station on Taka-shima-dai hillside the **Hongaku-ji Temple** still exists. The temple became the temporary U.S. consulate in 1856 when Townsend Harris was permitted to move here from Shimoda. The details of a commercial treaty between the United States and Japan were agreed upon here, and in July of 1858 Harris was able to sign the first commercial treaty with Japan aboard a U.S. warship in the bay in front of Kanagawa. The old temple buildings was destroyed in the bombing raids of May 1945 with the exception of the front gate, and the present buildings are all of post-1945 construction. The temple is thus no more than a footnote to history today.

The second site is **Yokohama Station**, at which all Tokaido Line trains stop (with the exception of the Shinkansen trains, which take a different route and stop at Shin Yokohama Station to the west). Something should be said about this area, even though it is not central to the portions of Yokohama that are of major interest to visitors. Yokohama Station has virtually become a "city within a city." Shopping is a favorite Japanese pastime, and the underground mall and the department stores, particularly to the west of the station, are the delight of Yokohama's conspicuous consumers. **Takashimaya** has a store to the west of the station, where a number of hotels are located, while the **Porta Underground Shopping Mall** and the **Sogo Department Store** lie to the east of the rail line, as do the bus terminal and hotels. Sogo even has a museum of art, Japan's first in-house art museum in a department store, which hosts a variety of exhibitions (open 10:00 a.m. to 8:00 p.m.). Restaurants of all kinds may be found on either side of the station.

> ### GETTING THERE
> This walk starts at Ishikawacho Station, three short stops from Yokohama Station on the JR Negishi Line.

A tapestry of flowers at the Nihon Odori Flower Art Festival in Yokohama, held every May

FESTIVALS IN YOKOHAMA

Note: On the 1st, 15th, and 28th of each month the **Noge Fudoson festival** is held.

January 1 **Hatsumode** The first visit to shrines or temples to pray for good fortune in the New Year. It is particularly popular at the Iseyama Shrine.

Early January **Dezome-shiki** The Fireman's Festival at Nihon-odori in the Naka-cho district for a display of fire equipment and acrobatics by firemen.

January or February **Shunsetsu (Chinese New Year)** A delightful New Year's Festival is held in Chinatown.

February 3 or 4 **Setsubun** A ceremony marking the end of winter and the beginning of spring. Roasted beans are scattered in temples and shrines to drive out evil and to welcome in good fortune.

Early February to early March **Yokohama**

International Doll Festival A viewing of dolls from around the world at the Doll Museum.

Late February (and Late September) **Motomachi Charming Sale** Held twice a year in Motomachi Shopping Street.

Mid-to-late February **Plum Blossom Viewing** At the Sankei-en Garden and other parks in Yokohama.

Late March to early April **Cherry blossom time** in the Sankei-en, Nogeyama Park, Kamonyama Park, Minato Mirai 21 area and elsewhere in Yokohama.

Mid-to-late April **Tulip time** in Yokohama Park and Yamashita Park.

Late April **International Street Performers' Festival** Performers from all around the world present their acts at the Isezaki Mall, Bashamichi, Minato Mirai area and Noge shopping street.

Late April **Spring Fair of Flowers** in Yokohama Park.

Late April to early May **An exhibition of flower beds** in *Yamashita Park*.

Early May The summer-long **Port Festival** begins with a costume procession starting at Yamashita Park.

Ice Cream Memorial Day (Bashamichi March) A stall opens along to Bashamichi-dori. On an origin memorial day, Bashamichi Ice Cream is given.

May 14–16 **Iseyama Kodai Jingu Shrine Festival** Stalls line the entry to the shrine. In odd-numbered years a *mikoshi* (a portable shrine) is paraded about the grounds.

Late May to early June **Iris viewing** at Sankei-en garden.

Late May to early June **Yokohama Kaiko Kinen Bazaar** The traditional bazaar which continues from 1920. There is a lot of booth which sells various items in Yokohama Park.

June 1st weekend **Port Opening Festival** Features a concert on the sea stage in Seaside Park in Minato Mirai; evening fireworks; and a bazaar at Yamashita.

First Sunday in June **Jamokamo Matsuri** A 30-foot (10-meter)-long straw snake is carried through the city to absorb "evil," which "evil" is then removed by burning the straw snake. The festival is centered on the Shinmei Shrine in Tsurumi ward.

Mid June **Short-Short Film Festival** The U.S. Academy Award official recognition, the greatest international short film festival in Asia. Brilliant Short Shorts Theater near Shin-takashima or Minatomirai station.

Mid-July **Fireworks display** in Yamashita Park closes the Port Festival.

August **Kanagawa Shinbun** Fireworks display over the bay in front of Yamashita Park.

First or second Sunday in August **Ouma-nagashi (Setting Afloat of Horses)** Large straw effigies of horses are set afloat in the bay to do away with illness or bad luck. At the Honmoku Shrine.

Mid-August **Kuan Yu Celebration** In Chinatown, fireworks, lion, and dragon dances.

Late-August **Kanazawa Festival** Fireworks

over the sea in front of the Umi-no-koen Park.

Late August **Honmaku Jazz Festival** at Honmaku baseball field.

Late August **Tsurumi River Festival** Fireworks over the river at the Tsukudano Park.

September 1 **Shio Matsuri (Ocean Current Festival)** To ensure a plentiful catch of fish and the safety of fishermen at Kanazawa Fishing Port.

September 13 or 15 **Osan-no-miya Matsuri** An autumn festival in which the Hie Shrine *mikoshi* (portable shrine) is carried about.

October 1 **Chinese Independence Day Festival** in Chinatown, a parade of dancing lions and dragons.

October 10 **Double-ten Celebration** In Chinatown, a parade of dancing lions and dragons.

Early October **World Festa Yokohama** The festival where one can experience the culture of the world. Enjoy local food, music and dance, selling of folkcrfats in Yamashita Park.

Mid-October to end of November **Yokohama Jazz Promenade** The greatest jazz festival in Japan. **Chrysanthemum display** at the Nogeyama Koen Gardens.

Late October **Yokohama International Festa** Enjoy local food, music, and workshop in Zo-no-hana Park.

Late October and into November **Chrysanthemums on view** at the Sankei-en Garden.

Late October **Basha-michi Festival** Rickshaw and open carriage rides to recall early Meiji days in Yokohama. Yokohama Marathon starts at Yamashita Park.

November on a few occasions **Cock Festival** (Tori-no-ichi). At the Otori Shrine, bamboo garden rakes (for good luck) and *daruma* dolls (which can bring good luck) are sold.

Walking Tour 21

YAMATE-CHO
The Yamate Bluff–A Haven for Westerners on Higher Ground

1. **Motomachi and the Italian Garden**
2. **The Foreigners' Cemetery**
3. **Harborview Park and French Hill**

The great Yokohama conflagration of 1866 destroyed much of the city, laying waste almost 50 percent of the Kannai downtown, where the main foreign business and residential area was located. The downtown would be rebuilt, but in the future it was to become primarily the business and commercial portion of the city and not a residential area. **Yamate (the Bluff)**, the high ground to the south of Kannai, would see Western-style houses arising as the Europeans and Americans moved to this higher ground. Here on the Bluff, as the residents called their new

residential area, homes, churches, mission schools, and even a cemetery for foreigners would be developed. There was another reason for the move to the Bluff–and that was fear. The political unrest in Japan between the Japanese who favored the opening to the West and those opposed it was reaching a crisis. On a snowy March morning in 1860, as the Japanese premier, Ii Naosuke, and his guards left his mansion to walk the brief way to the shogun's castle in Edo, he was ambushed and slain by opponents of the policy he implemented. That same year, the translator of the British ambassador was slain by those opposed to foreigners, and in 1861 the same misfortune befell Dutchman Henry Heusken, the translator for Townsend Harris, the American ambassador. In September 1862, Charles Richardson, an Englishman, was slashed to death by the bodyguards of the lord of Satsuma for not paying the required respect to the daimyo and his entourage on the Tokaido Road. In retaliation, when admission of guilt for the act and adequate recompense for the death were not forthcoming, the British navy shelled the main town of the lord of Satsuma. Then in 1864 two British officers were murdered in Kamakura by two fervent haters of foreigners.

As a result of the 1864 murders, the French moved 250 troops into Yokohama, while the British stationed more than 1,000 troops in the city, and the heights of the Bluff provided space for the necessary military encampments. Then came the 1866 fire, which seriously damaged Kannai. This catastrophe led the Japanese government to permit the Europeans and Americans to lease ground on the Bluff for homes for the foreign community. It was a great relief to Western civilians to live close to the military encampments in the event that more violence from Japanese radicals should threaten Western

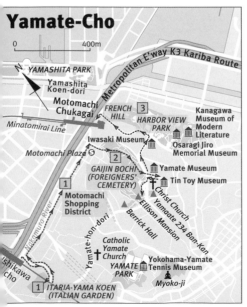

lives. Americans and Europeans could thus work in Kannai during the day and then retreat to the safety of the Bluff at evening. The Bluff was to remain primarily a foreign residential enclave for the next 50 years.

☐1 MOTOMACHI AND THE ITALIAN GARDEN

The Bluff can be approached from either the overhead walkway to French Hill (Furansu-Yama) from the street behind Marine Tower (see Walk 20) or from the south exit of Ishikawacho Station on the JR Negishi line, the same station where Walk 20 began. From the rail station, the walk leads through **Motomachi**, the area in which the fishermen of the pre-1859 era lived. In the period after 1859, Motomachi became the chief shopping district for both residents and ship's crews who came ashore in Yokohama. The shops were at first run by foreigners, but in time Japanese merchants would take over. Today the shops of the Motomachi shopping street on the south side of the Nakamura River stretch from the Negishi line toward the harbor, and the shops are a far cry from those of the 1860s and later, for now the 200 or more stores specialize in expensive wares, much of them from overseas. Here are boutiques, coffee shops, restaurants, and shops concentrating on the latest of fashions.

A brief diversion may be made before or after viewing Motomachi. Just ten minutes by foot to the south of Ishikawacho Station, on the hill above the Negishi Line's Yamate tunnel, is **Itaria-yama Koen**, the Italian "Hill" Garden that takes its name from the fact that the Italian consulate was located here after 1880. The park consists of a European-style garden with waterfalls and other water features, and a European-style house that is open to the public. (The gardens are open from 9:30 a.m. to 5:00 p.m., closed on Mondays and the day after national holidays. Admission is free.)

☐2 THE FOREIGNERS' CEMETERY

Returning toward the station and then east along the Motomachi shopping street, at Motomachi Plaza a road leads uphill to the **Gaijin Bochi**, the Foreigners' Cemetery, which is encircled by a road. (Twenty minutes on foot from Ishikawacho Station.) Here through the years some 4,000 foreigners from 40 different countries have been buried. The first foreigner to be interred in Yokohama was Robert Williams, a marine on one of Commodore Perry's ships, who died in 1854 after being hit on the head with a stone

The Gaijin Bochi (Foreigners' Cemetery) overlooking the waters of the Yokohama Bay area

thrown by a Japanese while the marine was onshore. (His body was later disinterred and moved to the cemetery next to the temporary American consulate in Shimoda.) The Foreigner's Cemetery reflected the sensibilities (or lack thereof) of the foreign community of the day, for Jews and Chinese were buried in a separate portion of the burial grounds. No Japanese were interred here, and at a later date a separate cemetery for the Chinese was opened farther to the south. To the Japanese, the cemetery is rather exotic, with its stone angels over graves, tombstones with crosses, and other elements of Victorian mortuary taste. (The Foreigners' Cemetery is open to visitors on Saturdays and Sundays from late March to November 30 from noon to 4:00 p.m. A donation of at least ¥200 is required to enter.) Those buried here included many of the important individuals of the early foreign community, and one of the more noted graves is that of Edmund Morell, who died in 1871. Morell engineered and supervised the construction of the first railroad in Japan, which stretched from Tokyo to Yokohama and opened in 1872, the year after Morell's untimely death. Appropriately enough, the 1934 gravestone, which replaced an earlier stone over Morell's grave, is in the shape of a railroad ticket.

Many Victorian-style houses may still be found on the Bluff, although the catastrophes of 1923 and 1945 reduced their number greatly. On the far (south) side of the cemetery is the **Yamate Museum** (Yamate Shiryokan) in a 1909 wooden house, the oldest extant wooden building on the Bluff. The house preserves the interior of the late 19th-century home of a well-to-do Japanese family who lived in Western style. The museum contains much in the way of memorabilia of the early days of the Bluff, with everyday items from the West as well as ukiyo-e prints of foreign life of Meiji times (1868–1912) in Yokohama. (The museum is open from 11:00 a.m. to 4:00 p.m. but closed Mondays. Entry is ¥200.) Between the Yamate Museum and the Christ Church (Protestant, originally 1863, destroyed in 1923 and since rebuilt) is a street leading away from the cemetery to the south. At its end is the **Tin Toy Museum** (Buriki-no-omocha Hakubutsukan), which specializes in tin toys from the 1890s to the present (open daily from 9:30 a.m. to 6:00 p.m., until 7:00 on weekends; entry is ¥200). Adjacent to it is Christmas Toys, a sales shop given over to Christmas-related items–although a very few

Japanese are Christians, they do celebrate the trappings of the commercial and secularized version of Christmas, just as do Westerners overseas.

Beyond Christ Church, following the road to the west along Motomachi Garden, which adjoins the Foreigners' Cemetery, one comes to the **Ellison Mansion**, a 1926 structure designed by the Czech architect Antonin Raymond, who assisted Frank Lloyd Wright in design elements of the 1920s Imperial Hotel in Tokyo. This clapboard building houses photographs that illustrate what life was like before the catastrophes of the 20th century changed the Bluff forever.

3 HARBORVIEW PARK AND FRENCH HILL

Returning past Christ Church and the Yamate Museum, the road continues toward Harbor View Park and French Hill. Along the way is the **Iwasaki Museum**, which exhibits costumes from ancient Egyptian times on, and there are displays of art as well as of Art Nouveau glass. It also has materials of the former Goethe Theater, which enlivened life on the Bluff for many years with productions of Shakespeare's plays, including the first ever performance of Hamlet in Japan, before the theater too became but a memory. Japanese visitors are fascinated by the fact that one can don costumes of past years to be photographed–for a fee. (Open from 9:40 a.m. to 6:00 p.m. daily except Mondays and the day after national holidays. Entry ¥300.)

Beyond the museum is the International School and then **Harbor View Park** (Minato-no-Mieru Oka Koen), the "Hillside Garden Overlooking the Port" created in 1962 at the end of the Bluff to take advantage of its excellent vista. This was the location of the British military barracks in the early years of the city. During the day one can look across the bay to the far side of the Yokohama Bay Bridge, the entire Kannai section of downtown Yokohama, and the Yokohama Port Symbol, a 158-foot (48.19-meter)-tall tower completed in 1986 at the Honmoku piers to mark the opening of the port of Yokohama. The park provides a charming view of the city at night when the lights of Yokohama shine forth. Across from the park to the south is a memorial museum to a noted Japanese author, the **Osaragi Jiro Memorial Museum** (Osaragi Jiro Kinenkan). A number of Osaragi Jiro's novels are concerned with life in Yokohama, but he was also fascinated with

Harborview Park with the Yokohama Bay Bridge in the background

France and with French life, as can be seen by some of his possessions in the museum where his 30,000 books and a model of his study are on view. The museum is obviously for those with a particular interest in Japanese literature, but it does have a coffee shop that may appeal to those who do not have a penchant for novels in Japanese. (Open from 10:00 a.m. to 5:30 p.m., but closing at 5:00 p.m. between October and March. It is closed on Mondays. Entry is ¥200.) Nearby is another specialized museum, the **Kanagawa Museum of Modern Literature** (Kenritsu Kanagawa Kindai Bungaku-kan) a further street to the south. Its collection is obviously primarily in Japanese. (Open from 9:30 a.m. to 5:00 p.m. except on Mondays. Entry fee varies with the exhibition.)

Turning north along the road that parallels the western edge of Harbor View Park, French Hill becomes a continuation of the park toward the Kannai portion of the city. (French Hill was an encampment area for French troops in the 1860s to 1875.) The Bluff as a Victorian residential enclave for foreigners pretty much came to an end in the 1920s. World War I had occupied the Western nations in their war efforts, and the Japanese, who

were not so involved, were able to expand their commercial ties with Asia at the expense of the Western nations. Thus European and American trading interests found new competition from the growing Japanese commercial and industrial complex, which tended to become monopolistic and interlocked. The 1923 earthquake was a further discouragement to the continuation of the foreign community, and the Bluff as a foreign residential area began its slow decline.

This concludes the tour of Yamate-cho. An overpass leads from French Hill down to the streets behind the Marine Tower on the waterfront. The steps from the overpass, on the other side of the elevated expressway over the Nakamura River, can bring one down to the street that leads to **Ishikawacho Station** for a train back to Tokyo, or one can enjoy the Kannai section of Yokohama with its many restaurants before leaving the city.

> ## *GETTING THERE*
> This walk starts at the south exit of Ishikawacho Station, three short stops from Yokohama Station on the JR Negishi Line.

Walking Tour 22

SANKEI-EN GARDEN AND HASSEI-DEN FOLK MUSEUM

A Classic Garden Filled with Teahouses, and the Hall of the Eight Sages

1. **Sankei-en Garden**
2. **Honmoku Civic Park**
3. **Hall of the Eight Sages**

Beyond the Yokohama Bluff (Yamate-cho), there are two sites to the south of the city center that are of interest. Unfortunately, they are at a sufficient distance that they cannot be properly included in a walking tour of the Bluff, but they can be easily reached by bus from the city. Bus #8 runs from Yokohama Station to the Sakuragicho rail station and to the canopied bus stop #2 between the station and the Port Museum in Minato Mirai. Then it goes down Honcho-dori and through the diversified housing and commercial area to the south of the Kannai section of the city, an interesting modern area, before reaching the destination of this tour, the Sankei-en Garden. In April, many of the streets south of the central portion of the city are delightfully enlivened with the white blossoms of the cherry trees that line the roadways.

The **Sankei-en Garden** is at the southeast end of Yokohama on a raised sector above former Honmoku Beach and Negishi Bay. It arose as a magnificent planned garden, but also became the home to a number of ancient and historic buildings that were moved to the garden beginning in the early 1900s. The Sankei-en (Three Glens Garden) was created in the late 19th century by Hara Tomitaro (1868–1939), a Yokohama businessman of taste who was a poet, a fine calligrapher, and a classical Chinese scholar. This local entrepreneur had grown wealthy in the silk trade, which for many of the early years of Yokohama history was the financial basis for the port's prosperity. As his wealth increased, he took over some 43 acres (17 hectares) of land about Honmoku-yama (Honmoku Hill), and he gave it the name of the pseudonym he used as a poet, that of Sankei (Three Glens), to become the Sankei-en (Three Glens Gardens).

The Sankei-en is rich in many flowering trees and shrubs, including flowering cherry trees of a number of varieties, apricot trees, azaleas, and wisteria, and its ponds display water lilies and lotus plants. To all these natural beauties Hara Tomitaro added a number of historic edifices (now numbering 16 buildings) brought from various areas of central Japan. Within all this loveliness, in 1920 he built his traditional *shoin*-style retreat, the Haku-un-Tei (White Cloud Residence) alongside the ancient gate to the Inner Garden of the complex. In 1906 he opened the gardens to the public for their enjoyment, although he continued to live in his original mansion and after 1920 in his retreat villa in the Inner Garden until his death in 1939. Responsibility for the Sankei-en was assumed in 1953 by the Sankei-en Hoshokai, a private foundation that will ensure the continued proper management of this unusual garden and park of historic buildings, and by 1958 the new organization had restored the landscaped grounds, which had suffered from wartime neglect, and the gardens were fully reopened to the public.

1 SANKEI-EN GARDEN

After taking bus #8 to Honmoku Sankei-en-mae bus stop, a ten-minute walk brings one to the garden entrance. On leaving the bus, the intersection just before the bus stop should be taken to the left past an interesting housing complex of Western style private homes that are just before the garden entry. (The gardens are open from 9:00 a.m. to 5:00 p.m. Entry is ¥500.) From the entry gate the path leads between the main pond on the left and the Lotus Pond on the right, which is followed

Sankei-en Garden in the fall

by the Water Lily Pond, also on the right. Behind this latter pond, hidden away by greenery, was the mansion in which Hara Tomitaro originally lived.

Continuing, through the **Inner Garden** (Nai-en) ticket gate, one then proceeds through the **Go-mon**, a 1708 gate from Kyoto that opens onto the Inner Garden proper. To the right, just inside the Go-mon Gate, lies the **Haku-un-tei**, the White Cloud Residence, a *sukiya*-style house that Hara built as his retirement villa in 1920. (Unfortunately, it is not open to the public.) As an educated individual (he attended Waseda University in Tokyo) and a friend of artists and internationally minded cohorts, he made his home a center for an intellectual group in the 1920s and 1930s. Many of their members were assassinated by the nationalistic militarists of those years, who did not approve of internationalism or non-Japanese ideas. The path diverts to the left and then continues over a small bridge that crosses one end of the good-sized pond that stands before the Rinshun-kaku complex (described below). On the left is the **Tenzui-ji Juto Oido**, a modest wooden building noted for the intricate carving on its exterior door. This small building was created at the request of Toyotomi Hideyoshi in 1591 at the Daitoku-ji Temple in Kyoto to house the *juto* to

Omandokoro, his mother. A *juto* is a monument or offering of respect. In this case it was erected by Hideyoshi to celebrate his mother's longevity after her recovery from an illness and as an offering for the eventual peace of her soul. It was only moved here from the Daitoku-ji in 1960, long after Hara's death, and thus the present association managing the Sankei-en Garden is further enriching Hara's project.

A small covered bridge is crossed over a branch of the pond, and on the right is the **Rinshun-kaku Villa**, which was brought here in 1917. Composed of three units, this villa once belonged to a branch of the ruling Tokugawa clan (1603–1868), and it was first erected in 1649 on the Kii Peninsula beyond Osaka by Tokugawa Yorinobu as his second residence. It is noted as being the only intact villa in the architectural style popular with the daimyo, the lords of feudal fiefdoms in Japan in the 1600s. As with such noble villas, a visiting daimyo would first be admitted to the *hikae-no-ma*, a "reception room" of four chambers in which he would await admittance to the owner's inner villa. From the *hikae-no-ma*, the visitor would be welcomed to the *sekken-no-ma*, the "official" part of the villa where the resident feudal lord would greet and meet with his visitors. The last portion of the villa was the *okugata*, the inner private quarters of the lord and his family, and this consisted of five rooms. The villa has *fusuma* (sliding interior panels to subdivide rooms) decorated by noted artists of the Kano school of painting of the 17th century (Kano Tanyu, Kano Yasunobu and Kano Tsunenobu).

Among the 20 rooms of the villa, the Tengaku (Celestial Music Room) in the women's quarter is noted for its transom grills above its doorways since the wood carving to this music room includes flutes and pan pipes. The room also contains a *katomado*, a bell-shaped doorway that was typical of temple architecture rather than domestic buildings. The Suninoe room is the only one with furnishings and with colorful paintings on the *fusuma*, and it and the adjacent Naniwa room were used for receiving guests on formal occasions.

The path continues uphill beyond the villa by means of a series of steps to the **Gekka-den Guest House**, built by Tokugawa Ieyasu as a waiting room for daimyo at the Fushimi Castle outside of Kyoto in 1604, a year after he became shogun and began his rule over all of Japan. The Fushimi Castle was the stronghold of Ieyasu's predecessor, Toyotomi Hideyoshi, and it was noted for its many rooms in the lush Momoyama style of architecture and decoration. Many of the units of the castle were dispersed when the castle was later dismantled, and the Gekka-den eventually was obtained for the Sankei-en and established here in 1917. Beyond the Gekka-den is the **Kinmo-kutsu Teahouse**, an anomaly among these ancient buildings, since it was constructed in 1918 at Hara's request, and it received its name from the fact that the post that forms part of its tokonoma was created from a handrail that once belonged to the Kinmo-kaku Gate of the Daitoku-ji Zen monastery in Kyoto. (The pillar of a tokonoma is best if it is made from a rare or unusual or historic piece of timber.) As can be deduced from the number of teahouses on the grounds of the Sankei-en, Hara had a passion for *cha-no-yu*, the traditional tea ceremony.

Coming back down the hillside and crossing over a branch of the pond once more, the Choshu-kaku is approached. The **Choshu-kaku Teahouse** was built in 1623 by Iemitsu, the third Tokugawa shogun. This irregular, two-story tea pavilion was designed by Shogen Sakuma, and he placed the roof, the second-floor balcony, and the railing off-center

according to the design tenets preferred for teahouses. The building once stood in the Nijo-jo Castle in Kyoto, the official residence of the Tokugawa shoguns in the emperor's capital.

The path continues past the Choshu-kaku to the **Shunso-ro Teahouse**, which was created in 1621 by Urakusai, also known as Oda Nagamasu, the brother of the mid-15th-century civil ruler of Japan, Oda Nobunaga.

Sankei-en Garden & Hassei-den

0   100m

N

5
4
3

INNER GARDEN (NAI-EN) 6
2
7
8

C
G
(G

Yokohama Pottery Center

SHANGHAI-YOKO FRIENDSHIP GA

Honmoku St
Koen-mae Bus

Urakusai served Toyotomi Hideyoshi, his brother's successor after Nobunaga died. Then in 1586, taking residence in Kyoto, he shaved his head as a Buddhist monk and took the name of Urakusai, by which he has since been known. He studied the tea ceremony under the great tea master, Sen-no-Rikyu, and he began his own tea ceremony school, which was continued after his death. At one time, he

had his mansion in Edo (Tokyo) outside the shogun's castle, and that area of modern Tokyo has retained his name as Yurakucho. This teahouse was also known as the Kyuso-tei, the "Nine-Window Arbor" due to the number of windows in the structure. (Teahouses were often called *arbors*.)

Just before the path regains the main route leading to the exit of the Inner Garden, the

1. **Haku-un-tei (White Cloud Residence)**
2. **Tenzui-ji Juto Oido**
3. **Rinshun-kaku Villa**
4. **Gekka-den Guest House**
5. **Kinmo-kutsu Teahouse**
6. **Choshu-kaku Teahouse**
7. **Shunso-ro Teahouse**
8. **Renge-in Teahouse**
9. **Sankei Memorial Museum**
10. **Sankei-en Temmangu Shrine**
11. **Tomyo-ji Main Hall**
12. **Taishunken Teahouse**
13. **Yokobue-an Teahouse**
14. **Yanohara Farmhouse**
15. **Tokei-ji Butsu-den**
16. **Rindo-an Teahouse**
17. **Sanju-no-to Pagoda**
18. **Shofukaku Observatory**

Sankei-en's pagoda glimpsed from the main pond

Renge-in Teahouse is on the right, a structure created in 1917 for Hara's pleasure. The path now passes by the large pond in front of the Rinshun-kaku and arrives at the 1988 **Sankei Memorial Museum**, which exhibits examples of Hara Tomitaro's calligraphy and brush paintings, an outgrowth of his studies in Chinese civilization. Video displays offer a color tape of the *Four Seasons of the Sankei-en*, as well as other scenes of the garden. Rest rooms are available in this building.

A number of ponds lie within the Inner and the Outer Gardens, with paths along and across them, thereby offering an opportunity to stroll and to enjoy the varying aspects of the Sankei-en. On leaving the Inner Garden, one is back at the main pond that was passed en route to the Inner Garden gate. A monument to Hara lies before three small refreshment stands, where one may obtain tea and other light refreshments. In the **Outer Garden**, the path to the left forks, and one takes the left fork onto **Nakano-shima Island** with its Kankatei Arbor and panoramic views, then on to the opposite shore via Kashinbashi Bridge. Before one is the old **Sankei Temmangu Shrine**, since every establishment needs a Shinto shrine to house the guardian deity of the land. To the left, the path goes to the exit gate, but instead this

tour follows the path to the right, along the narrow neck of the pond. The **main hall of the Tomyo-ji Temple** appears on the left. It was moved here from the town of Kamo in Kyoto Prefecture in 1914. Adjacent is the **Taishunken Teahouse**, where refreshments may be obtained. Farther along the path is another teahouse built by Hara, the **Yokobue-an,** followed by the 1650 **Yanohara Farmhouse,** a huge, three-story building in the *gassho* style, a style noted for its steep roof that is often compared to hands clasped in prayer. The building was disassembled and moved here from Shokawa village in Gifu Prefecture in 1960, when the town was to be submerged by a new dam. The house was obviously the home of a wealthy, extended farm family in the Hida mountain country of the Japanese Alps. One-half is in the luxurious *shoin* style, which was enjoyed by powerful daimyo and aristocrats, while the other half is in the traditional rural Hida architectural style. This traditional architectural design created a three-storied, steeply pitched, thatched-roof structure built without nails and with its beams secured by thick straw ropes The path then leads to the 1509 **Tokei-ji Butsu-den**, the Buddha Hall, from the Tokei-ji Zen sect temple in Kamakura. This is the temple that was known as the "Divorce Temple," since a woman who took refuge here could, after an appropriate time, be considered divorced from her husband. From here, the path descends and crosses the Kankakyo footbridge, continuing past the 1970 **Rindo-an Tea Ceremony House** donated by the modern Sohen School of the Rindo Tea Ceremony Association. Heading uphill, one comes to 15th-century **Sanju-no-to**, a three-story pagoda of the former Tomyo-ji Temple that is a companion to the main hall visited down below. Standing 82 feet (25 meters) tall, it was built within the temple grounds in 1457 and is the oldest pagoda in the Kanto region. Continuing uphill, the **Shofukaku Observatory** is reached. An early Hara family mansion built in 1890 once stood here, with a view over the Negishi Bay, but it was destroyed in the air raids of 1945. A new utilitarian structure was built in its place in 1964, its second floor providing a view over Negishi Bay; the view is no longer as outstanding as it once was, since the outlook is one of oil refineries and other industrial units as well as a new elevated highway created on landfill. The former beach has been obliter-

A closer view of Sanju-no-to Pagoda

ated and a good portion of the bay filled in below the hill on which the viewpoint stands.

Descending from the belvedere, taking a left and then a sharp left, one comes to the south gate of the Sankei-en.

2 HONMOKU CIVIC PARK

From the south gate, one can cross over a waterway to the Honmoku Shimin Koen, the **Honmoku Civic Park**, which has the **Shanghai-Yokohama Friendship Garden**. This is a classical Chinese-style garden with a permanently ensconced Chinese Pleasure Barge, a building in a traditional Chinese architectural style on an island in the lake. The building exhibits decorative art objects from China. Also in the Civic Park is a huge swimming pool, which refreshes up to 7,000 people at the same time. This may be a belated attempt by the government to make up for the loss of the seafront beneath the park, when the beach was sacrificed to industrial progress and employment.

3 HALL OF THE EIGHT SAGES

Just outside the Honmoku Civic Park is the **Hassei-den Kyodo Shiryokan** (Hall of the Eight Sages). The Hassei-den is a two-story, octagonal, ferroconcrete building that was an attempt to recreate the Yumedono of the

Horyu-ji Temple south of Nara, a building dedicated to Prince Shotoku, who brought Chinese learning and Buddhism to Japan. The Hall of the Eight Sages was built in 1932 on the Hachioji-hama headland by Adachi Kenzo as a national center for spiritual education. The date of 1932 is significant, since this is the period when the militaristic ultranationalists in Japan were directing the nation in the path that led to World War II. Adachi Kenzo (1864–1948) was an ultranationalist who became the Home Minister for Spiritual Training. The Hall of the Eight Sages has a collection of farming and fishing materials on its first floor, which were meant to bring to mind a simpler era in Japanese life before industrialism took hold. On the second floor are eight life-sized figures of the sages: Sakyamuni, the Buddha and progenitor of the Buddhist faith; Confucius, who set the moral tone for society and government; Socrates, as one of the earliest of Western philosophers; Jesus, as a prophet of mercy and justice; Prince Shotoku, who brought the light of Chinese learning and Buddhist thought to Japan; Kobo Daishi, the priest who gave Japan the artistic and religious beliefs of Tantric Buddhism; Shinran, who popularized Amida Buddhism and the help Amida can give to his followers and brought the truths of Buddhism in a simplified form to the mass of the Jap-anese people; and Nichiren, whose dogmatic form of Buddhism and fiercely nationalistic spirit perhaps foretold the rigidity and aggressive nature of Japanese state Shinto after 1868. In the midst of these eight sages selected by Adachi Kenzo is a large mirror, which, he said, was a symbol of the universe. (Open 9:30 a.m. to 4:00 p.m., closed on third Wednesday of each month and national holidays. No entry charge.)

A bus can be taken back to the heart of Yokohama from either the Honmoku Shimin Koen-mae bus stop from the Hall of the Eight Sages or from the Honmoku Sankei-en-mae bus stop from the Sankei-en. The bus from the former bus stop, or a taxi from the Hall of the Eight Sages, can bring one to Negishi Station for a train back to town.

GETTING THERE
This walk begins at the Sankei-en Garden, which are reached by the #8 bus from Yokohama Station.

KAMAKURA OVERVIEW
Visiting the Famous Temples and Shrines of the Ancient Minamoto Capital

One of the attractions for city dwellers is the seaside, and Tokyo is fortunate in that it has a number of towns and resorts by the sea that are within easy reach. Kamakura is the town that has the most to offer such visitors on a day trip, and these enticements can be enriched as well by brief visits to specific sites in towns but a few minutes from Kamakura. Kamakura, only 25 miles and one hour from Tokyo and reached in even less time from Yokohama, is a seaside resort that attracts residents of the area's large cities as well as to tourists from throughout the world. Surrounded by evergreen hills on three sides, with its fourth side open to a sandy beach and the waters of Sagami Bay, it is little wonder that it is crowded on weekends and during the summer. But Kamakura has manmade attractions as well: great Zen temples, a huge bronze Buddha image meditatively towering over the suburb of Hase, and a broad promenade in Kamakura that runs from the sea to the great vermilion shrine to the Shinto God of War on a rise overlooking the city. There are 118 Buddhist temples and 41 Shinto shrines (only a selection of which are described below, since only the major sites are of interest to most visitors from overseas), as well as other attractions of a more popular seaside resort nature.

Kamakura was the center of Japanese government from 1192 to 1333, when members of the Minamoto clan ruled as shoguns, the civil rulers of the nation, and then when the Hojo clan served as regents for the shoguns and ruled behind the scene. It is quite appropriate, given the military nature of the government that went by the name of Bakufu (Tent Government), that Hachiman, the Shinto deity of war, was the tutelary god for Kamakura. This benign-looking town has a history of military mayhem, clan rivalry, the assassination of enemies or family members lusting for power—and even the killing of members of the imperial family. It is a tale of intrigue and double-dealing, but also of great temples that offered the latest in Buddhist thought from China as well as the glory of impressive architecture and lovely gardens. It even boasts one of the few places in Japan where, in past centuries, an abused or unwanted wife could find surcease from her woes and the end to her marriage—in a nunnery, where, after a comparatively brief stay, she could be free of an uncaring husband. It goes without saying

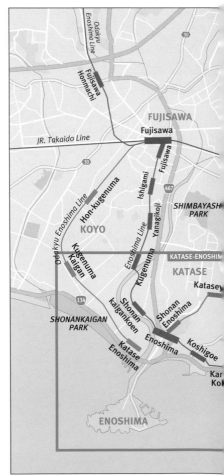

that the temple was quickly labeled the "Divorce Temple," a name that has endured.

In Tokyo, the Yokosuka Line can be taken to Kamakura from Tokyo Station. Trains to Zushi, Yokosuka, and Kurihama all stop at Kita-Kamakura (North Kamakura) and Kamakura Station. Coming from Tokyo or Yokohama on the Yokosuka Line, there is a choice of the same entries into Kamakura as well. On either route, it is possible to alight from the train at Kita-Kamakura to visit two of the city's great Zen temples and the "Divorce Temple" mentioned above. If the train is taken to the next station, Kamakura Station, the great Wakamiya Oji promenade to the central Shinto shrine overlooking the city and sea is at hand. For the purposes of this tour, we shall begin at Kamakura Station and explore the Central and Kita-Kamakura (North Kamakura) area before traveling to Hase and its great Buddha. This tour is very long and to be fully enjoyed would require an overnight stay in Kamakura. It can, however, be broken up and portions skipped depending on one's taste and stamina. For visitors who prefer a shortened walk, the North Kamakura portion may be omitted, although this means missing two of the five great Zen temples of Kamakura. Alternatively, one may choose to visit only a few highlights, such as the Wakamiya Oji and the Tsurugaoka Hachiman-gu and Kamakura-gu Shrines in Central Kamakura, the Kencho-ji and Engaku-ji Temples in North Kamakura, and the Great Buddha in Hase.

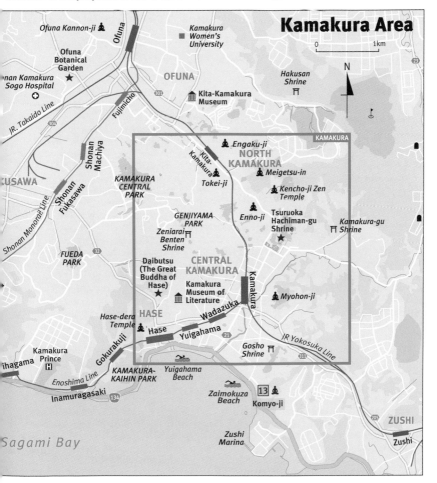

Walking Tour 23

KAMAKURA AND HASE
The Famous Temples and Shrines of Central and North Kamakura and a Great Bronze Buddha

1. **Hongaku-ji Temple**
2. **Wakamiya Oji**
3. **Wakamiya Shrine**
4. **Tsurugaoka Hachiman-gu**
5. **Shirahata Shrine and Yoritomo's Grave**
6. **Egara Tenjin Shrine**
7. **Kamakura-gu**
8. **Kencho-ji Temple**
9. **Enno-ji Temple and the Kings of Hell**
10. **Tokei-ji Temple (the Divorce Temple)**
11. **Engaku-ji Temple**
12. **Zeniarai Benten Shrine (diversion)**
13. **Komyo-ji**
14. **The Great Buddha of Kamakura**
15. **Hase-dera Temple**

On leaving Kamakura Station to the east, a square before the station marks the beginning of **Komachi-dori** with its red torii in the far left corner of the square. Komachi-dori is a narrow street headed to the northern part of Kamakura, and it was once the main street of the medieval city when it was lined with the residences of samurai and the shops of merchants. Komachi-dori is still a shopping street, with several hundred shops offering a variety of items meant to tempt tourists and visitors down from Tokyo or Yokohama for the day. It also boasts a monument to the 13th-century priest Nichiren, a volatile and often politically indiscrete Buddhist reformer of whom more will be said below. Across the station square in the middle of its far side is a street that leads to Wakamiya Oji, the impressive ceremonial avenue running from the sands of Yuigahama Beach and Sagami Bay to the vermilion Tsurugaoka Hachiman-gu Shrine on the hillside at the end of this broad avenue. It is one of those peculiarities of time that Wakamiya Oji became a dividing mark between temples of the Nichiren Buddhist sect to the east and temples of the Rinzai Zen sect to the west.

1 HONGAKU-JI TEMPLE
Across Wakamiya Oji, where Komachi-dori crosses it to the south, is the **Hongaku-ji Temple**, created in 1436, which sits on the site where the priest Nichiren lived on his return from exile in 1274 on the island of Sado in the Japan Sea, having first offended and then been forgiven by the Hojo Regents, who ruled Japan from Kamakura. Nichiren's enmity toward Zen Buddhism had not sat well with Zen's Hojo adherents. Two centuries later in 1407 a portion of the ashes of this anti-establishment monk was deposited at this temple, and it thus became and has remained an important pilgrimage site for adherents of the Nichiren sect of Buddhism. The temple grounds also have the **grave of Masamune**, a famed medieval swordsmith. Each year this Buddhist temple holds a demonstration of sword making in Masamune's honor, and the sword smith at work is always clad in the white robe of a Shinto priest. The demonstration is thus a ceremony with Shinto religious overtones held on the grounds of this dissident Buddhist sect. This admixture of the elements of Japan's two major faiths marks the ability of the Japanese to amalgamate diverse beliefs, an ability that has always characterized the Japanese consciousness and that often puzzles visitors from Europe and America, where religious beliefs are frequently more rigid and less open to compromise.

2 **WAKAMIYA OJI**

Since the early 1200s there has been but one place to begin an exploration of Kamakura, and that is at the beginning of the **Wakamiya Oji**, the Young Prince's Way. This ceremonial path was created in 1180 by Minamoto Yoritomo, the first Kamakura shogun, as an offering to the gods for the successful pregnancy of his wife, Masako. The young prince who was born thereafter was Minamoto Yoriie, the second and luckless Kamakura shogun. The Wakamiya Oji begins at the waterfront at **Yuigahama Beach** and heads inland for 1,530 yards (1,400 meters) to the Tsurugaoka Hachiman-gu, the Hachiman Shrine of Kamakura, on the hillside ahead. The crescent shaped beach that stretches along Sagami Bay was used as an archery and riding practice ground in the days of the Kamakura shoguns, and today it is one of the most popular summer beaches for the greater Tokyo area. The broad, straight Wakamiya Oji avenue that begins at the beach was planned with the laws of perspective in mind in order to make it appear to be even longer than it is. Originally, it was 30 feet (9.1 meters) wide at the stone torii near its beginning but only 12 feet (3.7 meters) wide at the third, vermilion torii in front of the Hachiman Shrine, thereby providing the impression of greater length.

Today, Wakamiya Oji is a commercial roadway up to the first red torii, where it becomes two narrow roads on either side of a raised promenade between the two roads. The side roadways were lowered in the late 1800s to accommodate the level of other local roads as Kamakura moved into the modern era, and they are now lined with commercial buildings. The avenue's impressive length, with the sea at its southern beginning, its great vermilion shrine on the hillside on its northern end, and the green hills surrounding the city on three sides, was meant to awe any visitor to the shogun's government of the 13th and 14th centuries. Given the military dictatorship that the Kamakura government was, the fact that its great shrine was dedicated to Hachiman, the Shinto God of War, gave proper indication to any visitor of its warlike nature.

Running as straight as an arrow, the Wakamiya Oji has a 33-foot (10-meter)-tall stone torii erected in 1618 at the seaside to mark the beginning of the path to the Hachiman Shrine, and two more vermilion torii lie astride the path en route to the grounds of the shrine. The raised pedestrian route between the two vermilion torii is lined with azaleas and cherry trees, and in early April the way is enriched with the color of their blossoms. The start of the pedestrian route is guarded by two very large stone *koma-inu* (Korean lion-dogs) placed there in order to prevent evil from encroaching on the path to the Hachiman Shrine. Beyond the second vermilion torii, where the side roadways end and the stone paved approach to the shrine begins, are two low bridges on either side of the larger, major **Taiko-bashi** (Drum

The start of the pedestrian route guarded by two large koma-inu *and a vermilion* torii

Bridge), all three of which cross a stream that connects a pond on either side of the bridges. The Taiko-bashi is an exceedingly steep, arched, "half moon" bridge, so steep that it would be a challenge to mount it if it were not closed to the public—and even a greater challenge to descend the opposite side without injury. It is claimed that success in crossing the bridge will assure that one's wish will be granted, the most appropriate wish being for a safe arrival at the foot of the far side of the bridge!

The Gempei-ike, the **Gempei Ponds** (*Gempei* is the word for the two clans described below), on either side of the bridges, have symbolic significance. Masako, shogun Yoritomo's wife, saw the ponds as symbolizing the defeat in the 1100s of the Taira clan, which had ruled Japan before being conquered by her husband. Masako had three islands set in the pond on the right and four islands in the pond on the left. The right-hand pond is the Genji-ike, the **Genji pond**, the pond of the victorious Minamoto clan of Yoritomo, while the other pond is the Heike-ike, the **Heike pond**, that of the defeated Taira clan. What does this symbolism mean? The Genji pond has three islands, and the Japanese word for three, *san*, can also mean "birth," while the Heike pond has four islands, and the Japanese word for four, *shi*, can also mean "death." To make the point even clearer, the Genji pond has lotus plants that bloom with white flowers, a symbol of purity, while the lotus of the Heike pond have a red bloom, symbolizing the Taira blood that was spilled in 1185 at the battle of Dan-no-ura when the clan was defeated. (The lotus plants bloom from late July to mid-August.) A small bridge leads to one of the islands on either side of the bridges; the island on the right holds a shrine to the Shinto deity Benten.

The Minamoto defeat of the Taira, as symbolized in the two ponds, was brought to an even unhappier conclusion in time. In these ponds in 1333, the conqueror of the last Minamoto/Hojo regent washed his sword of the blood of the head of the last Hojo regent he had decapitated, after the regent along with his soldiers had committed ceremonial suicide (*seppuku*) in the nearby Harakiri Yagura (literally, Harakiki Tomb) cave. Thus, the Minamoto period of rule that began in blood at Dan-no-ura in 1185 came to a bloody end in 1333 at Kamakura, and the city lost its role as the de facto seat of national governance.

Behind the Heike pond, on the left, is the

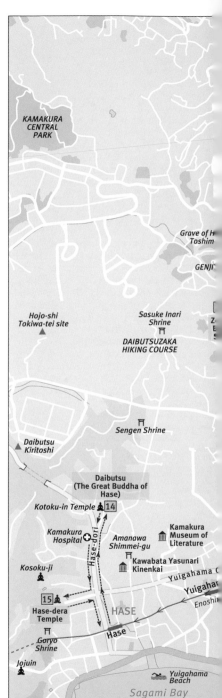

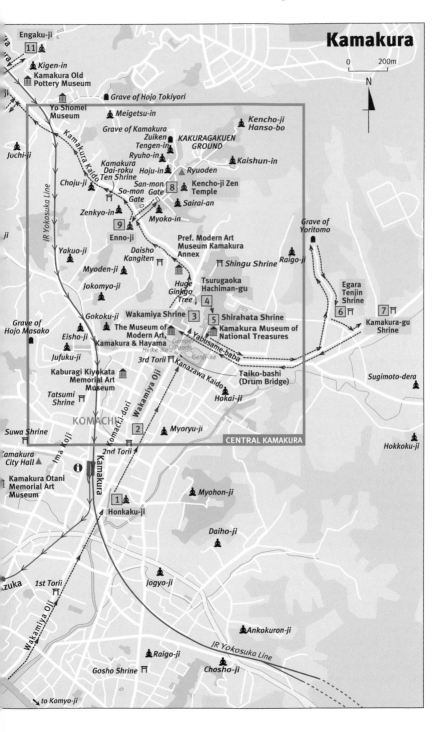

Kamakura

0   200m

N

Engaku-ji
11
Kigen-in
Kamakura Old
Pottery Museum

Grave of Hojo Tokiyori

Yo Shomei
Museum
Meigetsu-in
Grave of Kamakura
Zuiken
Tengen-in
Ryuho-in
Kamakura
Dai-roku
Ten Shrine
Hoju-in
Choju-ji
San-mon
Gate
So-mon
Gate
Zenkyo-in
Myoko-in
Enno-ji
Yakuo-ji
Daisho
Kangiten
Myoden-ji
Jokomyo-ji
Huge
Ginkyo
Tree
4
Gokoku-ji
Wakamiya Shrine
3
The Museum of
Modern Art,
Kamakura & Hayama
Eisho-ji
Jufuku-ji
Kaburagi Kiyokata
Memorial Art
Museum
Tatsumi
Shrine
KOMACHI
Suwa Shrine
2
Myoryu-ji
Kamakura
City Hall
2nd Torii
Ima-koji
Kamakura
Kamakura Otani
Memorial Art
Museum
1
Honkaku-ji

KAKURAGAKUEN
GROUND
Kencho-ji
Hanso-bo
Kaishun-in
Ryuoden
Kencho-ji Zen
Temple
Sairai-an
8
Pref. Modern Art
Museum Kamakura
Annex
Shingu Shrine
Raigo-ji
Grave of
Yoritomo
Egara
Tenjin
Shrine
6
Tsurugaoka
Hachiman-gu
Shirahata Shrine
5
Kamakura Museum of
National Treasures
Yabusame-baba
3rd Torii
Kanazawa Kaido
Taiko-bashi
(Drum Bridge)
Hokai-ji
Sugimoto-dera
Kamakura-gu
Shrine
7
Hokkoku-ji
CENTRAL KAMAKURA

Grave of
Hojo Masako

Kamakura Kaido

JR Yokosuka Line

Komachi-dori

Wakamiya Oji

Genpei-
Ponds-
Genpike
Heike-ike

Jochi-ji

9

Myohon-ji
Daiho-ji

1st Torii
Jogyo-ji
Wakamiya Oji
Raigo-ji
Gosho Shrine
Chosho-ji
Ankokuron-ji
JR Yokosuka Line
to Komyo-ji

The Shimo Haiden Lower Shrine Prayer Hall, with a giant gingko tree to the left, said to be 1,000 years old

1951 ferroconcrete **Museum of Modern Art, Kamakura & Hayama** (Kanagawa Kenritsu Kindai Bijutsukan) created by Junzo Sakakura, a student of Le Corbusier. In typical Corbusier fashion, the building is set on *pilotis* (columns) in the water. A new wing was added to the museum in 1966, and the original building now houses the museum's numerous temporary exhibitions. The museum's collection consists of Japanese and Western art from the 19th century, and it includes sculptures, paintings in oil, watercolors, and prints. (Open from 9:00 a.m. to 5:00 p.m. except on Mondays, the day following a national holiday, and the New Year period. Entry varies with the exhibition, from ¥700 to ¥900.)

A narrow road, the **Yabusame-baba**, the Road of the Mounted Archers, crosses the Wakamiya Oji. Since the Kamakura shogun rule was a military government, Yoritomo's

men had to perfect the arts of war. Thus there were contests in which mounted archers galloped at a high speed past targets, shooting their arrows at the targets as though they were shooting at enemies. Today, in April and in September, the Yabusame contests are still held in medieval costume, and the affair attracts huge crowds to this narrow road along which the contest takes place. To the left on the Yabusame-baba is the **Kamakura Museum of National Treasures** (Kamakura Kokuhokan), a reinforced concrete building created in 1928 to house fragile art pieces from area temples, shrines, and private collections, a precaution brought about by the damage to the area and artistic artifacts in the Great Kanto Earthquake of September 1, 1923. The museum was built in the *azekura* or log-cabin style of the Shosoin Treasury in Nara, albeit in modern reinforced

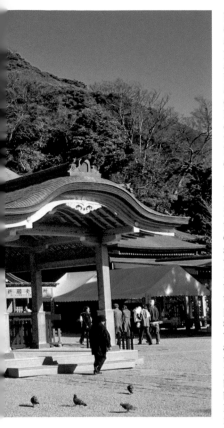

brother's line wiped out. This spot, it is claimed, is where the original Haiden platform stood on which Yoritomo forced his brother's pregnant mistress to dance–in the hopes that she would have a miscarriage and lose his brother's baby. In defiance of Yoritomo, Shizuka Gozen, his brother's mistress, sang of her love for Yoshitsune while performing her dance. Yoritomo was enraged and was only prevented from harming Shizuka by his wife Masako. Eventually, when Shizuka's baby boy was born, it was immediately put to death at Yoritomo's order.

A broad staircase beyond the Haiden leads upward, and on the left is a huge gingko tree, 73 feet (22 meters) tall and 23 feet (7 meters) in girth, supposedly planted one thousand years ago. In reality, this is but an offspring of the original tree. The tree has historical significance, for it is indicative of the blood vengeance that was all too typical of the Kamakura Minamoto clan and their relatives, the Hojo clan, who succeeded them. Behind the huge tree in 1219 hid Kugyo, the high priest of the Tsurugaoka Shrine who was the son of the second, ineffectual shogun Yoriie, who had retired to a monastery and then been assassinated. Twenty-eight-year-old Sanetomo, the brother of Yoriie, became the third Kamakura shogun, displacing Yoriie, and thus bad blood existed within the family. This was blood Yoriie's son vowed to spill. Sanetomo had been warned to wear armor under his robes of state on his visit to the Hachiman Shrine, but he had disregarded the advice. As Sanetomo left the grand staircase from the shrine to walk down Wakamiya Oji in two feet of snow on January 27, 1219, Kugyo, disguised as a woman, sprang from behind the tree and struck off the head of his young uncle. Kugyo escaped with the head, which was never found. Needless to say, Kugyo was later captured and killed. The result was the takeover of governance by the Hojo regents, relatives of Minamoto Yoriie and Sanetomo (through their mother Masako, who was a member of the Hojo family). The strange situation came into being whereby the emperor reigned but did not rule, and his appointed shogun ruled in name only, while the Hojo regent for the shogun had the real governmental power.

concrete. Its collections contain over 2,000 items from the years 1192 to 1573, which are shown a few at a time, and exhibits are changed four times a year. The treasured art objects include Japanese sculpture, Chinese and Japanese paintings, and decorative arts in enamel and metals. A pamphlet in English is available. (Open from 9:00 a.m. to 4:30 p.m. except on Mondays, national holidays, and the New Year period. Entry ¥300.)

Closing the end of Wakamiya Oji, before the monumental stone staircase to the Tsurugaoka Hachiman-gu Shrine, is the wall-less, roofed **Shimo Haiden**, the Lower Shrine Prayer Hall, a stage-like structure. A roofed ablution basin stands on the left before the Haiden. Unfortunately, Minamoto Yoritomo, the ruling shogun, had a violent hatred for his younger and more popular brother, Yoshitsune. He was determined to have him killed and have his

3 WAKAMIYA SHRINE

To the right of the bottom of the stairs is the 1624 **Wakamiya Shrine**, the Young Prince's Shrine, the junior shrine to the grand shrine

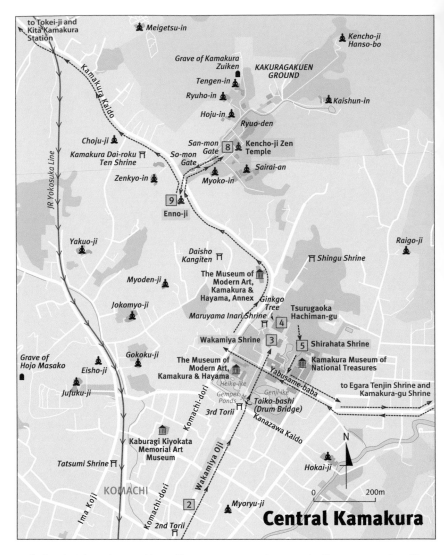

to Tokei-ji and
Kita Kamakura
Station

Meigetsu-in

*Kencho-ji
Hanso-bo*

*Grave of Kamakura
Zuiken*

**KAKURAGAKUEN
GROUND**

Tengen-in

Ryuho-in

Kaishun-in

Hoju-in

Ryuo-den

Kamakura Kaido

Choju-ji

*San-mon
Gate*

8 *Kencho-ji Zen
Temple*

*Kamakura Dai-roku
Ten Shrine*

*So-mon
Gate*

Zenkyo-in

Myoko-in

Sairai-an

JR Yokosuka Line

9

Enno-ji

Yakuo-ji

Raigo-ji

*Daisho
Kangiten*

Shingu Shrine

Myoden-ji

**The Museum of
Modern Art,
Kamakura &
Hayama, Annex**

*Ginkgo
Tree*

*Tsurugaoka
Hachiman-gu*

Jokomyo-ji

Maruyama Inari Shrine

4

Wakamiya Shrine

3

5

Shirahata Shrine

**Kamakura Museum of
National Treasures**

*Grave of
Hojo Masako*

Gokoku-ji

**The Museum of
Modern Art,
Kamakura & Hayama**

Eisho-ji

Heike-ike

Yabusame-baba

Jufuku-ji

*Gemper
Ponds*

Genji-ike

to Egara Tenjin Shrine and
Kamakura-gu Shrine

*Taiko-bashi
(Drum Bridge)*

3rd Torii

Kanazawa Kaido

**Kaburagi Kiyokata
Memorial Art
Museum**

N

Tatsumi Shrine

Hokai-ji

KOMACHI

0   200m

2

Myoryu-ji

Central Kamakura

2nd Torii

at the head of the staircase. A large Shinto
sacred rope hangs on its façade, while
two large, stone lanterns stand before the
building. The shrine is dedicated to Emperor
Nintoku, the son of the Emperor Ojin (who is
also seen as the incarnation of Hachiman, the
Shinto god of war). Nintoku, whose gigantic
tomb is outside of Osaka, is said to be a "good
emperor." Looking out over the countryside
from his palace, he noted the absence of
smoke coming from the chimneys of his
people's houses. He recognized that this

meant they were in dire poverty and could not
afford fuel, so he rescinded taxes in order not
to burden them further.

4 TSURUGAOKA HACHIMAN-GU

Returning to Wakamiya Oji, at the top of the
61 steps comprising the monumental
staircase at the end of this broad avenue is
the **Tsurugaoka Hachiman-gu**, the
Hachiman Shrine to the tutelary deity of the
city of Kamakura. It was originally situated
close to the sea when it was founded in 1063

by Minamoto Yoriyoshi as a branch of the Iwashimizu Hachiman-gu, the important Hachiman Shrine honoring the Shinto god of war near Kyoto. In 1191 Minamoto Yoritomo, the first of the Kamakura shoguns, moved the shrine to its present location on the rise overlooking Kamakura, since, as has been indicated, Hachiman served as the tutelary deity for the ruling military Minamoto clan.

Shinto mythology can be quite complicated and often less than rational (what myths of any religion are rational?). Thus the shrine to Hachiman also celebrates both the Emperor Ojin, who is said to have reigned from 270 to 319, and his mother, the Empress Jingu (from whom the English word *jingoist* is derived). The Empress Jingu was a fearsome warrior in her own right. Legend claims that, pregnant and due to deliver at the time of her war with Korea, the empress put a stone behind her sash to delay the birth of her child—the future Emperor Ojin, who remained in her womb many months beyond term. As politically "modest" as she was warlike and determined, she ruled as regent for 69 years, refusing to ascend the throne as queen. (Despite this modesty, history has always referred to her as Empress Jingu.) It is little wonder, given this background, that in Shinto mythology Emperor Ojin and Hachiman, the God of War, became identified as one and the same being. Thus Hachiman, the emperor Ojin, and the Empress Jingu are the deities of this shrine.

The 1191 shrine was reconstructed in the 17th century by the Tokugawa shoguns, and after a fire in 1817 it was once more rebuilt in 1823 in the lush Momoyama period (1580-1630) architectural style. As with most Shinto shrines, within the colonnaded square of the shrine are the linked main shrine buildings, the Haiden (Prayer Hall) at which prayers are offered, and the Honden (the structure that holds the spirits of the deities). At one time, as a joint Shinto-Buddhist site, there was a bell tower, a pagoda, and other Buddhist halls, but these were all removed by the Meiji government in its antagonism to Buddhism after 1870.

The brilliant vermilion shrine is entered through a large gateway, the Romon, guarded on either side of its entry by the images of the armed Shinto guardians Udaijin and Saidaijin. About the two main structures is a gallery in which many of the shrine's treasures are on view. Here are seven *mikoshi* (portable shrines), bows and arrows, medieval armor, saddles, kimono, screens depicting

battles, maps of old Kamakura, and two wooden images, one of them being of the goddess Benten. Two gold-mounted swords given by Emperor Go-Shirakawa to Yoritomo, five silk robes given by the Emperor Kameyama in 1281, a war drum with a design of golden dragons that once belonged to the murdered Prince Morinaga, a canopied boat ornamented with mother of pearl that the emperor of China gave to Toyotomi Hideyoshi in the 1590s, and even relics of Yoshitsune, Yoritomo's despised brother, have found a home here. (Legend has it that once the shrine even held the skull of Yoritomo as a youth!) The *mikoshi* are used at the shrine's annual festival on September 15-16, when the deities of the shrine are taken on procession through the town in these portable units. (The shrine treasures are on view from 9:00 a.m. to 5:00 p.m. April to October and from 9:00 a.m. to 4:00 p.m., from November to March. Entry ¥200.) The shrine reception hall can be entered from the east side of the complex, and here visitors so desiring can be exorcised of evil spirits. To the west of the main shrine is an area at the roadway to Kita-Kamakura where new automobiles may be exorcised against various modern dangers caused by evil spirits.

5 **SHIRAHATA SHRINE AND YORITOMO'S GRAVE**
Returning to the foot of the 61 steps that led to the Tsurugaoka Hachiman Shrine, turning left, and continuing to the east of the Wakamiya Shrine, a left turn brings one to the **Shirahata Shrine**, the White Flag Shrine, the white flag or banner being the symbol of the Minamoto. *Hachiman* in Chinese means "eight banners," and eight white banners are said to have descended from the heavens at Usa in Kyushu where the original shrine to Hachiman was established. Since Hachiman was the protecting deity for the Minamoto clan, the clan banner was white in honor of its guardian deity. This White Flag Shrine is dedicated to the spirits of Yoritomo and his son Sanetomo, the first and third of the Kamakura shoguns of the Minamoto line, and within the shrine is an image of Yoritomo. The shrine was rebuilt in 1897, and it has a large, ostentatious Momoyama-style roof at the entry to the shrine building: the building and its closed doors to the shrine are covered with black lacquer with gold trim. An ablution unit stands to the right for use by worshippers.

The way to the **grave of Yoritomo** is along a continuation of Yabusame-baba to the east (away from Wakamiya Oji), the narrow Archers' Road that crosses the path from the Yoritomo shrine. Turning to the left onto Yabusame-baba, the road becomes a city street with schools and private houses along it. (English language direction signs mark most of the route.) A series of turns alternating between the left and then the right lead to a street to the north with a stone torii at its end and then a series of steps up the hillside. Tiles set in this street are of the white banner, the Minamoto symbol. Up the steps is the modest grave of Yoritomo, the first Kamakura shogun. The modesty of the grave belies the mausoleum that may have once been here, since war and political vengeance have obliterated the original grave markings. Today a small moss-covered stone pagoda, 5 feet (1.6 meters) tall, is surrounded by a low stone balustrade, a stone lantern on either side, as the tomb was restored in 1779 by order of Prince Shimazu. Flowers and burning incense often are left by visitors to the grave. These stones both mark the grave and overlook the site of Yoritomo's one-time palace on the flat land below the tomb. Virtually all of Kamakura was destroyed in the battle in the 1330s that saw the overthrow of the Minamoto/Hojo rule of Japan.

6 EGARA TENJIN SHRINE

Leaving Yoritomo's grave site, the first street to the left should be taken, following signs pointing the way to the Kamakura-gu Shrine (described later in this tour). But first a street headed toward the hills leads to the **Egara Tenjin Shrine** to Sugawara Michizane, the patron of intellectual activities and scholarship. A red torii and then steps lead up to the buildings of this shrine that no medieval capital with cultural and intellectual pretensions could omit. It is still favored by students, who come to pray for success in their studies, leaving their *ema*, wooden prayer plaques, with their plea for success written upon the back.

At the top of the steps from the street a simple wooden gate gives on to the flat ground on the hillside on which the shrine is located. A 900-year-old gingko tree is to the right of the gate, and once the grounds had many *ume* (plum) trees, the favorite tree of Michizane. This is one of the few shrines that predate the shrine to Yoritomo, although the actual date of its creation is not known. According to legend, on August 25, 1104, there was a tremendous storm, and a scroll descended from the heavens to the present shrine site with a picture of Michizane upon it. Thus, tradition claims, the shrine was born. The old divine painting is still preserved, and most of the shrine's treasures now are in the Treasury of the Kamakura-gu Shrine, since many of the early treasures were lost to fires. The painting on the scroll depicts Michizane in court costume, holding a *shaku* (a symbol of imperial or religious authority). In time Yoritomo made the Egara Tenjin Shrine his tutelary shrine to protect his nearby palace, and then, much later, in the 1590s Toyotomi Hideyoshi restored and enhanced the shrine.

The Honden, the Spirit Hall of the shrine, is in vermilion with two closed, black-lacquered

On the grounds of the Kamakura-gu Shrine

ANNUAL EVENTS IN THE CENTRAL KAMAKURA AREA

January 1–3 **Hatsu-mode** The first visit of the year to the Shinto Hachiman-gu and Kamakura-gu Shrines to begin the New Year.

January 5 **Joma-Shinji** Expels the devils using holy archery below the Hachiman-gu Shrine.

February 3–4 **Setsubun** A coming of spring ceremony in which beans are scattered in shrines and temples to drive out evil spirits.

April (2nd Sunday) **Kamakura Festival** At the Tsurugaoka Hachiman-gu, a week-long festival from Sunday to Sunday. The first day a procession in historical costumes proceeding from Wakamiya Oji and Shizuka-no-mai commemorates Shizuka's defiant dance before Yoritomo. The last day is a Yabusame archery display from horseback.

May 5 **Iris Festival at Hachiman-gu**.

Late-July **Yuigahama Beach** after nightfall: a fireworks display, one night in mid-August

August 7–9 **Bonbori Matsuri (Paper Lantern Festival)** At the Hachiman-gu Shrine, walking through a large straw hoop guarantees freedom from various illnesses during the coming year.

August 16 **Emma Festival at Enno-ji**.

August 20 **Annual festival at the Kamakura-gu** Commemoration of the death of Prince Morinaga.

September 15–16 **Annual festival at Tsurugaoka Hachiman-gu** At noon on the 15th, a procession of *mikoshi* leave the Hachiman-gu Shrine to "air" the shrine deities. On the 16th at 1:00 p.m., Yabusame-Shinji mounted horsemen shoot arrows at a stationary target as they gallop past at full speed. Below the Hachiman-gu Shrine.

Early October **Takigi Noh** By torchlight at the Kamakura-gu Shrine.

The 1st Sunday of October **Doll Festival at Hongaku-ji**.

Early November **Showing of the temple treasures** at the Engaku-ji and the Kencho-ji, from 9:00 a.m. to 4:00 p.m. Entry is ¥500

November 1–15 **Chrysanthemum display** At the Hachiman-gu Shrine.

December 17–18 **Year-end market** At the Hase-dera.

---

doors, the sole decoration on the structure being a faded gold panel with the name of the shrine, Tenman-gu, in calligraphy upon it. As with all shrines to Michizane, there are many, many *ema* on racks, posting prayers or wishes for intellectual success from worshippers of Michizane, the most brilliant man of his age. Due to court intrigue, Michizane was banished in 901 from Kyoto to Kyushu, where he died two years later. Various catastrophes following his demise were interpreted as the result of his restless spirit, and thus 45 years after his death he was deified as Tenjin, the Deity of Heaven.

7 KAMAKURA-GU

Beyond the Michizane shrine, a path going off diagonally to the northeast leads to the **Kamakura-gu** Shrine, in a grove of trees. (It is a ten-minute walk from the Wakamiya Oji path.) This shrine is devoted to one of the bloody episodes in Kamakura history. Ironically, though, it wasn't erected out of true sorrow, but as a political act in 1869 by the new militaristic government of the Meiji era,

supposedly by imperial order. (The emperor was but a 15-year-old youth who was being used by the victors in the overthrow of the Tokugawa shogun for their own political purposes.) While the shrine ostensibly honors an imperial prince slain in the year 1335, it was but another stone in the Meiji attempt at deifying the modern Japanese emperor, which was to have serious repercussions for the Japanese and the world six decades later. The shrine originally was a Zen Buddhist temple, the Toko-ji, but was taken over by the government after 1868 in order to turn it into a Shinto shrine to fit its political and religious goals.

The story of the murdered prince involves the fall of the Kamakura military government (1192–1333), the attempt by the emperor of that day, Emperor Go-Daigo, to rule in fact as well as in name, and the desire of Ashikaga Takauji to rule as shogun in place of the Hojo regents he had defeated. In the complex political and military maneuvering involved, Prince Morinaga, the third son of Emperor Go-Daigo, raised an army to defend his father's right to rule, for Morinaga desired to

The magnificent Kencho-ji Zen Temple in North Kamakura

serve as his father's shogun. With the permission of the emperor, his father, the prince was defeated and imprisoned in a cave for seven years by Ashikaga Takauji, since Takauji had poisoned the emperor's mind against his son with false charges. The prince's pleas to his father were never delivered. Morinaga then became the victim of a last and futile attack by the Hojo army against Takauji's brother, Ashikaga Tadayoshi. Tadayoshi was in charge of his royal prisoner, and when at one point it appeared that the Hojo forces would trap the Ashikaga defenders in Kamakura, he had the prince slain before temporarily retreating from the city. The prince was beheaded and the head cast aside. (The spot where the head was thrown is now railed-in as a memorial spot.)

A path from the street leads to a stone torii marking the entry to the grounds of the shrine. Ahead lies the Haiden, a place for worship in front of the fence-enclosed Honden, the Main Hall, where the spirit of Prince Morinaga is enshrined. The Honden is not open to the public. A path to the left of the buildings goes beyond the enclosed area and up steps to the cave in which Morinaga was held. (A fee must be paid before entering this area.) The low opening of the barred cave– which is 13 feet (4 meters) deep and has an area of 130 square feet (12 square meters)– does not permit for a viewing of the interior. Steps lead down from the cave to a park-like area with a huge memorial stone and to the Treasury where, behind glass walls, some of the shrine's collections can be observed. This includes the usual armor, bows and arrows, pikes, and other military ware of the medieval era, but an 1893 sculpture of a large wooden horse with a wooden image of Morinaga in armor, holding a case of arrows and grasping a long bow, is one of the main objects in the display. There is also the inevitable large, unattractive portrait of Emperor Meiji, a not very handsome individual. Other paintings depict the story of the doomed life of Prince Morinaga. The prince is buried atop Richikozan Hill, which lies 220 yards (200 meters) east of the shrine and up 170 steps to the prince's tomb. An annual ceremony has been held since the 1870s at the shrine on August 20, the date of the prince's beheading.

At this point the tour continues to Kita-Kamakura (North Kamakura). It is best to return to the foot of the steps to the Tsurugaoka Hachiman-gu at the end of Wakamiya Oji, which can be done by taking the southwest road from Kamakura-gu until it meets the main east-west road that in turn should be followed west back to Hachiman. Without mounting Hachiman's steps, one should now continue to the west to Komachi-dori. Just before this street are two points of interest. First, there is the **Maruyama Inari Shrine**, which is surrounded by red flags. This shrine is dedicated to the Shinto deity of commerce, and thus it attracts many worshippers desiring success in business affairs. Beyond, at Komachi-dori, is a spot where priests of the shrine will exorcise evil spirits from new cars. From here one can walk through the tunnel that pierces the hill to the north to Kita-Kamakura and its most interesting temples. The **Kencho-ji Temple** is 711 yards (650 meters) from the Tsurugaoka Hachiman-gu at the far end of the tunnel, and it is the next site to be visited in the second portion of the tour of Kamakura.

8 KENCHO-JI ZEN TEMPLE

Just beyond the roadway tunnel, a path on the right leads to the **Kencho-ji** Zen temple. A series of Zen temples were created in the 1200s under the Hojo regents, acting on behalf of the Minamoto shoguns. These regents were to favor the Zen teachings that refugee Chinese priests were bringing from the mainland as they and other Chinese intellectuals fled the persecution of Kublai Khan and his Mongol forces, which were conquering the Song dynasty of China. Zen practices and doctrines had a great appeal to the Hojo regents, because of Zen's simplicity, its disciplined training, and its reliance on one's inner self. Hojo Tokimune (1226–1263), the second Hojo regent, became an avid student of Zen and the sponsor of Zen temples, and even took monastic orders just prior to his death. The Japanese military of the Kamakura period were greatly attracted to the faith that would become the basis of Bushido, the Japanese art of war.

On the fall of the Song dynasty, from 1251 to 1253, regent Hojo Tokeyori established a new temple just to the north of Kamakura, the Kencho-ji, for refugee Zen priest Rankei Doryu (1213–1278). The priest is also known by his Chinese name of Lan-hsi Tao Lung. The Kencho-ji was to become the first and foremost among the Five Great Zen Temples of Kamakura. The glory of the temple has been too often despoiled by fire, civil war, and earthquakes; the 1415 conflagration leveled the temple structures, and rebuilding could not be undertaken due to the civil wars that were impoverishing the nation. The Kencho-ji had to wait almost 200 years before proper reconstruction could take place, and then it was rebuilt by a Tokugawa shogun under Priest Takuan in the 1600s. It suffered tragically again on September 1, 1923, when the Great Kanto Earthquake once more leveled most of its buildings, which had once numbered 50 units. Today a smaller Kencho-ji has ten sub-temples and the main buildings described below. Previously, the grounds of the temple were far more extensive than at present, and a symbol of the loss sustained can be seen in the secular high school that now separates the temple from the highway. Nonetheless, the temple remains the headquarters of the Kencho-ji branch of the Rinzai sect of Zen Buddhism.

Rankei Doryu not only served the Hojo regent as the founding abbot of the Kencho-ji, but he was virtually a minister of state, informing the regent of conditions in China and then acting as the go-between when representatives of Kublai Khan came with their demand that Japan prostrate itself before China or face invasion. For his knowledge, his spirituality, and his Buddhist learning, the priest was granted the title of Daigaku Zenji, Great Zen Master, and on his death he was buried on the hillside behind the temple he had served. At the main highway, the temple is entered through a modest wooden gateway, the **So-mon** (General Gate) from 1754 that once stood at the Hanju Zanmai-in Temple in Kyoto, where the imperial family mortuary tablets are kept. It was moved here in 1943, 20 years after the earlier gate had been destroyed by earthquake. The name of the temple on a plaque with gold lettering is in the calligraphy of the Emperor Go-Fukakusa. Situated in a magnificent grove of cryptomeria (Japanese cedar) trees, the temple buildings are enhanced by their lovely surroundings. The path that leads to the **San-mon** main gate is lined in early April with blossoming cherry trees. Built in 1754, the gate is also called the Tanuki-mon, the Badger Gate, from a legend that a badger turned itself into a monk so as to help in building the gate, a transformation by which the badger could repay the monks for their kindnesses to him. The upper floor of the gate holds the images of the Five Hundred Rakan, early disciples of the Buddha (not open to view). To the right of the San-mon is the Bonsho, the great bronze bell, 6 ½ feet (2 meters) tall and 15 feet (4.6 meters) in diameter, which was cast in 1255 and is said to be the second oldest bell in Kamakura. It is hung within a thatched-roof belfry, and it bears an inscription by the temple founder, Rankei Doryu. A path alongside the belfry leads to the Zen-do, the Zen Hall, and other private (non-public) monastic areas.

Beyond the San-mon is the Butsu-den (Buddha Hall) in the Chinese Song style of architecture. Both the Butsu-den and the Kara-mon (Chinese Gate) were mausoleum buildings of the shoguns in the great Zojo-ji Temple in Edo (Tokyo), and they were taken apart and moved here in 1647. The path to the Butsu-den Hall is enclosed with juniper trees whose seeds the first abbot is said to have brought from China and planted here 750 years ago. Today the trees are 39 feet (12 meters) tall and have a girth of 20 feet (6 meters). Within the hall is the famed statue of the seated, wood-lacquered (originally gilded) image of Jizo, the deity who protects travelers, children, and pregnant women. He holds the *shakujo* in one hand, the staff with rings that jangle as Jizo walks so as to scare away insects, lest they be walked upon and inadvertently killed in violation of the Buddhist precept against the taking of life. In his other hand he holds the jewel that is said to make wishes come true. Behind the image are 1,000 small, gilded Jizo images arranged in tiers.

Within the head of the main Jizo image was an even smaller Jizo (now in the temple Treasury), which, it is said, once saved a man's life. The victim was brought before the executioner for his misdeeds, and twice the executioner swung his sword with great force against the miscreant's neck to sever his head. Both times the blade was blunted and did no damage to the victim. When the culprit was examined, a small image of Jizo was found hidden in the topknot of his hair–and that small image had two marks upon the nape of its neck, such as the executioner's blade should have made upon the condemned man's neck. Since Jizo had protected the individual, the culprit was pardoned and freed.

Within the Butsu-den are a number of artistic treasures including a remarkable Kamakura period (1192–1333) seated, wooden image of Regent Hojo Tokeyori, founder of the temple, at age 33, holding a *shaku*, a symbol of office. Another painted and lacquered image is of Prince Shotoku, the founder of Buddhism in Japan. A portrait on silk of Rankei Doryu, the first abbot of the temple is among several paintings, including one by Kano Motonobu of the early 1600s and one by Mincho, another noted artist. The tombstone of the first abbot is kept here, having been removed and placed within the hall. Behind the Butsu-den is the 1814 rebuilt **Hatto** (Dharma Hall or Hall of the Law), a building that is used for *zazen* (seated meditation) training and practice by laymen. (It is sometimes called the **Ryuo-den**, the Dragon King Hall, since it has a dragon painted on its ceiling.) All major public ceremonies of the temple are held in this building, the largest wooden building in eastern Japan.

A path at the side of the Hatto leads to the Kara-mon, the Chinese Gate of 1646 in the Song style, and beyond it is the Hojo, the Main or Abbot's Hall. As with the San-mon, the Hojo originally belonged to the Hanju Zanmai-in Temple in Kyoto, and it was once used as the abbot's residence. The Hojo is *tatami*-matted, and thus shoes must be removed before entering it. A large drum on the far left, and a bronze bowl struck for its note during services, is on the right in the area before the altar. Mortuary plaques are located on either side of the altar. Behind the Hojo is a pond and garden by the famed landscape master, Muso Soseki, but unlike most Zen gardens, which are *karesansui* (dry gardens of stones), this garden is a contemplative garden, with its walkways around the pond meant to be conducive to meditation. The pond is in the shape of the ideograph for "mind," and thus is known as the Shin-ji Ike (Mind Character Pond). Farther up the hillside is the Hanso-bo, the Shinto shrine that protects the monastery, a structure brought from the Hoko-ji Temple in Shizuoka in 1890.

Between the San-mon and the Butsu-den, a path leads to the right to the Suzan-mon Gate and the monastic residences, Zen-do meditation hall, Kaisan-do (Founder's Hall), and administrative offices of the monastery. This portion of the grounds is not open to the public as it is the training area in meditation for the monks. (The temple is open from 8:30 a.m. to 4:30 p.m. Entry ¥300. From November 1–3 the temple shows its treasures, including the painting of the first abbot and the wooden image of the founding regent.)

9 ENNO-JI TEMPLE AND THE KINGS OF HELL

Across from the Kencho-ji on the other side of the main roadway is the **Enno-ji Temple** from the year 1250, the temple of the King of Hell. If nothing else, the contrast between the quiet, meditative Zen temple across the way and this temple, identified with the fear of being condemned to Hell, illustrates the great diversity of beliefs that Buddhism can encompass. Once located near the seacoast, the temple was destroyed in the 1701 earthquake and tsunami and subsequently reconstructed beyond the hills surrounding Kamakura. Up steps to the temple grounds, the temple has in its the square hall statues of the ten Kings of

Hell presided over by Emma, the Supreme King of Hell. Emma sits scowling (he really is an unpleasant looking fellow) in a recessed area at the rear of the small hall, with one of the subservient kings in attendance on either side of his recessed space. To the right and left, against each of the two side walls are the other kings: on the left from the rear are Taizan, Toshi, Godo, Keirin, Hyoto, and Gokan. On the right are Sotei, Shinko, and Henjo (Shoko has been removed to the Fine Arts Museum). These ten unwholesome looking worthies are the ones who weigh the life of the deceased and recommend the appropriate punishment to Emma for his decision. It is Emma who passes the final judgment as to which of the six levels of Hell the deceased is deserving.

By contrast, at the entrance to the hall is a small image of a seated monk, the Zen priest Chikaku, who established the temple and who sits here with great forbearance. Next to him is the figure of Datsueba, the Robe-Stealing Hag. This less-than-wholesome personage is the one who relieves the newly dead of their clothes as they gather at the Sai-no-kawa River, the Buddhist equivalent of the River Styx. She is also the misanthrope who forces little children, deceased before their time, to remain at the edge of the river, in limbo, where they have to pile up stones, a task they must accomplish before being released from this netherworld. Datsueba, of course, kicks over the pile of stones so laboriously built by the children. (This is why at some temples one will see small piles of stones erected by worshippers as symbols of assistance to the dead children.) Jizo, the patron and protector of children, helps the children in their time of need in this trying task of piling up stones. Thus an image of Jizo can sometimes be observed in the opposite front corner of the temple from the image of the seated, founding monk. Given the unpleasant company (the Zen monk excluded), it must understandably be a relief to Jizo when, from time to time, he is removed to the Fine Arts Museum for exhibition as a piece of sculpture. In the garden before the temple, a three-foot-tall image of Jizo stands next to the temple bell. A low table covered with a red cloth and shaded by a bamboo umbrella is where tea is served for a fee. (The temple is open from 9:00 a.m. to 4:00 p.m., but closed at 5:00 p.m. from December through February Entry is ¥200.)

MEIGETSU-IN, THE TEMPLE OF THE CLEAR MOON Farther along the roadway to the north and uphill to the right is the **Meigetsu-in**, the Temple of the Clear Moon. Despite its lovely name, this is not a temple on which much time (if any) need be spent– except in June when its pink, blue, and white hydrangeas are in bloom. The acres of color are so attractive at this time that the temple grounds are inundated by Japanese visitors. Behind the temple is the grave of Ashikaga Takauji who overthrew the Minamoto/Hojo shogunate in 1333 and moved the Shogun's government back to Kyoto. (The temple is open from 6 a.m. to 6:00p.m. during the flowering of the hydrangea. Entry ¥300.)

⑩ **TOKEI-JI TEMPLE (THE DIVORCE TEMPLE)**

Farther along to the north, the Jochi-ji Temple is passed on the left before one comes to steps and a path, also on the left, leading into the **Tokei-ji Temple**, better known perhaps as the "Divorce Temple." Until the very late 19th century, a man could get rid of his wife by returning her to her family at any time he wished. A wife had no such release from the trials of an unhappy marriage or an overbearing mother-in-law whose house she shared with her husband. In 1285, one small window of hope was opened for abused or unhappy wives when the nun Kakusan, the widow of Hojo Tokimune, turned her nunnery into a place of refuge for women in need of relief. This practice of providing a place of refuge for women was finally enacted into law by Hojo Sadatoki (1271–1311), so that a woman who was able to escape to this nunnery and reside there for three years could have her marriage dissolved. Legend holds that if a woman arrived at night after the nunnery gate was closed, she need only throw her shoe over the nunnery wall to claim refuge. The temple thus had another popular nickname, the Kakekomi-dera, the "Run-In Temple." At one time there were three inns before the temple to receive an overflow of marital refugees who had "run in."

In actuality, the nuns in the temple did try to resolve differences between husbands and wives, a form of marriage counseling, so as to save marriages that, on the woman's part, was not that easily dissolved, since she had little possibility of financial security once a divorce took place. Until 1873, this and one other temple in Japan were the sole resource for a woman in marital distress. A more modern divorce law was thus legislated by the Meiji government in that year, and the nunnery had come to outlive one of its main purposes. As a

A stone image of Buddha at Tokei-ji Temple

result, on the death of the last abbess in May 1902, the Tokei-ji became a monastic branch of the Engaku-ji Temple instead of a nunnery, and it has since been headed by a male abbot. In its time, it was one of the five nunneries in Kamakura. The temple had another nickname, that of the Matsu-ga-oka (Pine Tree Hill) Imperial Palace, so called from the fact that the fifth chief nun, Yodo-ni, was the daughter of the Emperor Go-Daigo. The 20th chief nun is remembered also since she was the young daughter of the luckless Toyotomi Hideyori, the only son of Hideyoshi. When her family was exterminated at the fall of Osaka Castle in 1615, she alone survived, and Tokugawa Ieyasu permitted her to live so long as she became a celibate nun.

Steps lead up from the highway to the ticket booth (Open from 8:30 a.m. to 5:00 p.m., closed 4:00 p.m. from November through February. Entry is ¥100) with a long, tree-lined path ahead. On the left is the temple bell under a moss-covered, thatched roof, while ahead on the right a small wooden gateway leads to a square, wooden building with a ball on its top, a usual symbol of a memorial hall. Within the rear center of this hall is the temple's main image, a 14th-century Sho Kannon in wood. (A Sho Kannon is the simple image of the Deity of Mercy without the many arms or additional faces about its crown that embellish later such representations of the deity.) The Kannon is attributed to the noted sculptor Unkei, and its long necklace reaches to its feet, which rest on a lotus,

which in turn is on a golden lion. To the right side of the hall in an alcove off the center is an image of a nun, obviously the founding nun of the temple. The path from the entry gate continues straight ahead before it diverges to the right and left. A 3-foot (4-meter)-tall seated Buddha is located at the end of the straight path. To the left, a walk leads to a small structure where tea can be obtained, while the path to the right leads to the 1978 fireproof, concrete temple treasury, the **Matsu-ga-oka Hozo** (Pine Tree Hill Treasury), which is both a museum and a library, the latter noted for its collection of Zen texts, much of it donated by the Zen scholar of the 20th century, Suzuki Daisetz (1870–1966). The museum consists primarily of a large room with displays of the temple treasures including a Muromachi period (1333–1578) Suigetsu Kannon ("Kannon Gazing at the Moon's Reflection") and an unusual lacquered box with the Roman Catholic "HIS" inscribed upon it. In addition there are sutras (religious writings), inlaid bowls, and lacquer boxes and trays. A smaller area has examples of calligraphy from the temple's library collection. (The Treasury is open from 9:30 a.m. to 3:30 p.m., closed Mondays. Entry is ¥300.)

The path continues uphill into the woods on the slope of Mt. Shoko. There are graves on both sides up a double flight of steps to a small platform with the tombs of the abbesses and the nuns. On the far right is a small cave with the tomb in a pagoda shape of the foundress, the wife of the Regent Hojo Tokimune who founded the Engaku-ji Temple across the highway. Among those buried here is the fifth head nun, the daughter of the Emperor Go-Daigo for whom the one-time Matsu-ga-oka Imperial Palace (Pine Tree Hill Palace) was built. Her grave is in a large cave carved from the rock and with a large torii in front of it. In addition, the daughter of Toyotomi Hideyori (the granddaughter of Toyotomi Hideyoshi, who was Tokugawa Ieyasu's predecessor) is buried here. Suzuki Daisetz, the modern religious writer, is also buried here.

11 ENGAKU-JI TEMPLE

Across from the Divorce Temple and a little farther up the road toward Kita-Kamakura Station is the **Engaku-ji Temple**, one of the most impressive of the Zen temples in Kamakura. Unhappily, the Yokosuka Rail Line cuts right through what was the entrance to the Engaku-ji Temple, separating its

Byakurochi (White Heron Pond) from the main portion of the temple's hillside grounds. The pond is historically important, since it received its name from the fact that a white heron settled here, thereby signifying to the temple's founding abbot, Mugaku, that the spirit of Hachiman, the resident *kami* (Shinto deity) of the city, had shown his approval of the establishment here of Mugaku's Zen temple, the second of the Five Great Zen Temples of Kamakura. (The temple is open from 8:00 a.m. to 5:00 p.m., but closes at 4:00 p.m. from November through March. Entry ¥300.)

This Rinzai Zen temple of the Engaku-ji School of Zen was begun in 1278–1282 by Hojo regent Tokimune, who appointed Mugaku Sogen (1226–1286), a Chinese refugee priest from Song China, as its first abbot. (Mugaku Sogen's honorific title was Bukko Kokushi.) It is a temple whose Zen doctrines accept the "sudden" rather than "gradual" approach to enlightenment. To this purpose it has employed the use of the koan (riddles) method to move novice monks to enlightenment. Tokimune, as regent, was fascinated by the approach of Zen to religion and life, an attitude equally held by other samurai of the time. Zen's disciplined intellectual and spiritual training, and its simplicity in contrast to the ostentation of the aristocratic court of the emperor in Kyoto, were appropriate not only for a monk but for a warrior, since it led to concentration on that which was important–in religion or in war. Zen's indifference to death and the dangers that beset life also appealed to the military mind.

Tokimune had the temple created both in the hope of spreading Zen doctrine and as a reaction to the attempt by the troops of Kublai Khan, the Mongol conqueror and emperor of China, to invade Japan. Two such invasions of the island of Kyushu were attempted by the Chinese, and many Japanese soldiers died in the repulse of the invaders. Their success was sealed by a storm, a *kamikaze* or Divine Wind, which scattered and sank the Chinese fleet, drowning many of its warriors. Thus this temple was also created to solace the souls of those Japanese who had died in the late 1200s in the two battles. So important to Tokimune was this new temple that he helped in the excavations of the foundations of the first buildings. To his delight, the diggers uncovered a stone chest that held the Engaku-kyo sutra, the sutra of Perfect Enlightenment. No better omen for the future of the temple could be had, and thus the temple was named for the discovered sutra. Of the 42 buildings

The San-mon at Engaku-ji Temple dates to 1783. A curiosity is that it was built without nails.

FESTIVALS AT ENGAKU-JI

January 1–3 **Dai-hannya Kito-e** At the Hojo, the reading aloud of the sutra titles of 600 volumes of the Prajuaparamita sutra.

February 15 The **memorial day** on which Gautama Buddha passed from this world and achieved Nirvana. At the Butsu-den.

April 8 **Hana Matsuri-e (Flower Festival)** At the Hojo Gotan-e in honor of the Buddha's birthday.

June 18 **Kannon Senbo** At the San-mon, confession to Kannon, the bodhisattva of great compassion, mercy, and love.

August 16 **Thanksgiving Day** At the Hojo Segaki-e, the *O-Bon* celebration in honor of the annual return of the spirits of the dead.

October 3 **Kaisan Kokushi Maisaiki (Founder's Day)** At the Butsu-den and the Shari-den.

October 5 **Daruma Taishi Maisaiki** At the Butsu-den, the anniversary of the death of Bodhidharma.

October 14–15 **Shari-ko-shiki** At the Hojo, memorial service in honor of the Buddha's tooth.

The three days around November 3 **Homotsu Kazeire** At the Hojo, airing and showing of the temple treasures.

December 15 **Jodo-e** At the Butsu-den, the memorial day of the Buddha's Enlightenment.

December 31 **Joya Nenju** At the Butsu-den and Benten-do, New Year's Eve service.

that graced this hillside, fire, civil war, and earthquakes have left but 17 structures standing today, many of them modern or relocated from other temples. Only the main gate and the temple bell have survived the onslaughts of nature and man. The Great Kanto Earthquake of September 1, 1923, was particularly devastating to the temple. Nonetheless, the Engaku-ji remains one of the Five Great Zen Temples of Kamakura.

Steps lead from just beyond the rail station to the small, roofed gate of the temple, the So-mon, beyond which lies the ticket booth and then farther steps to the San-mon, the main Mountain Gate that begins the north/ south axis of the temple complex. The San-mon was rebuilt without nails in 1783, and the steps leading up to it are complemented by the alternate "female slope," which provides an easier access to the gate. The huge gate was rebuilt by priest Daiyu Kokushi, who refounded the temple; its name, Engaku Kosho Zenji, appears on the gate on a plaque in the calligraphy of retired emperor Fushimi. The two-story gate is decorated with carvings of lions and dragons, and its second floor (not open to the public) has a Kannon image and images of *rakan*, disciples of the Buddha. To the left of the San-mon are caves and grottos, which are off limits to visitors, while to the right a path and then 137 steps lead to the Great Bell of the year 1301, which is 8½ feet (2.5 meters) tall and 55 inches (1.4 meters) across. It is the largest bell in Kamakura and is noted for its sonorous tone and the beauty of its shape. It was donated by Regent Hojo Sadatoki for the welfare of the nation.

Beyond the San-mon is the 1963 Butsu-den, the Buddha Hall, rebuilt in reinforced concrete, the earlier hall having been destroyed by fire in 1284, again in 1526, and finally in 1923 by the earthquake of that year. Within is the image of the Hokan Shaka Nyorai, the original Buddha, as well as an image of Emma, the King of Hell, by the sculptor Unkei. The ceiling is decorated with a modern painting of clouds and a dragon by Seison Maeda. To the left is the Senbutsu-jo, the Buddha Selection Hall, from 1699, with a heavy thatch roof. Its very plain interior with tatami flooring has one standing image at the rear with a golden lantern hanging on either side of the image. Farther up the hillside on the left is a modern building brought here from Tokyo in 1928. This is the Kojirin, a hall for the practice of *zazen* (Zen seated contemplation) by laity. Its origins go back to 1868, at the beginning of the Meiji era, when the government initiated its persecution of Buddhism. The temple began to train laity as itinerant and lay practitioners of Zen meditation, so that the faith would not be lost. Under freer conditions after 1945, the practice has been retained so as to spread the understanding of Zen and its doctrines and practices.

Up the slope of the hillside, the path leads on the right to the Hojo, the Abbot's Hall, and the monastic buildings for the monks, which are open to the public during the first week of November when temple treasures are traditionally "aired" and are on public view. (The

One of several ornate ponds at Engaku-ji Temple

airing is entitled *mushi bosho*–"expel insects.") The temple Hojo or lecture hall is the traditional hall of the abbot, and it is used today for religious ceremonies. In its garden are the Edo-period (1603–1868) Hyaku Kannon, one hundred stone sculptures of Kannon, the Deity of Mercy, some of which were damaged in the 1923 earthquake and have been moved here for safekeeping. Once they were at a branch temple of the Engaku-ji, the Shoei-in, but in the late 20th century they were moved to the walled garden of the Hojo. The Hojo has a large, unusual vent over its traditional kitchen area, and a dormitory behind the building is lined with windows of many panes. The buildings look out upon a lovely garden containing a pond, a small flat-stone bridge, trees, raked gravel, and bushes that compose the garden.

The path up the hillside slope continues to the oblong-shaped Myoko-ike, a pond whose name translates as the lovely "Lake of the Sacred Fragrance." Up some steps beyond the pond, a path to the left leads to the Shari-den, the Relic Hall of the temple. The hall lies behind two gateways, the entry to the first covered gate being closed to the public since this is one of the more sacred halls of the temple. Built in 1285 by Hojo Sadatoki, the son of Tokimune, the Hojo regent who founded the temple, it has a large, heavy cypress

thatch roof is in the Song style of Chinese architecture of the pre-1200 era. Fire destroyed the thatch roof in 1558, but it was replaced in the same style, as was done once more after the 1923 earthquake. The most important relic within the Shari-den is a tooth of the Buddha, a gift obtained by Minamoto Sanetomo from the Nonin-ji Temple in South China. The tooth is kept within a quartz reliquary. Within the building is the statue of priest Mugaku, the first abbot, but the Shari-den is only open the first three days of each year. Behind the Shari-den is the Kaisan-do, the Founder's Pavilion, which is a shrine to the first abbot, and beyond it is the Keiko-byo, the grave of Regent Hojo Tokimune, the founder of the temple.

Farther up the hillside is the thatch-roofed Butsunichi-an on the left (entry charge), a tea pavilion where *matcha*, green tea, is served for a fee. Opposite is the Hakuroku-do, the Cave of the White Deer. Legend reports that a herd of divine white deer issued from the cave and paused to attend to the inaugural sermon that the founding priest was giving on the opening day of the monastery. Just above the tea pavilion is a building where are enshrined the statues of Hojo Tokimune, his son Sadatoki, and his grandson Takatoki, the last Hojo regent. A series of additional steps bring one higher on the hillside and to the Obai-in, the branch Temple of the Yellow Plum Blossoms, at the top of the path. The widow of Hojo Tokimune, the nun Kakusan-ni, here had a Kegon pagoda built for the eternal bliss of her late husband, the regent who died on the day that he took holy orders. At a later date, the Ashikaga shoguns, who had defeated the Hojos, had the Obai-in sub-temple constructed at the same spot in honor of Muso Kokushi, the priest and landscape artist who was responsible for temples and gardens in Kamakura as well as in other cities of the realm. The main image of the temple is that of Yakushi Nyorai, the Healing Buddha, while to the right of the Buddha is the seated image of Muso Kokushi. An additional small building holds an image of Kannon.

This brings one to the end of the path, and a return to the main gate can be made by retracing the way down the hillside. This tour will continue to the Great Buddha at Hase, A return to Kamakura Station in the center of the city can be made by bus or train from the foot of the hill at the entry pond. Before leaving, one other shrine and one temple are worth mentioning, even though they are somewhat off the beaten track.

12 ZENIARAI BENTEN SHRINE (DIVERSION)

The **Zeniarai Benten Shrine** is in the western foothills of the city and is best reached by taxi, which should take five minutes from Kamakura Station. Created in 1185, it resulted from a dream by Yoritomo that his regime would flourish if a shrine to the goddess Benten were established at a particular spring in his capital. The shrine was created, and it is entered by way of a natural tunnel and then a manmade "tunnel" of many vermilion torii contributed by the faithful. The attraction of the shrine is its ability to double one's money. The name of the shrine means "money washing" shrine, and if one places one's money in a wicker basket and moves it around in the spring water in the small pool in the shrine's cave, the money will double or triple in time. Of course, this is primarily efficacious on the Day of the Snake in the Chinese zodiac calendar. Fortunately such days occur every twelve days. (It is questionable whether this benefit applies to Traveler's Checks.) The shrine is in a gorge with many shrines, caves, teahouses, and those who can tell your fortune. In other words, particularly on the Day of the Snake it is a crowded and joyous day of celebration tinged with the hope of newfound riches.

13 KOMYO-JI

The other temple is the **Komyo-ji**, on a hill overlooking the beach and the sea. To visit, it is best to take a taxi or bus (from bus stand #1 at the plaza before the station) from Kamakura Station, This temple was founded in 1243 by Hojo Tsunetoki, and it has been reconstructed in traditional style but in reinforced concrete. It is primarily noted for its lovely gardens. A Jodo (Amida) temple located at the eastern end of the seafront, it has main gate from the 1500s that is the largest of all in the temples in the city, and a sub-temple building flanks each side of its courtyard. The very large Main Hall holds a golden Amida image, while the Senju-in on the left side of the courtyard holds a 1,000-arm (Senju) Kannon image. An elevated walkway leads to the Kaisan-do, the Founder's Hall behind the Main Hall, and from it there are walks in the garden, established by the noted landscape artist Kobori Enshu, can be enjoyed. The lotus in its large pond flower in June and July. To the right of the Main Hall is the *karesansui* (dry garden) named Garden of the Three Divinities and the Five Founders. The Three Divinities are Amida and his assistant Bodhisattvas Seishi and Kannon, while the Five Founders are the five Chinese patriarchs who began the Jodo or Amida sect. Boulders represent the three divinities, while rocks represent the five patriarchs. The temple has its annual festival between October 12 and 15. (Open 9:00 a.m. to 5:00 p.m. No entrance charge.)

14 THE GREAT BUDDHA OF KAMAKURA

Most visitors to the Great Buddha at Hase begin their journey from Kamakura Station. The small train line, the Enoshima Electric Railway (aka Enoden), which begins at the rear of the station, connects the cities of Kamakura and Enoshima, and Hase Station is the third station stop after the beginning of the line in Kamakura, 1.3 miles (2 kilometers) away. At Hase Station, the main street leading inland from the railway should be taken one mile (1.5 kilometers), a ten-minute walk, to the **Kotoku-in Temple**, which is the home of the Great Buddha, a sight that can be seen as one approaches the temple.

The Daibutsu, or **Great Buddha**, was the main image of the Kotoku-in Temple when it

Right: *The iconic image of the Great Buddha (Daibutsu) at Kotoku-in Temple in Hase*

was cast in 1252, and it is an image of the Amida Buddha, the Buddha of Eternal Light, the Buddha of the Western Paradise of the Jodo sect of Buddhism. The wall-enclosed grounds of the temple are entered (after paying the ¥200 entry fee) through a gateway with a Nio guardian on either side to prevent evil forces from entering the sacred grounds. A large straw sandal hangs in a niche on the sides of the gateway, footgear that a Nio might wear. Within the grounds a purification basin stands on the left of the path to the Buddha image.

This most impressive seated image of Amida Buddha is 37 feet (11.31 meters) tall and weighs 93 tons. Seated on a lotus throne that is on a stone platform, the image holds its hands in its lap, palms upward and the thumbs touching, representing the *mudra* (position) of "Steadfastness of Faith." Its serene face with half-closed eyes is most attractive in its contemplative mood, and it shows the repose and calmness of its nature, which is the goal of a true believer. The eyes were of gold, and a silver boss on its forehead originally would have shone forth as a symbol of religious illumination when the body of the image was in its initial gilded state. The boss would have been no small thing since it weighed 30 pounds (13.6 kilograms). In 1923 the *mudra* of "Steadfastness of Faith" showed itself in a way other than planned by its designer, for in the earthquake of September of that year the quake caused the image to rock back and forth—but it did not move or fall from its base.

The Daibutsu was created from sheets of bronze that were cast separately and then soldered together by its caster—attributed variously to Goroemon Ono, Hisatomo Tanji, or Shigemitsu Mononobe—a task that took five years. The stylized curls on the image's head had to be cast separately and then attached to the head of the figure. The curls number 656 in all. The image is hollow within, and it is possible to enter the image (for an additional ¥20; open from 8:00 a.m. to 4:30 p.m.) and to climb a staircase so as to be able to look out the two windows in its upper back between the shoulder blades.

The project was conceived by a monk by the name of Joko ,who began a subscription among the common people for its construction in 1238, and the first image was a wooden one that existed between 1238 and 1247. Then in 1252 the wooden image was replaced by the present bronze figure. The Daibutsu originally sat within the temple's Main Hall,

whose structure was 450 feet square (40 meters square) and supported by 63 gigantic wooden columns. Despite it being so far inland from the sea, a storm in 1369 damaged the hall, and then a tidal wave that swept inland in 1495 destroyed the temple that covered the image. Ever since, the Daibutsu has sat in the open air within a portico set back from and about it on three sides. The stone bases for the columns remain in place, and thus give an impression of the size of the building. The image is second in size in Japan only to the larger Daibutsu of Nara, which is taller by 16 feet (5 meters). The image at Hase is a far more attractive one than the Buddha in Nara, for the latter image was repaired badly in the past after it was damaged by earthquakes and fires. (The Kamakura Daibutsu can be visited between 8:00 a.m. and 5:30 p.m. from April to September from 8:00 a.m. to 5:00 p.m. from October to March. Entry is ¥200.)

15 **HASE-DERA TEMPLE**

Midway back toward the railway station, a street leads off to the right and is signed for the **Hase-dera Temple**, with its noted Kannon. Legend recounts that such a Kannon image was sculpted from a huge camphor tree for the Hase-dera Temple near Sakurai in Nara Prefecture by priest Tokudo Shoin in the year 721. The legend further relates that the Nara image was carved from the lower half of the camphor tree, while the Hase image was sculpted from the upper half of the tree. It is further claimed that the finished upper image was set adrift in the sea near Osaka so that it might find its way to a place that was in need of its ministrations. Fifteen years after it was launched, it came ashore at Hase just beyond Kamakura, and a temple was created for it. There are skeptics who say that it was only carved some time after the year 1600, while others see it as being created as early as the year 1200. Steep stone steps lead up to the Amida and Kannon Halls of the temple, passing some one thousand small stone images of Jizo en route. Jizo has various qualities, and one of them is that as the Mizuko Jizo he looks after still-born or aborted children or children who died at an early age. (Abortion has always been a means of birth control in Japan.) Thus parents who have been bereaved make offerings to the images, sometimes in the form of bibs or head coverings.

The noted Kannon within the temple is a Juichimen Kannon, that is, a Kannon with ten

Hase-dera Temple. The temple is known for its 11-headed image of Kannon.

small heads about its main crown, signifying the Deity of Mercy's attempt to seek out all those in need of help. The 30-foot (9.3-meter)-tall wood image was covered with gold leaf at the behest of Ashikaga Takauji, the first Ashikaga shogun after the 1330s. The image is housed today in a hall that is fire- and earthquake proof, yet the structure has been designed in such a manner that it looks like the other buildings on the temple grounds. Additional images of Kannon and other deities are in the hall as well. A miniature shrine holds an image of Tokudo Shoin, the alleged carver of the main Kannon image. The adjacent small Amida Hall houses a seated image of Amida, since this, as with the Daibutsu Temple, is a Jodo sect temple that reverences Amida, the Buddha of the Western Paradise. The image was ordered created by Minamoto Yoritomo in 1194 as a protector against evil spirits. The nearby temple bell is dated August 8, 1264, and it is the third largest bell in the area after that at the Engaku-ji and the Kencho-ji. (The temple is open from 8:00 a.m. to 5:00 p.m. but closes at 4:30 p.m. between October and February. Entry ¥300.)

From the temple grounds, there is a good view over the Yuigahama Beach, which runs in a crescent shape before Kamakura. The beach was used by Yoritomo's military for archery and riding practice in medieval times, but today it is one of the favorite summertime beaches for local residents. A head-land separates Yuigahama Beach on the east and Inamuragasaki Point on the west. The point, which takes one of the surrounding mountains that enclose Kamakura right into the sea, was strategic for the defense of Kamakura in the shoguns' times, since only at low tide could a section of the beach provide a passageway into the town. In 1333, during the war between the emperor's forces and those of the Hojos, Yoshida Nitta, the imperial general, is said to have thrown a golden sword into the sea in the hope of pleasing the Sea God and so gaining his entry into Kamakura. The waters did recede a full kilometer (two-thirds of a mile), and the imperial forces were thus able to enter the city across the sands beyond the point and defeat the Hojo forces, thereby ending the rule of the Kamakura government.

If one wishes, one can reach the **Zeniarai Benten Shrine**, mentioned earlier, either on foot or by taxi from Hase. Otherwise, from the Hase-dera Temple one can return to Hase Station and then back to Tokyo via Kamakura Station. Alternatively, one can continue to Enoshima for Walk 24.

GETTING THERE
This walk starts at Kamakura Station, which is just under one hour from Tokyo Station on the Tokaido Line.

Walking Tour 24

KATASE AND ENOSHIMA ISLAND
A Surly Monk, a Legendary Kannon, and a Famed Nude Goddess

1. **Nichiren and the Kamakura Execution Grounds**
2. **Enoshima Island**

Visitors to the island of Enoshima most often route their journey through Kamakura Station, which can be reached via the Tokaido Line from Tokyo or the Shonan Shinjuku Line from Yokohama. The small Enoshima Electric Railway (aka Enoden) train line begins at the rear of Kamakura Station and connects the two cities of Kamakura and Enoshima. With its nude image of Benten, the goddess of music and of good luck, among other attributes, and the popular and more secular attractions of a typical seaside resort, Enoshima makes for both a historically interesting and (if you avoid the weekend crowds in summer) laidback tour, either as a day trip on its own or as an extension to a trip to the Great Buddha at Hase at the end of the previous walk.

1 NICHIREN AND THE KAMAKURA EXECUTION GROUNDS

From the Enoden Railway's Enoshima Station, the first sight on this tour is just 110 yards (100 meters) to the northeast. The **Ryuko-ji Temple** commemorates a miracle that saved the life of Nichiren, who was mentioned in connection with the Hongaku-ji Temple where Komachi-dori crosses Wakamiya Oji in Kamakura. Nichiren was an unusual Buddhist monk in that his fervid dislike of other Buddhist sects and his invective directed toward the government had raised questions as to his mental stability. Where the other sects of Buddhism were concerned, his remarks were vituperative. "Zen," he said, "is the teaching of the Devil." "Jodo (Amida Buddhism) will lead straight to Hell." "Shingon will ruin the country." Since the regent, Hojo Tokimune, was an ardent follower of Zen, such remarks did not endear

this dissident monk to the secular authorities, and in 1271, he was condemned to die.

The beach at Katase was the execution ground of the Kamakura shoguns. Here, on September 12, 1271, Nichiren was forced to kneel and bow as the executioner prepared to strike off his head. Then, as his followers aver, a bolt of lightning struck and shattered the sword from the hand of the executioner as he was about to strike. So miraculous an occurrence was significant, and thus Nichiren was reprieved from the death sentence and condemned to exile on the island of Sado in the Japan Sea instead. Nichiren had been proclaiming the doom of the nation if his words were not followed and if his form of Buddhism were not made the state religion. A few years after he was sent into exile, the troops of Kublai Khan attempted to invade the southern Japanese island of Kyushu and were only driven off with heavy losses by a storm that sprang up and endangered their invasion fleet. Nichiren's forecast of doom seemed to have some validity to it when the Chinese fleet and troops appeared, and thus he was pardoned and allowed to return to Kamakura. The emissaries sent by Kublai Khan in 1275 demanding obeisance from Japan were decapitated at this spot at Katase, and their heads were sent back to the Khan in gift boxes. The first unsuccessful invasion of Kyushu followed. A second set of emissaries in 1279 carrying the repeated message were also executed. The second Chinese invasion by 150,000 troops, which followed in 1281, might have succeeded had not the *Kamikaze*, the Divine Wind, sprung up and destroyed the Chinese fleet and military. In his usual modest manner, Nichiren proclaimed that the gods had answered his prayers, and thus the nation was saved.

In 1337, Nichiren's followers built the first temple at the spot of his near-execution, the

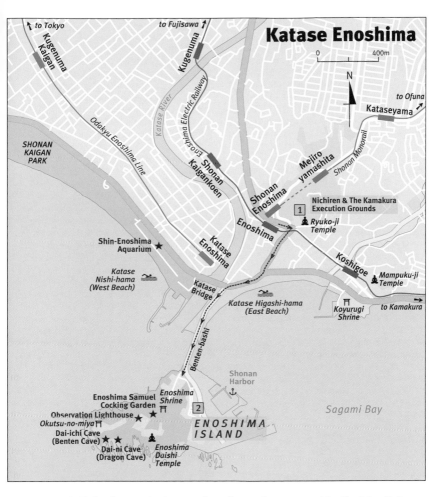

Ryuko-ji Temple. Today the complex is a noted one, with its Hondo (Main Hall) being one of the largest in the Kamakura area. At the foot of the steps are various large memorial stones, one of which (in Japanese) details Nichiren's miraculous escape from beheading. The entry gate has the traditional Nio guardians on either side of the gate, and then steps mount to the more ornamental gate with its richly carved sides. In 1971, on the 700th anniversary of Nichiren's miraculous escape from death, the huge second gate at the foot of the temple steps was dedicated. This white gate has a green and red ceiling with a dragon on it (the temple's name, *Ryuko-ji*, means "Dragon Temple") and, on the terrace in front of the Hondo, a modern statue of Nichiren enhances the temple com

plex, as does a pure white Shari-den (Relic Hall) in Thai style, holding relics of the historic Buddha. In 1910 a five-story pagoda was erected (the only one in Kamakura) on the hill behind the temple, and it and the Hondo alone survived the 1923 earthquake. A concrete azekura (log cabin–style) Treasury building holds the important treasures of the temple, and the temple bell is also in this forepart of the hillside temple. To the right when facing the Hondo are the monastic quarters for monks and the temple administration building. On September 11–13, the temple holds a grand festival on the anniversary of the date on which Nichiren's life was spared by divine intervention. It is a boisterous celebration with much beating of gongs.

MAMPUKU-JI TEMPLE The Mampuku-ji is merely a footnote to history. Here in 1185, at the mountain ridge that blocked the seaward entrance to Kamakura, Minamoto Yoshitsune, the brother of Yoritomo, resided while awaiting permission to enter Kamakura to visit his brother, who was now shogun in both name and fact. Yoshitsune had been responsible for many of the military victories that had put his brother in power, but Yoritomo was insanely jealous of his more attractive sibling. Permission to enter Kamakura was denied, and before long Yoshitsune was being pursued by his brother's forces intent on killing him. The letter Yoshitsune wrote to Yoritomo, pledging his allegiance to his brother, has since been known as the "Kashigoe Appeal," from the location of the Mampuku-ji Temple in Kashigoe, where the letter was written. A draft of the "Kashigoe Appeal" is held by the temple.

② ENOSHIMA ISLAND

The Katase-Enoshima area is a popular beach resort for people from Tokyo, and it can be overcrowded in season. It has all those things that attract residents from large cities: beaches, sea water, an aquarium, a botanic garden, a zoo, an observation tower from which Mt. Fuji can be seen—and even the famed "nude" image of the Indian goddess of beauty, Benten. Almost all of this is on an island of 45 acres (18 hectares) with a circumference of 1.6 miles (2.5 kilometers) and which rises to the grand height of 185 feet (60 meters). The Katase River on the mainland separates the Higashi-hama (East Beach) from the Nishi-hama (West Beach). The west end of Katase Bridge (over the Katase River) has the two-story **Shin-Enoshima Aquarium** (Suizoku-kan), which offers a huge tank with 350 species of sea life as well as dolphin shows, a penguin enclosure, and hands-on activities for kids. (Open 9:00 a.m. to 5:00 p.m., but opening at 10:00 a.m. between December and February. Entry ¥2,000).

A harbor on the north side of the island, **Shonan Harbor**, was created to protect the **Katase Beach** from erosion and to serve fishermen and tourists, and in 1964 it served as the yacht basin for the Olympics of that year. The island itself is reached over a 656-yard (600-meter)-long divided bridge, the Benten-bashi. This leads to the main street, which offers what one would expect of a resort: *ryokan* for overnight stays and souvenir shops for mementos of a visit to the beach. Hydrofoils from the harbor reach Atami in 1

hour, Ito in 1 hour and 15 minutes, and Oshima Island, with its active volcano, out in the Pacific Ocean in 2½ hours.

One cannot escape the influence of Minamoto Yoritomo in the Kamakura area, and here he commissioned the priest Mongaku to create the Kogan-ji Temple in 1182. It was not sudden piety that led to the commission, but the desire for the gods to permit him to have victory over the northern Fujiwara clan at Hiraizumi. The temple was a good investment, for he did conquer the Fujiwara, and the temple continued on its religious way until the advent of the Meiji government in 1868, when it was confiscated and turned into the **Enoshima Shrine**, a Shinto shrine complex comprised of three small shrines, dedicated to three female Shinto deities. The 185-foot (55-meter) height to be climbed beyond a red torii can be daunting (it involves some 300 steps to be mounted), but in 1959 an outdoor escalator in four stages of 350 feet (106 meters) in length was created to make for an easier ascent. The escalator ends at the base of an **observation tower** (Sea Candle), a 17.5-acre (7-hectare) area that has a **Botanical Garden** (Enoshima Samuel Cocking-en) with 300 kinds of tropical plants (open from 9:00 a.m. to 8:00 p.m.; entry ¥200), a small zoo, and a weather station.

A stone lantern on the waterfront drive to Enoshima

Enoshima Island with the unmistakable Mount Fuji hovering in the distance

Three Shinto shrines at the head of the 300 steps replace the original Buddhist temple of the year 1182. The first, on the left, is the Hetsu-no-miya and the most important of the three shrines. It holds three Benten images in its octagonal-shaped treasure house. One image is said to be 1,400 years old; another image is reputed to be from the 700s and has eight arms; while the third one is claimed to be 600 years old. This last one is the famed Hadaka (Naked) Benten, which once was enshrined in the cave on the south side of the island. Benten is a female deity originating in India, and she represents beauty; she is also one of the seven gods of good luck, and the only female deity in that group. The second shrine, the Nakatsu-no-miya, to the right has a very large bronze torii of 1747 before it and large stone lanterns given by a rather unusual set of patrons from old Edo (Tokyo): timber wholesale merchants, owners of Kabuki theaters, and owners of red-light establishments. The third shrine, the **Okutsu-no-miya,** is farther up the hill, and it comes after a restaurant with a panoramic view over the sea. The **observation tower** atop the hill permits for a view to the Hakone range of mountains as well as Mt. Fuji, and the tower is topped by a light, which makes it a lighthouse as well. It stands 177 feet (54 meters) tall, and on its observation deck one is 374 feet (114 meters) above the sea.

Returning to the base of the island and to its south side, the caves that have been carved by the waves can be seen. The **Dai-ichi Iwaya Cave** (First Cave or Benten Cave), which origi-

nally held the nude Benten image, is 39 feet (12 meters) high, with an opening 11.5 feet (3.5 meters) wide. The cave branches within, and the left hand chamber holds a copy of the Benten image. Not far beyond is the **Dai-ni Iwaya Cave** (Second Cave or Dragon Cave), where the dragon who controlled the fall of rain was said to dwell. Falling stone within the cave has led to its being closed to the public. Modern commercialism, of course, has seen to it that the dragon has not departed, for in another cave there is an electronic dragon who roars and whose presence offers some validity to old legends.

Back at Enoshima Station, the Enoden Rail Line can be taken back to Kamakura or on to Fujisawa, where a Japan Rail train can be taken to Atami or Odawara and beyond. The monorail line can be taken to Ofuna for a connection with the JR Yokosuka line to Yokohama and to Tokyo. The Odakyu Rail Line can also be taken to Shinjuku Station in Tokyo. In **Ofuna**, an 82-foot (25-meter)-tall Kannon image can be seen from the rail station. Begun in 1939, it was not completed until 1960. Within it are several altars, since it serves as a Buddhist temple. (Open 9:00 a.m. to 5:00 p.m. Entry ¥300.) Also in Ofuna are the Shochiiku Company film studios, one of the largest motion picture companies in Japan.

GETTING THERE

This walk begins at Enoshima Station, which is three stations from Kamakura Station on the Enoshima Electric Railway.

Walking Tour 25

YOKOSUKA

A Japanese Admiral, an English Sailor, and an American Commodore

1 **Mikasa Park and Battleship *Mikasa***
2 **Sarushima Island (Monkey Island)**
3 **The Grave of William Adams**
4 **Yokosuka City Museum**

Yokosuka is a city that is primarily known as a naval base, its naval installations having had their beginnings in the 19th century under a French engineer who helped in the planning of the port. A major naval base for the Japanese Imperial Navy through World War II, after that war it became an important base for the American navy. As with all such installations, military security keeps a portion of the harbor beyond public visitation. There are, however, sites that are open to and of interest to the public.

1 **MIKASA PARK AND BATTLESHIP *MIKASA***
In the public **Mikasa Park** on the waterfront is the **battleship *Mikasa***, the flagship of the Japanese navy under Admiral Heihachiro Togo (1847–1934) that played so important a part in the Russo-Japanese War of 1905. Today the retired battleship is a public monument and a museum to one of the great successes of the new Japanese navy. Built in 1902 by the Vickers Shipbuilding Company of England, the *Mikasa* was the headquarters ship of

The battleship Mikasa *in Mikasa Park*

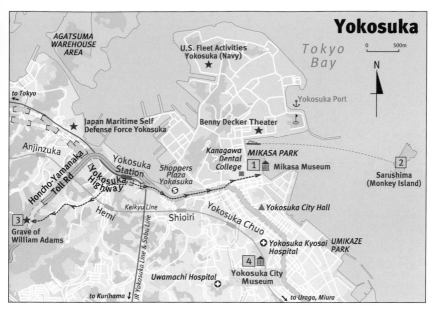

Admiral Togo in the 1905 battle of the Tsushima Straits, when much of the Russian Far Eastern navy was decisively defeated. Thirty-five out of thirty-eight Russian ships were lost to capture or sinking, while only three Japanese torpedo ships were sunk.

The battleship *Mikasa* was decommissioned in 1923 as a result of the Washington Naval Conference, which set a limit on the size and number of naval vessels to be held by the major international governments. Since 1961, the ship has been restored and "grounded" in a concrete base as a memorial to the 1905 victory, and it now contains the **Mikasa Museum** to Admiral Togo on its middle deck. Of interest also is the great disparity between the quarters for the officers and enlisted men in the Japanese military of the past. (The Mikasa Museum is open from 9:00 a.m. to at least 4:30 p.m. Entry is ¥500.) Mikasa Park and the battleship can be reached from Yokosuka Station on the JR Yokosuka line (from Tokyo and Kamakura), which is 1 mile (1.6 kilometers) from the ship, or by the Keihin Kyuko Railway's Yokosuka Chuo Station (from Yokohama), which is 875 yards (800 meters) northeast of the park, a ten-minute walk.

2 SARUSHIMA ISLAND (MONKEY ISLAND)

A ferry from Mikasa Park takes one in ten minutes to **Sarushima Island** (Monkey Island), 1.5 miles (2.5 kilometers) southeast of Yokosuka. The island was a former secret Japanese naval fortress that commanded the entry to Yokohama and Tokyo Bays. Today it is a park, with more than 70 subtropical plants and with monkeys and deer, and it is a pleasant place for relaxation.

3 THE GRAVE OF WILLIAM ADAMS

The other site of interest, to foreigners in particular, is **the grave of William Adams** (c.1564–1620), the English sailor who became marooned in Japan when his ship was wrecked on the Japanese coast at the beginning of the 1600s. The grave is two-thirds of a mile (1 kilometer) southwest of Anjinzuka Station on the Keihin Kyuko Electric Railway and 1 mile (1.5 kilometers) northeast of the JR Yokosuka station. Adams, a native of Gillingham in Kent, was a shipwright, a sailor, and a sailing captain. In 1598 he became the chief pilot of one of five ships owned by a Netherlands Trading Company. Of the five ships, his was the only one that made it successfully to the Pacific Ocean, but then it was wrecked off the coast of Kyushu at Bungo on April 19, 1600. Becoming a confidante of Tokugawa Ieyasu, he taught Ieyasu math, navigation, gunnery, and shipbuilding. Refused permission to return to England, he was given a Japanese wife and set to work

The harbor in Uraga. It was from here, in 1860, that the first Japanese ambassador to the U.S. set sail.

building ships for Ieyasu, the first ones being created in the village of Ito on the Izu Peninsula. Granted a fief in the Miura Peninsula, he was given the Japanese name of *Anjin Miura*, "Pilot of Miura." Adams died at Hirado, near Nagasaki while visiting the British "factory" (trading post), and his and his wife's ashes were said to be interred on a portion of their estate after their deaths.

A pair of obelisks stand over the grave of Will Adams and his wife, Oyuki, but there are questions as to whether they are really buried here. In 1905 the prefecture had the grave site explored and no remains were found. Nonetheless, every April 14 there is a memorial service at the grave site by British and Dutch officials, representatives of the U.S. and Japanese naval forces, and the mayor of

Yokosuka. The grave site on Mt. Hataka (682 feet [208 meters]) can be reached from the Keihin Kyuko line by crossing under the rail tracks and taking the road uphill. In time, a sign points to the left to Tsukayama Park, and this path will lead to the grave site, which is behind a fence. Obviously, a taxi can also be taken to the site and held for a return.

4 YOKOSUKA CITY MUSEUM

The **Yokosuka City Museum** (Yokosuka-shi Shizen Jinbun Hakubutsukan), which is south of Yokosuka Chuo Station, is an archeological and natural history museum, but it does have materials relating to Commodore Perry and Will Adams. One of the curiosities of the collection is a temple chair of the type used by the representatives of the shogun to seat

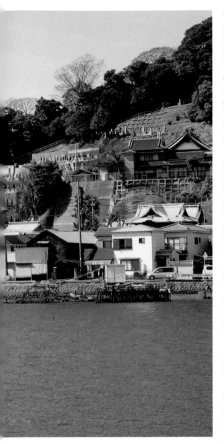

when he sailed with two sloops into the bay at this then small village. His proffered letter from the American president was refused acceptance. Seven years later, in 1853, Commodore Matthew Perry also dropped anchor here in order to present a letter from President Fillmore of the United States requesting the opening of political and commercial relations between the two countries. The letter was then presented at Kurihama, located another 5.4 miles (9 kilometers) beyond Uraga, on July 14, 1853. The Japanese officials agreed to meet with Commodore Perry in 1853 at this small seacoast village, having had carpenters spend the night creating a wooden and cloth covered reception hall for the momentous meeting. Here on July 14, 1853, Perry presented the president's letter, making it clear that he would be back within a year for a positive response to the president's request. He did return the following March (in less than a year), landed at the tiny fishing village of Yokohama, and (four years later) political and commercial relations between the two countries were agreed upon by the 1858 Treaty of Kanagawa. A monument commemorating the event was raised in 1901, and the presiding American present was Admiral Rogers, a grandson of Commodore Matthew Perry. One mile (1.5 kilometers) south of the Kurihama rail stations is a museum that describes the events of 1854. Each July 14, Kurihama celebrates the event with the **Black Ship Festival**, "Black Ships" (Kurofune) being the name by which the mid-19th century Japanese described the American steamship flotilla.

Kurihama can be reached by either the Japan Rail Yokosuka or the Keihin Kyuko rail lines. The Yokosuka line leaves from Tokyo Station (see the Kamakura rail instructions in the overview for Kamakura) for Kita Kamakura, Yokosuka, and Kurihama. The Keihin Kyuko line goes from Tokyo to Yokohama and so on to Yokosuka and KeiKyu Kurihama Station, which is a three-minute walk from JR Kurihama Station.)

Commodore Perry at their meeting to discuss the opening of relations between the two countries. Since chairs were generally not used by the Japanese up to this time, this temple chair was the only kind available for the occasion. (Open 9:00 a.m. to 5:00 p.m., closed Mondays and the New Year period. No admission charge. A taxi provides the easiest means of access to the museum.)

URAGA AND KURIHAMA–AN AMERICAN COMMANDER AND THE BLACK SHIPS

Two other sites are of historic interest but do not warrant a visit. The first is the town of **Uraga**, which is 4 miles (6.6 kilometers) farther along the rail line from **Yokosuka Chuo Station**. In 1846 Commodore Biddle of the U.S. Navy attempted unsuccessfully to open relations between Japan and the United States,

---

GETTING THERE

This walk begins at Mikasa Park in Yokosuka, which is within walking distance of two stations: Yokosuka Station on the JR Yokosuka Line, which gives direct access to Tokyo and Kamakura, or Yokosuka Chuo Station on the Keihin Kyuko Line for direct access from Yokohama.

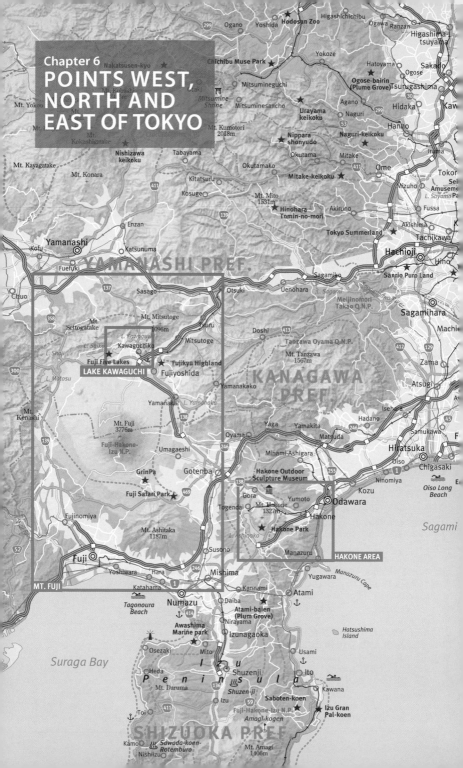

Ogano
299
Yoshida
Hodosan Zoo
Higashichichibu
Ogawa
Ranzan
Higashima-
tsuyama

Nakatsusen-kyo
Chichibu Muse Park ★
Yokoze
Hatoyama
Ogose
Sakado

Mt. Yokoo
Mt. Kabushio
**Ogose-bairin
(Plume Grove)** Tsurugashima
30
Kaw

Mitsumineguchi
Agano
Naguri
299
Hidaka

Mitsumine
Shrine
Mitsuminesancho
**Urayama
keikoku**
53
Hanno
Iruma
Tokor

Mt. Kayagatake
Mt. Kumotori
2018m
**Nippara
shonyudo**
Okutama
Mitake
411
Ome
Mizuho
Sei
Amuseme
L. Sayama Pa

Mt. Konara
Mt.
Koknshigatake
Tabayama
Okutamako
Okutama
Mitake-keikoku ★
Fussa

Nishizawa
keikoku
Kitatsuru
Mt. Mito
1531m
**Hinohara
Tomin-no-mori**
Akiruno
Akishima

411
Kosuge
Hachioji

Enzan
139
Tachikawa

Kofu
Katsunuma
Tokyo Summerland ★
Hino

Yamanashi
YAMANASHI PREF.
Sagamiko
Sanrio Puro Land

Fuefuki
137
Sasago
Otsuki
Uenohara
L. Sagami
Meijinomori
Takao Q.N.P.

Chuo
358
Mt. Mitsutoge
1096m
Tsuru
Doshi
413
Tanzawa Oyama Q.N.P.
Sagamihara
Machi

Mt.
Settogatake
L. Kawaguchi
Mitsutoge
Mt. Tanzawa
1567m
412
129
Zama

L. Shibire
Kawaguchiko
**KANAGAWA
PREF.**
Atsugi

L. Shoji
Fuji Five Lakes
★ **Fujikyu Highland**
Yamanakako
Hadano
246
Isehara
Samukawa

300
LAKE KAWAGUCHI
Fujiyoshida
45
F

L. Motosu
Yamanaka
L. Yamanoka
Yaga
Yamakita
Matsuda
Hiratsuka
Oiso
1
Chigasaki

Mt.
Kenashi
139
**Mt. Fuji
3776m**
138
Oyama
Minami-Ashigara
255
Ninomiya
Kozu
Oiso Long
Beach

**Fuji-Hakone-
Izu N.P.**
Umagaeshi
246
**Hakone Outdoor
Sculpture Museum**
Odawara
Sagami

GrinPa ★
Gotemba
138
Gora
Yumoto

Fuji Safari Park ★
469
Togendai
Mt. Hakone
1327m
Hakone

Fujinomiya
Susono
Hakone Park ★
Manazuru
HAKONE AREA

Mt. Ashitaka
1187m
L. Ashinoko

52
Fuji
Yoshiwara
Hara
246
Mishima
Yugawara
Manazuru Cape

MT. FUJI
Katahama
1
Kannami
Atami
Hatsushima
Island

Tagonoura
Beach
Numazu
Daiba
**Atami-baien
(Plum Grove)**

**Awashima
Marine park**
Nirayama
Izunagaoka

Osezaki
Mito
Izu
Usami

Suraga Bay
Heda
u
Shuzenji
Ito

Mt. Daruma
Peninsula
Shuzen-ji
136
Kawana

Toi
Izu
Saboten-koen
**Izu Gran
Pal-koen** ★

411
Fuji-Hakone-Izu N.P.
59
Amagi-kogen

Kamo
**Sawada-koen-
Rotemburo**
Mt. Amagi
1406m

Nishiizu
SHIZUOKA PREF.

Walking Tour 26

THE HAKONE REGION
Mountains, Spas, and Thermal Eruptions

1. **Odawara**
2. **Hakone-Yumoto**
3. **Miyanoshita**
4. **Gora**
5. **The Hakone Ropeway**
6. **Togendai on Lake Ashinoko**
7. **Hakone-machi**
8. **Moto-Hakone**

Only an hour from the heart of Tokyo (57 miles or 95 kilometers distant) is one of the most interesting day trips away from the bustle of the busy metropolis. The destination is the **Hakone National Park**, a district of mountains, spas, thermal activity, and the longest cable-car ride in Japan–all of which exist within the crater of an extinct volcano some 25 miles (40 kilometers) in diameter. The volcano itself may be gone, having blown itself into extinction some 400,000 years ago (according to geologists), but hot springs, spas, and sulfurous steam from bubbling hot mud still exist in various sections of the immense, still-active crater. The crater itself lies between the Izu Peninsula and the Pacific Ocean on one side and the majestic height of Mt. Fuji on the other side, the latter visible on clear days from particular vantage points within the Hakone region or as reflected in the waters of **Lake Ashinoko**.

Hakone is not only a spa area but a mountainous region 2,625 feet (800 meters) above sea level that has played its part in Japanese history. In Heian times (795–1185) aristocrats found its hot springs to have a curative effect, and around these same hot springs spas were created in modern times. In the medieval period, a castle built at **Odawara** became the stronghold of a branch of the Hojo clan, members of the ruling military government during the Kamakura period (1185–1333). At the end of the 1400s, the Hojos still held sway over the Kanto Plain, and their castle was one of the best defended strongholds on the Tokaido route between Kyoto and the future city of Edo (Tokyo), that is, between the emperor's capital and the shogun's seat of power. Later, from the early 1600s until 1868, the important **Hakone Barrier** (Hakone Sekisho Ato), or Checkpoint, saw guards of the Tokugawa government search each traveler passing through the mountain pass en route to and from Edo. Two things were forbidden: to smuggle guns into Edo or for the daimyo, the great lords of the nation, to try surreptitiously to smuggle their women out of Edo. Either act would have been a clear indication of an incipient revolt by dissident daimyo.

One can reach this area–replete with names as intriguing as the Valley of the Greater Boiling (Owakudani) and the Valley of the Lesser Boiling (Kowakidani)–either by the Kodama Shinkansen train from Tokyo Station to the Odawara Station, before transferring to a local line bound for Hakone-Yumoto Station, or by the Odakyu Electric Railway's "Romance Car" from the Shinjuku Station in Tokyo, which takes 90 minutes to reach the Hakone-Yumoto Sation. (A train departs each of the stations for the Hakone region every 30 minutes.) The less expensive and slower Tokaido rail route from Tokyo takes 90 minutes to Odawara.

1 ODAWARA
If you take the Kodama Shinkansen train to Odawara, it is but a ten-minute walk from the station to the four-story **Odawara Castle's donjon**, visible from the station platform. The castle may have hoary antecedents, but the present structure is a rebuilding from a 1960 restoration. While it appears to be an authentic medieval castle from the outside, the interior (as with so many of these postwar restorations) does not reflect its earlier austere condition. In the past it was the strong-

The four-story donjon of Odawara Castle

hold from the 1400s of the Hojo clan, who held sway over the great Kanto Plain of which Tokyo is now the heart. Seized by Toyotomi Hideyoshi in the late 1580s as he tightened his control over all of Japan, it, as were other Japanese castles, was slighted after 1868, when the new Meiji government, acting in the name of the emperor, saw to the destruction of any centers of possible armed danger to their regime. The restored castle today is similar to other such reconstructed strongholds in that it now sits in a public park and offers cultural attractions ranging from a Folk Crafts Museum and a zoo on the castle grounds to a museum of local history on the castle's first three floors. Special exhibitions are held three times a year in a separate gallery between the third and fourth floors. The castle's apricot trees blossom in February, while its cherry trees come into bloom in April, enhancing what appears to be a fortress centuries old. (Open daily from 9:00 a.m. to 5:00 p.m. except during the New Year period. Admission ¥400 for the donjon; ¥300 for the museum or ¥600 for a combined donjon and museum ticket.) It is easiest to take a taxi from the rail station to the castle, where a steep flight of steps must be mounted to the donjon.

2 HAKONE-YUMOTO

The **Hakone Tozan Railway**, a funicular rail line into the Hakone region begins at Odawara Station, and it can be taken in 13 minutes to Hakone-Yumoto, 9.6 miles (6 kilometers) from Odawara. The funicular train can be found at platform 11 and 12 of Odawara

Station; the two platforms are at the end of the platform, between tracks 7 and 8. The railway right-of-way at times climbs a 20 percent grade, and there are three switchbacks en route at which the train stops and then reverses direction to climb ever higher.

Hakone-Yumoto, 13 minutes by train from Odawara, is at the confluence of the Sukumo and Hayakawa Rivers, the outlets of the waters of Lake Ashinoko. The town is one of the oldest spas in the Hakone region. Its hot springs range in temperature between 95 to 133 degrees Fahrenheit (35 to 56 degrees centigrade). One public spa is just beyond the rail station, while a free bus from the station takes one to a more plush spa (*onsen*) with separate outdoor baths for males and females. In 1590, the town and its **Soun-ji Zen Temple** were the headquarters for Toyotomi Hideyoshi when he undertook the successful siege of the nearby Odawara Castle, as he wrested control of all Japan from local feudal lords. Soun-ji Temple was established in 1521 by Hojo Soun (1432–1519), the lord of Odawara Castle, in his will, and Hojo Soun's portrait on silk is still retained in this, the Hojo family temple. In its heyday, Soun-ji was one of the largest temples in eastern Japan, but with the fall of the Hojos it soon fell into decay. Only a few buildings remain today, and the temple is probably more noted for the fact that five of the Hojo lords are buried in its precincts.

Two reminders from Tokugawa days (1603–1868) remain in Hakone-Yumoto: one is a small stretch of stone pavement from the old

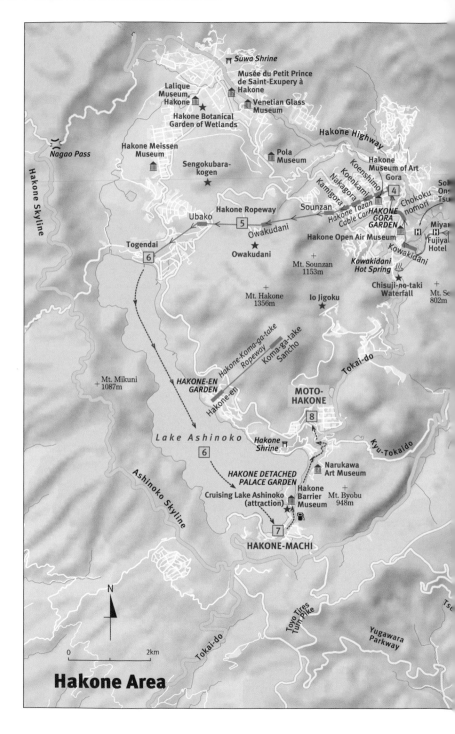

Hakone Area

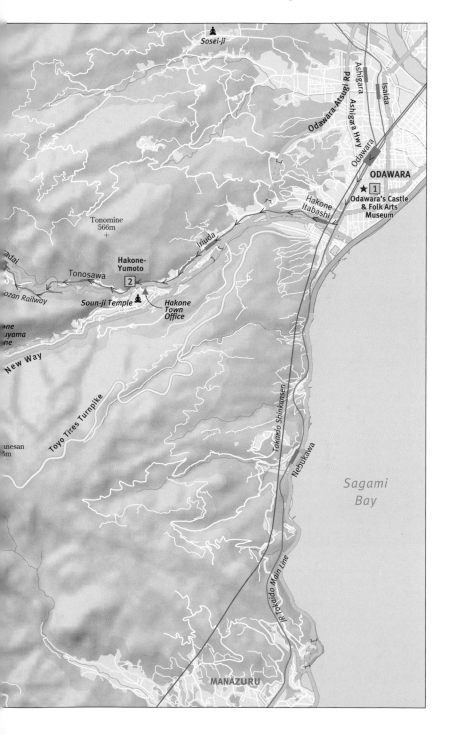

Tokaido highway at the west end of town, originally laid down in 1619 and not stone-paved until 1862; and the other is the colorful Daimyo Gyoretsu, the Feudal Lord's Procession, which takes place each November 3rd. This procession reflects an aspect of the behavior of the nation's daimyo between the 1600s and 1868 that was strictly regulated by the Tokugawa shoguns, even to the comings and goings of such lords en route to and from Edo. The honor and prestige of the daimyo had to be preserved by the proper number of guards and servants to accompany them on the every-other-year procession between their fiefdom and Edo and then on their return home. A slow and impressive ceremonial march for the entourage was de rigeur as they approached and left a town. Today, each November this bit of history is remembered when some 400 townspeople in medieval garb repeat a daimyo processional with a slow march in 40 minutes from Hakone-Yumoto to Tonosawa, two-thirds of a mile (1 kilometer) away. A return procession in state is made in the afternoon to Hakone-Yumoto. **Tonosawa** itself is a lovely spot on the Hayakawa River, with simple thermal springs. It has a thatch-roofed Amida temple from the 1600s that one can reach in 40 minutes from Hakone-Yumoto. Buddhist stone images lead to it through a field of azaleas. The summit of the mount above the village, at an altitude of 1,857 feet or 566 meters, is noted for its view.

3 MIYANOSHITA

If Hakone-Yumoto is 328 feet (100 meters) above sea level, by the time the train gets to **Miyanoshita**, 20 minutes later, the 1,312-foot (400-meter) level has been reached. Miyanoshita is one of the hot spring spas that Westerners began to patronize after Japan was opened to the rest of the world in the 1870s, and the **Fujiya Hotel**, which had its debut in 1878, became the headquarters for a restful spa vacation for these visitors from abroad. The hotel was the first Western-style hotel in Japan, and there all the aspects of Western civilization were available, including a library with the best in English literature, a billiard table, and afternoon tea–or something stronger. The hotel combined Japanese and Western elements in its structure: a vermilion handrail on its interior steps to the lobby provides a Shinto touch, while a dragon is entwined along the uppermost railing. Furnishings, of course, were the best that

Victorian England could provide. One could walk along paths laid out through the woods, and the more ambitious could climb **Mt. Sengen** at 3,830 feet (1,153 meters). The town became the most popular spa in the Hakone range of mountains, and it is still noted for its hotels, *ryokan* (Japanese inns), and antique and souvenir shops such as one expects to find at spas or resorts.

Today the less ambitious can drive around the countryside, or, in five minutes by bus, visit **Kowakidani** (Valley of the Lesser Boiling), alive with hot springs of a tempera-ture of 150 degrees Fahrenheit (70 degrees centigrade), with sulfurous fumes emanating from cracks in the ground. The valley sports a nickname of Ko-Jigoku (Little Hell), since the noxious fumes emanating from a cave in the vicinity provided a vision to earlier ages of the nature of the realm ruled over by King Emma, the Buddhist deity of the damned. The **Sokokura Onsen Tsutaya Hot Spring** is but 550 yards (500 meters) northwest of Miyanoshita Station, and a stone bathhouse here was used in 1590 by Hideyoshi's soldiers wounded in the attack on Odawara Castle. The cascade of the **Chisuji-no-taki** (Waterfall of a Thousand Threads) is a little to the south, and the loveliest time to visit this delightful waterfall is in April, when both azaleas and cherry blossoms enrich the area with their colorful blossoms. (The Fujiya Hotel is reached by descending the hill from the rail station, then turning left for a few minute's walk along a street of shops.)

4 GORA

The Hakone-Tozan Railway continues for another 10 minutes and 5 miles (3 kilometers) from Miyanoshita to its terminus at Chokoku-no-mori Station in **Gora**, a town 1,969 feet (600 meters) high, which boasts three amenities. Just five minutes away from the Gora terminus of the railway is the first, the **Hakone Gora Garden** (Hakone Gora Koen), where a rose-covered entryway leads along a brick path to an exotic bird-garden (with parrots and peacocks), an alpine plant garden, and a nature museum. A pond with a very large fountain and an un-usual number of rocks give the park the popu-lar name of Rock Park. The garden is noted for its springtime display of azaleas and cherry blossoms, and it boasts a traditional teahouse and even tea bushes. (Open 9:00 a.m. to 5:00 p.m. all year. Admision is ¥500.)

Ten minutes south of Gora is the second

amenity, the **Hakone Open Air Museum** (Chokoku-no-Mori Bijutsukan, the "Sculpture in the Woods Museum"), which can also be reached in three minutes from the Chokoku-no-mori Station just before Gora. This museum exhibits some 100 late 19th- and 20th-century sculptures, primarily by Western artists, both under the sky and indoors, with selections by Moore, Rodin, Bourdelle, Arp, Calder, and other modern American and European sculptors. Indoors are paintings by Renoir, Vlaminck, Utrillo, Chagall, and modern Japanese painters. There is one room for the studies by Manzu for the doors of St. Peter at the Vatican, while a Picasso room holds over 200 works. (The Open Air Museum is open from 9:00 a.m. to 5:00 p.m. daily. Admission is ¥1,600.)

To the southwest of Hakone Gora Koen is the third attraction, the **Hakone Museum of Art** (Hakone Bijutsukan), established in 1952, with a collection of pictures and Chinese and Japanese porcelains. It is most easily reached from the second stop of the cable car, which begins in Gora at the Koenmae stop. The grounds of the museum are a pleasurable sight, since they are covered with moss shaded by bamboo and Japanese maple trees. The museum is a branch of the MOA Museum in Atami and was begun by the founder of that museum, Okada Mokichi. It consists of two buildings, the smaller one to the right of the entry exhibiting the techniques of Japanese ceramics with the tools of the craft, samples of clay, shards from ceramic kilns, and photographs of potters at work. The larger building up a slope offers an overview of Japanese ceramics through the ages from Jomon and Yayoi times through to objects of Shino, Seto, Oribe, Inari, Kutani, and other Japanese ceramic wares. At one time the museum held examples of Chinese, Korean, and Near Eastern ceramics, but these have now been moved to the Atami museum. (Open 9:30 a.m. to 4:30 p.m., although it closes at 4:00 p.m. from December through March. Closed Thursdays and the New Year period. Admission is ¥900.)

On August 16, the Daimonji-yaki ceremony on Mt. Myojo takes place at the conclusion of the O-Bon period when the spirits of the dead, who have returned for the annual visit to their family homes, are returned to the other world. A huge fire in the shape of the character Dai ("Great"–standing for the importance of Buddhist law) is burned on the mountainside

The Hakone Ropeway carries passengers over fuming, sulfurous valleys.

in the evening, the crossing element of the *Dai* character being 354 feet (108 meters) long. The event can be observed from Gora, and fireworks and folk programs in the town enliven the festive occasion. Gora, as with other towns in the area, is a spa, and it sits on the slopes of **Mt. Sounzan**, a section of terrain still underlain with seismic and thermal activity. (Interestingly, hot water for a number of the spas is piped from Owakudani, farther along the route to Lake Ashinoko.) Because of its altitude, when the weather is clear, there are extensive views of the peaks of the Hakone range as well as a view of the Pacific Ocean from Mt. Sounzan.

⑤ THE HAKONE ROPEWAY

At Gora the funicular railway ends and the cableway begins. The cableway's cars make a few stops before arriving at the top of Mt. Sounzan in nine minutes. There the Hakone Ropeway goes to Togendai at the shore of Lake Ashinoko. This ropeway is the longest such means of transportation in Japan, extending 1.6 miles (2.5 kilometers) down to Togendai. The 2-½-mile (4-kilometer) route is traversed in thirty-three minutes by a number of gondolas (cable cars) which can hold no more than ten passengers each.

From Sounzan, after a 13-minute run, the cable car stops at **Owakudani**, where one may get off before continuing to the terminus at the lake. En route, the car is as high as 2,000 feet above the seething thermal valley below. If Kowakidani is known as "Ko-jigoku" ("Little Hell"), Owakudani is known as "O-jigoku" ("Big Hell"). Sulfurous fumes pour from crevices in the ground and from fractured rocks, since this is the crater of the

Snow-capped Mount Fuji beyond Lake Ashinoko and the red torii gateway of Hakone Shrine

one-time Mt. Kamiyama. Hot springs bubble forth from the ground, and some of these waters are captured and piped to some of the 12 spa towns down the valleys. In places at Owakudani the mud of the earth boils continuously. Every tourist locale must have its specialty, and here eggs can be purchased that have been boiled in the volcanic waters, their shells turned black by the chemicals of the boiling waters. A path from the ropeway station leads into the active thermal area, where the sulfurous fumes and boiling mud can be experienced firsthand.

6 TOGENDAI ON LAKE ASHINOKO

The cableway continues on from Owakudani, stopping at the Ubako Station en route to the lake. The descent to **Lake Ashinoko** (Lake of Reeds) is the longest such cable-car ride in Japan, and at **Togendai** on the lake one has a choice of boats to Hakone-machi and Moto-Hakone. A few of the boats are of a type that would delight children—one being a pirate ship with figures of pirates at various places on the deck or rigging. Lake Ashinoko is 2,376 feet (723 meters) above sea level, occupying a former volcanic crater. It has an 11-mile (17.5-kilometer) circumference and is 138 feet (42 meters) deep. The lake is a fisherman's, swimmer's, and boater's delight, and on clear days an inverted reflection of Mt. Fuji can be seen on its surface. Such a view is best seen on clear mornings from Hakone-machi or Moto-Hakone. (The waters of Lake Ashinoko eventually find their way into Sagami Bay near Odawara.) Refreshments and souvenirs can be purchased before boarding one of the boats at Togendai and heading in 30 minutes to the far end of the

lake to Hakone-machi or Moto-Hakone, the two towns being but five minutes apart by bus (two-thirds of a mile or one kilometer).

7 HAKONE-MACHI

Hakone-machi is a summer resort, and the old Hakone Barrier (Hakone Sekisho) or "Travelers' Checkpoint," stood nearby from 1618 to 1869. Here all travelers to and from Edo (Tokyo) had to present their "passport" and their reasons for traveling along the Tokaido (Great Eastern Highway). A monument marks the site of the original barrier, and just five minutes from the dock is the 1965 replica of the old checkpoint, now sitting across the road from its original site and still guarded by life-sized mannequins in medieval garb. Recent scholarship indicates that for a proper bribe guards would show individuals the holes in the fences where it was possible to slip past the barrier. The **Hakone Barrier Museum** (Hakone Sekisho Shiryokan) is adjacent to the rebuilt barrier, and here old passports, documents, everyday utensils used by travelers, coins, daimyo seals, palanquins, and armor are on display. The descriptive labels, unfortunately, are in Japanese only. (Open 9:00 a.m. to 5:00 p.m., closing at 4:30 in the winter. A ¥500 admission fee to the museum also permits for admission to the barrier.) The **Hakone Detached Palace Garden** (Onshi Hakone Koen) adjacent to the museum was once the site of an imperial villa, and it offers a pleasant place to stroll through the woods. On clear days, it is possible to see the reflection of Mt. Fuji on the waters of the lake from this site. Beyond the former imperial villa is the **Suginami-ki**, the "Cryptomeria

Lined Road," **a stretch of the old Tokaido road** that still runs 1.25 miles (2 kilometers) alongside the modern roadway. The huge ancient cryptomeria (cedar) trees that line the old road were planted in 1618.

8 MOTO-HAKONE

Moto-Hakone lies ahead, 1 mile (1.5 kilometers) and five minutes by bus, and it too is the terminus not only of the boats from Togendai but also the buses that run to Atami, Odawara, Mishima, and Numazu with their rail stations, as well as to other towns of the region. Nearby (a 15-minute walk, 550 yards or 500 meters) on the heavily wooded hillside is the **Hakone Shrine** (Hakone Jinga). It is said that the shrine was founded in the year 757 by the priest Mangan (710–784) as a Buddhist temple and that it was here that Yoritomo, the future shogun of the Kamakura government, took refuge after being defeated near Odawara. Until 1868, this was a center for the activities of Shugendo peripatetic Buddhist monks, but in its anti-Buddhist bent, the new Meiji government turned the temple into a Shinto shrine. A red torii standing near the water and the present shrine buildings are said to have been redone at an earlier date (1667). A **Treasure Hall** next to the shrine has a wooden figure of Priest Mangan, said to have been carved during the Heian times (710–1133). Old scrolls concerned with the early years of the temple and other antiquities are also on view. (Open from 9:00 a.m. to 4:30 p.m. Admission is ¥500.) A picturesque torii gate stands out in the lake, albeit its picturesque quality belies its concrete fabric. Moto-Hakone also has the small Narukawa Art Museum (open all year from 9:00 a.m. to 5:00 p.m.; admission ¥1,200), which offers changing exhibits of modern Japanese prints and also has a pleasant café.

The **Hakone Festival** (Kosui Matsuri) takes place here from July 31 to August 1. During the festival thousands of lanterns, alight with flaming candles, are set afloat on the lake, and ceremonial rites are observed by shrine attendants from boats in the lake. The service—and the offering of red rice to the dragon of the lake—is said to take place to appease the nine-headed dragon who dwells in its waters—but what comes to us as folklore or Shinto myth was much more likely an attempt by the Meiji rulers to change the summertime Buddhist O-Bon ceremony for the dead into a Shinto or folk rite. Fireworks in the evening close the festival.

FESTIVALS

May 2–3 **Odawara Hojo Godai Festival** The festival at the castle grounds includes a Feudal Lord's Procession on May 3.

July 31 **Kosui-sai** The "Lake Festival" in which lanterns with candles are floated on the Lake Ashinoko.

August 5 **Torii-yaki Matsuri** A huge wooden torii is built out on Lake Ashinoko and then is burned while thousands of lanterns are set afloat on the lake.

August 16 **Daimonji-yaki** A huge Dai character is burned on Mt. Mojo. A fireworks display and folk entertainments are held near Gora station.

November 3 **Daimyo Gyoretsu** Feudal Lord's Procession at Hakone-Yomoto.

One other attraction is in the area, and that is **Hakone Garden** (Hakone-en), which is 15 minutes away by bus or by boat. Hakone-en is a leisure center with swimming pools, golf, a camping site, bowling alleys, and other sports possibilities. It also has an aquarium and International Village, with buildings in the style of 29 different countries and examples of their folk art. It is obviously not an attraction for most foreign visitors, and it appeals primarily to Japanese vacationers (open 9:00 a.m. to 5:00 p.m. year-round; entry fees). A cable car from Hakone-en rises in eight minutes to the top of **Koma-ga-take**, 4,355 feet (1,327 meters) above sea level, where a superb view of Mt. Fuji and Lake Ashinoko may be obtained in fair weather. From either Hakone-machi or Moto-Hakone, a bus can be taken back to Odawara (43 minutes) and thus the train to Tokyo. A different bus can be taken to Atami (80 minutes) or Mishima, and in either city a train can be obtained for Tokyo. If time permits, one could always visit the most interesting MOA Museum in Atami before returning to Tokyo.

GETTING THERE

This walk begins at Hakone-Yumoto Station on the Odakyu Line and can be reached from Shinjuku Station in Tokyo on the "Romance Car" service in 90 minutes.

Walking Tour 27

MOUNT FUJI
Climbing the Sacred Mountain

If there is one symbol of Japan worldwide, it is that of cone-shaped **Mount Fuji**. It is the sacred mountain Fuji-san that millions of Japanese aspire to climb. In fact, in the brief two months of July and August, when the mountain is officially open to climbers, more than 200,000 people hike to the top of the highest mountain in Japan from its fifth station (Go-gome), which they have reached by bus from the rail station at which they arrived. One can climb the mountain at any time through-out the year, but the huts en route and food service are available only in July and August. Moreover, the cold, icy winds and snow make the trek dangerous during much of the year.

Romantic as Mt. Fuji appears, and as thrilling as a climb to its top at 12,388 feet (3,776 meters) may be, the romance can somewhat lose its bloom when one is faced with climbing single file behind a line of other pilgrims seeking the same thrill in reaching the crest of the sacred mount. In July and August, the paths are lined with climbers in a stream befitting a city rush hour, and the detritus of the slope and the debris left behind by these thousands each day make a mockery of the sacred nature of Fuji-san.

Hikers on the barren slopes of Mount Fuji are rewarded with a magnificent view.

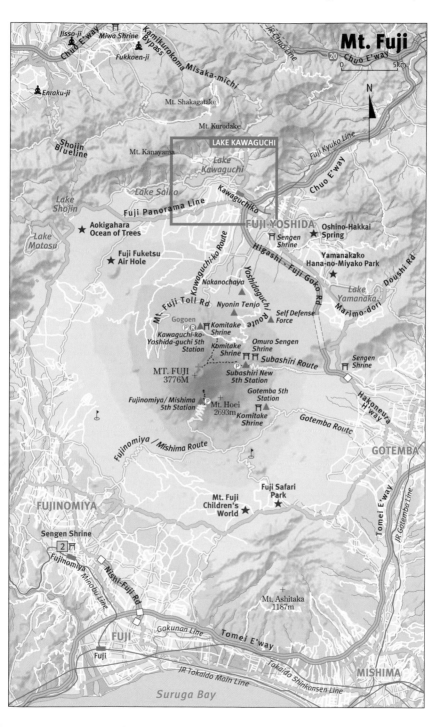

Overnight hut on the trail up to the peak offer shelter and hot meals.

While Mt. Fuji is within less than two hours from Tokyo and thus qualities as a day trip, this description is more informative than practical. It would really require an overnight stay in an area hotel and a very early ascent of the mountain if one truly wished to reach the summit and be back before nightfall for a return to Tokyo.

Mt. Fuji is a remarkable sight, particularly from a distance. There it stands in all of its glory and beauty, its cone snow-covered in all but midsummer, its base forming an almost complete circle some 22 to 25 miles (35 to 40 kilometers) across the plain from which it rises. So sacred was the mount that until Meiji times (1868) no woman was permitted on it except once every 60 years, lest the sacred mountain be defiled. The justification for this ban was that the goddess of the mount was female and a jealous spirit and thus might erupt in fire and brimstone if another female approached its sacred top. It is presumed that the name *Fuji* comes from the early Ainu, an indigenous people who once inhabited much of the main island of Honshu and who were eventually driven north to the island of Hokkaido by the Japanese after the 700s. The word is thought to mean "fire," an appropriate name for a volcanic mountain noted for its 18 recorded eruptions in historic times, the worst being in the years 800 and 864 and the last major explosion occurring in

1707, when the ash from the explosion inundated Edo (Tokyo) 63 miles (100 kilometers) away with ash 6 inches (15 centimeters) deep.

① CLIMBING MOUNT FUJI

There are five popular trails up the mountain, and of the ten stations (*gome*) in which Mt. Fuji is divided, it is at the **fifth station (Gogome)** that most climbers begin their trek, having arrived there by the 2-½-hour bus journey from the nearest rail station. It takes from five to nine hours to reach the summit of the crater, which is 4 miles (6 kilometers) from the fifth station, but it only takes three to five hours to descend, generally by the Sunabashiri (Sand Sliding Slope). **Kawaguchi-ko** (Lake Kawaguchi) is the best rail stop for access to Mt. Fuji from Tokyo, and it can be reached by means of the JR Chuo or the JR Fuji Kyuko line from Shinjuku Station in Tokyo in two hours. A bus from the Shinjuku Station reaches the town in ten minutes less than two hours, while the bus from Shinjuku Station to the fifth station takes 2 hours and 25 minutes directly. If the **Subashiri Slope** is used for a descent, the bus from the new fifth station (Shin go-gome) takes one to the Gotemba rail station for a return to Tokyo in one and three-quarters hours.

Many hikers plan to stay overnight at one of the huts between the fifth station and the summit of the mountain so that they can rise at 3:00 a.m. and thus reach the summit as the sun appears on the horizon of the Pacific Ocean to the east. These cabins are crowded and offer a minimum of comfort (including traditional Japanese toilets and not those of a modern variety). Reservations for sleeping space must be made in advance through a travel agent, and the food available is traditional Japanese fare; foreigners may wish to carry their own food (and drinking water) for the trek. The conditions of the climb are not idyllic: the surface of the slope consists of loose volcanic rubble, and the average temperature during the day in July and August on the mountain is in the 41–43 degrees Fahrenheit (5–6 degrees Celsius) range.

Sturdy boots, gloves and warm clothing are a must when attempting this climb.

Warm clothing, sturdy boots, and gloves to protect the hands when one slips on the volcanic grit are essential—as is rain gear, since the weather is not always dry. Protection against the sun and ultraviolet light is also recommended. The view also may be less than expected since Fuji is often cloud-covered. The above may sound discouraging, but it is only realistic as to the conditions on the mountain.

At the summit, the crater (Nai-in or "Sanctuary") is almost circular in shape, measuring 550 feet (150 meters) across. The bottom of the crater is 772 feet (220 meters) below the top of the eight peaks that form the blasted crater. The path circling the crater is 164 feet (50 meters) above the bottom. It is thought that a lake once filled the 246-foot (75-meter)-wide bottom; today it is the refuse of visitors' lunches and soft drink and beer cans that rest at the bottom of the crater. Two paths 2 miles (3 kilometers) long permit the circling of the eight peaks of the top of the mountain. The path skirting the edge of the crater is the easier one, since the other involves some climbing. A concrete weather observation center has been built on the side of one of the peaks, its radar scope able to detect typhoons more than 500 miles (800 kilometers) from Japan.

An exhilarating early-morning view above the clouds

There are two springs near the summit. At the foot of the northwest peak is the **Kinmei sui**, the icy cold Gold Sparkling Waters, while to the north of the Koma-ga-take peak is the **Gimmei sui**, the Silver Sparkling Water.

2 SENGEN SHRINE

Prior to 1868, the goddess of Mt. Fuji was worshiped as both a Shinto and a Buddhist deity the **Sengen Shrine** at the foot of the mountain. (From the 1100s, Buddhist lore held the crater to be the entry to the other world.) After 1868, the new Meiji government removed all Buddhist elements from the shrine and the worship of the goddess, and by government decree the shrine became a pure Shinto shrine, with the goddess now known as the Shinto Konohanasakuya-hime, the "Flowers Upon the Tree Blossoming Princess." Each August 26 and 27, the Sengen Jinja, the shrine to the goddess, is celebrated in the town of **Fuji-Yoshida** at the foot of Mt. Fuji. The date marks the closing of the summer climbing season of the mount, and the ornate shrine holds a noted festival, the Yoshida-no-hi Matsuri, the Fire Festival of the Sengen Shrine. Dozen of bonfires 23 feet (7 meters) high and 3 feet (1 meter) in diameter are lit throughout the city. Bonfires are also lit on the **Yoshida Trail** outside the mountain huts This torch festival honors the goddess whose spirit is paraded through the streets of the city in a vermilion-lacquered *mikoshi* that is in the shape of Mt. Fuji and weighs 2,475 pounds (1,123 kilograms). The portable shrine is carried by many young men with much high spirits on their part and on the part of the crowds that gather for the festival.

3 LAKE KAWAGUCHI

Fuji-Yoshida is but seven minutes by train from Lake Kawaguchi, and it can also be reached directly by train from the Shinjuku Station in Tokyo. Of the Fuji Five Lakes (Fuji-go-ko) area, **Lake Kawaguchi** (Kawaguchi-ko) is the one most worth visiting. It is the rail station for the bus to the fifth station of Mt. Fuji, and, in good weather, it offers a lovely view of Fuji from its northern shore, with the cone reflected upside down in the waters of the lake. It is the second largest of the Five Lakes and the most beautiful, and at 2,697 feet (809 meters) above sea level it is an ideal recreational resort in all seasons. This hot springs resort has spas (*onsen*) and amenities for tourists, including a number of museums. Of particular interest is the **Kubota Itchiku Museum**, which is devoted to the work of the master textile artist who revived the lost *tsujigahana* technique for silk dying that was a hallmark of Japanese craftsmanship in the 14th to 16th centuries. Kimonos created by

The goddess of Mt Fuji is paraded through the streets each August in the town of Fuji-Yoshida.

Lake Kawaguchi is the most beautiful of five lakes at the base of Mt. Fuji.

Kubota Itchiku for wear and as artworks are on display. The **Kawaguchi Museum of Art** has a permanent collection of paintings and photographs of Mt. Fuji as well as rotating exhibitions of works by Japanese and foreign artists. The **Kawaguchi Music Forest** is a theme park with European-style gardens. Local buses provide access to these attractions and to the other lakes in the Fuji-go-ko.

GETTING THERE

The Mount Fuji area is best accessed via Kawaguchiko Station, which is two hours from Tokyo's Shinjuku Station on the Kaiji Express, changing at Ootsuki for the Fujisan Express. Buses also run between Tokyo and Shinjuku Stations and Kawaguchiko.

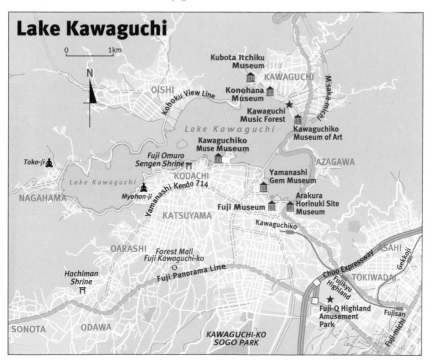

Walking Tour 28

KAWAGOE
Little Edo–A Vision of Old Tokyo

1 **Yamazaki Art Museum and Kameya Sweet Shop**
2 **Choki-in Temple**
3 **Chuo-dori**
4 **Kawagoe City Museum**
5 **Kita-in Temple**

Some 25 miles (42 kilometers) beyond Tokyo on the Musashi Plain, a scant hour away by train from Shinjuku Station, lies the city of **Kawagoe**. Kawagoe won the favor of the early Tokugawa shoguns in the 1600s as a castle town meant to protect the northern approaches to Edo. It was in an area rich in natural resources, and a powerful daimyo whom the shogun could trust was placed in charge. For more than 100 years, the Matsudaira clan ruled from their fortified stronghold, which served as an outer defense for the shogun's capital.

Kawagoe is one of the few cities to retain a semblance of its Edo-period (1603–1868) flavor. Known as **Little Edo** (Ko-Edo) even then, it preserves in an area north of the modern city its ancient main street lined with buildings of the past, which were created in the traditional *kura* or "fireproof storehouse" style. Happily, the city center was spared the bombings of 1945, which enabled a small portion of the city to still reflect that bygone era. Fire was always the bane of Japanese citizens and towns, particularly of merchants and the wealthy, whose possessions were in constant danger of destruction. Stone was too expensive a material for buildings other than the castles of the daimyo, the great lords who ruled over parts of feudal Japan. The average house or shop was made of wood with a thatched or wood-shingled roof. Cooking was done over small open fires, and sparks from such fires were an ever-present danger, since they could set dry wood or thatch aflame and destroy not

only one building but whole sections of a town. Hence, the well-to-do and the merchant class built their clay-walled shops or residences in the *kura zukuri* style that provided fireproofing to safeguard their treasure.

Kura zukuri buildings were usually two stories tall and constructed with a wood framing at their core, which was then packed and covered with damp clay with a fibrous material as a binder. The walls were a foot or more in thickness and were then covered outside with a white plaster as a waterproof external surface. The walls of the more well-to-do citizens were covered with diagonal black tiles with white plaster joints, which enhanced their attractiveness. Narrow windows bore iron shutters that could be closed in time of danger, and the only doorway had a heavy iron door. Even these metal-protected openings could be covered over with thick layers of clay so as to completely enclose the structure against the threat of fire. The sloping roofs were covered with heavy clay tiles, often richly ornamented, sometimes with dragon-head tiles as a protection against the god of fire. It took from six months to a year to build such a structure, because of the time required for the successive layers of clay to dry and harden.

In 1660 Tokugawa Ietsuna, the then shogun, issued an order that the roofs of all buildings had to be tiled as a protection against sparks from fires. Such decrees were enforced with greater or lesser effectiveness. In 1893 a fire devastated a major portion of Kawagoe. When the flames had subsided, only the *kura* and one wooden structure from 1792 remained in the old town. In the rebuilding of the old portion of the city, the *kura* style of architecture therefore won favor both for shops and homes. As a result, the old main street of Kawagoe, **Chuo-dori** (Central Street), serves today as a museum for a building style of the past that has long since disappeared in most modern cities of Japan, though only 30 of the

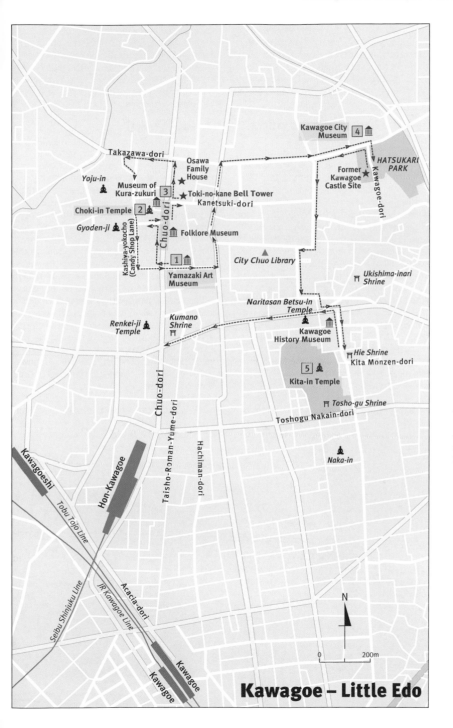

Takazawa-dori

Yoju-in

Museum of
Kura-zukuri `3`

Choki-in Temple `2`

Gyoden-ji

Kashiya-yokocho
(Candy Shop Lane)

Osawa
Family
House

★ Toki-no-kane Bell Tower
Kanetsuki-dori

Folklore Museum

`1`
Yamazaki Art
Museum

Chuo-dori

Kawagoe City
Museum `4`

HATSUKARI
PARK

Former
★ Kawagoe
Castle Site

Kawagoe-dori

City Chuo Library

*Ukishima-inari
Shrine*

Naritasan Betsu-in
Temple

Kawagoe
History Museum

Hie Shrine
Kita Monzen-dori

*Renkei-ji
Temple*

*Kumano
Shrine*

`5`
Kita-in Temple

Tosho-gu Shrine

Toshogu Nakain-dori

Naka-in

Kawagoeshi

Tobu Tojo Line

Hon-Kawagoe

Chuo-dori

Taisho-Roman-Yume-dori

Hachiman-dori

Seibu Shinjuku Line

JR Kawagoe Line

Acacia-dori

Kawagoe

Kawagoe

N

0   200m

Kawagoe – Little Edo

more than 200 *kura* that existed in Kawagoe are still in place. Tokyo once had many such structures, but these were mostly destroyed in the Great Kanto Earthquake of 1923. Now, it is the old portion of Kawagoe, with its concentration of *kura*, that resembles the Edo depicted in woodblock prints from before 1868.

are changed every few months. Since houses were so perishable, and since the Japanese concentrated their art displays in the small tokonoma (alcove) of their house, few objects were shown at any one time. Extra treasures were thus kept in the family *kura* and rotated according to the season, as is the case here.

1 YAMAZAKI ART MUSEUM AND KAMEYA SWEET SHOP

On arriving at the rail station in Kawagoe, a taxi can be taken directly to the **Yamazaki Art Museum** (Yamazaki Bijutsukan), which is just off Chuo-dori. Much of Kawagoe is a modern, sprawling city, and it is its small, ancient heart one wishes to visit. The first building of note is the art museum (open from 9:30 to 4:30 except on Wednesdays, the last two days of the month, and the New Year holiday; admission ¥500). This small museum is housed in three *kura*, and it has an unusual sponsorship, since it is an outgrowth of the **Kameya Sweet Shop**, an enterprise that dates back to the late 1700s and was once the supplier of sweets to the Matsudaira lords of the local castle. One *kura* contains the cherry-wood candy molds used in making Japanese sweets. Another *kura* holds family treasures from the past, while the third contains modern Japanese paintings, scrolls, and *byobu* (painted screens) of Gaho Hashimoto, an artist of Meiji times (1868–1912), which

2 CHOKI-IN TEMPLE

Leaving the Yamazaki Art Museum and the Kameya Sweet Shop, a turn to the right and then right again at the corner places one on Chuo-dori. *Kura zukuri* (*kura*-style) buildings can be found on both sides of the street, interspersed with a few non-*kura* structures. Chuo-dori is on a north-south axis, north being the direction taken as one turns the corner from the Yamazaki Museum. On the left (west) side of the street as one heads north, a fascinating *kura zukuri* building with its heavy tile roof is at the first narrow lane to the left. A walk down the lane leads to **Choki-in**, a small temple with a tiny garden with a stream before the temple grounds. At its end, in front of the temple hall is an unusual skeleton-like figure in bronze, a Buddha image of the Ghandara-style of Central Asia. Walking back along the lane to the main street permits a closer examination of the heavy *kura*-style building at the corner. To the left on Chuo-dori are a few shops (selling pottery, knives, and artworks) in interesting *kura zukuri*–style buildings.

One of the many old buildings that have given Kawagoe its "Little Edo" moniker

3 CHUO-DORI

Crossing Chuo-dori to its east side, the Hattori Minzoku Shiryokan (**Folklore Museum**) is to the right in an old structure amid newer buildings. (Open 9:30 a.m. to 4:00 p.m., closed Mondays except on national holidays, and from December 25 to January 2. Free entry.) Once a shop that made and sold parasols and *geta* (wooden clogs, which elevated the feet above the dirt or mud), it now serves as a small museum of Kawagoe's past and is operated by the city. Brochures (some in English) and postcards and books (primarily in Japanese) are on sale. A courtesy map of the city with descriptions in English of the major sites in old Kawagoe is presented to visitors, an invaluable guide to the old part of the city. At the rear of the shop is a large diorama, which shows Kawagoe as it was.

Farther along Chuo-dori at a corner beyond the museum, a turn to the right brings one before the **Toki-no-kane**, a very tall, wooden bell tower first built 350 years ago. Rebuilt in the style of the Edo period after the 1893 fire, its large bronze bell in the Japanese style (no clapper but a wooden beam with which it is struck from the outside) is still rung at 6:00 a.m., 3:00 p.m., and 6:00 p.m. daily. Returning to and crossing Chuo-dori to its west side, to the right (north) is the Kura-zukuri Shiryokan, or Museum of Kura-zukuri. (Open 9:00 a.m. to 5:00 p.m., closed Mondays, or Tuesday if Monday is a national holiday. Admission is ¥350.) Here three *kura* behind the entry shop exhibit memorabilia from premodern days when this was still a castle town, including the tools used in the creation of the plaster ornamentation of the *kura*. Fire fighting equipment (an important element in any wooden town), candy molds, and a house of former times can be explored. The main building (rebuilt after the 1893 fire), through which one enters, was once the Koyama family tobacco wholesale shop. The custom of smoking tobacco was one of those Western concepts introduced to Japan by the Portuguese in the 16th century. The upper reaches of this early building can be reached by a winding stairway. Beyond the museum, north along Chuo-dori is the Osawa-ke, the **Osawa Family House**. The oldest building in the city, dating from 1792, it is a rarity, since so few wooden houses have survived fires or modernization. It was once the home of a kimono merchant. (Open 9:30 a.m. to 5:00 p.m. Closed Mondays. Admission is ¥200.)

At the next corner a turn to the left onto Takazawa-dori and then left again at the next street on the left brings one to **Kashiya-yokocho**, a narrow street that bears the name of **Candy Shop Lane**. Once this narrow street was populated with numerous candy shops that made Japanese sweets available for the tastes and pocketbooks of the common people. Of 70 such shops, some 10 still survive today. At the end of this lane one is at an east-west through street, and a turn to the left puts one before the Tanakaya café and restaurant and facing Chuo-dori again.

4 KAWAGOE CITY MUSEUM

Continuing east past Chuo-dori and the Yamazaki Art Museum until this street ends at a north-south street, turn left and walk north past three intersections, none of them through streets, until you reach Takazawa dori. A right turn leads in a few minutes to the modern **Kawagoe City Museum**, which is worth a visit (open 9:00 a.m. to 5:00 p.m., closed Mondays, or Tuesday if Monday is a national holiday, and closed over the year end and New Year holiday; admission is ¥200). This well-planned museum in a modern building, built to resemble the *kura*-style on an extended scale, traces the history of the region from the earliest of times to the present. The prehistoric era is illustrated with artifacts from archeological explorations and includes *haniwa*, clay sculptures, *magatama* used for jewelry, and early primitive tools. The section on medieval times offers everything from a warrior's armor to Buddhist sculpture and an early bronze temple bell. One gallery is set up to resemble a street of shops before the modern era and illustrates the shops and crafts of the pre-1868 period. A folklore section shows not only the tools used by craftsmen but a full-sized *kura* cut-away to illustrate its structure. Note-worthy at the museum (and at the Kumano Jinja shrine in the center of the town) are examples of *dashi* festival floats, 25 of which are paraded, along with local citizens in costumes of the past, in the town's annual festival in mid-October. At night at festival time the *dashi* are illuminated with paper lanterns.

KAWAGOE-JO HONMARU GOTEN The

street heading south from Takazawa-dori upon leaving the museum is Kawagoe-dori, which leads to the former Kawagoe castle site. While Tokyo, as Edo, dates its beginnings to the

Some of the 500 Rakan statues at the Kita-in Temple. Each one has a different face.

mid-1400s when Ota Dokan built his castle there, on the site where the present Imperial Palace now stands, Kawagoe was another place that Ota Dokan fortified, and it too had a castle, built by Dokan in 1457. The **Kawagoe-jo Honmaru Goten** (Main Ward of the Palace at Kawagoe Castle) is all that remains on the site and is a bit of a disappointment. Those castles that had not been wrecked in war or dismantled by the shogun's order after 1603 have usually succumbed to fire, and the story is no different in Kawagoe. The castle is now gone, and in its place in the midst of playing fields, stands the curved gabled entryway and a large reception room of the one-time dwelling of the lord of Kawagoe Castle, a structure that dates only to 1848. (Open 9:00 a.m. to 5:00 p.m., closed Mondays, but if Monday is a national holiday, the site is open on Monday but closed the following day. Admission is ¥200.)

5 KITA-IN TEMPLE

After retracing one's steps from the former castle site back to **Takazawa-dori**, turn left onto **Takazawa-dori** and left again (now heading south) at the next intersection, then take the sixth turning on your left followed by the first street on your right. This will bring one to the **Kawagoe History Museum**, while across from it is the **Naritasan Betsu-in Temple**. (The city map is most helpful here.) Naritasan Betsu-in, or Naritasan Temple, is an 1850 branch of the important shrine to the Buddhist deity Fudo in Narita near the Tokyo International Airport. It was created by a local merchant who had been to Narita to pray for relief from his growing blindness. There in the Fudo temple his failing eyesight was restored in answer to his prayers. Naturally, the main image in the temple that the merchant created in Kawagoe is that of Fudo. Of

greater interest to many worshippers is the image of Binzuru-sama, a seated figure who has medical curative powers that are much in demand. By making an offering, saying a prayer for the amelioration of one's illness, and touching the portion of the image's body that corresponds to the ailing portion of one's own body, a cure will be effected. Outside of the temple, within the temple grounds, is a very small garden with a stream, a pond, and turtles. (On the 28th of each month a market is held on the grounds, and a variety of small antiques and other articles of lesser value are for sale.)

Continuing to the south of Naritasan Temple, one arrives at **Kita-in**, the major temple of old Kawagoe. In some ways, Kawagoe even predates Ota Dokan and his castle of the 1400s, for in 830 the noted Buddhist priest Ennin built the first of the many units of Kita-in at the site of the present temple. Ennin was to become the head of the Tendai sect of Buddhism in Japan in 854, and thus Kita-in became the important Tendai sect headquarters in the Kanto region of Japan. Destroyed by fires and wars on various occasions, it reached its height of glory when the priest Tenkai became its abbot in 1588. Tenkai became a confidant of Ieyasu, the first Tokugawa shogun, and Kita-in was enriched by this relationship. Although Tenkai was the abbot of Kita-in, a temple that was dear to him, his value to the Tokugawas was such that he was soon brought to Edo, where he created the huge Kanei-ji Temple, which covered most of what today is Ueno Park. Ueno lay to the northeast of Edo, and it is from that direction that evil always flows under the rules of Chinese geomancy.

Tenkai built Kanei-ji as a protection to the Tokugawa capital. When Tokugawa Ieyasu died, Tenkai remained an important advisor to Ieyasu's son Hidetada, and then to his grandson Iemitsu, the third shogun. When in 1638 Kita-in was destroyed by fire, Tokugawa Iemitsu saw to its rebuilding as a gesture of esteem to Abbot Tenkai. Not only did he ensure the survival of the temple, but he made it a present of a number of rooms from the Kyakuden structure of his castle in Edo, rooms that today form parts of six temple buildings here in Kawagoe. In the mid- and late-19th century, the castle in Edo was destroyed by fire, and so these rooms are the only remaining portions of the shogun's castle. The buildings given by Iemitsu include the room in which Iemitsu is said to have been born. The *shoin* (residential portion) of the structure is decorated with paintings done by artists who worked under Kano Yoshinobu, and these include many *byobu* (painted screens), including one of 24 screens depicting 25 17th-century craftsmen at work. The Jigen-do Hall (named for the abbot's posthumous title) on a slight rise houses a red, robed, wood image said to be an image of Abbot Tenkai, which was created within two years of his death at 108 in 1643. (One of the ironies of fate is that Kanei-ji in Ueno Park in Tokyo was destroyed in the last battle between former Tokugawa adherents and the new Meiji government in 1868. Later a new Main Hall for Kanei-ji was installed on a portion of the former temple grounds, that replacement being one of Tenkai's temple buildings from Kawagoe.)

The 500 *rakan* (followers of the Buddha) in the courtyard of the temple (the entry fee to the museum includes a visit to the *rakan*) were carved between 1782 and 1825, all of them with individual faces indicating the many moods to which mankind is subject. The images are approximately 16 inches (40 cm) tall and are in various poses. Elevated in their midst are images of three Buddha figures seated in contemplation. The **Kita-in** (open from 8:50 a.m. to 4:30 p.m. from March 1 to November 23 and until 4:00 p.m. the rest of the year; ¥400) puts on special exhibitions within the temple grounds. On January 3 each year the temple is the site of Kawagoe's second-largest festival, the Daruma Doll Festival. Anyone who buys a daruma doll (supposedly depicting Bodhidharma, who brought Zen Buddhism east from India) from one the many vendors should draw a pupil in one of its blank eyes and make a wish. When the wish is realized, you draw a pupil in the second eye. Next to Kita-in is the **Tosho-gu Shrine** (which is open on Sundays, national holidays, January 1–5, April 17, and August 17). This small, ornate shrine is one of the many built in honor of Tokugawa Ieyasu after his death, and, in a sense, they all form branches of the great mausoleum in Nikko where Ieyasu's remains were enshrined. The treasures of the shrine are on public view during Golden Week at the end of April and the beginning of May.

Returning to the intersection where Naritasan Temple is located, a left turn (to the west) will bring one back to Chuo-dori. The bus that runs south on this street goes back to the **Kawagoe Station** for a return to **Shinjuku** in Tokyo.

FESTIVALS

January **Daruma-Ichi Festival** At Kita-in, in which small images of the red, roly-poly representation of the founder of Zen Buddhism are sold. The custom is to paint in one pupil in the image's eyes when one wishes to achieve some goal. The image supposedly understands that its other eye will not be inscribed until the wish is achieved.

February 3 **Setsubun** At Kita-in. Symbolizing the end of the winter season, beans are scattered about the halls of the temple to rid the temple of evil spirits and to bring in good spirits.

Early April **Goma Ceremony** At Kita-in. The burning of prayer sticks to make the prayers inscribed on them effective.

Last Sunday in May **Plant Fair** At Kita-in.

Last week-end of July **O-bon** Lanterns are placed to guide the spirits of the dead back to their netherworld after their annual visit to homes. Parades with *mikoshi* and lanterns take place.

Mid-October **Kawagoe Matsuri** A festival held on the third Saturday and Sunday of October that honors the deity of Hikawa Shrine, the patron deity of the city. Twenty-four floats, of which 17 wheeled floats are replicas of those dating back to Edo days in Tokyo that were part of the Kanda Matsuri in the capital. On the Saturday the floats are on display in their local areas, and on the Sunday they progress in a grand festival through the town.

November 1–23 **Chrysanthemum Festival** Many varieties of chrysanthemums are on display at Kita-in.

GETTING THERE

Kawagoe Station, 30 minutes from Ikebukuro (which is less than 10 minutes from Shinjuku on the JR Yamanote Line) in Tokyo on the Tobu Tojo Line, is the nearest station to the start of this walk. From the station, take a taxi to the Yamazaki Art Museum (Yamazaki Bijutsukan) to begin the walk.

Walking Tour 29

NARITA

Shinsho-ji Temple in Narita and the National History Museum in Sakura

1 **Shinsho-ji Temple**
2 **National Museum of Japanese History**

Narita is known to any visitor to Japan as the primary passenger air terminal in the greater Tokyo region for arrivals from and departures for overseas. What is probably not known is that it is also one of the largest terminals for fresh fish that have arrived by air freight from around the world—fish bound for the famed Tsukiji fish market in Tokyo. For most visitors to Japan, Narita is but a way

station en route into Tokyo. This is a mistake, however, for there are a number of very interesting sites within 15 to 30 minutes of the airport that are worth seeing and worthy of a return visit from Tokyo if one cannot stop for a visit on arrival in Japan. The first site of interest, of course, is the great Shinsho-ji Buddhist temple in Narita City, and it dates its inception back to the tenth century.

1 **SHINSHO-JI TEMPLE**
In 939, Taira-no-Masakado, the strongman of the Kanto region, declared his independence

Shinsho-ji Temple in Narita. People commonly call the temple Narita-san.

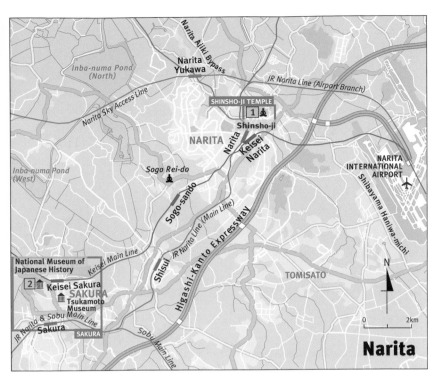

Narita

of the government at Kyoto. In fact, he went one step further: he declared himself to be emperor of Japan instead of the generally recognized emperor in Japan's capital. Obviously, such a challenge had to be met, and the Fujiwara chief minister of the emperor had the military mount a campaign against the rebel. The government's army was making little headway, and so in Kyoto Emperor Sujaku, threatened by the pretender's claim to imperial power, made his contribution to the battle by borrowing an image of the deity Fudo said to have been carved by the great priest Kukai (Kobo Daishi) and held by the Jingo-ji Temple on Mt. Takao in Kyoto. He sent the priest Kanjo with the Fudo image to accompany the military forces. Kanjo first underwent a three-week prayer and fire ceremony to guarantee the success of the military expedition against Masakado. The emperor even sent a sacred sword, the Amakuni-no-tsurugi, to seal the outcome.

With such supernatural guardians, poor Masakado had little chance of victory, and soon his head was being carried to Kyoto as a trophy of war. Legend recounts that one

stormy night his head flew back from Kyoto to join his body in its grave in what today is Tokyo, Masakado being nothing if not resolute both in life and death. The existence of the shrine to Masakado in the Tokyo financial district, over the rebel's supposed grave, today no doubt verifies this miracle.

The image of Fudo not only helped to assure success for the imperial forces in the year 940, but the image then became so heavy that it could not be moved, thereby making it obvious that it did not want to return to Kyoto but preferred to remain in the Kanto region. Thus a temple was raised to the deity in Kosu, near Narita, where the final battle against Masakado had taken place. As temples and deities often do, in 1705 Fudo was relocated to a newer and grander edifice built to house this deity, and this new unit was created in the town of Narita. **Shinsho-ji**, or Naritasan, as it is often called, became a popular temple for pilgrims of the Shingon sect of Buddhism as time went by. Today Shinsho-ji sits in its park of 42 acres (17 hectares) as one of the more important temples dedicated to Fudo (originally the Hindu deity Acala, one of the

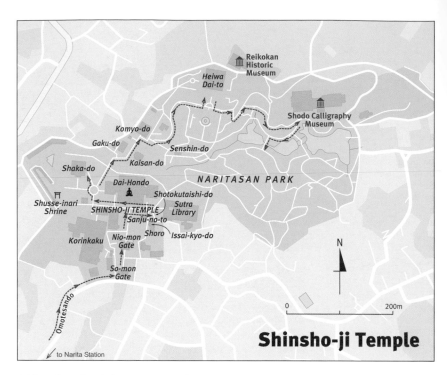

Shinsho-ji Temple

deities whose duty it is to conquer evil). Images of Fudo usually hold an upright sword in one hand and a rope with which to snare the forces of evil in the other. Since Fudo is often encircled in flames, he is rather a fearful looking being.

The temple lies 15 minutes, 875 yards (800 meters), to the north of the Keisei Narita train station or three-quarters of a mile (1.2 kilometers) from the Japan Rail station, and it is approached via the shop-filled Omotesando (Street Before the Temple). On this street between the rail stations and Shinsho-ji is the **Narita Tourist Pavilion**, which exhibits two of the floats used in the Narita Gion Festival, which takes place from July 7 through July 9. The pavilion also has five large screens that display Gion festival activities. Exhibits show items used on pilgrimages to the Fudo temple during the Edo period (1603–1868). A free tea ceremony is held here from 10:30 a.m. to noon every Thursday. Tourist information is naturally available. (Open from 9:00 a.m. to 5:00 p.m., closed Mondays but open that day on national holidays and then closed the next day. No entry charge.)

As a pilgrimage destination for adherents to the Shingon branch of Buddhism, Shinsho-ji receives some 12 million visitors annually from all over Japan. When approaching the temple complex, on the left side of the lower courtyard and up a set of steps is the 1974 **Korinkaku**, a huge residence hall for pilgrims who come to participate in ascetic practices. A small temple museum lies within the building, and it can be entered from the grounds of the upper level of the temple complex. In the courtyard there is a sacred well for ablutions, and its cold waters are poured by pilgrims over their bodies as a rite of penance, even in the coldest of weather in the winter. The rite calls for circumambulating the main hall of the temple 100 times in the white pilgrim's wrapper, counting the rounds on white threads. Fasting is another of the practices to be observed during such periods of pilgrimage.

Stalls selling primarily religious items line the approach to the steps that take one up to an upper court, and on either side of the path is a very large bucket for the holding of water as a precaution against fire, six smaller buckets being stacked in pyramid shape above the huge bucket. These buckets are more ornamental than functional. The temple grounds proper are entered through the 1831 **Nio-mon gateway,** with its images of the Nio guardians on either side of the passageway through the gate, and a large paper lantern hangs in the opening of the gate. Beyond the gateway, stairs lead to a vast terrace on which is the ferroconcrete **Dai-Hondo** (Great Main Hall) of 1968, which was created in tradition-al temple architectural style. Golden doors lead into the Dai-Hondo, and within the tem-ple a glass wall separates the front part of the building from its inner altar area. Surrounding the columns of the interior are golden hangings, with additional golden hangings pendant from a canopy over the altar. At the altar is the sacred image of Fudo Myo-o, accompanied by Kongara and Seitaka, who are usually associated with him.

It is said that the great Shingon priest Kukai (774–835) carved the image of Fudo, and it was this very image that was led into the battle that defeated Masakado. Within the Dai-Hondo, the Goma fire ceremony occurs five times a day, when the wooden prayer sticks on which visitors write their prayers or wishes are ceremonially burned so as to make their prayers efficacious. At the back of the Dai-Hondo, open doors look into an altar with an image of the Buddha with an associ-ate bodhisattva on either side. Additional buildings surround the Dai-Hondo: to the right when facing the Dai-Hondo is the **Sanju no to** (three-story pagoda) of 1712, which has gone through reconstruction on various occasions since that time, the latest occurring between 1981 and 1983. Its end rafters are carved as dragons, and the panels on its sidewalls have carvings of the sixteen rakan, disciples of the Buddha. The pagoda is a colorful building, since not only is it lac-quered in the familiar vermilion, but wave-like colorful paintings enhance the underside of each of the pagoda roofs. Enshrined in the lower level of the pagoda are the five Tathagata, who are endowed with the five wisdoms of the Buddha.

To the right is the 1722 **Issai-kyo-do,** with its bell-shape Zen-type windows on either side of its doorway. This library of sutras (Buddhist scriptures) holds the temple's entire Issai-kyo Sutra in a revolving library case. The revolving case is set up on crouch-ing figures that support the unit. A complete turning of the sutra drum by a pilgrim is equal to a complete reading of the sutras, and

The Great Pagoda at Shinsho-ji

the action is one that brings merit to the pilgrim. These sutras were a gift from the Dalai Lama of Tibet in 1731. The 1706 **Shoro** (Belfry) to the right of the sutra building has the temple bell. To the left of these units and set back a short distance is a vermilion hexa-gonal **Shotokutaishi-do,** which holds a more than life-sized image of Prince Shotoku, a censer in his hand (the prince is credited with making Buddhism a major force in Japanese life in the 600s A.D.). The 1858 **Shaka-do** to the left when facing the Dai-Hondo, was the former Hondo, or Main Hall, before 1968, and it retains an image of the historic Sakyamuni, or Buddha. The building is noted for the intricate carvings of the 500 *rakan* followers of the Buddha on the exterior walls. To the left of the temple grounds is the **Shusse-inari Shrine**, which serves as a Shinto protector for this Buddhist temple.

The ground behind the Dai-Hondo and the Shaka-do is on a higher level, and a stone retaining wall behind the Dai-Hondo displays numerous stone images of Buddhist deities in bronze. Water cascades down the wall into a small pond. A hermit image is seated in a cave-like opening, and the 36 disciples of the Buddha who are said to be capable of saving the faithful from worldly desires are placed about the wall. A stairway to the rear right of the Dai-Hondo brings one into **Naritasan Park**. The first portion of the park has many memorial stones detailing gifts bestowed upon the temple. (Public restrooms are to the left of the lower level of the staircase.) A stairway to the rear left of the Dai-Hondo (to the rear right of the Shaka-do) leads to the upper level, which has additional temple buildings. To the right on this upper level is the 1938 **Kaisan-do (**Founder's Hall), which enshrines the spirit of Kanjo, the priest who brought the Fudo image from Kyoto to Narita in the 940s. Opposite the Kaisan-do is the two-story roofed building, open on all sides, which serves as the **Gaku-do**, or Votive Hall, the

building that holds religious pictures generally painted on wood panels, given to the temple. The seated image in the structure is of the Kabuki actor Danjuro VII, for this is the family temple of the Ichikawa family of Kabuki actors. The 1701 **Komyo-do** (Inner Sanctuary), behind these last two buildings holds an image of the Dainichi Nyorai, the Great Sun, the cosmic Buddha in whom all the cosmic forces are one. To the right is a double Shinto shrine in vermilion. Farther to the rear and to the right is the 1983 Heiwa Dai-to, the **Great Pagoda**, a very tall pagoda with a square first floor topped by a round upper level under a huge roof. Within it on the lower level to one side is the **small museum** with materials on the temple and on the town.

A pond at Narita-san, complete with ornamental carp, maple trees, and stone lantern

It holds, among other items, some of the temple's treasures, not only the Amakuni-no-tsurugi sword that the emperor sent as a sacred symbol in the battle against Masakado but also the image of the Namikiri Fudo that it is said Kobo Daishi carved from the wood of the boat that brought him back from his studies of esoteric Buddhism in China. The sword receives its name from the blacksmith who created it for Emperor Mommu in the 700s.

The 41-acre (16-hectare) Naritasan Park is noted for its cherry and apricot trees, and its Japanese and English gardens (open from 8:30 a.m. to 4:00 p.m. daily). A rivulet, cascades, and a pond enhance the park, and a formal garden is just below the Heiwa Dai-to Pagoda. The **Shodo Bijutsukan**, a museum

devoted to calligraphy, is within the park grounds, and it exhibits some of the finest examples of Japanese calligraphy (open 9:00 a.m. to 4:00 p.m.; admission ¥500).

2 NATIONAL MUSEUM OF JAPANESE HISTORY

Only 15 minutes to the west of Narita on the Keisei rail line is the town of **Sakura**. It can be reached from Narita or from the Keisei Ueno rail terminal in Tokyo, or in 45 minutes by the Japan Rail Sobu line from Tokyo Station. The town itself has an historic past of which it is duly proud, but in recent times the **National Museum of Japanese History** (Kokuritsu Rekishi Minzoku Hakubutsukan) has become a major attraction in the community. Sakura was once a castle town under the dominion of the local lord. The castle is gone (today the National Museum is on its grounds), but some of the old samurai houses still exist within the town. Two of these houses, **the Kawahara, Tajima and the Takei family houses**, have been restored, and within them the furnishings and belongings of a samurai family are on display and bring a lively quality to the buildings. (Open from 9:00 a.m. to 5:00 p.m. Closed Mondays unless a national holiday, in which case they close the following day. Admission ¥210. Take the bus from the #3 depot of the bus terminal at the Sakura Keisei Station or the bus from the #1 or #2 depot at the JR rail station to the Miyakoji-machi bus stop, from which it is eight minutes on foot.

Three minutes on foot from the above bus stop is the **Tsukamoto Museum**, with a small, frequently changing public exhibition of some 20 items from its collection of 400 samurai swords and 250 sword sheaths. (Open 9:00 a.m. to 4:00 p.m. Closed weekends, national holidays and Mondays. Entry is free.) Three minutes from the bus stop in another direction is the **Shinto guardian shrine of the town**. The most noted aspect of the shrine is the huge cryptomeria (cedar) tree that is reputed to be 1,200 years old. The tree is 89 feet (27 meters) tall and has a circumference of 26 feet (8 meters). It is the largest tree in the Kanto region, despite its top having been blasted by lightning and suffering other natural calamities. The shrine's annual festival occurs from October 14 through 16, with a colorful procession of *mikoshi* and festival floats. The town also has the first private hospital built in Japan in 1843. Part of a newer hospital building, it is

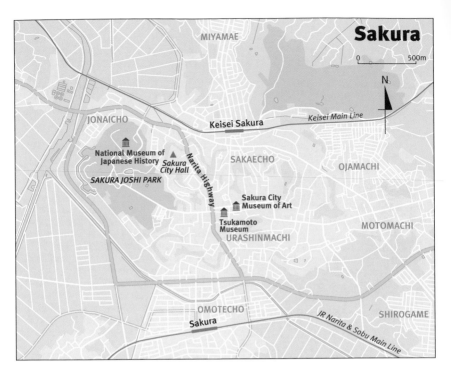

historically important, since some of the first of Dutch medical studies were put into practice here in the 19th century, revolutionizing Japanese medicine, which heretofore had depended on Chinese medical lore.

The gem of the town, however, is its 1981 two-story **National Museum of Japanese History**. Organized on 13 historical and 6 folklore themes, the museum holds more than 106,000 items and offers scale models of ancient tombs, villages, and palaces as well as artifacts from the entire past history of the nation. The first gallery is devoted to the prehistoric era of the Jomon and Yayoi cultures, while the second is on the era of the court at Kyoto in the 9th to the 16th centuries. The third gallery covers the Tokugawa/Edo Period (1603–1868). The fourth is devoted to an ethnographic view of Japanese civilization, while the fifth covers Japanese life and towns in their various aspects in the modern period. The museum is meant both for the pleasure of general public and as a research center for scholars of the Japanese past. The detailed models, the display of numerous artifacts, and the fine explanatory descriptions (in English) provide a rich in-

sight into Japanese history and customs. (Open from 9:00 a.m. to 5:00 p.m. March through September and until 4:30 p.m. October through February. Closed Mondays unless a national holiday, in which case it closes the following day. Closed during the year end and the New Year holiday. Admission is ¥420.) The museum is a 15-minute walk from the Keisei Sakura Station or 10 minutes by bus from the #1 depot of the bus terminal in front of the Keisei Station. Get off at the Kokuritsu Hakubutsukan bus stop and then a five-minute walk. A bus from the #1 depot at the JR station for Tamchi Shako leaves one at the Kokuritsu Hakubutsukan bus stop as well. In all cases, a taxi from the station is probably the easiest way to get to the sites.

GETTING THERE

This walk can begin at either Keisei Narita Station on the Keisei Line (connecting to Narita Airport in 10 minutes and Tokyo's Ueno and Nippori in just over an hour) or JR Narita Station on the Sobu Line (75 minutes from JR Tokyo Station).

Hatsumode celebration in Narita

FESTIVALS IN THE NARITA REGION

January **Hatsumode** First visit of the year to temples and shrines to pray for a good New Year.

February **Setsubun** The throwing of beans to drive out evil spirits and to welcome in good spirits, a celebration of the end of winter. At Shinsho-ji Temple in Narita.

Late February, early March **Plum Blossom Festival** Plum blossom viewing festival that includes outdoor tea ceremony in Naritasan Park.

April 3 **Flower Viewing Dance (Odori-Hanami)** in Narita City.

April **Cherry Blossom Viewing** in all area parks.

Early July **Gion-e** A procession of festival floats at Shinsho-ji Temple.

Early July Hidrangea Festival in Sogo Rei-do Temple

August, first Saturday **Kashima River Paper Lantern Festival** in Sakura.

Early September **Otaiya-sai Night Festival** Sogo Rei-do Temple.

October 14, 15, 16 **Shrine Go-Reisai Annual Festival** Sakura.

October The Narita Fireworks Festival in Inba-numa Pond.

November **Chrysanthemum Festival** Shinsho-ji and Sogo Rei-do Temples

December **Otaki-Age** Fire festival at the Shinsho-ji Temple.

The 3rd Sunday of each month Antique Fair in Shinsho-ji Temple

Tokyo General Information

GETTING TO TOKYO

There are various international airports in Japan for arrivals from overseas, the main terminals being: Narita for Tokyo, Nagoya for central Japan, and Osaka for the rest of Japan. With a new international terminal having opened in October 2010, Haneda Airport 30 minutes from Shinagawa in Tokyo, is also gradually increasing its number of international routes. There are airports in Sapporo, Fukuoka, Nagasaki, and many other cities too, but these are generally not arrival points from outside of Asia. If arriving at an airport other than Narita or Haneda, it is possible to use the train network or one of the numerous domestic flight routes to get to Tokyo after clearing immigration and customs. At Narita, foreign currency can be changed at counters just beyond the customs area or in the lobby outside of the customs area. You can also you overseas ATM cards at most larger post offices in Tokyo and at many banks and even convenience stores.

TRANSPORTATION FROM NARITA INTO THE CITY

Narita Airport is approximately one hour from Tokyo. Tickets for limousine buses can be obtained in the lobby just outside the customs area and the buses depart from the curb outside the lobby almost every 10 minutes. In approximately one hour, depending upon traffic, the bus goes to the Tokyo City Air Terminal (TCAT) where a taxi can be taken to one's hotel. Some limousines go directly to individual hotels in Tokyo, and information as to the limousine desired can be obtained at the ticket counter. Trains to central Tokyo depart from the basement level of the airport and train tickets can be obtained there. The **Keisei** trains go to Ueno Station while the **Japan Rail** trains go to Tokyo Central Station. In either case, a taxi or trains can be taken from the Tokyo stations to one's hotel.

TRANSPORTATION WITHIN TOKYO

Within Tokyo one has a choice of taxis, trains, subways, and buses. Since not all buses indicate their route or destination in English on their front, the use of subways, trains or taxis is recommended.

Taxis: Taxis can be hailed on the street, and taxi doors are opened automatically by the driver for entry or departure from the vehicle. Taxis are metered, and the drivers do not expect a tip. Not all taxi drivers speak English, and if you do not know the Japanese name of your destination, it's best to have the front desk at your hotel write your destination on a piece of paper that you can give to the taxi driver.

Subways: There are two subway systems in Tokyo: Tokyo Metro and Toei, both with various branches. Tickets are purchased from vending machines in the subway station lobbies, and a signboard usually indicates the cost of a ticket to specific stations. The ticket is placed in the slot at the turnstile, and it is then returned through another slot. **The ticket must be retained for use to exit the turnstile at your destination.** On leaving the station of your destination, the ticket is again deposited into the turnstile. If the correct amount has been paid, the barrier to exiting is activated and the ticket is not returned on departure. If the fare for the ticket was for less than is required, the guard can be paid the difference needed, or you can use one of the "fare adjustment machines" always situated just inside the ticket gates. If in doubt as to the cost of your ride, choose the least expensive ticket and then pay the difference to the guard at the exit of your destination. If you are staying in Tokyo for a length of time, it might be easier to buy an electronic Pasmo or Suica pass, which can be charged with as much money as you see fit and then swiped against scanners on the ticket gates upon entering and leaving a station to automatically deduct the fare. Pasmo (issued by Tokyo Metro) and Suica (issued JR) can be used on any Toei, JR, or Metro line, and even on many bus routes. They can also be used on many drinks vending machines and in some shops.

Trains within Tokyo: The heart of Tokyo is circled by the JR Yamanote Line, part of the Japan Rail system. There are other JR lines that serve parts of the city: the yellow Sobu Line, the orange Chuo Line and the blue Keihin Tohoku Line. As with the subway system, tickets must be purchased from vending machines, and the same instructions as to the use of tickets (or Pasmo and Suica) applies as described under the "Subway" entry above.

Maps and General Information: Maps of the city, information on sights and events, and maps of the transportation lines in the city can be obtained from your hotel or from the Tourist Information Office in Tokyo, which is located one-minute from the Nihombashi exit of Tokyo Station. They also have a Web site: www. tictokyo.jp/en/

SHOPPING

Tokyo has shops to suit almost every taste and budget, from high-end fashion boutiques and department stores to shops dealing in traditional crafts and all manner of quirky souvenirs. Harajuku and Shibuya cater to the young, trendy set and are where you'll find the latest in teen fashions and trends. More conservative is Ginza, still Tokyo's premier shopping district, which is home to the Mitsukoshi, Matsuya, Wako, Matsuzakaya, and Printemps department stores as well as flagship stores for such international brands as Luis Vuiton, Chanel, and Cartier.

Equally fashionable, but with a more contemporary feel, are Aoyama and Omotesando, home to numerous famous brands, tiny backstreet boutiques, and the chic Omotesando Hills shopping mall. Shinjuku and Ikebukuro too have plenty of shopping options, with giant department stores, home electronics, the latest fashions, and almost everything else in between to be found along their crowded streets.

In Akihabara the focus is on home electronics and gadgetry, and besides the numerous small specialty stores you'll find many large duty-free stores offering discounts on the latest tech. Akihabara also caters to Japan's *otaku* (geeks) and is awash with manga- and anime-related stores.

For souvenirs, the area along and around Nakamise-dori in Asakusa is rife with small stalls selling cheap T-shirts and plastic samurai swords, but among all that are also good places to pick up edible souvenirs such as rice crackers and sweet *ningyo-yaki*, as well as traditional craft ware that includes exquisite Kiriko glassware. You'll also find similar on Omotesando at Oriental Bazaar, a three-story shop aimed at tourists, where the items range from expensive antique furniture and used kimono to sushi-shaped USB sticks.

EATING OUT

With its vast range of cuisines and number of high-quality, yet usually affordable restaurants, Tokyo is a gourmand's dream. Sushi, the food most associated with Japan, doesn't get much better than in Tsukiji, where the early-morning and lunchtime sushi bars offer high-quality fare at good prices. In nearby Ginza, you'll also find fine sushi restaurants, as well as upmarket restaurants specializing in other traditional cuisines, such as tempura, *teppanyaki*, and *kaiseki-ryori*.

Cosmopolitan areas such as Roppongi, Omotesando, and Aoyama have no shortage of great places to eat and drink, with options ranging from traditional Japanese to fashionable modern Japanese fusion to cool European and Asian restaurants.

Representing what the Japanese call B-grade gourmet—affordable, no-frills but tasty fare—are dishes such as ramen, *yakitori*, and *gyudon* (beef bowl). You'll find these all over the city, but for the best range of ramen head to Yokohama and its Ramen Museum, a collection of ramen shops representing regional variations from around the country. For good *yakitori* try the restaurants under the elevated rail tracks between Yurakucho and Shimbashi Stations, or the back streets near Rokku Broadway and Hanayashiki Amusement Park in Asakusa.

The Okubo and Shin-okubo areas of Shinjuku Ward (near Kabuki-cho) are known for their Asian restaurants, especially those specializing in Korean barbecue (*yakiniku*) and Southeast Asian cuisines. Yokohama's Chinatown is not surprisingly the place to go for a good variety of Chinese flavors.

One thing to remember with restaurants is that even in Tokyo (especially away from international areas such as Roppongi) many still don't take credit cards. Be sure to check before ordering.

ENTERTAINMENT AND CULTURE

With Kabuki-za in Higashi Ginza undergoing renovation until 2013, Tokyo is temporarily without its star theatrical attraction. However, the Shimbashi Enbujo in Ginza and the Kokuritsu Gekijo near the Imperial Palace are two good alternatives for taking in a Kabuki performance. The latter also puts on Bunraku (puppet theater) performances from time to time, while Noh, another highly stylized form of traditional theater, is best experienced at the National Noh Theater in Sendagaya. These theaters offer an "earphone guide" that provides commentary, explanations, and translations of dialogue and lyrics. For something a bit different but just as traditional, head to the theaters on Rokku Broadway in Asakusa. Engei Hall in particular has numerous comic performances of Manzai ((stand-up comedy performed by a duo) and Rakugo (comic storytelling performed by a single performer alongside other traditional storytelling and comic acts.

In a modern city like Tokyo, there are of course numerous contemporary distractions. In particular, Tokyo is blessed with a vibrant arts scene, which is most accessible in and around Roppongi, with sights that include the Mori Art Museum atop Roppongi Hills, the Suntory Art Museum and Design Site 21_21 in Tokyo Midtown, and the nearby National Art Center. In east Tokyo, Ueno is home to a wonderful collection of museums and galleries, including the highly recommended Tokyo National Museum, National Science Museum, National Museum of Western Art, and Shitamachi Museum.

For entertainment that is especially popular with younger generations, Akihabara provides some of the city's most cutting-edge gaming arcades, while the areas around Tokyo Dome and Odaiba are also full of good family amusements. Just outside of Tokyo, in Urayasu in neighboring Chiba Prefecture (about 30 minutes from central Tokyo), are the hugely popular Disney World and Disney Sea amusement parks.

TOKYO'S TRADITIONAL AND MODERN FACES
It's often said that Tokyo is a city of contrasts, a place where glistening skyscrapers loom over centuries-old temples and deep-rooted traditions sit comfortably with incredible technological advancements. For a glimpse of traditional Tokyo, head first to Yanesen, an area that encompasses the Yanaka, Nezu, and Sendagi neighborhoods in northeastern Tokyo. The narrow streets here are dotted with small temples and shrines, mom-and-pop stores, and charming old cafés and restaurants. As an alternative, the Tsukishima, Asakusa, and Shibamata areas also retain much of their old Edo charm. The modern side is visible almost everywhere you go but is best seen in the very center of the city, among the towering buildings of Shiodome or at the sleek Roppongi Hills and Tokyo Midtown urban redevelopments. To visit Shibuya Crossing or Shinjuku Station at morning or evening rush hour is to experience the modern crowded metropolis at its most hectic.

HOLIDAYS AND FESTIVALS IN TOKYO
The exact dates of some of holidays and events change from year to year—particularly those shrine events, which are keyed to the lunar calendar. An up-to-date listing is always available from any tourist information office or from the Web site of the Japan National Tourism Organization (www.jnto.go.jp).

January
1 **Hatsumode** The first visit of the year to a shrine to pray for good luck in the new year. A national holiday.
2 **Ippan-sanga** Reception of the public by the emperor and family. Palace grounds.
6 **Dezome-shiki** Firemen's parade and display. At Tokyo Big Sight.
8 **Dondo-yaki** The ceremonial burning of New Year's decorations at the Torigo-e Shrine.
15 **Seijin-no-Hi** (Coming of Age Day). A national holiday. A celebration of the coming of age at 20.
Mid-January **Hatsubasho** The first sumo tournament of the new year. At the Kokugikan Stadium in Ryogoku.

February
3 **Setsubun** End-of-winter festival featuring the throwing of beans to drive out bad luck and attract good fortune. Bean throwing services at Kanda Myojin Shrine, Zojo-ji Temple, Senso-ji Temple, Hie Shrine, and many other shrines and temples.
4 **Commemoration** of the day on which the 47 Ronin committed seppuku (ceremonial suicide). Sengaku-ji Temple.
8 **Harikuyo** Service for worn-out needles. Held at shrines across the country, including Awashima-do Shrine next to the Senso-ji Temple in Asakusa.
11 **National Foundation Day.** A national holiday. A celebration of the supposed accession to the throne in 660 B.C. by Emperor Jimmu, the supposed first emperor.
Mid-February **Display and sale of dolls** in the Asakusabashi wholesale district in preparation for the Doll Festival.
Mid-February to mid-March **Hakubai-sai** White plum blossom festival. Yushima Tenjin Shrine.

March
3 **Hina Matsuri** (Doll Festival). Dolls are displayed, particularly those depicting the ancient imperial court.

19 **Kinryu-mai**. Golden Dragon Dance at the Senso-ji Temple in Asakusa.

20 **Shubun-no-Hi** (Vernal Equinox Day) A national holiday to show respect for growing things in nature and to welcome in spring.

April

Early to mid-April **Cherry Blossom Viewing.** Particularly in Ueno Park, Sumida Park, Chidorigafuchi Park, Korakuen Garden, Yasukuni Shrine.

8 **Hana Matsuri** Celebration of the birthday of the Buddha. Children's procession at the Tsukiji Hongan-ji Temple, the Senso-ji Temple, the Zojo-ji Temple, and other Buddhist temples.

13-15 **Spring Festival** At the Zojo-ji Temple.

17 **Ueno Tosho-gu Taisai** Traditional music and dances are performed in honor of Tokugawa Ieyasu at his memorial shrine.

21-23 **Spring Festival** At the Yasukuni Shrine.

Fourth Sunday **Confucius Festival** At the Yushima Seido Shrine.

Late April to early May **Azalea Festival** At the Nezu Shrine.

28 **Fudo Ennichi Festival** At the Fudo Temple in Fukagawa.

29 **Midori-no-Hi** (Green Day) A national holiday. The first day of Golden Week. A series of holidays in which hotels, buses, trains, temples, shrines, and parks are most crowded, since all of Japan is on vacation this week.

May

3 **Constitution Day** A national holiday celebrating Japan's post World War II constitution.

5 **Kodomo-no-Hi** (Children's Day) A national holiday.

5 **Suiten-gu Shrine Festival**. Parade of *mikoshi*, dances on the *kagura* stage, sales at stalls. At the Suiten-gu Shrine.

Kanda Matsuri (in odd-numbered years) Seventy *mikoshi* are paraded through the streets of Kanda, Otemachi, and Nihombashi.

Mid-May **Sumo Tournament.** Fifteen-day tournament at the Kokugikan Stadium.

Third weekend **Sanja Matsuri** Festival and *mikoshi* procession at and around the Asakusa Kannon Temple.

24-25 (or the closest weekend) **Yushima Tenjin Shrine Annual Festival.**

End of May **Azuma Odori** Dances by Shimbashi geisha at the Shimbashi Embujo Theater.

Late May to early June **Iris Blooms** At the Meiji Shrine.

31 **Potted Plant Fair** At the Sengen Shrine at the Senso-ji Temple in Asakusa.

June

9 (or nearest Sunday) **Yomatsuri.** A procession of *mikoshi*, including a four-ton unit that takes 200 men to handle. A nighttime festival at the Torigo-e Shrine.

9-16 **Sanno Matsuri** The great Hie Shrine festival held in even-numbered years. The procession on June 15 circles the palace and moves from Ginza to Kyobashi.

15 **Sanno Matsuri procession** described above.

July

1 **Nagoshi Harai** At the Torigo-e Shrine where walking through a straw ring can protect one against illness during the hot summer season.

9-10 **Hozuki-ichi** Chinese lanterns and ornamental plants are sold in the Senso-ji Temple area of Asakusa. The plants can serve to banish insects.

13-15 **Bon Odori** Dances during the Festival of the Dead at the Tsukuda-jima Sumiyoshi Shrine.

Mid-July to mid-August **Evening Festival** at Ueno Park.

13-16 **Mitama Matsuri** A service for the war dead who are enshrined at the Yasukuni Shrine.

Last Saturday **Sumida-gawa Hanabi Taikai** Fireworks display over the Sumida River.

August

6-8 **Tsukuda Matsuri.** A procession held every third year (2013, 2016, etc.) in which a *mikoshi* is taken aboard a flat barge for a procession on the Sumida River.

15 **Memorial service** attended by the emperor at the Tomb of the Unknown Soldier.

13-16 **O Bon Celebration** The annual welcoming home of the spirits of the dead for a few day's visit.

15 **O Bon lanterns** are set adrift on the Sumida River in the Kototoibashi Bridge area at the end of the O Bon festival to send the spirits of the dead back to their abode.

Mid-August **Fukagawa Matsuri** The Fukagawa festival occurs every third year (2014, 2017, etc.) with a procession of 100 *mikoshi*—at the Tomioka Hachiman-gu Shrine.

Last Saturday **Asakusa Samba Carnival**. A

street parade in Asakusa that features thousands of samba dancers from all over Japan. Runs from the afternoon into the evening.

September

1 **Memorial Service** for victims of the 1923 earthquake at the Earthquake Memorial Hall.
15 **Keiro-no-Hi** (Respect for the Aged Day). A national holiday.
Mid-September **Sumo Tournament** for 15 days at the Kokugikan Stadium.
20-21 **Nezu Gongen-sai** A parade of *mikoshi* and the setting up of stalls at the Nezu Shrine.
23 **Shunbun-no-Hi** (Autumnal Equinox Day) A national holiday. Services for the dead are held at temples.

October

First Saturday **Kakunori** A festival of log-rolling acrobatics in the Sendaibori River at the Kurofunabashi Bridge in Fukagawa.
10 **Health and Sports Day** A national holiday.
17-19 **Autumn Festival** at the Yasukuni Shrine.
Mid-October to mid-November **Chrysanthemum Displays** at temples and shrines.
18 **Asakusa Kannon Matsuri** Golden Dragon Dance and special offerings of chrysanthemums at the Senso-ji Temple in Asakusa.

November

3 **Bunka-no-Hi** (Culture Day) A national holiday.
3 **Tokyo Jidai Matsuri** (Tokyo Historical Parade) A festival and parade to celebrate the Edo period, held at Senso-ji Temple in Asakusa.
Day of the rooster in the Chinese calendar **Tori-no-Ichi** (Lucky Rake Festival) Lucky rakes can be purchased at stalls to "rake in good fortune." Otori Shrine in Asakusa and other shrines.
15 **Shichi-Go-San** A celebration at which children aged 3, 5, 7 (boys of 5 and girls of 3 and 7) are taken to shrines to receive a blessing.
23 **Kinro Kansha-no-Hi** (Labor Thanksgiving Day) A national holiday.

December

5 **Osame-no-Suiten-gu** A festival at the Suiten-gu Shrine.
14 **Gishi-sai**. A service in memory of the 47 Ronin on the anniversary of their killing Lord Kira. Sengaku-ji Temple.
14 **Memorial Service** To console the spirit of Lord Kira, killed by the 47 Ronin. At the site of Lord Kira's mansion in Ryogoku.
Mid-December–December 27 **Year's End Fair** at Senso-ji Temple in Asukusa when New Year's decorations are for sale.
17-19 **Hagoita-Ichi** Battledores for sale at the Senso-ji Temple in Asakusa.
23 **Emperor's Birthday** A national holiday. The emperor greets well-wishers from the palace reception building.
28 Last official day of work before the beginning of the week-long New Year holiday that starts on December 29.
31 **Joya-no-Kane** The ringing of temple bells 108 times at midnight to absolve mankind of the 108 earthly desires or passions of humanity.

DAY TRIPS BY TRAIN

Whether one is a visitor to or a resident of Tokyo, there are times when one feels the urge to get out of town. Few cities offer the variety of interesting destinations that are available in such close vicinity to its metropolitan district as does Tokyo. With a Japan Rail Pass one can reach these varied destinations easily, even obtaining a reserved seat on the train just before departure other than on national holidays. A timetable in English that is issued by the Japan National Tourist Organization (JNTO) provides the train schedules for all of the locations mentioned in this guide The wise traveler purchases an *o-bento* lunch on the train platform before boarding the train—or often can purchase one on the train, particularly on Shinkansen routes. This provides not only for a more flexible traveling and dining schedule, but it frees one from spending time in restaurants when one is anxious to visit famous places. By traveling with a Rail Pass, the JNTO Timetable, a camera, and an *o-bento* lunch, one can easily savor the fascinating towns, castles, and museum villages beyond the confines of Tokyo.

Index

All maps are listed in bold type.

Photo Credits

000zzz/Dreamstime.com: 277
Andrew Holmgren/Dreamstime.com: 179
Angelaostafichuk/Dreamstime.com: 178
Aryu/Dreamstime.com: 138
Bogdan/Dreamstime.com: Front cover, 100, 273
bunkyo: 173
Danilo Mongiello/Dreamstime.com: 56
Edcelmayo/Dreamstime.com: 226
Eric Oey: 260, 261
Eg004713/Dreamstime: 242
Hirofumi Iwasaki/Dreamstime.com: 214
Hirotaka Ihara/depositphotos: 103
Ian Walker/Dreamstime.com: 112
Irfannurd/Dreamstime.com: 181, 201
J. Henning Buchholz/Dreamstime.com: 96
Japan Photo Library (JNTO): 49, 68, 70, 71, 73, 88, 116, 157, 211, 255, 270
Japanese Gallery, London: 8
Jarnogs/Dreamstime.com: 237
Library of Congress Prints and Photographs Division, 9, 11
Mfharrison/Dreamstime.com: 140
Mihai-bogdan Lazar/Dreamstime.com: 171, 198, 222–223, 233
Mike Kwok/Dreamstime.com: 103, 107, 114, 191
Neale Cousland/Dreamstime.com: 5, 256

Nob50/ Dreamstime.com: 19
Oblachko/Dreamstime.com: 77
Odakyu Electric Railway/JNTO: 243,
Omers/ Dreamstime.com: 18
Paylessimages/fotolia: 130
photolibrary.jp: 15, 23, 26, 29, 33, 34, 35, 36, 38, 39, 43, 46, 48, 49, 50, 52, 57, 59, 78, 82, 83, 85, 87, 95, 97, 99, 109, 113, 123, 129, 133, 144, 147, 150, 154, 155, 163, 174, 179, 182, 201, 203, 207, 215, 219, 244, 251, porschelegend/fotolia: 153
Salladart/Dreamstime.com: 4, 274
Sean Pavone/Dreamstime.com: 258
Sergey Pristyazhnyuk/Dreamstime.com: 239
Shirototoro/Dreamstime.com: 262
Stardust1978/Dreamstime.com: 94
Stephen Bures/Dreamstime.com: 56
Takashi0106/fotolia: 246
Tifonimages/Dreamstime.com: 228
TommL/iStockphoto, 1
Valeria Cantone/Dreamstime.com: 22
Xiye/Dreamstime.com: 167
Y. Shimizu/JNTO: 69, 200
Yasufumi Nishi/JNTO: 2–3, 20, 120, 127, 136, 145, 160, 192, 193, 196, 204, 209, 232, 235, 266, 268
Yuryz/ Dreamstime.com: 66, 112, 148

The Tuttle Story: "Books to Span the East and West"

Most people are surprised to learn that the world's largest publisher of books on Asia had its humble beginnings in the tiny American state of Vermont. The company's founder, Charles E. Tuttle, belonged to a New England family steeped in publishing. And his first love was naturally books—especially old and rare editions.

Immediately after WW II, serving in Tokyo under General Douglas MacArthur, Tuttle was tasked with reviving the Japanese publishing industry. He later founded the Charles E. Tuttle Publishing Company, which thrives today as one of the world's leading independent publishers.

Though a westerner, Tuttle was hugely instrumental in bringing a knowledge of Japan and Asia to a world hungry for information about the East. By the time of his death in 1993, Tuttle had published over 6,000 books on Asian culture, history and art—a legacy honored by the Japanese emperor with the "Order of the Sacred Treasure," the highest tribute Japan can bestow upon a non-Japanese.

With a backlist of 1,500 titles, Tuttle Publishing is more active today than at any time in its past—inspired by Charles Tuttle's core mission to publish fine books to span the East and West and provide a greater understanding of each.